SAGE was founded in 1965 by Sara Miller McCune to support the dissemination of usable knowledge by publishing innovative and high-quality research and teaching content. Today, we publish over 900 journals, including those of more than 400 learned societies, more than 800 new books per year, and a growing range of library products including archives, data, case studies, reports, and video. SAGE remains majority-owned by our founder, and after Sara's lifetime will become owned by a charitable trust that secures our continued independence.

Los Angeles | London | New Delhi | Singapore | Washington DC | Melbourne

INDIA HIGHER EDUCATION REPORT 2017

Thank you for choosing a SAGE product!
If you have any comment, observation or feedback,
I would like to personally hear from you.

Please write to me at **contactceo@sagepub.in**

Vivek Mehra, Managing Director and CEO, SAGE India.

Bulk Sales

SAGE India offers special discounts
for purchase of books in bulk.
We also make available special imprints
and excerpts from our books on demand.

For orders and enquiries, write to us at

Marketing Department
SAGE Publications India Pvt Ltd
B1/I-1, Mohan Cooperative Industrial Area
Mathura Road, Post Bag 7
New Delhi 110044, India

E-mail us at **marketing@sagepub.in**

Get to know more about SAGE

Be invited to SAGE events, get on our mailing list.
Write today to **marketing@sagepub.in**

This book is also available as an e-book.

INDIA HIGHER EDUCATION REPORT 2017

Teaching, Learning and Quality in Higher Education

Edited by

N. V. Varghese
Anupam Pachauri
Sayantan Mandal

Los Angeles | London | New Delhi
Singapore | Washington DC | Melbourne

First published in 2018 by

SAGE Publications India Pvt Ltd
B1/I-1 Mohan Cooperative Industrial Area
Mathura Road, New Delhi 110 044, India
www.sagepub.in

SAGE Publications Inc
2455 Teller Road
Thousand Oaks, California 91320, USA

SAGE Publications Ltd
1 Oliver's Yard, 55 City Road
London EC1Y 1SP, United Kingdom

SAGE Publications Asia-Pacific Pte Ltd
3 Church Street
#10-04 Samsung Hub
Singapore 049483

**National Institute of Educational
Planning and Administration (NIEPA)**
17-B, Sri Aurobindo Marg
Opposite Adchini
New Delhi–110016

Published by Vivek Mehra for SAGE Publications India Pvt Ltd, typeset in 10.5/13 pts Bembo by Zaza Eunice, Hosur, Tamil Nadu, India and printed at Chaman Enterprises, New Delhi.

Library of Congress Cataloging-in-Publication Data

Names: Varghese, N.V., editor. | Pachauri, Anupam, editor. | Mandal,
   Sayantan, editor.
Title: India higher education report 2017: teaching, learning and quality in
   higher education/edited by N. V. Varghese, Anupam Pachauri, and Sayantan
   Mandal.
Description: New Delhi, India; Thousand Oaks, California: SAGE, 2018. |
   Includes bibliographical references and index.
Identifiers: LCCN 2018013019 (print) | LCCN 2018028256 (ebook) | ISBN
   9789352807185 (Web PDF) | ISBN 9789352807178 (E pub 2.0) | ISBN
   9789352807161 (hardback: alk. paper)
Subjects: LCSH: Education, Higher—India. | Educational equalization—India.
Classification: LCC LA1153 (ebook) | LCC LA1153 .I4685 2018 (print) | DDC
   378.00954—dc23
LC record available at https://lccn.loc.gov/2018013019

ISBN: 978-93-528-0716-1 (HB)

SAGE Team: Rajesh Dey, Sandhya Gola, Shobana Paul and Ritu Chopra

Contents

Part III: Quality Management

List of Tables

List of Figures

List of Abbreviations

AC	academic council
AFT	American Federation of Teachers
AHELO	assessment of higher education learning outcomes
AICTE	All India Council on Technical Education
AIIMS	All-India Institute of Medical Sciences
AISHE	All India Survey on Higher Education
AIU	Association of Indian Universities
AMU	Aligarh Muslim University
API	academic performance indicator
AQAR	annual quality assurance report
ARWU	Academic Ranking of World Universities
ASCs	academic staff colleges
ASOS	academic staff orientation scheme
ATIs	advanced training institutions
AUBR	assessment of university-based research
BCom	bachelors in commerce
BEd	bachelors in education
BCI	Bar Council of India
BHU	Banaras Hindu University
BoM	board of management
BoS	board of studies
CAT	Common Admission Test
CBCS	choice-based credit system
CCA	continuous and comprehensive assessment

CEC	Consortium for Educational Communication
CFTIs	centrally funded technical institutions
CGPA	cumulative grade point average
CHE	Centre of Higher Education
CINQF	Council of Implementation of National Qualification Framework
CIS	course of independent study
CP	comprehensive project
CPD	continuing professional development
CPE	Centre for Potential for Excellence
CPI	cumulative performance index
CPRHE	Centre for Policy Research in Higher Education
CSR	corporate social responsibility
CWCU	Centre for World-Class Universities
CWUR	Centre for World University Ranking
DBT	direct benefit transfer
DCI	Dental Council of India
DGE&T	Directorate General of Employment and Training
DGT	Directorate General of Training
DST	Department of Science and Technology
EC	European Commission
EEE	Effective Education for Employment
EHEA	European Higher Education Area
EQA	external quality assurance
EQAR	European Quality Assurance Register
EQC	examining quality culture
EQF	European qualification framework
ESG	European standards and guidelines

EU	European Union
EUA	European Union Association
EUREQA	empowering universities to fulfil their responsibility for quality assurance
FDC	faculty development centres
FGD	focus group discussion
GER	gross enrolment ratio
GO	graduation outcome
HE	higher education
HEEACT	Higher Education Accreditation Evaluation Council University Ranking
HEIs	higher education institutions
HRDCs	Human Resource Development Centres
IA	internal assessment
IAMR	Institute of Applied Manpower Research
ICAR	Indian Council for Agricultural Research
ICC	Implementation Core Committee
ICRIER	Indian Council for Research on International Economic Relations
ICSSR	Indian Council of Social Science Research
ICT	information communication technologies
IGNOU	Indira Gandhi National Open University
IIE	Indian Institute of Education
IIMs	Indian Institutes of Management
IIScs	Indian Institutes of Science
IISERs	Indian Institutes of Science Education and Research
IITs	Indian Institutes of Technology
ILO	International Labour Organization
INFLIBNET	Information and Library Network

IQA	internal quality assurance
IQAC	internal quality assurance cell
ISTE	Indian Society for Technical Education
JNU	Jawaharlal Nehru University
LMS	learning management system
LOI	letter of intent
MCI	Medical Council of India
MQR	minimum qualifications regulation
MCQ	multiple choice questions
MGAHV	Mahatma Gandhi Antarrashtriya Hindi Vishwavidyalaya
MHRD	Ministry of Human Resource and Development
MKU	Madurai Kamaraj University
MOL&E	Ministry of Labour and Employment
MOOCs	massive open online courses
MSD&E	Ministry of Skill Development and Entrepreneurship
MSU	Maharaja Sayajirao University of Baroda
MSW	masters in social work
NAAC	National Assessment and Accreditation Council
NBA	National Board of Accreditation
NC	national coordinators
NCERT	National Council of Educational Research and Training
NCGTC	National Credit Guarantee Trustee Company
NCME	National Council on Measurement in Education
NCTE	National Council for Teacher Education
NCVT	National Council for Vocational Training
NEA	National Education Association
NEP	new education policy

NET	national eligibility test
NHEQF	National Higher Education Qualification Framework
NIEPA	National Institute of Educational Planning and Administration
NIRF	National Institutional Rankings Framework
NITI	National Initiative for Transformation of Institutions
NKC	National Knowledge Commission
NLRC	national level review committee
NMEICT	National Mission on Education Through ICT
NPE	national policy on education
NPM	new public management
NPTEL	National Programme on Technology Enhanced Learning
NQF	national qualification frameworks
NSDA	National Skill Development Agency
NSDC	National Skill Development Corporation
NSDF	National Skill Development Framework
NSQF	National Skill Qualification Framework
NTTCs	national teachers training centres
NUEPA	National University of Educational Planning and Administration
NVEQF	National Vocational Education Qualification Framework
OBE	outcome based education
ODE	open and distance education
OERs	open educational resource
OI	outreach and inclusivity
OPs	orientation programmes
OS	overall score
OU	open university

PBAS	performance-based appraisal system
PD	professional development
PDGHE	postgraduate diploma in higher education
PG	postgraduate
PGDDE	PG diploma in distance education
PIs	principal investigators
PL	professional learning
PMKVY	Pradhan Mantri Kaushal Vikas Yojana
PMMMNMTT	Pandit Madan Mohan Malaviya National Mission on Teachers and Teaching
PoA	programme of action
PPP	purchasing power parity
PPP	public–private partnership
PS	number of publications reported in Scopus
PSE	post-secondary education
PTR	Pupil–teacher ratio
PU	Panjab University
PUBMED	number of publications reported in Pubmed
PW	number of publications reported in Web of Science
QAu	quality audit
QA	quality assurance
QF	qualification frameworks
QIF	quality indicator framework
QIP	quality improvement programme
QS	Quacquarelli Symonds
QS Asia	Quacquarelli Symonds Asian Ranking of Universities
QSWUR	Quacquarelli Symonds World University Ranking Systems
RCs	refresher courses
RECs	regional engineering colleges

RPP	research and professional practice
RQFs	regional qualifications frameworks
RUSA	Rashtriya Uchchatar Shiksha Abhiyan
SADC	Southern African Development Community
SCDL	Symbiosis Centre for Distance Learning
SCHE	State Council of Higher Education
SCIE	Science Citation Index-Expanded
SGPA	semester grade point average
SME	subject matter expert
SPAs	Schools of Planning and Architecture
SPI	semester performance index
SSC	sectoral skill council
SSCI	social science citation index
SSDM	State Skill Development Mission
SSR	self-study report
SV	skill vouchers
SWAYAM	Study Web of Active Learning by Young and Aspiring Minds
TEIs	teacher education institutions
THE BRICS	Times Higher Education Ranking of Universities in Brazil, Russia, India, China and South Africa
THE World	Times Higher Education Ranking of World Universities
TLCs	teaching–learning centres
TLR	teaching, learning and resources
UA	external assessment conducted by the university
UG	undergraduate
UGC	University Grants Commission
UKPSF	UK Professional Standard Framework
UPE	university with potential for excellence
US	United States

USIEF	United States–India Educational Foundation
UTQ	university teaching quality
VET	vocational education and training
VPN	virtual private network
WRO	Western regional office
WTO	World Trade Organization
WUR	world university ranking
WURS	world university ranking systems

Preface

Investing in education is rewarding. Research evidence in the recent decades shows that investing in the quality of education is more rewarding to nations and individuals than extending the number of years of stay in schools. Investing in the quality of education results in higher rates of economic growth. Higher education graduates from good quality institutions enjoy a preference in hiring for employment and higher earnings, which encourages households to invest more in education and children and youth to stay for longer periods of time in schools and universities.

The increasing social demand for education combined with the willingness to invest by public authorities and students has resulted in the fast expansion and massification of the higher education sector in many developing countries such as India. The expansion process, no doubt, has contributed to increasing access to higher education. Increasing student diversity and improved representation of the under-represented groups is a sign of the possibilities of levelling-off of social inequalities in access to higher education. The increasing student diversity calls for moving away from the traditional ways of teaching–learning processes and classroom practices.

The higher education institutions of today are compelled to enhance quality to remain competitive. However, enhancing the quality of an expanding system continues to be a major challenge facing higher education in most countries. The establishment of external quality assurance mechanisms, the move towards constructing world-class universities and the popularity of global ranking of universities put pressure on the institutions to improve quality, attain global reputation and remain relevant. The quality parameters influence student choice of institutions of study, resource mobilization capacity and survival of institutions in the context of globalization and market competition.

The low learning levels, poor quality and declining employment prospects of higher education graduates have been inviting criticism in India. The pressure is for effective interventions in quality to ensure curriculum coherence, productivity of teachers and learning outcomes to regain the confidence and credibility of the sector. India, like most countries, has set up external quality assurance mechanisms to accredit institutions, established internal quality assurance cells to monitor quality at institutional levels, developed a national higher education ranking methodology and put in place initiatives to establish world-class universities/eminent institutions.

India established the National Assessment and Accreditation Council (NAAC) and National Board of Accreditation (NBA) in 1994 as external quality assurance agencies. The NAAC and NBA have been carrying out accreditation in general and technical higher education. NAAC takes into account seven criteria for their assessment. They are curricular aspects; teaching, learning and evaluation; research, consultancy and extension; infrastructure and learning resources; student support and progression; governance, leadership and management; and innovations and best practices. As of 2017, nearly 60 per cent of the universities and 25 per cent of the colleges are accredited.

NAAC prepared the guidelines for the establishment of internal quality assurance cells (IQAC) in 2007. IQACs are envisaged as the post-accreditation quality assurance measures to be initiated at the institutional levels. While external quality assurance (EQA) intervention is mostly once in five years, the IQAC is a regular system of monitoring quality operating within the institutions of higher education. The experience with regard to the functioning of the IQACs indicates that they have not become effective agents of change and quality monitoring at the institutional levels. The Centre for Policy Research in Higher Education (CPRHE) study on the effects of accreditation and functioning of IQAC cells shows good scope for improving these interventions to make them more effective.

The present *India Higher Education Report* (IHER 2017), the third in the series initiated by the CPRHE of the National University of Educational Planning and Administration (NUEPA), raises some of important issues pertaining to quality of higher education in India. The series is envisaged to provide an in-depth analysis of some of the critical dimensions of higher education in India, with contributions from eminent scholars engaged in research, policy and planning in the area of higher education. The first report—IHER 2015—provided a comprehensive account of the higher education situation in the country, focusing on various challenging issues facing the higher education sector in India. The second report—IHER 2016—focused on issues related to equity and diversity in higher education.

IHER 2017 is devoted to the theme of quality and teaching–learning in higher education. The themes included in this book cover a wide range of areas pertaining to different aspects of the theme of quality and teaching–learning in higher education. The CPRHE has succeeded in mobilizing well-known scholars in the area to address these issues. We are grateful to the authors of various chapters for their valuable contributions and for their continued support. I take this opportunity to place on record my deep appreciation of my faculty colleagues at CPRHE/NIEPA, Dr Anupam Pachauri and Dr Sayantan Mandal, for their sustained efforts and contribution to prepare this book.

N. V. Varghese

Acknowledgements

The CPRHE has published the first and second issues in the *India Higher Education Report* (IHER 2015 and IHER 2016) series. We are happy to present the third book—IHER 2017—titled *Teaching, Learning and Quality*. IHER 2017 discusses various aspects of quality concerns in higher education in India, focussing on quality assurance, rankings, research and teaching–learning in India. This book, as the previous ones, is the outcome of support received from various intellectuals and institutions and the efforts put in by the CPRHE.

IHER 2015 was a comprehensive book covering various issues and challenges facing higher education in the country. It was felt that the subsequent issues should focus on specific themes. IHER 2016 on the theme of Equity is the second in the series and has been published by SAGE. The proposal for the third IHER theme, that is Teaching, Learning and Quality, was discussed and approved in the executive committee (EC) meeting of the CPRHE in 2016. We would like to express our sincere thanks to members of the EC of the CPRHE.

We remain grateful to our previous vice-chancellors, Professor R. Govinda and Professor J. B. G. Tilak, for their guidance and support at every stage in the progress of the preparation of the IHER series.

The current book of the IHER includes chapters by some of the leading academics and policy-makers in higher education. They not only contributed their individual chapter but also contributed substantially to shape the current volume through their extensive comments on chapters by other authors. We gratefully acknowledge the valuable contribution of all the authors.

We are grateful to the registrar, NIEPA, Shri Basavaraj Swamy, publication officer, Dr Pramod Rawat, and his team for their support in facilitating the publication process and procedures.

We thank the SAGE team, especially Mr Rajesh Dey, Ms Sharmila Abraham and Ms Supriya Das, who interacted with us at different stages in the processing of the document for publication.

We are also grateful to all colleagues in CPRHE, Professor Mona Khare, Dr Nidhi S. Sabharwal, Dr Garima Malik, Dr Jinusha Panigrahi and Dr Malish CM, for their continuous support and several rounds of review comments. Ms Anuneeta Mitra must be thanked for the support with checking the references in the report.

Ms Anjali Arora, Mayank Rajput and Monica Joshi extended all logistics support to organize peer review meetings and contacting the authors. We gratefully acknowledge their support to the efforts to prepare this book.

N. V. Varghese
Anupam Pachauri
Sayantan Mandal

Chapter 1

Teaching, Learning and Quality in Higher Education in India
An Introduction

N. V. Varghese, Anupam Pachauri and
Sayantan Mandal

INTRODUCTION

Higher education has become a sought after experience that every secondary school graduate would like to have. Apart from seeing higher education as a stepping stone to a lucrative career and as a resource contributing to economic growth and social well-being, it is also seen as a source of learning how to develop a better self. Studies show that compared to high school graduates, college graduates have longer life spans, greater economic stability, better employment prospects and higher earnings. Many countries have reached a level of educational development where one may feel left out without a post-secondary level of education.

The share of labour force with higher education degrees is increasing globally, and more so in the developed countries. The share of the postgraduate degrees increased to 14 per cent in Britain and the USA as of 2015 (*The Economist*, 2015). Employers are willing to hire more and more higher education graduates and pay more for them since the employers believe that graduates from good universities are more productive and, hence, it is economically rewarding to employ them. The premium enjoyed by the higher educated in the labour market that has not declined even in the context of massification, no doubt, is a major reason for the continued massive expansion of the sector in the recent past. In other words, a larger number of students are investing longer periods of time in schools and universities in this century than in the past centuries.

The plan of this chapter is as follows: The next section discusses the reasons behind a sudden surge in the interest in quality in education followed by a discussion on the definitions of quality of higher education. The succeeding section highlights the issue of challenges to quality posed by the growing student diversity in any massifying system followed by sections on Indian efforts to improve quality in higher education and an introduction to the chapters included in this volume.

QUALITY CONCERNS IN HIGHER EDUCATION

The sources of economic growth and social well-being indicate the importance of investing in human beings and in their education (Easterly, 2002). While research evidence in the 1960s and the 1970s showed that investing in education is rewarding, the research evidence in the 1990s show that investing in quality of education contributes more to higher rates of economic growth and social returns (Hanushek, 1995). In fact, variations in rates of economic growth can be better explained by the quality of education provided in the country (Hanushek, 2005).

Quality forms the foundation on which the reputation of higher education institutions stands. Guarding global reputation is not only of academic interest but also of financial necessity for many universities. Consumer perceptions, influenced by national and international rankings, have a significant impact on student choices and institutional behaviour (OECD, 2005). Many students, domestic and international, choose institutions and invest their hard-earned resources only in return for a quality education from an institution of good reputation. Fee income forms a good share of the total income of several institutions (University Alliance, 2014). The corporate sector and production units are also equally interested in the quality of workers that they employ. The quality of graduates from the universities is an asset for many corporate houses to compete in the global market. The contribution of high quality higher education to human resource development and to economic growth is undoubtedly underlined by empirical studies (Hanushek & Woessmann, 2015).

The external pressure experienced by the university has gone up because of increasing international competition, public accountability, increased student enrolment and social economic dynamics. These factors also challenge universities to maintain quality and remain competitive. Although higher education has been forced into accepting quality assurance, there is still a mismatch between what universities have been prepared to provide and what the public actually expects them to provide. Further, the university is increasingly challenged to demonstrate its relevance, contributions and accountability to governments, funding agencies and to the people (Otara, 2015).

Higher education no longer focuses solely on the interests of the élite but plays a role in educating the majority of a nation's population to fit in the emerging dynamic world (Otara, 2015). The major challenge facing higher education systems the world over is to improve the quality of an expanding system. Most countries have set up external quality assurance (EQA) mechanisms to accredit institutions and established internal quality assurance cells (IQACs) to monitor quality at institutional levels. The university ranking exercises and national initiatives to establish world-class universities are manifestations of increased interest in the quality of higher education.

Recent discussions on quality of higher education point to the need for focusing on talented students, effective teachers, increased financial flows, and autonomy to improve teaching–learning processes and enhance learning outcomes. Advances in technology and reliance on technology have helped the globalization of higher education by making teaching–learning a globally connected process. Quality and standards have become global benchmarks to assess learning outcomes of national higher education systems across countries.

Enhancing the quality of an expanding and diverse system has become the major challenge facing most of the countries across the globe. The need for flexible, contextual and innovative learning approaches and delivery methods to address diversity on the one hand and reaching the targets set to achieve global standards on the other are the two forces that influence national priorities and institutional initiatives to enhance quality of higher education. The discussions on quality issues at the national and institutional levels are linked to discussions on improving one's position in the global rankings, creating world-class universities, enforcing accreditation and EQA standards, and promoting internal quality assurance (IQA) mechanisms. The focus is also shifting from indicators of improving access to enhancing learning outcomes.

ON DEFINING QUALITY

Quality is a multidimensional concept and, hence, it is not amenable for a simple and one-dimensional definition. Quality is seen as exceptional, conforming to standards, fitness for purpose, effectiveness in achieving institutional goals and customer's needs (Green, 1994). Many definitions tend to be stakeholder-driven definitions of quality (Schindler, Puls-Elvidge, Welzant & Crawford, 2015). There are four groups of stakeholders that are commonly considered while defining quality: (a) providers, (b) students, (c) users of outputs (employers) and (d) employees of the sector (academics and administrators) (Srikanthan & Dalrymple, 2002). The approach to quality by each of the stakeholders may vary.

One approach is to define quality as purposeful. Institutional products and services conform to a stated mission/vision or a set of specifications, requirements or standards, including those defined by accrediting and/or regulatory bodies. Another approach is to define quality as exceptional. Exceptional implies that the graduates achieve distinction and exclusivity through the fulfilment of high standards. Yet another definition focuses on the transformative dimension of quality. Transformative implies that the institutions effect positive change in student learning, and personal and professional potential. The accountability aspect of the system is also used as a definition of quality. Institutions are accountable to stakeholders for the optimal use of resources and the delivery of accurate educational products and services with zero defects (Bogue, 1998; Green, 1994; Harvey & Knight, 1996; Nicholson, 2011; Peterson, 1999).

It can be seen from the discussions that different stakeholders attempt to focus on varying aspects of quality in their definitions. For example, the professoriate will define quality focusing on the quality of research work carried out by an individual or an institution. The professional bodies tend to focus on professional standards and skills attained by the graduates. Students may focus on the quality of teaching and learning process that they experience. Despite the co-existence of multiple definitions of quality, some of the elements focused on in the definitions remain common (Ewell, 2010). One positive trend noticed over the years is that the meaning of quality in higher education remained relatively stable despite new definitions emerging (Schindler et al., 2015). An assessment of quality of an institution or a study programme balances between the elements included in the various definitions of quality. This is what many of the EQA exercises do in practice. The EQA agencies clearly identify the specific dimensions of quality such as teaching, research, infrastructure, teaching–learning conditions, etc. to be assessed when the assessment teams visit institutions.

It may be important to understand the differences between quality assurance, quality control, quality assessment and quality audit. Quality assurance is a process-focused activity and refers to a continuous process of evaluating the quality of higher education systems, institutions or programmes. This evaluation is done based on a commonly agreed upon criteria. Quality control is a product-focused concept, focusing on whether or not the outputs and outcomes are of expected quality. Quality assessment or quality review implies the actual process of external evaluation of an institution or programme. It focuses on the methods and mechanisms relied on to review quality aspects of an institution or programme (Campbell & Rozsnyai, 2002). A quality audit reviews the existing quality-assurance mechanisms in an institution and assesses the adequacy of these mechanisms to assure quality.

Quality assurance can be external and internal. EQA refers to the process of quality assurance carried out by an external body to determine whether the institution or programme is meeting the standards that have been set apriority. The work carried out by the accreditation agencies belongs to EQA. The IQA refers to policies and mechanisms existing in an institution for ensuring the quality and standards of its programmes.

Accreditation is the most commonly understood and widely used method of EQA. It is a process employed by a public or private body to evaluate the quality of a higher education institution or programme to formally certify that it (the institution or programme) has met certain predetermined standards. Accreditation makes an assessment and a kind of benchmarking based on a set of pre-determined quality criteria. It is thus the only method within the quality assurance spectrum that makes an explicit judgement about the degree to which an institution or programme actually meets pre-determined standards and quality.

The accreditation process is broadly seen in three steps. The first step is the preparation of a self-study of the institution or programme conducted by the institution itself. The second step involves a visit by a team of experts selected by the accrediting agency. The visiting team reviews the documents and the veracity of evidence with reference to the claims made by the institution in the self-study reports. The team holds discussions with the academic and administrative staff, and prepares a report to be submitted to the accreditation agency. Finally, the third step entails an examination of the reports by the accreditation agency to finally certify the quality level and accredit the institution or programme.

QUALITY AND DIVERSITY

Growing student diversity is a characteristic feature of any massifying higher education system. When the system expands and inequality indicators show a decline, there will be more students from disadvantaged groups in higher education institutions. Maintaining quality in a massifying system marked by diversity is a challenge faced by most higher education systems in the world. The student diversity is characterized by diverse social, economic, lingual and regional backgrounds as well as academic interests and work aspirations. The public authorities have responded to the challenges of student diversity by introducing diversity in academic study programmes in the university system.

The emergence and expansion of non-university institutions offering vocationally oriented courses reflects one of the successful strategies in this context. The training of skilled workforce in polytechnics in Finland, establishment of universities of applied sciences in Switzerland and differentiated higher education systems in the USA, Japan and Korea among others show how some countries have addressed student diversity in an expanding system (OECD, 2006).

The ideal institutions are those which succeed in combining equity with quality, giving opportunities for a good quality education to all children (Guimaraes de Castro, 1998). However, in reality, this is rarely successfully implemented. Empirical research based on a meta-analysis of large numbers of studies of class-size effects has shown that the more the number of students in a class, the lower the level of student achievement (Glass & Smith, 1979). It is argued, based on micro-level data, that educational quality is compromised as class size increases.

The problem is more acute and challenging when classrooms have students belonging to varying ethnic and social backgrounds, and schooling experience. The massification process worldwide has resulted in extending higher education opportunities to disadvantaged groups and first-generation learners. The changes in student composition challenge the traditional attitude towards teaching–learning process and its forms. The expansion of the system not accompanied by efforts to provide facilities and the quality enhancing measures targeting student diversity may result in declining quality.

INDIAN APPROACH TO QUALITY IN HIGHER EDUCATION

India's concern for quality is reflected in its approach to higher education. The committees and commissions appointed in the post-Independence period underlined the importance of quality in higher education. Till the end of the past century, these committees consistently expressed their fear that expansion of the higher education system will lead to a decline in quality and standards. The University Education Commission of 1948 considered that higher education was for the talented, and was concerned about the possible erosion in quality if enrolment increased and the system expanded (MOE, 1962).

The Education Commission of 1964–1966 was also in favour of limiting access to higher education for fear of erosion in quality. They were in favour of selective admissions to higher education institutions so as to maintain quality. The commission argued for a cautioned expansion of enrolment in the universities, and that too accompanied by an increase in the number of competent teachers and improvement in the facilities (NCERT, 1970). *The Challenge of Education* document of 1985 (MOE, 1985) and the *National Policy on Education* of 1986 also argued for a consolidation rather than a quantitative expansion of the system. For the committees and commissions, protecting the university education from degeneration and poor quality was the foremost concern rather than the expansion of higher education (Mathew, 2016).

This approach to quality changed from the turn of this century. The committees appointed in the past two decades argued for an expansion of the system. For example, the Birla-Ambani Committee 2000 (GOI, 2000), the National Knowledge Commission 2006 (GOI, 2006) and the Narayana Murthy Committee 2012 (GOI, 2012) among others did not favour a policy of limited expansion of the system for fear of erosion of quality. In fact, they underlined the importance of an expanded higher education sector to improve global competitiveness of the economy.

Interventions for Quality Improvement

The interventions to improve quality can be seen at several fronts. The focus has been on teachers and improvements in teaching, learning and research, although the commissions and committees also laid emphasis on revision of curriculum and student assessment methods.

The quality culture of an institution is rooted in its faculty and in their teaching competencies and research capacities. The committees and commissions have discussed about teaching–learning processes in the traditional mode of teaching as a teacher-centric activity revolving around the curriculum, textbooks, teachers and lectures. This situation is gradually changing in most of the institutions. With massification, the diversity in institutions and classrooms has become more apparent. It is no longer a selective group of 'talented' students as envisaged by the committees. Further, with increasing reliance on technology, the role of teachers, teaching and learning is transforming.

Higher education institutions are no longer a preserve of the élites. The massification process has attracted a large number of students from disadvantaged groups and first-generation learners with wide variations in pre-college experiences, in terms of language, course contents, and socialization with technology and people. In many institutions and classrooms, the students from disadvantaged groups form the majority. The changes in student composition challenge the traditional forms of teaching–learning process and call for a different approach and methodology of teaching–learning process. The student diversity brings along with it differences in the pre-college academic experiences which impact teaching–learning and learning outcomes in higher education (Sabharwal & Malish, 2017).

The other factor influencing teaching–learning process is technology. The new generation students are 'net' generation learners and depend more on online learning resources than on the traditional library resources and printed books (Varghese & Mandal, 2016). The e-learning and virtual campuses offer students alternatives to the traditional face-to-face learning conditions. The online discussions, assessments and projects/collaborative work replace the traditional face-to-face teaching and learning. The massive open online courses (MOOCs) have changed the landscape of higher education globally. The SWAYAM (Study Web of Active Learning by Young and Aspiring Minds—Indian version of MOOCs) is launched with a high level of expectation. The digital learning has been envisaged to become an integral part of the teaching–learning process in higher education in India.

Although technology has changed the role of teachers, as discussed earlier, the teacher continues to be the most important factor facilitating and promoting learning among students. Therefore, teacher recruitment to ensure quality teachers is of prime concern in higher education. Teaching needs to become more learner-centric and follow a constructivist approach for effective learning (Mandal, 2017). A teacher of today is a manager of student learning, a computer and networker—skilled in inter-personal relationships—and a democrat in the classrooms in addition to his or her traditional role as a course designer, supervisor, assessor, evaluator and subject expert (Wright, 2011).

At a time when the global pressure to enhance the quality of higher education is increasing, there is a decline in the academic profession in India. Some attribute this decline to dilution of academic rigour and ethos of academic profession (Jayaram, 2003). This together with shortages of teachers and large-sized classrooms are posing challenges to maintain good quality in higher education. A high teacher-student ratio (of 1:23) when compared with universities in other countries (Tilak & Mathew, 2015) puts tremendous pressure on teachers in teaching and evaluating the students.

Teaching is not the most attractive profession for young graduates. The salary levels and service conditions remain low when compared with other professions requiring the same qualification levels. Besides the non-stability of employment in academics, the other constraint is the limited possibilities of professional and institutional mobility for those in the system. Once placed in academic caste system, it is very difficult to move (Altbach, 1977). This factor also acts as a deterrent for aspiring academics who would like to join the teaching profession.

Unfortunately, India does not have any systematic induction or in service programme focusing on pedagogical aspects in higher education. The University Grants Commission (UGC) introduced an academic staff orientation scheme (ASOS) and established at least one academic staff college in each state following the recommendations of the 1986 Policy on Education. Further, the UGC introduced a national competitive examination—the National Eligibility Test (NET)—as a basic requirement for recruiting teachers.

As a follow-up to the recommendations of the Mehrotra Committee report of 1986 (UGC, 1986), the UGC has been conducting a national-level eligibility test (NET) for prospective university teachers (Varghese, Malik & Gautam, 2017). Variations among institutions in terms of basic facilities, teacher qualifications and competencies, and student profiles are wide. These variations will have their implications in learning outcomes and quality of higher education.

The most recent efforts towards improving the quality of higher education are through a mission established by the Ministry of Human Resource and Development (MHRD). The Pandit Madan

Mohan Malaviya National Mission on Teachers and Teaching (PMMMNMTT) mission introduced during the Twelfth Five-year Plan (2012–2017) focuses on inputs for enhancing learning outcomes and quality of higher education, relying on mobilizing a large number of high quality professors from top ranking institutions in the country (Varghese, Pachauri & Mandal, 2017).

EQA AND IQA SYSTEMS IN INDIA

International experience shows that many countries created EQA mechanisms to carry out accreditation and quality audits. India established accreditation agencies in 1994—the National Assessment and Accreditation Council (NAAC) for university sector working under UGC and the National Board of Accreditation (NBA) working under the All India Council for Technical Education (AICTE). While NAAC accredits institutions, the NBA accredits programmes.

The quality assessment by NAAC is accomplished through a process of self-study and peer review using well-defined criteria. The main purpose of assessment and accreditation is the improvement and enhancement of quality, recognizing excellence, accountability, information and benchmarking. Assessment is mainly based on seven major criteria: (a) curricular aspects; (b) teaching–learning and evaluation; (c) research, consultancy and extension; (d) infrastructure and learning resources; (e) student support and progression; (f) organization and management; and (g) healthy and innovative practices.

Accreditation of institutions and programmes in India used to be voluntary. This may be one of the reasons for a very slow progress in accreditation. The Twelfth Five-year Plan showed that only about one-third of the universities and about one-fifth of the colleges have been accredited at the end of the plan period. This trend will change since the UGC has linked accreditation with funding and the AICTE has made accreditation by NBA mandatory for all technical institutions.

The focus in quality assurance has shifted from EQA to IQA mechanisms. It is expected that the IQA mechanisms can help in addressing the requirements of national EQA agencies, and respond to the requirements for internal quality monitoring and management. In practice, the IQA systems can address issues related to teaching–learning more effectively than EQA systems. The IQA mechanisms today typically comprise of self-studies and evaluations of units/departments; monitoring and review of academic programmes; carrying out student surveys on teaching effectiveness; student and staff satisfaction surveys; analyzing student progression and so on.

In many cases, the IQA cells operate more like units collecting information and presenting the information on an agreed-upon format. Their effectiveness in terms of monitoring quality and teaching–learning processes is not yet evidenced. One of the reasons for this limited functioning of the IQA cells is the human resources available to them and their understanding of the role of the IQACs. Mostly IQACs end up conducting only the activities which are mandatory in nature, confining themselves to collecting and storing data that they receive from each of the departments (Pachauri, 2017). Many of them are not clear about their roles and responsibilities to facilitate the monitoring of quality and extending academic support. There is a need to orient those responsible for managing the IQACs. In other words, there is a need to strengthen IQA cells so that they will be able to play a more effective role in monitoring and improving quality at the institutional levels.

IHER 2017: TEACHING, LEARNING AND QUALITY

The India Higher Education Report 2017: Teaching, Learning and Quality consists of three broad themes in its conceptual frame. The first theme covers the chapters with focus on 'rankings, research and quality'; the second theme focuses on 'teachers and teaching–learning'; and the third theme covers the chapters focusing on 'quality management'.

Rankings, Research and Quality

Institutions are becoming increasingly aware of their global standing because the universities realize that they are situated in a global marketplace. In India, there is a sense of disquiet voiced by the chancellors, businesses and policy-making circles that none of the Indian universities figure in the top 200 universities of the world. The methodological problems with the rankings have been widely recognized but still the rankings seem to have stayed on and are influencing institutions. National governments aspire for their higher education institutions to compete globally and become academically attractive to international students and researchers.

G. D. Sharma, in Chapter 2 titled 'World University Ranking Systems: Are They Indicators of Quality?', compares indicators and methodologies of several world university rankings. Some of the rankings give a substantial importance to the reputation of the institution, while others focus more on research and publications.

India launched its national rankings of higher education institutions in 2015. Analyzing the National Institutional Ranking Framework (NIRF) 2017 ranking indicators and scores, Chapter 3 by Furqan Qamar, titled 'Measuring Performance of Higher Education Institutions and the National Institutional Ranking Framework', highlights that even the top-ranking institutions do not fulfil all the quality parameters. Further, the gap in rank scores between the top rank institutions and the bottom rank institutions amongst the top 100 institutions is wide on various indicators such as teaching, learning, resources, research and professional practice. In addition, any change in the weightage given to parameters could change the place of the institutions in ranking. The ranking, however, could be useful in identifying the quality gaps in the institutions, and designing appropriate policy and support environment to fill those gaps.

Research in universities is a stepping stone to improve the quality of teaching. Chapter 4, 'Research on Higher Education in India', by N. Jayaram shows that the progress of educational research in the universities has been uneven in India. The development of publicly funded researches and research institutes, and their growth trajectory and policy development help explain the paradigms and set the course for the recent developments. The critical analysis examines the increasing gap between policy and research in higher education, with its possible consequences.

Teachers and Teaching–Learning

Although teaching and learning are considered core to improve quality, research evidence on teaching–learning processes and classroom practices in higher education are limited, if not rare. The higher education classrooms around the world are changing from lecture-based and teacher-centric modes to more interactive and student-oriented teaching processes. New teaching strategies and new modes of technology mediated teaching–learning process are slowly but steadily gaining acceptance. MOOCs and other open source course platforms are increasingly supporting the extension of technology in teaching and learning. Besides planning for provision of teachers, the professional development of teachers in higher education and availability of resources is an issue, which this theme addresses.

One of the major and most crucial issues in the massifying Indian higher education is the severe shortage of teachers. The lag in public and institutional policies has made the situation critical where even after having a sufficient supply of eligible candidates, nearly half of the sanctioned teaching posts are vacant or are filled by temporary ad hoc faculties with low pay and no benefits. Analyzing this concern with an economic lens, Chiranjib Sen, in Chapter 5 titled 'Availability and Shortages of Teachers in Higher Education', argues that some of the common perceptions need to reviewed, and a series of strategic planning could provide a solution in this front.

In Chapter 6, titled 'Professional Development of Teachers in Higher Education', Santosh Panda examines the design of the continuous professional development (CPD) for teachers in higher education in Indian context. The chapter discusses the notion of professionalism and its implications for the profession of teaching in higher education. The design of several schemes and programmes for teachers' professional development including the implementation structure are analyzed to show their strengths and limitations. Further, in view of the provisions and resources, the schemes for professional development are discussed to arrive at the CPD framework for higher education teachers.

Chapter 7, titled 'Critical Perspectives of Teaching–Learning in Indian Higher Education', by Sayantan Mandal provides a first-hand account of the classroom teaching and learning in Indian colleges and universities. By analyzing the differences in teaching approaches and learning patterns, the author argues that teaching, learning and classroom practices have immense scope of improvement in view of changes in technologies and need for democratizing teaching–learning processes.

In Chapter 8, 'Developing e-Content for Massive Open Online Courses: An Experience of Teaching–Learning Centre', Vimal Rarh discusses the digital initiatives in India, with a focus on Indian MOOCs. Describing the process of e-content development in India and its development, the chapter focuses on the process in which it is blended with the national-level programme on teacher development. The challenges confronted by the Indian MOOCs are varied and context-specific. The analysis of the issues and challenges to this in its conception, planning and implementation phases provide a picture of Indian specificities of MOOCs, which is further discussed with selected case studies.

In Chapter 9, 'Student Assessments in Higher Education', K. Pushpanadham focuses on the roles of the policy actors, academia and other stakeholders in reshaping student assessment in Indian higher education. With specific case studies of student assessment patterns in different types of higher education institutions—general, technical, management and medical—the chapter analyses the complex and varied nature of assessment practices in the Indian system.

Providing students with more subject choices is a recent phenomenon in India. M. Rajivlochan and Meeta Rajivlochan elaborate the development of choice-based credit system (CBCS) in Indian higher education and the hurdles it faces at different levels to implement it. Chapter 10, 'Choice-based Credit System and Semester System in Indian Higher Education', argues that the policies and rigid compartmental structure of HEIs make the challenge complex.

Quality Management

Enhancing the quality of an expanding and diverse system has become the major challenge facing most countries across the globe. The focus of quality assessment is shifting from indicators of improving access to enhancing learning outcomes. The management 'of' and management 'for' quality at the institutional level is crucial and requires institutional efforts through devising policies, structures, mechanisms, processes and accountability frameworks. The IQACs linked to institutional governance for quality could play a vital role in achieving excellence.

In Chapter 11, 'Quality and Accountability in Higher Education', Mariamma Varghese explores various conceptions of quality with reference to the institutional accountability system, and how quality and accountability relate to institutional structures, governance and management. The author argues that quality and accountability are different facets of the higher education system. It is very important to consider the questions of who is accountable, to whom and how, and accordingly develop appropriate structures, rules and indicators. Calling for primary focus on students while devising accountability systems, the author urges institutions for individual as well as collective responsibility in view of their vision and mission.

Chapter 12, 'Managing Quality at Institutional Level', by B. S. Madhukar argues that even when the institutional assessment exercises are effectuated, through EQAs and IQA mechanisms, they do not bring desired outcomes due to lack of institutional culture. Drawing from international experience and developments in QA, B. S. Madhukar discusses the importance of institutional culture in having effective QA and quality improvement.

Anupam Pachauri, in Chapter 13 titled 'Effects of External Quality Assurance and Internal Quality Assurance on Indian Higher Education Institutions', discusses the effects of EQA and IQA on institutions, along with the dimensions of systematization of norms, procedures and structures; inclusion of diverse voices and perspectives; finance; and human resources. IQACs have been envisaged as an essential component of higher education institutions for the maintenance, enhancement and improvement of quality. The IQAC is expected to be the link between the EQA agency—in this case NAAC—and the institutions. The structure and function of IQAC has been broadly suggested by NAAC. In addition, instituting IQAC is a mandatory requirement for the institutions for going for the second and subsequent cycles of NAAC accreditation and assessment. Anupam Pachauri draws from a national research project at the Centre for Policy Research in Higher Education (CPRHE) of the National University of Educational Planning and Administration on the institutional effects of EQA and IQA.

In Chapter 14, 'Finance and Quality: The Reshaping of Higher Education', Aarti Srivastava focuses on funding and investment for quality improvement in higher education institutions. University budgets reveal to a great extent how and where the funds are being routed, and their relationship with various activities contributing to quality of the institution such as student welfare, research infrastructure and so on. The analysis of plan and non-plan grants is undertaken to show their impact on institutional quality. Analyzing budgets of a centrally funded university, the author highlights how institutions prioritize different aspects of quality.

In the last chapter of this volume, 'Qualification Frameworks for Improving Quality and Relevance of Education', N. V. Varghese brings out the importance of the national qualification frameworks (NQFs), and discusses their effect on learning outcomes and competency-based training. The author argues that NQF could be one of the measures to regain confidence of the employers and public in the national system of education. The NQFs also serve an important function of enabling comparisons of systems and qualifications, thus facilitating cross-border movement of students.

REFERENCES

Altbach, P. G. (1977). In search of Saraswati: The ambivalence of the Indian academic. *Higher Education*, 6(2), 255–275.

Bogue, G. (1998). Quality assurance in higher education: The evolution of systems and design ideals. *New Directions for Institutional Research*, 99, 7–18.

Campbell, C., & Rozsnyai, C. (2002). *Quality assurance and the development of course programmes*. Bucharest: UNESCO-CEPES.

Easterly, W. (2002). *The elusive quest for growth: An economist's adventures and misadventures in the tropic*. Cambridge, MA: MIT Press.

Ewell, P. (2010). Twenty years of quality assurance in higher education: What's happened and what's different? *Quality in Higher Education*, 16(2), 173–175.

Glass, G. V., & Smith, M. L. (1979). Meta-analysis of research on the relationship of class-size and achievement. *Evaluation and Policy Analysis*, 1(1), 2–16.

GOI (Government of India). (2000). *Report on a policy framework for reforms in education. Prime Minister's Council on Trade and Industry.* New Delhi: Government of India. (Also known as the Birla-Ambani Report).

———. (2006). *National knowledge commission report of the working group on undergraduate education.* New Delhi: National Knowledge Commission. Retrieved 14 January 2017, from www.knowledgecommission.gov.in

———. (2012). *Committee on corporate sector participation in higher education: Report of N. R. Narayana Murthy committee.* New Delhi: Planning Commission, Government of India.

Green, D. (Ed.). (1994). *What is quality in higher education?* London, UK: Society for Research into Higher Education & Open University Press.

Guimaraes de Castro, M. H. (1998). *Education for the 21st century: The challenge of quality and equity.* Brasilia: Esplanada dos Ministérios.

Hanushek, E. A. (1995). Interpreting recent research on schooling in developing countries. *World Bank Research Observer, 10*(2), 227.

———. (2005). Why quality matters? *Finance and Development, 42*(2), 15–19.

Hanushek, Eric A., & Woessmann, L. (2015). *Knowledge capital of nations: Education and economics of growth.* Cambridge, MA: MIT Press.

Harvey, L., & Knight, P. T. (1996). *Transforming higher education.* London, UK: Society for Research into Higher Education & Open University Press.

Jayaram, N. (2003). The fall of the Guru: The decline of the academic profession in India. In P. Altbach (Ed.), *The decline of the Guru: The academic profession in developing and middle-income countries* (pp. 199–230). New York, NY: Palgrave Macmillan. doi:10.1057/9781403982568

Mandal, S. (2017). *Teaching learning in higher education in India—A synthesis report.* New Delhi: CPRHE–NIEPA.

Mathew, A. (2016). Reforms in higher education in India: A review of recommendations of commissions and committees on education. *CPRHE Research Paper Series: Research Paper 2.* New Delhi: CPRHE–NIEPA.

MOE (Ministry of Education). (1962). *The report of University Education Commission 1948–1949.* New Delhi: Ministry of Education, Government of India.

———. (1985). *Challenge of education: Policy perspective.* New Delhi: Ministry of Education, Government of India.

NCERT (National Council for Educational Research and Training). (1970). *Education and national development: Report of education commission (1964–66).* New Delhi: National Council for Educational Research and Training.

Nicholson, K. (2011). *Quality assurance in higher education: A review of the literature.* Retrieved 18 September 2017, from http://cll.mcmaster.ca/COU/pdf/Quality%20Assurance%20Literature%20Review.pdf

OECD (Organisation for Economic Cooperation and Development). (2005). *Guidelines for quality provision in crossborder higher education.* Paris: Organisation for Economic Cooperation and Development.

———. (2006). *Higher education: Quality, equity and efficiency.* Paris: IMHE, Organisation for Economic Cooperation and Development.

Otara, A. (2015). Internal quality assurance in higher education from instructors perspectives in Rwanda: A mirage or reality? *Journal of Education and Human Development*, *4*(2, June), 168–174.

Pachauri, A. (2017). *Quality in higher education in India: A study of external and internal quality assurance at the institutional level—A research synthesis report.* New Delhi: CPRHE-NIEPA.

Peterson, J. C. (1999). *Internationalizing quality assurance in higher education.* Washington, DC: Council for Higher Education Accreditation.

Sabharwal, N., & Malish, C. M. (2017). *Diversity and discrimination in higher education: A study of institutions in selected states of India—A research synthesis report.* New Delhi: CPRHE-NIEPA.

Schindler, S., Puls-Elvidge, S., Welzant, H., & Crawford, L. (2015). Definitions of quality in higher education: A synthesis of the literature. *Higher Learning Research Communications*, *5*(3), 3–13.

Srikanthan, G., & Dalrymple, J. (2002). Developing a holistic model for quality in higher education. *Quality in Higher Education*, *8*(3), 215–224.

The Economist. (2015). Excellence v equity. *The Economist Special Report*, 26 March.

Tilak, J. B. G., & Mathew, A. (2015). Promotion in the academic profession in India: Upward mobility of faculty in higher education. *Changing Academic Profession* (RIHE International Seminar Reports, No. 23). Hiroshima University, Japan: Regional Institute of Higher Education.

University Alliance. (2014). *How do we ensure quality in an expanding higher education system?* London: University Alliance.

UGC (University Grants Commission), Government of India. (1986). *Report of the committee on revision of pay scales of teachers in universities and colleges* (also known as Mehrotra Committee). New Delhi: University Grants Commission, Government of India.

Varghese, N. V., Malik, G., & Gautam, D. (2017). Teacher recruitment in higher education in India: An analysis of NET results. *CPRHE Research Paper Series* (Research Paper No. 8). New Delhi: CPRHE-NIEPA.

Varghese, N. V., & Mandal, S. (2016). *Report of the international seminar on teaching learning and technology*, New Delhi: CPRHE.

Varghese, N. V., Pachauri, A., & Mandal, S. (2017). *Pandit Madan Mohan Malviya National Mission on Teachers and Teaching: An evaluation report.* New Delhi: MHRD.

Wright, P. M. (2011). Exploring human capital: Putting 'human' back into strategic human resource management. *Human Resource Management Journal*, *21*(2, April), 93–104.

PART I

Rankings, Research and Quality

Chapter 2

World University Ranking Systems
Are They Indicators of Quality?

G. D. Sharma

INTRODUCTION

World university rankings (WURs) have become a highly discussed theme in recent times after the publication of results of WUR by Times Higher Education (THE) and Academic Ranking of World Universities (ARWU). The debate in India also centres on the absence of Indian institutions in the world rankings. Universities from the developing world are rarely found in the world ranking list (*TOI*, 2016). This raises the question: does WUR represent ranking of world universities or does it represent only a set of universities from selected countries? An equally important question is whether the parameters and methodology used by WUR agencies reflect wide variations of university systems across countries. This chapter attempts to discuss the methodology of rankings followed by different agencies and their global relevance.

UNIVERSITY SYSTEMS IN THE WORLD

The development of university system can be seen in terms of different waves. The first wave was around the fifth century AD, when the first universities in the world were established in the Indian sub-continent, in Nalanda, Taxshila and Vikramshila. The second wave was the establishment of universities in the 9th and 10th centuries in Egypt and Morocco around 857 AD and 970 AD in Africa and Arab—or Maghreb. The third wave was in Italy in Bologna followed by in Spain and UK around 1088 and 1096. All the universities across the three waves represented three religious orientations, namely, Hindu, Islamic and Christian. The fourth wave university system is identified with experimentation and exploration mainly by the academics from the third wave university system, and this development took place in the USA. The fifth wave denotes the development of the university system mainly in the British and French colonies, under the influence of fourth wave universities.

The first wave and the beginnings of universities can be traced to the 5th century AD. Taxshila offered courses in more than 60 subject areas and attracted students from countries such as Babylonia, Greece, Arabia and China. The university of Nalanda established in the 5th century AD in the kingdom of Magadha (present state of Bihar in India) had many students from China, Korea, Japan, Tibet, Mongolia, Turkey, Sri Lanka and Southeast Asia The third oldest university was Vikramshila (783 AD) located in the present state of Bihar in India.

The second wave of establishment of universities are found in Morocco and Egypt. The University of Kaureen or University of al-Karaouine or al Quaraouiyine was established in 859 AD by Fatima Al Fihri, the daughter of a wealthy merchant. The university taught language, logic, medicine, mathematics and astronomy along with the Quran and Fiqh (Islamic jurisprudence). In Egypt, Cairo Al Ahzar University was set up as early as 970 AD. Established as a madrasa, it consisted of primary to tertiary levels, focused on Islamic education.

The first and second wave universities represented civilizations in the Asian World and African Muslim World. They focused on religion, logic, medicine, mathematics, astronomy and jurisprudence. The third wave of the university system came from Europe—Bologna, Italy—founded in 1088 AD, which is oldest in Europe. Among others, the top 10 oldest universities of the world presently in operation and ranked by the QS are given in Table 2.1.

Table 2.1 *Top Ten Oldest Universities in the World*

Name of the University	Founding Year (AD)
University of Al Azhar, Egypt	970
University of Bologna, Italy	1088
University of Oxford, UK	1096
University of Salamanca, Spain	1134
University of Sorbonne (presently University of Paris), France	1160
University of Cambridge, UK	1209
University of Padua, Italy	1222
University of Naples Federico II	1224
University of Siena, Italy	1240
University of Coimbra, Portugal	1290

Source: https://www.topuniversities.com

The fourth wave universities were established after 1500 AD. In Asia, the University of Santo Tomas, Philippines, was established in 1611; the University of Harvard, Massachusetts, in the USA in 1636; and the University of Sydney, Australia, in 1850. The fifth wave universities came to be set up in 1857: in India, the Bombay University in the Presidency of Bombay; Madras University in the Presidency of Madras; and Calcutta University in the Presidency of West Bengal. These universities were poor replica of the British university system. The setting up of Banaras Hindu University (BHU) and Aligarh Muslim University (AMU) was an attempt to resurrect the first and second wave university system and amalgamate it with the modern British university model. Similar trends have also been seen in many of the erstwhile colonial countries ruled by the British and the French that attempted to combine indigenous knowledge resources with the Western knowledge systems.

The estimates by Webometrics indicate that, as on 2016, there are about 40,000 higher education institutions (HEIs) (Webometrics, n.d.). However, not all of the HEIs appear in the popular ranking systems. In the following passages, we examine the methodology of selected systems of university rankings. When one is looking into the rankings of universities in the world, it is the third/fourth wave universities that seem to have gained pre-dominance in the WUR system. It may be pertinent to dwell briefly on all these wave systems of world universities and system of ranking.

World university ranking systems (WURS): The rankings of the world universities are a recent phenomenon. The first ARWU was published by Shanghai in 2003 which was followed by the Quacquarelli Symonds (QS) ranking of world universities published in 2004 and the THE ranking of world universities, 2009.[1] The most recent one is the WUR by Centre for World University Ranking (CWUR) in Jeddah, Saudi Arabia, in 2012. These rankings follow certain parameters, methodology of survey/data collection and techniques of ranking based on parameters and data collected through various sources. It may be pertinent to briefly mention the parameters and methodology followed by each of them.

Quacquarelli Symonds World University Rankings (QSWUR): The QSWUR assesses universities on 11 performance indicators relating to research, teaching, employability, internationalization, facilities, online/distance learning, social responsibility, innovation, arts and culture, inclusiveness and specialist criteria (Table 2.2). To be eligible for inclusion, institutions must teach at both undergraduate and postgraduate level, and conduct work in at least two of five broad faculty areas (arts and humanities, engineering and technology, social sciences and management, natural sciences, and life sciences and medicine; QS WUR, 2017).

THE TIMES HIGHER EDUCATION WORLD UNIVERSITY RANKINGS

THE's WUR uses 13 performance indicators, grouped into five categories. Institutions are excluded if they do not teach at undergraduate level or if their research output is below a certain threshold (THE, 2017; see Table 2.3).

---

[1] Before 2009, the QS and the THE rankings were combined.

Table 2.2 *Metrics for QS Ranking and Weightage in Overall Score*

Metrics for QS Ranking	Weightage in Overall Score (in %)
Academic reputation based on global survey of academics	worth 40% of the overall score
Employer reputation based on a global survey of employers	10
Student-to-faculty ratio	20
Research citations per faculty member	20
Proportion of international faculty	5
Proportion of international students	5

Source: QS WUR (2017).

ACADEMIC RANKING OF WORLD UNIVERSITIES

Also widely known as the Shanghai Ranking, the ARWU assesses six performance indicators, all relating to research excellence (Table 2.4). The ranking considers all institutions with Nobel Laureates, Fields Medallists, highly cited researchers, papers published in *Nature* or *Science*, or a significant number of papers indexed by the Science Citation Index-Expanded (SCIE) or Social Science Citation Index (SSCI; ARWU, 2017).

CENTRE FOR WORLD UNIVERSITY RANKING

CWUR uses eight objective and robust indicators to rank the world's top 1,000 universities (CWUR, 2017; see Table 2.5).

COMPARATIVE ANALYSIS OF WUR SYSTEMS

A comparative analysis of the ranking systems reveals that there is an emphasis on performance of the university in terms of Nobel Prizes and awards to alumni or their employment in high position in Forbes ranked companies. Two of the WUR systems, namely, THE and

Table 2.3 *THE Ranking and Weightage in Overall Score*

Categories for THE Ranking		Weightage in Overall Score (In %)	
Teaching	Reputation survey	15	30
	Staff-to-student ratio	4.5	
	Doctorate-to-bachelors ratio	2.25	
	Doctorates-awarded-to-academic-staff ratio	6	
	Institutional income	2.25	
Research	Reputation survey	18	30
	Research income	6	
	Research papers published per faculty member	6	
International outlook	International-to-domestic-student ratio	2.5	7.5
	International-to-domestic-staff ratio	2.5	
	International research collaborations	2.5	
Industry-income	Based on income earned from industry, relative to the number of academic staff employed, and adjusted for purchasing power parity (PPP)		2.5

Source: THE (2017).

QS, rely on survey of reputation. In the case of QS, almost half of the scores are based on the reputation survey, whereas in THE, it is only 33 per cent. Furthermore, there is emphasis on publications and citation index. In case of CWUR, almost half of the score are for awards to the alumni and present faculty members. In ARWU system, the awards to alumni and present faculty account for 30 per cent of the score. Research publication and citation have weightage of 40 per cent. QS WUR gives 20 per cent of the score for teacher–student ratio and another 20 per cent for research publication and citation. International faculty and students get a small score say 5 per cent or so.

Table 2.4 *ARWU Ranking and Weightage in Overall Score*

Metrics for ARWU Ranking	Weightage in Overall Score (in %)
Alumni	10
Based on the number of alumni of an institution who have won Nobel Prizes and Fields Medals, with greater weight given to more recent recipients.	
Awards	20
Based on the number of staff affiliated with an institution who have won Nobel Prizes in physics, chemistry, medicine and economics, and Fields Medals in mathematics, with greater weight given to more recent recipients.	
Highly cited researchers	20
Based on an institution's number of highly cited researchers, according to the latest list published by Thomson Reuters.	
Papers in *Nature* and *Science*	20
Based on the number of papers published in these two influential journals, drawing on a four-year period. For institutions specialized in social sciences and humanities, this category does not apply.	
Papers indexed	20
Based on the number of papers indexed in the SCIE and SSCI in the preceding calendar year, with a double weighting for papers indexed in the SSCI.	
Per capita performance	10
The weighted scores of the other indicators, divided by the number of full-time equivalent academic staff.	

* Methodology and estimation technique followed by it is given in Appendix 2.1.

Source: ARWU (2017).

Table 2.5 *WUR and Weightage in Overall Score*

Metrics for Centre for World University Ranking	Weightage in Overall Score (in %)
Quality of Education	25
Measured by the number of a university's alumni who have won major international awards, prizes and medals relative to the university's size	
Alumni Employment	25
Measured by the number of a university's alumni who have held CEO positions at the world's top companies relative to the university's size	
Quality of Faculty	25
Measured by the number of academics who have won major international awards, prizes and medals	
Publications	5
Measured by the number of research papers appearing in reputable journals	
Influence	5
Measured by the number of research papers appearing in highly influential journals	
Citations	5
Measured by the number of highly cited research papers	
Broad impact	5
Measured by the university's *h*-index	
Patents	5
Measured by the number of international patent filings	

Source: CWUR (2017).

Let us see which of the universities are ranked in the top 10 by following these different systems, though broadly following similar parameters.

It is interesting to note that in spite of different parameters and different weights given to these parameters, the results of top 10 universities belonging to different countries remain more or less the same (Table 2.6). The exceptions are Switzerland and one additional university in UK in THE ranking. It is also important to observe that it is the fourth wave universities—with focus on experimentation and exploration—that are appearing in the list of top 10 universities. However, rank of universities in the top 10 list from one system to other also varies as could be seen from Table 2.7.

Let us examine how universities have been ranked within top 100 university lists by different WUR systems for 2016. Table 2.8 gives a picture of numbers of universities from different countries ranked by these systems in the list 11–100.

Table 2.8 reveals that again it is the fourth wave universities, particularly from the USA, and third wave universities, particularly from Europe, which dominate WURs. However, exceptions of finding some universities from groups other than these two have also been observed.

SUBJECT RANKING OF WORLD UNIVERSITIES

The ranking of universities by subject have been done by three systems of WUR, namely, QS, THE and ARWU. The parameters taken for

Table 2.6 Top 10 Universities Ranked by Different WUR Systems in 2016

Sl. No.	Country	QS	ARWU	THE	CWUR
1	USA	5	8	6	8
2	UK	4	2	3	2
3	Switzerland	1	0	1	0
Total		10	10	10	10

Source: QS, THE, ARWU and CWUR websites.

Table 2.7 List of Top 10 Universities Ranked by Different WUR Systems, 2016

	CWUR		Times HE
USA	Harvard University	USA	California Institute of Technology
	Stanford University		Stanford University
	Massachusetts University of Technology		Massachusetts University of Technology
	Columbia University		Harvard University
	University of California Berkeley		Princeton University
	University of Chicago		University of California Berkeley
	Princeton University		Harvard University
	Cornell University		Imperial College London
UK	Imperial College London	UK	University of Cambridge
	University of Cambridge	Switzerland	Eth Zurich Swiss Federal Institute of Technology Zurich
	10		10
	QS		ARWU

USA	California Institute of Technology
	Stanford University
	Massachusetts University of Technology
	Harvard University
	University of Chicago
UK	Imperial College London
	University College London
	University of Oxford
	University of Cambridge
Switzerland	Eth Zurich Swiss Federal Institute of Technology Zurich
10	

USA	Harvard University
	Stanford University
	University of California Berkeley
	Massachusetts University of Technology
	Princeton University
	California Institute of Technology
UK	Columbia University
	University of Chicago
	University of Cambridge
	University of Oxford
10	

Table 2.8 *Number of Universities by Countries Ranked Between 11 and 100 by WUR Systems*

Sl. No.	Country	THE	QS	ARWU	CWUR
1	USA	34	25	40	48
2	UK	9	14	6	5
3	Australia	5	6	6	3
4	Canada	2	4	4	3
5	France	1	2	1	4
6	Japan	2	5	4	6
7	China	4	4	2	2
8	Sweden	4	2	2	1
9	Netherland	5	5	2	2
10	Germany	9	4	3	2
11	Singapore	2	0	1	1
12	Switzerland	1	4	3	4
13	South Korea	2	3	0	1
14	Belgium	1	1	2	1
15	Denmark	1	1	2	1
16	Ireland	0	1	0	0
17	Russia	0	0	1	1
18	Finland	1	1	1	0
19	Taiwan	0	1	0	1
20	Israel	0	0	0	3
21	Hong Kong	2	4	0	0
22	Italy	0	0	0	1
Total		**85**	**87**	**80**	**90**

Source: Compiled by respective websites of WUR system.

subject ranking are the same as adopted for institutional ranking by the respective WURSs. The types of subjects covered by these systems of rakings are presented in Table 2.9.

The comparative analysis of the universities ranked top 10 by three of the earlier stated ranking systems for economics is presented here. The subject chosen for analysis is from the point of author's convenience than any other specific reason for this choice.

Table 2.10 reveals that, depending on the adopted parameters and methodology, ranking of universities differs among the three WURSs. The position of MIT, USA, is first in two systems of 'WUR by subjects', namely, QS and THE, whereas in ARWU, it figures at the fifth rank. The London School of Economics, UK, does not find place in the top 10 economics subject ranking list of THE. Harvard University, which ranked second in QS and first in ARWU, ranked fifth in the top 10 economics subject ranking list of THE. A good number of institutions commonly figure in the list of all the three WUR systems among the top 10 universities, including economics. US universities are dominating the list of top 10 universities in economics subject, followed by universities of the UK. Our observation of dominance of fourth wave and third wave universities also holds true for ranking of universities in the subject of economics.

A COMMENTARY ON WORLD RANKING OF UNIVERSITIES

It seems the WUR is basically a phenomenon of USA, Europe, Canada and similarly positioned countries in terms of university education. The methodology and coverage do not seem to capture the global picture. It can be argued that the ranking methodology is biased in favour of the structure and functioning of universities in USA and UK. Universities in the Middle East, Africa (other than South Africa) and the rest of Asian countries also do not appear on the list. A good number of them are rated very high by their countries assessment and accreditation system as also from the aspects of parameters and a system assessment as developed by International Quality Assurance in Higher Education Authority.

In view of the earlier observations, it may be pertinent to have a fresh look at the methodology of ranking of world universities by

Table 2.9 Subjects Considered in Various Ranking Systems

QS World University Ranking by Subjects	Time Higher Education Subject Ranking	Academic Ranking of World Universities System
Arts and Humanities: Subjects covered under this category are Architecture, Archaeology, Arts and Design, English Language and literature, Linguistics, Modern Languages, Performing Arts, History and Philosophy,	**Arts and Humanities:** Arts, Performing Arts and Design, Languages, Performing Arts and Design, Literature and Linguistics, History, Philosophy and Theology, Architecture, Archaeology	Mathematics
		Physics
		Chemistry
		Computer Sciences
	Business and Economics: Business & Management, Accounting and Finance OR Business and Economics, Business and Management and Accounting & Finance (Combined), Economics and Econometrics	Economics and Business
Engineering and Technology: Chemical Engineering, Civil and Structural Engineering, Computer Science, Electrical Engineering, Mechanical, Aeronautical and Manufacturing Engineering, Mineral and Mining Engineering	**Clinics and Pre-clinics Health:** Medicine, Dentistry and other Health	Chemical Engineering
	Computer Science: Computer Sciences -Engineering and Technology:	Civil Engineering
		Electrical and Electronics Engineering
Life Science and Natural Science: Agriculture and Forestry, Biological Sciences, Dentistry, Medicine, Nursing, Pharmacy and Pharmacology, Psychology, Veterinary Sciences	General Engineering, Electrical and Electronic Engineering, Civil Engineering and Chemical Engineering	Energy Sciences and Engineering
		Environmental Sciences and Engineering

Natural Sciences: Physics and Astronomy, Mathematics, Environmental Sciences, Earth and Marine Sciences, Chemistry, Materials Sciences, Geography

Social Sciences and Management: Accounting and Finance, Anthropology, Business Management, Sociology, Communication, Education, Politics, Development studies, Statistics, Law, Economic, Social Policy

Life Sciences: Agriculture and Forestry, Biological Sciences, Veterinary Science, Sport Science

Physical Sciences: Mathematics & Statistics, Physics and Astronomy, Chemistry, Geology, Environmental, Earth and Marine Sciences

Social Sciences: Communication & Media Studies, Education, Law, Politics and International Studies (Incl. Development Studies), Sociology, Psychology, Geography

Materials Science and Engineering

Mechanical Engineering

THE gives ranking across core missions—teaching, research, knowledge transfer and international outlook

The methodology followed is the same as followed for institutional ranking.

Source: Compiled by respective websites of WUR system.

Table 2.10 *Ten Top Ranking Universities in Economics Ranked by Three Systems of WURs*

Rank	QS	THE	ARWU
1.	MIT, USA	MIT, USA	Harvard University, USA
2.	Harvard University, USA	Stanford University, USA	University of Chicago, USA
3.	Stanford University, USA	University of Oxford, UK	UCL, Berkeley, USA
4.	Princeton University, USA	University of Chicago, USA	Princeton University, USA
5.	UCL, Berkeley, USA	Harvard University, USA	MIT, USA
6.	University of Chicago	North Western University, USA	University of Cambridge, UK
7.	London School of Economics, UK	University of Cambridge, UK	Stanford University, USA
8.	University of Oxford, UK	UCL, Berkeley, USA	London School of Economics, UK
9.	Yale University, USA	University of Pennsylvania, USA	New York University, USA
10.	University of Cambridge, UK	University of Columbia, USA	University of Oxford, UK

Source: Compiled by respective websites of WUR system.

THE. As stated earlier, the methodology broadly covers teaching–learning (30%), research volume and reputation (30%), citation (30%), international outlook of staff and students (7.5%) and industry income (2.5%). The methodology seems to be biased in favour of citation, research and reputation, which account for 60 per cent of the scores. The extent to which citation is auto-correlated with research volume needs to be verified.

It may be further noted that methodology excludes those universities which do not offer undergraduate programmes. Universities in many countries may be offering postgraduate and research programmes and not undergraduate programmes. Hence, these are out of coverage by WUR.

The area/aspect of international outlook and industry income is again a phenomenon of developed countries, as they are able to attract students and faculty because of high income and also higher opportunities for students to earn while learning. Again, this aspect is tilted towards developed countries.

Methodology of ranking is highly based on opinion surveys regarding the reputation of teaching and research excellence. The reputed universities located in the USA and the UK have an advantage since people perceive them to be better. In practice, it seems to promote the same set of institutions to be ranked high, that is, the popularity of these institutions, rather than the quality impacts ranking since the weightage for reputation is quite high. This aspect of ranking is debatable and may not be totally convincing.

Another criticism is that citation is an ineffective tool to assess influence and contribution of idea. Giving high weightage to citation as a measure of research results in reproducing same set of indicators such as faculty research productivity and publications, resulting in heavy bias in favour of universities having policy of publish or perish, and a culture of reproducing and referring to the same set of authors. Citation is not a very good measure of assessment of research and idea influence also because this indicator does not consider institutions with less than 200 publications a year.

University income and research income indicators tend to count two times the same aspect and therefore appear to be highly auto collinear. These also depend on policy and income levels of specific countries. Therefore, it is tilted more towards developed countries. This controversial point has been noted by the THE, but has been overlooked as suggested by their experts (THE, 2017). International outlook is again a feature of developed economies, which can attract students and faculty by giving scholarship and better pay packets as also giving opportunity to students to earn while they learn. This indicator goes against universities in developing and least developed economies.

An estimation of the total number of universities examined by the WURs is not available. Many of the universities of developing countries may not be taking part in the provision of data since they may not be fitting into the kind of methodology adopted by the ranking agencies. In other words, the rankings do not reflect the functions of universities in the developing countries. Hence, the universities from these countries are mostly excluded from the WUR.

The performance indicators and rankings of universities should basically incorporate graduation rates and value added by universities in terms of students' outcome of learning, students' employment and income, and students' cost of education and earning, and the performance evaluation has to be based on hard data and analysis giving reduced weights to perceptions and opinions.

LIMITATIONS OF WUR SYSTEMS

A detailed study of WUR was carried out and published in *College Post* (2013, July–September). The paper examined the methodology, discussed the results, gave inferences and raised doubts about the authenticity of the term WUR.

The comparative analysis of WUR systems reveals that the results based on opinion survey systems with certain weights differ from the results of data-based systems of ranking. It also reveals that parameters adopted by all the four WUR systems are more or less a reflection of what is happening in fourth and third wave university systems in terms of awards, research publications, citation index and alumni employment in companies, which are well known phenomena of universities in the USA and also in Europe. Universities which follow either the European or American model of education also find a place in the list. There are universities from about 22 countries that figure in the list of 11–100, but most of the ranked universities are from USA and European countries.

The list of universities beyond the ranking of 200 is very arbitrary and does not reflect the level of scores gained by these universities. Some WUR systems publish lists up to 500 ranked universities, but most of them are grouped into large chunks, without assigning a specific score. This type of rankings of universities raises doubt about the system of rankings of world universities. One of the ranking systems gives a list of universities ranked up to 1,000, out of 27,000 universities, but again, these are ranked in groups of large chunks.

In all the WUR systems, many parameters are auto-correlated, which over emphasizes the same parameter. Fifth wave universities have very little chance of getting any respectable position in the WUR systems owing to the nature of parameters and methodology adopted by WUR systems.

Some possibilities of inclusion and ranking in the WURSs are for those universities which have started and evolved their own system of knowledge generation, teaching and research, keeping in view national or international knowledge resources, and are responding to country's developmental needs. Therefore, one finds the Indian Institute of Science (IISc), Bangalore, India, which has developed good research and analytical process, and Jawaharlal Nehru University (JNU), which has focused on interdisciplinary teaching and research, figure in the list of universities ranked between 200 and 300. Similarly placed universities in other parts of world also figure in the same segment.

The methodology and coverage do not seem to capture the world higher education system. Universities may find place in WUR systems if they are patterned on the third and fourth wave university types, and not a mere poor replica of them. This is because the methodology of including universities in the ranking system as also of gathering data/information may not capture the vast variety of university systems in the world. Therefore, the nomenclature of WUR used by these WURSs is misleading. They are at best used as a marketing tool in education services to attract students to their campuses.

The important issue therefore is, what is the purpose of ranking and how are universities ranked? The matter of ranking of universities of world and its implications has also been debated in UNESCO. A report entitled *Rankings and Accountability of Higher Education: Uses and Misuses* was brought out by UNESCO (Marope, Wells & Hazelkorn, 2013). In a chapter 'University Ranking—Many Sides of Debate,' Mmanstestsa Morope and Peter Wells note that,

[C]omparisons and rankings substantially influence not only individual decisions, but also collective decisions. Specific to universities, the influence of comparisons and rankings goes beyond individuals' choices of universities to country policy, strategic and investment priorities, and even to countries' strategic positioning and the competiveness of their higher education institutions.

The question therefore seems to be less about whether or not universities should be compared and ranked, but the manner in which this is undertaken. Do the 'yardsticks' used to compare and rank universities fit the purpose? And what is this purpose? Is it clearly delineated and communicated to the *Potential* stakeholders? Where the latter is clear and transparent, it can be hoped that an informed and discerning stakeholder-user will understand the merits and limitations of the 'yardsticks', and can consequently benefit from an appreciation of both. These are the questions. (Marope et al., 2013, p. 9)

The matter, therefore, also needs to be debated in the context of large numbers of universities set up at several points of time and with varied objectives in different parts of the world. To ably comprehend all these and put it in an acceptable comparative format is a huge task.

CONCLUSION

The academic value of the ranking systems as systems of quality of universities in the world is seriously doubtful, as these systems tend to give more emphasis on past performance and very little coverage of the present system of quality in terms of the teaching–learning process and their contribution to national or global development. These ranking systems have emerged as very strong marketing tools. It has also become a handle in the hands of critiques to brow beat the country's system of higher education. It is also a dangerous tool to force universities to follow the model of US and European university systems, ignoring the vast needs of knowledge and research requirement of developing countries, which are having very diversified socio-economic and educational needs of people at large.

APPENDIX 2.1

A Hong Kong Shanghai ranking system

The ARWU was first published in June 2003 by the CWCU, Graduate School of Education (formerly the Institute of Higher Education) of Shanghai Jiao Tong University, China, and is updated on an annual basis. Since 2009, the ARWU has been published and copyrighted by Shanghai Ranking Consultancy, which is a fully independent organization on higher education intelligence and not legally subordinated to any universities or government agencies.

ARWU uses six objective indicators to rank world universities, including the number of alumni and staff winning Nobel Prizes and Field Medals, number of highly cited researchers selected by Thomson Reuters, number of articles published in journals *Nature* and *Science*, number of articles indexed in SCIE and SSCI, and per capita performance of the university. More than 1,200 universities are actually ranked by ARWU every year, and the best 500 are published.

Although the initial purpose of ARWU was to find the global standing of top Chinese universities, it has attracted a great deal of attention from universities, governments and public media worldwide. ARWU has been reported by mainstream media in almost all major countries.

ARWU and its content have been widely cited and employed as a starting point for identifying national strengths and weaknesses as well as facilitating reform and setting new initiatives. Bill Destler, the president of the Rochester Institute of Technology, drew reference to ARWU to analyze the comparative advantages that Western Europe and the USA have in terms of intellectual talent and creativity in his publication in the journal *Nature*. Martin Enserink referred to ARWU and argued in his paper published in *Science* that 'France's poor showing in the Shanghai ranking … helped trigger a national debate about higher education that resulted in a new law … giving universities more freedom'.

REFERENCES

ARWU (Academic Ranking of World Universities). (2017). *Academic ranking of world universities 2017*. Retrieved 9 August 2017, from http://www.shanghairanking.com/

College Post. (2013, July–September). *College Post, 14*(3), 3–21.

CWUR (Centre for World University Ranking). (2017). *CWUR university rankings*. Retrieved 12 August 2017, from CWUR: http://cwur.org/

Marope, P. M., Wells, P. J., & Hazelkorn, E. (2013). *Ranking and accountability in higher education: Uses and misuses*. Paris: UNESCO.

QS WUR (QS World University Ranking). (2017). *Methodology*. Retrieved 20 August 2017, from https://www.topuniversities.com/qs-world-university-rankings/methodology

———. (2017). *Top universities*. QS World University Ranking. Retrieved 10 August 2017, from https://www.topuniversities.com/university-rankings/world-university-rankings/2018

THE (Times Higher Education). (2017). *World university rankings*. Retrieved 11 August 2017, from https://www.timeshighereducation.com/world-university-rankings

TOI (*Times of India*). (2016). IITs lose ground in global ranking. *The Times of India*, 6 September. Retrieved 7 September 2016, from http://timesofindia.indiatimes.com/

Webometrics (n.d.). Retrieved 14 March 2018, from http://www.webometrics.info/en/node/24

Chapter 3

Measuring Performance of Higher Education Institutions (HEIs) and the National Institutional Ranking Framework (NIRF)

Furqan Qamar

INTRODUCTION

The report *India Ranking 2017* by the National Institutional Ranking Framework (NIRF) under the aegis of the Ministry of Human Resource Development (MHRD) was released in April 2017 (MHRD, 2017). The reactions to the ranking of higher education institutions (HEIs), as expected, varied. Those who got positions on the list as per their expectations are jubilant while those ranked below their expectations are sceptical about the parameters used and methodology applied by NIRF. Those who challenge the rationale for such a ranking at the national level argue that it necessarily duplicates the efforts put in by the global and regional rankings of universities.

The reaction of the academic community has also been mixed. Some are in favour of rankings and feel that such a ranking shall help students make informed choices about the institutions to seek admission. There are others who feel that rankings are a distraction and the governments should focus their attention on improving the quality of HEIs through enhanced investments, and by removing ban on creation and filling up the faculty positions. Data generated through the ranking process provide valuable insight to the policy planners and regulators, indicating possibilities of change (Qamar, 2017). There are also those who challenge the need for ranking by the government when the assessment and accreditation by the National Assessment and Accreditation Council (NAAC) is already mandatory for all HEIs (Gnanam, 2014). They feel that a likely mismatch between the NAAC grades and the NIRF ranks may just confuse the stakeholders all the more. A good majority of the academic community feels that the ranking shall serve the real purpose only if the governments and the regulatory bodies draw lesson from the findings and work to mitigate the quality gaps that are evinced from the ranking data.

It is important to understand the nuances involved in the NIRF ranking in the proper context. This chapter attempts to present a comprehensive analysis of the parameters and methodologies used by the three most popular and commonly referred global and regional rankings of universities, so as to identify the parameters and methodologies that have the potentials to pull down the ranking of Indian universities. In doing so, the chapter attempts a thorough review of the performance of Indian universities in global and regional rankings in relation to the top 100 universities of the world and the region, and discusses the implications of rankings on the quality and excellence in HEIs in the country.

RUSH FOR THE RANKINGS

By highlighting the acceptability, receptivity and reputation of HEIs, it is believed that rankings stimulate competition and provide critical information to various stakeholders in higher education. These enable policy planners, educational administrators and regulators to take measures to promote and incentivize quality. Indeed the rankings also empower alumni, students and prospective students and brighten their future prospects. Rankings have been chased in all countries including

India with the above-mentioned objectives. Former President Pranab Mukherjee, during his tenure, has been cajoling Indian HEIs to proactively prepare and participate in the global ranking process (*The Indian Express*, 2016). He sincerely believed that rankings can significantly improve the prospects of good placements for graduating students and provide a benchmark for continuous quality enhancement of Indian institutions of higher education (Konwar, 2014).

As rankings assumed importance, the number of agencies attempting and publishing rankings of HEIs have multiplied. The first worldwide league table that was closely watched and that emerged as the most credible and objective ranking of the world universities was developed by the Shanghai Jiao Tong University in 2003. This ranking largely focused on research completed by the institutions. This was followed by the Times Higher Education (THE) which launched its ranking in 2004 in partnership with Quacquarelli Symonds (QS). Reputation survey was the main focus in THE-QS rankings. In 2010, THE split from QS and created its own ranking methodology where citation database information is compiled in partnership with Thomson Reuters. QS has designed its rankings to look at a broad range of university activities employing six indicators. In 2009, QS launched the QS Asian University Rankings in partnership with *The Chosun Ilbo* newspaper in South Korea wherein it ranks in the top 200 Asian universities. Since 2011, QS began ranking universities around the world by subject. Even to this date, these are the most popular rankings of HEIs.

INDIAN UNIVERSITIES IN THE GLOBAL AND REGIONAL RANKINGS

While there are a number of agencies that rank the world universities, three agencies that are the most popular and are commonly referred to are (a) Shanghai-based Academic Ranking of World Universities (ARWU),[1] (b) QS World Ranking of Universities (QS World)[2] and (c) THE

---

[1] Academic Ranking of World Universities (ARWU). (n.d.). Retrieved from Academic Ranking of World Universities: www.shanghairanking.com

[2] QS. (n.d.). Retrieved from Quacquarelli Symond World University Ranking: www.topuniversities.com

Ranking of World Universities (THE World).[3] The regional rankings are relatively a new phenomenon as both QS as well as THE have started bringing out rankings of the Asian Universities. THE, in addition, also brings out the BRICS ranking. For the purposes of the present analysis, the following regional rankings have been used: (a) QS Asian Ranking of Universities (QS Asia); (b) THE Ranking of Asian Universities (THE Asia); and (c) THE Ranking of Universities in Brazil, Russia, India, China and South Africa (THE BRICS).[4]

However, these rankings are certainly not the only ones. There are many other rankings, albeit less popular or less popularized. These include (a) Russian ReitOR Ranking, (b) the Leiden Ranking (CWC Leiden),[5] (c) the Netherlands Ranking, (d) the Taiwan Higher Education Accreditation Evaluation Council University Ranking (HEEACT),[6] (e) the EU Assessment of University-Based Research (AUBR), (f) University Rankings by Academic Performance (URAP) in Turkey, (g) German Centre of Higher Education Development (CHE),[7] (h) the EU U-Multi Ranking (EU-UMap),[8] (i) the Centre for World University Ranking of Saudi Arabia, (j) U21 Ranking of Australia (Universitas),[9] (k) Assessment of Higher Education Learning Outcomes (AHELO) in France and the (l) Webometrics of Spain (Webometrics).[10]

---

[3] Times Higher Education (THE). (n.d.). Retrieved from Times Higher Education Ranking: www.timeshighereducation.co.uk

[4] Times Higher Education (THE). (n.d.). *THE BRICS and emerging economies*. Retrieved 27 Match 2018, from https://www.timeshighereducation.com/world-university-rankings/2017/brics-and-emerging-economies-university-rankings#

[5] CWC Leiden. (n.d.). Retrieved from CWC Leiden Ranking: www.leiden-ranking.com

[6] HEEACT. (n.d.). Retrieved from HEEACT World University Rankings: www.uzh.ch

[7] Centre for Higher Education (CHE). (n.d.). *CHE University Ranking*. Retrieved 27 March 2018, from http://www.che-ranking.de/cms/?getObjec=615

[8] EU-UMap. (n.d.). Retrieved from U-Map: www.u-multirank.eu

[9] Universitas. (n.d.). Retrieved from U 21 Ranking of National Higher Education System: www.universitas21.com

[10] Webometrics. (n.d.). Retrieved from Webometrics, Ranking Web: www.webometrics.info.en

In India, it was the media which started the process of ranking of colleges. In 1997, *India Today* published a survey on best colleges. In 2004, ORG-MARG identified the top 10 colleges in arts, science, commerce, law, engineering and medicine streams. *Businessworld* ranks business schools of the country. The Indian quality assurance agency, NAAC, assesses the universities and colleges and grades them. It also computes scores over several parameters which could have been used to rank universities, but NAAC desisted the idea and remained confined to grading only.

NIRF AND *INDIA RANKING 2017*: PARAMETERS AND METHODOLOGY

The world and the regional rankings do not fully fathom the realities of the Indian higher education system (Pahari, 2011). The foremost limitations of such rankings emanate from their parameters and methodologies, as elucidated in the preceding paragraphs. The second-most important set of limitations arise in view of the fact that only a minuscule number of students in India are able to pursue their higher education in the best HEIs. These do not account for even 1 per cent of the enrolment in higher education. The rest of the students are enrolled in a large number of universities and colleges situated across the length and breadth of the country. Those who seek admission to these institutions too require reliable information about the quality of these institutions to base their admission decision upon.

National Institutional Ranking Framework

The MHRD in 2015 took the initiative of bringing out a national ranking framework for HEIs in India. The first edition of the ranking was announced in 2016, but being a new initiative, only a limited number of universities and colleges participated in the same, and it was, therefore, dubbed as a dry run. The framework and methodology for NIRF was framed by two separate committees with some common members. One committee specifically developed the framework for the technical HEIs covering largely engineering and management education. The other committee built on the framework developed by the first committee to make it relevant for the multi-disciplinary universities and colleges that are constituent, affiliated or associated thereto.

In order to further improve upon the framework, a National Level Review Committee (NLRC) was constituted by MHRD. The framework was refined and modified for the computation of *India Ranking 2017*, based on the recommendations of the NLRC. The second edition of the ranking was announced in 2017, with somewhat changed parameters, in which a relatively larger number of universities and other HEIs, including colleges, participated. The modified framework resolved to compute a common ranking of all participating HEIs irrespective of the disciplinary domain. Further, the ranking was confined to only such HEIs which were of a reasonable size, thereby excluding a large number of small-sized universities, colleges and institutes. However, an exception was made in case of centrally funded HEIs, which were included in the ranking irrespective of their size.

The modified framework also brought under its ambit all HEIs including those teaching architecture, law and medical and so on, beside the colleges of higher education. While participation of universities and colleges increased significantly, *India Ranking 2017* admits that the participation of the architecture, law and medicine streams has not been very encouraging and, therefore, could not present rankings of these types of HEIs. Importantly, however, the quality of data collected during the 2017 ranking was found to be superior. The basis of discussion in this paper is largely based on the NIRF ranking 2017 as the same can be taken as a relatively better benchmark than NIRF 2016.

The NIRF 2017 presents ranking in the following categories:

1. NIRF 2017 provides overall ranking of all major HEIs including institutions of national importance (IITs, NITs and IISERs), universities (central, state, private, deemed), colleges (general higher education as well as professional and technical) and the stand-alone institutes offering postgraduate programme in management/business administration (IIMs and other ACTE [Association for Career and Technical Education] approved ones).
2. A separate ranking of universities which separates universities (central, state, private and deemed), colleges (general higher education as well as professional and technical) from the rest of HEIs, that is, the institutions of national importance (IITs, NITs, IISERs), colleges (general

higher education as well as professional and technical) and stand-alone institutes offering a postgraduate programme in management/business administration (IIMs and other ACTE-approved ones).

3. A specific but combined ranking of universities and colleges including departments, faculties and schools in universities offering programmes of studies in the disciplines of (a) engineering and technology, (b) management and business administration, and (c) pharmacy.

4. A separate ranking of general degree colleges has also been launched for the first time this year (2017).

Institutional Mechanism for NIRF Ranking

NIRF rankings are computed under the aegis of the MHRD of the Government of India. For the purpose, MHRD has constituted the Implementation Core Committee (ICC) which steers and oversees the development and revision of the framework and methodology, and also oversees the collection, compilation and collation of data and, finally, the production and dissemination of NIRF rankings. Collection, verification and cleaning of data; computation of matrices and indices; and then rankings of the HEIs are undertaken by the National Board of Accreditation (NBA), an autonomous body of the MHRD mandated to accredit technical programmes. NBA works in partnership and close coordination with the Information and Library Network (INFLIBNET), an inter-university centre under the University Grants Commission (UGC). Besides, Web of Science (Clarivate Analytics), Scopus (Elsevier) and the Indian Citation Index also partner in providing independent data on citation and impact. However, NBA is essentially the designated ranking agency.

Parameters and Sub-parameters Used for NIRF Ranking 2017

India Ranking 2017 is computed on the basis of a set of metrics for ranking of academic institutions encompassing five parameters, each of which cover four sub-parameters, except one which has five sub-parameters. Each parameter is assigned different weightage for the ranking of HEIs. Similarly, each sub-parameter also is assigned different weightage. The metrics are computed on the basis of two distinct data sets (see Table 3.1).

Methodology for Computation of Various Metrics

Methodology for computing various metrics and indices are thoroughly explained in Appendix 3.1. While the methodology is transparent and every institution itself can compute and verify its score for various metrics, there are a couple of metrics that are based on a function, and the value of that function has not been predetermined and is left to NIRF to decide.

Data Collection for NIRF

Data for the ranking are supplied by the participating HEIs on the NIRF portal. The portal provides an opening as well as a closing date for furnishing the required data, and the same is announced each year. Data supplied for NIRF are also required to be uploaded and made available for at least the next three years by the participating HEIs on their official website so as to promote transparency and public scrutiny, and also to enable 'easy cross-checking'. They are also expected to provide a dedicated email id to receive feedback on the data from the public and stakeholders. The institutions are expected to 'proactively and objectively examine the comments and feedback received to effect correction, if so warranted'. Failure to post the data on the website may debar an institution from being ranked for two years. In order to further ensure that the data supplied by the participating HEIs are reliable and that they do not resort to unethical practices, the NIRF has the power to undertake physical verification as well. Although the same is not a precondition to ranking, resistance and non-cooperation from the institution in this regard may also debar them from being ranked.

In addition to the data supplied by the participating HEIs, NIRF also directly accesses data from 'internationally available databases like SCOPUS, Web of Science and the Indian Citation Index or other suitable sources as it may deem fit'. Importantly, 'NIRF also reserves the right to modify any of the metrics if it deems fit to do so in the

Table 3.1 *Parameters and Sub-parameters Used by NIRF for Ranking Higher Education Institutions*

Sl. No.	Parameter	Marks	Weightage
1.	**Teaching, Learning and Resources (TLR)**	**100**	**0.30**
a.	Student strength including doctoral students (SS)	20	
b.	Faculty student ration with emphasis on permanent faculty (FSR)	30	
c.	Combined metric of faculty with PhD or equivalent with experience (FQE)	20	
d.	Financial resources and their utilization (FRU)	30	
2.	**Research and Professional Practice (RPP)**	**100**	**0.30**
a.	Combined metric for publications (PU)	30	
b.	Combined metric for quality of publication (QP)	40	
c.	IPR and patent: Filed, published, granted and licensed (IPR)	15	
d.	Footprints of projects, professional practice and executive development programmes (FPPP)	15	
3.	**Graduation Outcome (GO)**	**100**	**0.20**
a.	Combined metric for placement, higher studies and entrepreneurship (GPHE)	40	
b.	Metric for university examination (GUE)	15	
c.	Median salary (GMS)	20	
d.	Metric for graduating students admitted into top universities (GTOP)	15	
e.	Metric for number of PhD students graduated (GPHD)	10	

(Continued)

Table 3.1 (Continued)

Sl. No.	Parameter	Marks	Weightage
4.	**Outreach and Inclusivity (OI)**	100	0.10
a.	Percentage of students from other states: Regional diversity (RD)	30	
b.	Percentage of women: Women diversity (WD)	25	
c.	Economically and socially challenged students (ESCS)	25	
d.	Facilities for physically challenged students (PCS)	20	
5.	**Perception (PR)**	100	0.10
a.	Peer perception: Employers and research investors (PREMP)	25	
b.	Peer perception: Academic peers (PRACD)	25	
c.	Public perception (PRPUB)	25	
d.	Competitiveness (PRCMP)	25	
	Total	**500**	**1.00**

Source: NIRF (n.d.).

interest of rationalisation necessitated by the exigencies or the nature of the data encountered' and 'any changes so made will be notified at the time of announcing the rankings'. Accordingly, NIRF (a) invites institutions to register on the NIRF portal and submit their data online; (b) undertakes, wherever desirable and feasible, authentication of data either on its own or with the help of partner agencies; (c) extracts the relevant information from the authenticated data; and (d) computes various metrics and ranks institutions. Normally, NIRF displays the data supplied by the participating HEIs on its website after due processing for cross-checking by the institution, and the institutions are expected to check the same and report any anomalies. The institutions are also invited to check the data accessed by NIRF from independent sources as well.

Coverage and Exclusion from NIRF

As mentioned earlier, *India Ranking 2017* covers all HEIs with enrolment exceeding 1,000. The condition of minimum enrolment of 1,000 is not applicable in case of the centrally funded institutions/universities. Further, specialized mono-disciplinary institutions in engineering, medical, law, management and pharmacy and degree colleges are also covered, albeit for disciplinary rankings only, even if their student enrolment is less than 1,000.

NIRF also provides the universities an additional option that their schools, faculties, institutions and departments such as arts, humanities and social sciences, architecture, engineering and technology, medical and health, life sciences, management and business administration, and pharmacy can register and provide additional information for inclusion in the discipline-specific ranking. However, discipline-specific ranks of the HEIs are announced only in case of those disciplines for which a 'significant' number of institutions register and report data. The final decision on ranking of a discipline has therefore being taken by NIRF after analysing the data. Distance and open mode universities, and affiliating universities without teaching departments on the campuses have not been included in the ranking.

Newly established HEIs which have not yet produced a minimum of three batches of graduates have also been excluded from the ranking. The NIRF document also mentions that 'while score computations for the parameters are similar for both kinds of rankings (i.e., common or discipline-specific) on most counts, the weights are somewhat different on a few parameters, to take into account discipline-specific issues'. The percentile calculations, if done separately, for the two sets of rankings are supposed to be declared in the overall ranking.

Table 3.2 gives the number of various types of HEIs that participated in *India Ranking 2017*. Obviously, while the number of HEIs participating in the ranking has significantly gone up in 2017 as compared to 2016 and while most of the universities and institutions of national importance have participated in the ranking, the participation of other HEIs is still very low. It would, therefore, not be wrong to deduce that

Table 3.2 *Number of Different Types of HEIs Which Participated in* India Ranking 2017

Ranking	CUs+CFTIs	SU+DU+PU	Others	Total
Overall Ranking (Universities+INIs)	109	239	376	724
Engineering	56	163	788	1007
Management	25	95	422	542
Pharmacy	5	62	249	316
Architecture	4	17	21	42
Colleges	0	10	525	535
Arts	12	43	6	61
Medical	1	28	14	43
Law	4	28	11	43
Total	**216**	**685**	**2,412**	**3,313**

Source: Compiled from NIRF Ranking Report 2017, MHRD (2017).

while overall ranking and the ranking of universities could be fairly reliable, the same may not be true in case of other HEIs.

Analysis of NIRF Rankings

India Ranking 2017 reports data for Top 100 HEIs in its Overall Ranking and also data on Top 100 Universities in the University Ranking. This seriously limits a comprehensive analysis of institutions, as the scores on various metrics for all participating HEIs are not reported. These limitations notwithstanding, it is possible to attempt some meaningful analysis of the data, and the following section seeks to attempt the same.

TOP 100 HEIs IN *INDIA RANKING 2017* BY THEIR TYPE

The overall ranking of the top 100 HEIs comprise of 35 centrally funded technical institutions (CFTIs), 62 universities and 3 colleges. A closer analysis of the data, particularly when related to the total number of each of the different types of HEIs, reveal some interesting findings. It is obvious that while 69 per cent of the IITs, 57 per cent of the IISERs and 45 per cent of the IIMs could make to the top 100 in the overall ranking, only about 24 per cent of the central universities could make it to the top 100. It is surprising that none of the Schools of Planning and Architecture (SPAs) and the IIITs could find mention in the coveted list. It is equally surprising that the deemed universities with 20.33 per cent are neck to neck with the central universities, and the worst performers are the state universities and the private universities with only 6.13 per cent and 1.54 per cent making to the top 100 in the overall ranking. Going by the University Ranking 2017 alone, the proportion of the central and the deemed universities has been found to be the highest at 30.43 per cent and 30.08 per cent. In contrast, only 11.70 per cent of the state universities and a meagre 2.69 per cent of the private universities could make to the top 100 list of universities (Table 3.3).

Performance of HEIs in *India Ranking 2017*: Overall Scores and Scores on Various Parameters

Analysis of the overall and parameter-wise scores obtained by HEIs ranked at various positions offer some useful insight on the state of affairs of these institutions.

Overall Scores (OS): It is disquieting to find that not even a single HEI, even the one ranked first in *India Ranking 2017* could score 100. Most importantly, the gap between the scores obtained by the top ranking and those in the bottom ranks within the top 100 is disturbingly wide. HEIs ranked first could manage an OS of only 83.28, and the OS declines significantly for the one ranked lower, to the extent that for the HEI ranked 100th, the OS could not exceed 37.25. These clearly indicate wide quality gaps within the best ranked HEIs in the country (Table 3.4). Rank-wise data on the OS further elaborates on the finding (Table 3.5).

Scores on Teaching, Learning and Resources (TLR): TLR in the NIRF can be taken as the input-based parameter, and it reflects on the investment in the HEIs. An analysis of the scores obtained

Table 3.3 Types of HEIs Emerging as Top 100 HEIs

Higher Education Institutions (HEIs)	Total Number	Number in NIRF 2017		Percentage Ranked in Top 100	
		Overall Ranking	University Ranking	Overall Ranking (in %)	University Ranking
Indian Institutes of Technology (IITs)	26	18		69.23	
National Institutes of Technology (NITs)	31	3		9.68	
Indian Institutes of Science Education and Research (IISERs)	7	4		57.14	
National Institute of Pharmaceutical Education and Research (NIPER)	7	1		14.29	
Schools of Planning & Architecture (SPAs)	3	0		0.00	
Indian Institutes of Information Technology (IIITs)	18	0		0.00	
Indian Institutes of Management (IIMs)	20	9		45.00	
Total Centrally Funded Technical Institutions	**112**	**35**		**31.25**	
Central Universities	46	11	14	23.91	30.43
Deemed Universities	123	25	37	20.33	30.08
Private Universities	260	4	7	1.54	2.69
State Universities	359	22	42	6.13	11.70
Total Universities	**788**	**62**	**100**	**7.87**	**12.69**
Colleges		3			
Total HEIs in the Top 100	**900**	**100**	**100**	**11.11**	**12.69**

Source: MHRD (2017)

Table 3.4 *Maximum, Minimum and Average Score of Top 100 HEIs in* India Ranking 2017

Parameters	Maximum Score	Minimum Score	Average Score
Teaching, learning and resources (TLR)	83.11	36.34	55.78
Graduation outcome (GO)	98.71	47.70	68.91
Research and publication (RPC)	87.59	1.09	25.25
Outreach and Inclusivity (OI)	86.49	39.02	66.59
Perception (PR)	83.44	0.03	16.99
Overall Score (OS)	83.28	37.25	46.45

Source: MHRD (2017).

Table 3.5 *Overall Scores Obtained by HEIs in* India Ranking 2017

Ranks	Maximum Score	Minimum Score	Average Score
Top 10	83.28	58.92	66.30
11–20	58.25	51.75	55.00
21–30	51.46	48.27	49.69
31–40	48.19	44.99	46.35
41–50	44.95	43.50	44.18
51–60	43.35	42.48	42.98
61–70	42.46	41.37	41.82
71–80	41.36	40.31	40.83
81–90	40.10	38.73	39.36
91–100	38.68	37.25	37.98

Source: MHRD (2017).

by differently ranked HEIs on this parameter indicates that the best-ranked HEI could score 83.11, whereas the bottom-most amongst the top 100 could score a mere 39.03 (Table 3.6). Rank-wise analysis of TLR scores further reinforces the finding (Table 3.6).

Scores on Graduation Outcome (GO): Compared to the input-based parameter (TLR) and all other output-based parameters, HEIs

Table 3.6 *Teaching, Learning and Resources (TLR) Scores Obtained by HEIs in* India Ranking 2017

Ranks	Maximum Score	Minimum Score	Average Score
Top 10	83.11	47.85	61.56
11–20	78.28	43.48	58.892
21–30	77.67	36.34	59.496
31–40	79.17	44.43	62.956
41–50	56.68	41.33	48.822
51–60	75.08	36.7	53.334
61–70	72.99	40.32	55.472
71–80	72.76	39.35	53.177
81–90	71.99	37.11	52.923
91–100	64.13	39.03	51.181

Source: MHRD (2017).

have scored higher on the GO, which shows that they have largely been focussing on teaching and learning, and whatever resources are at their disposal, and they are making better use of those. However, there seems a significant scope of improvement in this regard as well (Table 3.7). The same trend gets better highlighted in the rank-wise analysis of the GO score (Table 3.7).

Research and Professional Practice (RPP): This parameter considers the number and quality of research publications, and intellectual property and patents, and is reflective of the intensity of research, publications and patents in the HEIs. This is one of the two parameters that should be a major concern for the HEIs as well as for the policy planners and regulators. Analysis of the data reveals that while the HEI ranked first in the OS could secure 87.59 on the RPP parameters, the score on this parameter plummets to an abysmal 1.09 down the rank (Table 3.8). Further analysis of this score by the ranks of HEIs indicates the gravity of the situation (Table 3.8).

Outreach and Inclusivity (OI): It is a critical parameter as it seeks to comment on the impact of a HEI on the society, and also to

Table 3.7 *Graduation Outcome (GO) Scores Obtained by HEIs in India Ranking 2017*

Ranks	Maximum Score	Minimum Score	Average Score
Top 10	98.71	58.34	80.616
11–20	91.42	62.91	78.324
21–30	95.76	52.74	69.603
31–40	91.98	57.2	69.043
41–50	89.89	57.82	71.916
51–60	93.17	51.78	66.288
61–70	80.31	47.94	64.564
71–80	71.52	51.27	63.798
81–90	82.16	55.08	62.962
91–100	79.64	47.7	62.029

Source: MHRD (2017).

Table 3.8 *Research and Professional Practice (RPP) Scores*

Ranks	Maximum Score	Minimum Score	Average Score
Top 10	87.59	33.96	62.739
11–20	56.61	13.85	41.254
21–30	44.1	12.47	29.505
31–40	31.32	6.04	18.981
41–50	36.82	6.59	25.954
51–60	40.79	6.36	20.334
61–70	29.26	1.09	15.644
71–80	29.05	1.47	15.142
81–90	26.87	1.89	10.955
91–100	23.36	1.56	11.944

Source: MHRD (2017).

assess their contribution in making higher education equitable and accessible by the deprived and marginalized section of the society. HEIs on this parameter too performed a little above average, and there is tremendous scope for improvement (Table 3.9).

Perception (PR): This is the second of the two parameters on which HEIs have fared very poorly—so much so that the PR score ranges from 83.44 for the best ranked university to as low as 0.03 for the one ranked 100th (Table 3.10).

The discussion clearly indicates that the HEIs in general performed poorly on all parameters (also see Appendix 3.2). Given the size and number of HEIs in the country, it was but natural to expect that at least the top 100 institutions shall be very close to scores of 100 and that they shall be neck to neck. Alas, the data disappoints in this respect.

Some Major Limitations of *India Ranking 2017*

Different parameters used for computing the OS also affect the ranking differently and are not necessarily totally synced. These are amply

Table 3.9 *Outreach and Inclusivity (OI) Scores Obtained by HEIs in* India Ranking 2017

Ranks	Maximum Score	Minimum Score	Average Score
Top 10	82.40	60.01	70.29
11–20	83.55	47.44	66.81
21–30	83.53	39.02	67.57
31–40	86.49	48.44	69.48
41–50	85.16	55.73	64.91
51–60	82.57	47.40	67.83
61–70	86.05	42.67	65.81
71–80	77.13	49.10	64.86
81–90	80.33	47.19	65.33
91–100	76.83	40.19	63.07

Source: MHRD (2017).

Table 3.10 *Perception (PR) Scores Obtained by HEIs in* India Ranking 2017

Ranks	Maximum Score	Minimum Score	Average Score
Top 10	83.44	28.79	58.58
11–20	59.91	6.92	26.11
21–30	49.96	3.53	23.09
31–40	24.61	3.79	10.14
41–50	23.31	0.89	8.73
51–60	18.99	0.67	8.42
61–70	23.96	1.94	9.92
71–80	20.95	0.72	10.82
81–90	30.64	0.59	10.03
91–100	14.31	0.03	4.04

Source: MHRD (2017).

evident in Figure 3.1 (Charts 1 through 5). So wide are the variations that if HEIs are ranked separately on each of the parameters used for computing the OSs, the ranking of HEIs would become altogether different in bulk of the cases, as is shown in Appendix 3.3. Needless to mention that given such wide variations in the OS and the parameter-wise scores, weightage plays a very important role in determining the ranking. If we change the weight of a particular parameter even by a fraction, the ranks of HEIs would become totally different than that it has obtained with the present weightage under NIRF.

CONCLUSION AND POLICY IMPLICATIONS

If the purpose of ranking is to identify the best 100 amongst all the HEIs that we have in the country, the Indian ranking initiative is a welcome initiative, and as time passes and increasingly larger number of HEIs present themselves for ranking, the quality, consistency and reliability of the best ranked institutions shall improve. If the objective is to enable students and employers to take informed decisions about admission and placements, the ranking suffers from the fact that the top

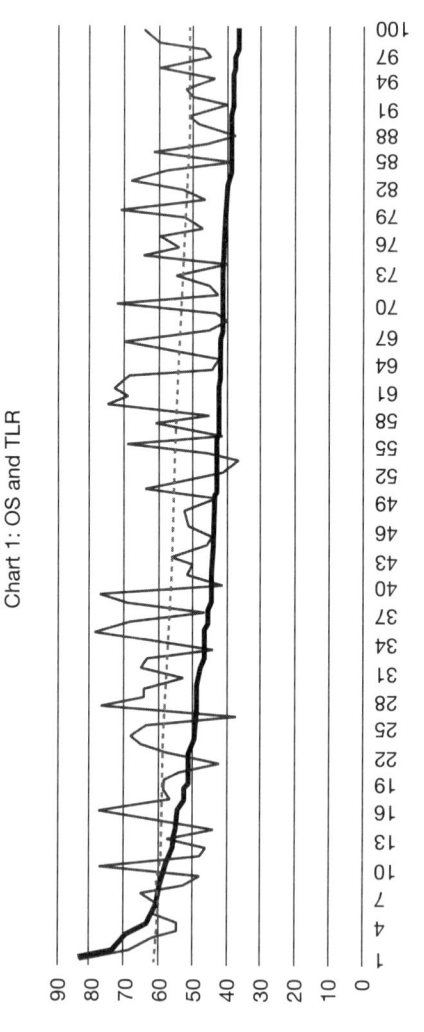

Figure 3.1 *Scores vs. Ranking: Combination of Parameters*

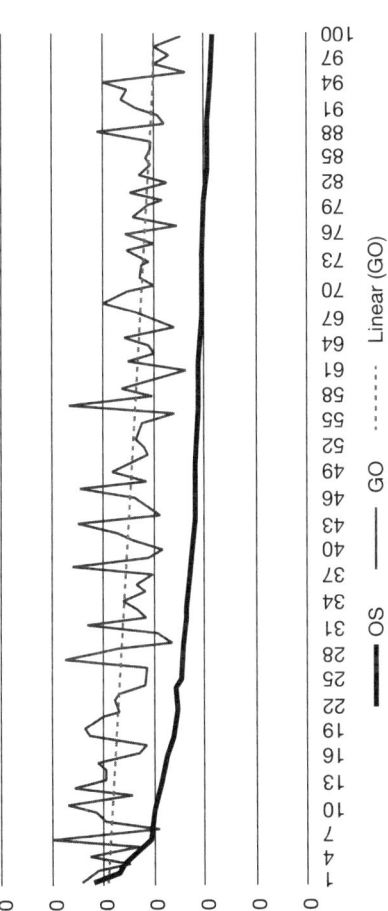

Chart 2: OS and GO

OS —— GO —— Linear (GO) ------

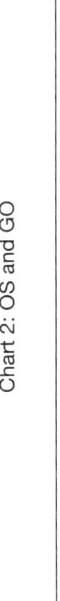

Figure 3.1 (Continued)

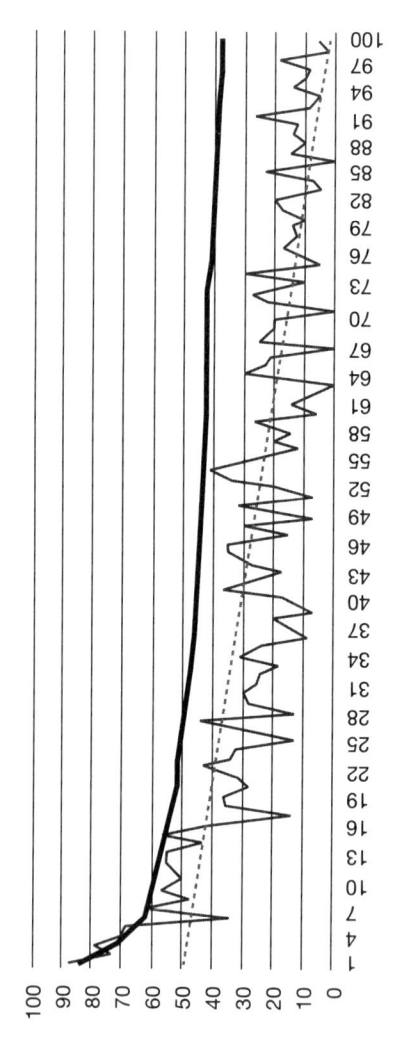

Chart 3: OS and RPP

OS ——— RPP ········ Linear (RPP)

Figure 3.1 (Continued)

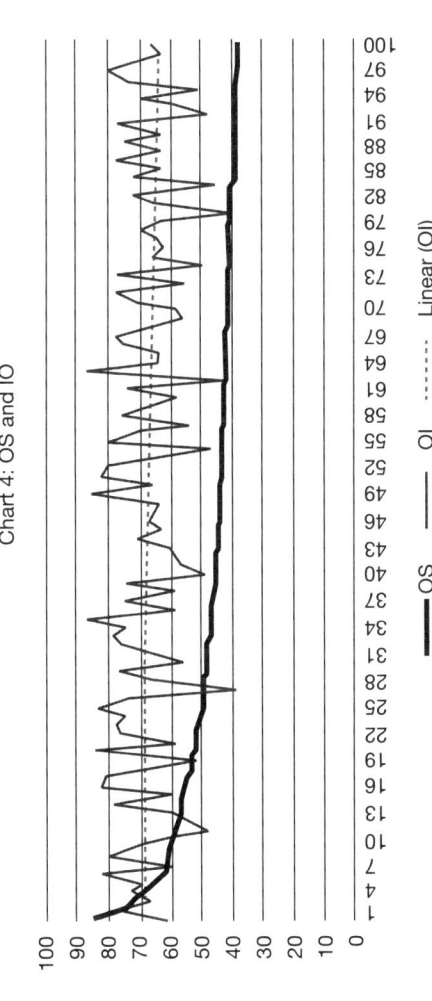

Chart 4: OS and IO

OS   IO   Linear (OI)

Figure 3.1 (*Continued*)

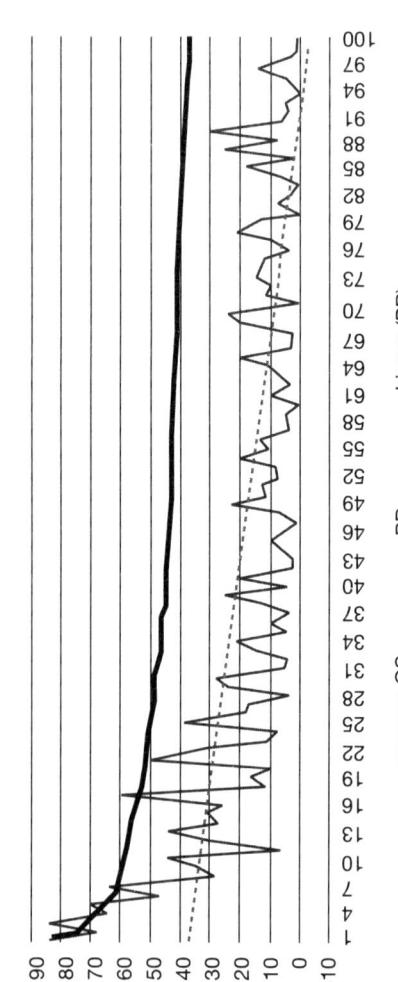

Chart 5: OS and PR

—— OS   —— PR   ------- Linear (PR)

Figure 3.1 (Continued)

100 institutions at best cater to less than one per cent of the students, and shall, therefore, not be considered very useful. Essentially, the objective of these rankings and scores should be to identify the quality gaps, and take policy and investment decisions to improve the overall quality of HEIs and higher education. From this point of view, *India Ranking 2017* provides plenty of insights to the policy planners in the country.

APPENDIXES

Appendix 3.1A *Metric 1: Teaching, Learning and Resources*

$$TLR = SS\ (20) + FSR\ (30) + FQE\ (20) + FRU\ (30)$$
$$SS = f(NT) \times 15 + f(NP) \times 5$$

The f(NT) and f(NP) are functions to be determined by NIRF and notified at the time of announcing ranks;

NT = Total number of students studying in the institution considering all UG and PG programmes, excluding the PhD programme. (Calculated on the basis of approved intake over the entire duration of the respective programmes);

NP = Total number of students enrolled for the doctoral programme till previous academic year.

$$FSR = 30 \times [10 \times (F/N)]$$

F = Full-time regular faculty in the institution in the previous year;

Regular appointment means faculty on full-time basis;

Faculty on contract basis/ad hoc basis for a period of not less than two years will also be considered;

N = Total number of students studying in the institution considering all UG and PG programmes, including the PhD programme. Thus, N = NT + NP.

Expected ratio is 1:10 to score maximum marks;

For F/N < 1:50, FSR will be set to zero.

(Continued)

Appendix 3.1A *Continued*

$$FQE = FQ + FE$$

$$FQ = 10 \times (F/95), \ F \leq 95\%;$$

$$FQ = 10, \ F > 95\%.$$

Here F is the percentage of Faculty with PhD (or equivalent qualification), over the previous three years;

$$FE = 3 \min(3F1, \ 1) + 3 \min(3F2, \ 1) + 4 \min(3F3, \ 1)$$

Rationale: Full marks for a ratio of 1:1:1

F1 = Fraction with Experience up to eight years;

F2 = Fraction with Experience between 8 + to 15 years;

F3 = Fraction with Experience > 15 years.

$$FRU = 10 \, p(BT) + 10 \min(4*BC/BT, \ 1) + 10 \min(4*BO/3BT, 1)$$

BT = Total average annual expenditure/student for the previous three years: (excluding expenditure on buildings);

BC = Average annual capital expenditure per student on academic activities and resources: (library, new equipment for laboratories, workshops, studios, other suitably identified academic activities) (excluding expenditure on buildings);

BO = Operational (or recurring) expenditure per student on faculty and staff salaries, maintenance of academic Infrastructure or consumables etc. on a per student basis: (excluding maintenance of hostels and allied services);

The function p is the percentile fraction.

Source: NIRF (2017).

Appendix 3.1B *Metric 2: Research & Professional Practice (RPP)*

$$RP = PU(30) + QP(40) + IPR(15) + FPPP(15)$$

$$PU = 30 \times p(P/F)$$

P is the number of publications = weighted average of two largest numbers given by Scopus, Web of Science, PUBMED, FT 45 (as feasible) over the previous three years.

$$P = 0.45P1 + 0.45P2 + 0.1PI$$

Let P1, P2=Two largest of {PW, PS, PUBMED, FT45,...etc.}*,

For discipline-specific rankings, the sources and weights will be suitably tuned, as felt necessary;

PW: Number of publications reported in Web of Science;

PS: Number of publications reported in Scopus;

PUBMED: Number of publications reported in PUBMED, etc.;

PI: Number of publications reported in Indian Citation Index.

It is felt that PW and PS would suffice. However, if additional sources need to be considered, this computation will be done only for the top 200 institutions. For others, a nominal value based on percentiles will be used.

F is the nominal number of faculty members as calculated on the basis of an FSR of 1:10.

$$QP = \{15 \times p\,(CC/P) + 12.5 \times p(NCI) + 12.5 \times p(TOP25P)\}$$

CC=Total citation count over previous three years;

P is total number of publications over this period as computed for PU;

$$CC = 0.45CCW + 0.45CCS + 0.1CCI$$

$$NCI = 0.5\,NCIW + 0.5\,NCIS$$

$$TOP25P = 0.5\,TOP25PW + 0.5\,TOP25PS$$

NCI: Field normalized citation index averaged over the previous three years.

TOP25P: Number of citations in top 25 percentile averaged over the previous three years.

$$IPR = IPF + IPG + I\,PP + IPL$$

$$IPF = 3 \times p(PF/F)$$

PF is the number of patents filed over previous three years.

$$IPG = 3 \times p(PG/F)$$

PG is the number of patents granted over the previous three years.

$$IPP = 3 \times p(PP/F)$$

PP: No. of patents published.

(Continued)

Appendix 3.1B *Continued*

$$IPL = 2 \times I(P) + 4 \times p(EP/F).$$

EP is the total earnings from patents etc. over the last three years.

$I(P) = 1$, if at least one patent was licensed in the previous three years or at least one technology transferred during this period; 0 otherwise.

F is the nominal number of faculty members as calculated on the basis of an FSR of 1:10.

Primary Data for EP: Institution to supply data on prescribed format.

$$FPPP = FPR + FPC + EDP$$

$$FPR = 5 \times p(RF)$$

RF is average annual research funding earnings (amount actually received in rupees) at institute level for the previous three years.

$$FPC = 5 \times p(CF)$$

CF is average annual consultancy amount (amount actually received in rupees) at institute level, for the previous three years.

$$EDP = 5 \times p(EP)$$

EP = Average annual earnings from full-time executive development programmes of a minimum duration of one year over previous three years.

Source: NIRF (2017).

Appendix 3.1C *Metric 3: Graduation Outcome (GO)*

$$GO = GPHE(40) + GUE(15) + GMS(20) + GTOP(15) + GPHD(10)$$
$$GPHE = 30 \times (Np/100 + Nhs/100) + 10p3$$

Np = Percentage of graduating students (both at the UG and PG levels) placed through campus placement, averaged over previous three years.

Nhs = Percentage of graduating students (both at the UG and PG levels) who have been selected for higher studies, averaged over the previous three years.

$$p3 = p(NE)$$

NE = number of sustained spin-off companies set up over the previous five years' period.

Primary Data for Np: To be sought from the institution in a prescribed format giving names of companies, number of students recruited by each, and the maximum, minimum, average and median salary, offered by each (required also for 3C).

Primary Data for Nhs: To be sought from the institution in the form of a prescribed Table giving names of Institutions students into which their students have been admitted (indicating the number of students in each).

Primary Data for NE: To be sought from the institution in a prescribed format giving names of companies (along with their creators' graduation profile) set up and sustained over the previous five years, in a prescribed format.

$$GUE = 15 \times \min [(Ng/80), 1]$$

Ng is the percentage of Students (as a fraction of the approved intake), averaged over the previous three years, passing the respective university examinations in stipulated time for the programme in which enrolled.

Primary Data: To be provided in a prescribed format

$$GMS = 20 \times p(MS)$$

MS = median salary of graduates from an institution.

Primary Data: To be made available by the institutions in the prescribed format giving names of companies, number of students recruited by each, and the maximum, minimum and median salary, offered by each. The overall minimum, maximum and median salary should also be provided.

$$GTOP = 15 \times p(ntop)$$

$$ntop = Ntop/Ng$$

Ntop = Number of graduating students who were admitted into a top university for higher studies in the previous year.

Ng = Number of graduating students in the previous year.

$$GPHD = 10 \times p(Nphd)$$

(Continued)

Appendix 3.1C *Continued*

Nphd = Average number of PhD students graduated over the previous three years.

Primary Data: Number of graduating PhD students as reflected in the approved annual report/convocation report to be provided in the prescribed format.

Source: NIRF (2017).

Appendix 3.1D *Metric 4: Outreach and Inclusivity (OI)*

$$OI = RD(30) + WD(25) + ESCS(25) + PCS(20)$$

RD = 25 × fraction of total students enrolled from other states + 5 × fraction of students enrolled from other countries.

$$WD = 10 \times (NWS/50) + 10 \times (NWF/20) + 5 \times (NWA/2)$$

NWF and NWS are the percentage of women faculty and students, respectively.

NWA is the number of women members in senior administrative positions, such as heads of departments, deans or institute heads.

Expectation: 50% women students and 20% women faculty and two women members in senior administrative positions required to score maximum marks.

Primary Data: To be provided in the prescribed format

$$ESCS = 25 \times (Necs/50)$$

Necs is the percentage of economically and socially challenged students.

Expectation: 50% economically and socially challenged students should be admitted to score maximum marks.

PCS = 20 marks, if the Institute provides full facilities for physically challenged students, as outlined. Else, in proportion to facilities.

Basis: Verifiable responses to questions.

Source: NIRF (2017).

Appendix 3.1E *Metric 5: Perception (PR)*

$$P = PREMP(25) + PRACD(25) + PRPUB(25) + PRCMP(25)$$

Peer Perception: Employers and research investors (PREMP): This is to be done through a survey conducted over a large category of employers and research investors, Professionals from reputed organizations, officials of funding agencies in government, private sector, NGOs, etc. Comprehensive list will be prepared taking into account various sectors, regions, etc. Lists to be updated periodically. This will be based on an online survey carried out in a time-bound fashion to ascertain preferences of employers and funding agencies.

Peer Perception: Academic Peers (PRACD): This is to be done through a survey conducted over a large category of academics to ascertain their preference for graduates of different institutions. Comprehensive list will be prepared taking into account various sectors, regions, etc. Lists to be updated periodically. This will be based on an online survey carried out in a time-bound fashion.

Public Perception (PRPUB): PRPUBLIC: Based on data collected online from general public, in response to advertisements. Would ascertain preference of general public for choosing institutions for their wards and friends.

Competitiveness (PRCMP): $PRCMP = 30 \times p(Naphd)$

Naphd = Number of PG and PhD Students admitted from top institutions in the previous year.
Primary Data: List of such students along with details of their institutions and year of graduation to be provided.

Source: NIRF (2017).

Appendix 3.2 *Overall and Parameter-wise Scores of the Top 100 Universities in the India Ranking 2017*

Overall Rank	HEI	OS	TLR	GO	RPC	OI	PR
1	Indian Institute of Science Bangalore	83.28	83.11	87.97	87.59	61.48	83.33
2	Indian Institute of Technology Madras	73.97	69.49	84.02	72.60	76.75	68.70
3	Indian Institute of Technology Bombay	71.78	64.68	70.07	78.14	65.80	83.44
4	Indian Institute of Technology Kharagpur	68.43	55.07	85.11	70.46	72.85	64.72
5	Indian Institute of Technology Delhi	64.18	55.45	65.92	68.48	68.69	69.53
6	Jawaharlal Nehru University	61.53	62.11	98.71	33.96	82.40	47.27
7	Indian Institute of Technology Kanpur	60.69	60.07	58.34	62.14	60.01	63.62
8	Indian Institute of Technology Guwahati	60.37	65.53	78.28	47.46	79.28	28.79
9	Indian Institute of Technology Roorkee	59.84	52.24	83.38	56.60	72.70	32.38
10	Banaras Hindu University	58.92	47.85	94.36	49.96	62.97	44.01
11	Jawaharlal Nehru Centre for Advanced Scientific Research	58.25	78.28	68.79	51.93	47.44	6.92
12	Jadavpur University	57.32	48.64	91.42	54.09	53.37	28.81
13	Anna University	56.50	46.25	79.31	54.58	60.01	43.94
14	University of Hyderabad	56.30	57.30	78.79	42.77	78.13	27.06
15	University of Delhi	55.37	43.48	82.06	56.61	58.60	30.76
16	Amrita Vishwa Vidyapeetham	54.70	62.90	65.77	39.49	82.17	26.12

17	Indian Institute of Management Ahmedabad	54.27	78.14	62.91	13.85	80.97	59.91
18	Savitribai Phule Pune University	52.81	56.39	85.13	35.03	72.26	11.20
19	Aligarh Muslim University	52.74	58.56	87.43	36.20	51.55	16.62
20	Jamia Millia Islamia	51.75	58.98	81.63	27.99	83.55	9.73
21	Birla Institute of Technology & Science-Pilani	51.46	54.83	73.88	31.26	58.50	49.96
22	Vellore Institute of Technology	51.36	41.65	75.57	42.87	75.99	32.95
23	Indian Agricultural Research Institute	51.20	58.22	74.11	33.60	76.79	11.52
24	Indian Institute of Technology Indore	50.23	65.42	63.50	32.43	74.58	7.17
25	Indian Institute of Management Bangalore	49.26	68.62	63.57	12.47	83.53	38.72
26	Indian Institute of Technology Hyderabad	49.07	63.51	62.91	28.02	72.21	18.06
27	Calcutta University	48.90	36.34	95.76	44.10	39.02	17.15
28	Tamil Nadu Agricultural University	48.84	77.67	75.33	12.56	63.48	3.53
29	Indian Institute of Science Education & Research, Pune	48.28	63.94	52.74	28.43	76.10	24.13
30	Manipal Academy of Higher Education-Manipal	48.27	64.76	58.66	29.31	55.51	27.67
31	Visva Bharati	48.19	53.56	86.74	25.23	67.26	4.71
32	Indian Institute of Technology Ropar	47.84	66.25	62.91	24.68	75.73	4.07
33	Siksha'O' Anusandhan University	46.72	63.31	66.02	17.17	78.18	15.57

(Continued)

Appendix 3.2 (*Continued*)

Overall Rank	HEI	OS	TLR	GO	RPC	OI	PR
34	National Institute of Technology Tiruchirappalli	46.57	44.43	71.92	31.32	73.68	20.92
35	Bharath Institute of Higher Education & Research	46.45	59.33	63.42	23.12	86.49	3.79
36	Homi Bhabha National Institute	46.45	79.17	66.98	8.75	58.08	8.70
37	Indian Institute of Technology Mandi	45.62	68.77	61.11	16.43	74.31	4.06
38	Osmania University	45.52	46.63	91.98	20.56	58.41	11.16
39	Indian Institute of Management Calcutta	45.17	70.17	62.15	6.04	74.17	24.61
40	Punjab Agricultural University, Ludhiana	44.99	77.94	57.20	16.51	48.44	3.83
41	Institute of Chemical Technology	44.95	41.33	69.31	36.82	55.73	20.69
42	Jamia Hamdard	44.84	52.44	73.99	27.86	57.57	1.87
43	Gauhati University	44.42	50.65	89.89	16.84	59.41	2.48
44	Indian Institute of Science Education & Research, Kolkata	44.38	56.68	57.82	27.13	70.00	6.79
45	Bharathiar University	44.29	45.67	63.73	35.58	62.60	9.11
46	National Institute of Technology Rourkela	44.02	43.93	67.94	34.18	65.97	4.00
47	Kerala University	43.95	50.61	89.18	14.62	64.47	0.89
48	Tezpur University	43.78	51.89	62.76	28.83	63.05	7.09
49	TATA Institute of Social Sciences	43.71	51.92	76.50	6.59	85.16	23.31

50	Shanmugha Arts Science Technology & Research Academy (SASTRA)	43.50	43.10	68.04	31.09	65.18	11.10
51	Indian Institute of Management Lucknow	43.35	63.94	62.69	6.94	82.57	12.92
52	Indian Institute of Science Education & Research, Mohali	43.27	55.38	62.99	17.55	80.48	7.52
53	Indian Institute of Technology (Indian School of Mines)	43.21	40.04	67.12	34.27	67.08	7.88
54	Panjab University	43.13	36.70	66.18	40.79	47.40	18.99
55	S.R.M. Institute of Science and Technology	43.07	45.80	64.33	25.07	78.65	10.80
56	Indian Institute of Space Science and Technology	43.06	69.46	51.78	11.63	70.33	13.45
57	Mysore University	42.83	41.59	93.17	20.10	53.51	3.44
58	National Institute of Pharmaceutical Education and Research, Hyderabad	42.74	61.28	60.78	14.30	75.15	3.90
59	Pondicherry University	42.70	44.07	72.73	26.33	65.61	4.67
60	Tamil Nadu Veterinary & Animal Sciences University	42.48	75.08	61.11	6.36	57.50	0.67
61	Sri Ramachandra University	42.46	68.16	47.94	14.10	73.02	8.86
62	Anand Agricultural University	42.26	72.99	70.24	5.89	42.67	2.75
63	Indian Institute of Management Udaipur	42.15	68.76	60.00	1.38	86.05	5.04
64	University of Madras	41.85	44.22	62.26	29.26	62.75	10.82

(Continued)

Appendix 3.2 (*Continued*)

Overall Rank	HEI	OS	TLR	GO	RPC	OI	PR
65	National Institute of Technology Surathkal	41.80	42.31	71.88	21.43	62.86	20.13
66	Indian Institute of Technology Bhubaneswar	41.75	57.89	51.73	20.92	74.82	2.66
67	Indian Institute of Management Tiruchirappalli	41.73	71.34	60.00	1.09	77.67	2.31
68	Sri Venkateswara University	41.48	45.88	68.72	24.43	64.57	1.94
69	Andhra University	41.38	40.32	80.31	18.59	55.75	20.72
70	Indian Institute of Technology (Banaras Hindu University), Varanasi	41.37	42.85	72.56	19.35	57.89	23.96
71	Indian Institute of Management Kashipur	41.36	72.76	60.00	1.47	70.17	0.72
72	Sathyabama Institute of Science and Technology	41.30	42.32	65.64	22.17	77.13	11.08
73	Indian Institute of Engineering Science and Technology, Shibpur	41.28	45.50	64.98	27.57	54.35	9.29
74	Jagadguru Sri Shivarathreeshwara University	41.18	55.34	61.55	10.32	76.67	14.99
75	Thapar University	40.78	39.35	70.16	29.05	49.10	13.17
76	Dr D. Y. Patil Vidyapeeth Pune	40.59	64.52	60.27	4.90	65.47	11.61
77	North Eastern Hill University	40.51	53.99	71.52	11.83	61.35	3.24
78	Indian Institute of Technology Gandhinagar	40.48	59.15	51.27	17.34	63.65	9.24
79	Kalinga Institute of Industrial Technology	40.47	46.39	68.53	12.75	69.17	20.95
80	Sri Sivasubramaniya Nadar College of Engineering	40.31	52.45	64.06	14.02	61.58	13.86

81	Guru Angad Dev Veterinary & Animal Sciences University	40.10	71.99	56.99	10.08	40.19	0.59
82	National Institute of Technology Warangal	40.05	46.02	68.74	17.53	64.94	7.43
83	Indian Institute of Technology Patna	39.87	52.27	55.08	19.13	71.52	2.80
84	Dr Y. S. Parmar University of Horticulture & Forestry	39.54	68.64	65.58	4.39	44.54	0.64
85	Indian Institute of Management Kozhikode	39.20	58.19	60.86	6.11	71.74	5.73
86	AMITY University	39.17	38.50	63.06	23.36	61.86	18.06
87	Indian Institute of Crop Processing Technology	39.15	62.29	60.86	1.56	76.83	1.42
88	PSG College of Technology	39.07	45.79	61.11	14.34	62.60	25.48
89	Banasthali Vidyapith	38.74	37.11	82.16	9.99	74.26	7.46
90	Bharati Vidyapeeth	38.73	48.43	55.18	12.95	62.17	30.64
91	Saveetha Institute of Medical and Technical Sciences	38.68	51.11	57.85	11.81	76.63	5.81
92	Annamalai University	38.59	39.03	68.64	26.87	47.19	3.67
93	Calicut University	38.45	50.30	72.68	8.81	57.08	4.74
94	Mizoram University	38.36	52.31	70.52	5.27	69.93	0.03
95	Kurukshetra University	38.26	43.43	79.64	13.44	50.37	2.33
96	Shiv Nadar University	37.95	59.15	47.70	9.43	73.23	5.24
97	Symbiosis International University	37.67	44.80	60.44	8.92	80.33	14.31
98	Indian Institute of Science Education & Research, Bhopal	37.32	46.13	53.21	18.21	70.78	3.00
99	Rajiv Gandhi Indian Institute of Management	37.28	61.42	60.00	1.89	62.21	0.57
100	KLE Academy of Higher Education and Research	37.25	64.13	49.61	4.90	65.54	0.69

Source: Compiled from the India Ranking Report 2017.

Appendix 3.3 *Overall and Parameter wise Ranks of the Top 100 Universities in the* India Ranking 2017

HEI	OS	TLR	GO	RPC	OI	PR
Indian Institute of Science Bangalore	1	1	9	1	71	2
Indian Institute of Technology Madras	2	13	14	3	20	4
Indian Institute of Technology Bombay	3	24	39	2	51	1
Indian Institute of Technology Kharagpur	4	51	13	4	35	5
Indian Institute of Technology Delhi	5	48	52	5	47	3
Jawaharlal Nehru University	6	33	1	25	7	9
Indian Institute of Technology Kanpur	7	36	86	6	73	6
Indian Institute of Technology Guwahati	8	21	23	13	12	18
Indian Institute of Technology Roorkee	9	59	15	8	36	14
Banaras Hindu University	10	68	3	12	62	10
Jawaharlal Nehru Centre for Advanced Scientific Research	11	3	41	11	94	64
Jadavpur University	12	66	6	10	89	17
Anna University	13	71	21	9	74	11
University of Hyderabad	14	45	22	16	15	20
University of Delhi	15	84	17	7	76	15
Amrita Vishwa Vidyapeetham	16	31	53	18	8	21
Indian Institute of Management Ahmedabad	17	4	65	70	9	7
Savitribai Phule Pune University	18	47	12	22	37	46
Aligarh Muslim University	19	41	10	20	90	36
Jamia Millia Islamia	20	40	18	37	4	52
Birla Institute of Technology & Science-Pilani	21	52	29	29	77	8

HEI	OS	TLR	GO	RPC	OI	PR
Vellore Institute of Technology	22	90	25	15	24	13
Indian Agricultural Research Institute	23	42	27	26	19	45
Indian Institute of Technology Indore	24	22	61	27	28	62
Indian Institute of Management Bangalore	25	18	60	75	5	12
Indian Institute of Technology Hyderabad	26	29	67	36	38	33
Calcutta University	27	100	2	14	100	35
Tamil Nadu Agricultural University	28	6	26	74	60	80
Indian Institute of Science Education & Research, Pune	29	27	94	35	23	24
Manipal Academy of Higher Education-Manipal	30	23	85	31	86	19
Visva Bharati	31	54	11	43	48	71
Indian Institute of Technology Ropar	32	20	66	45	25	73
Siksha`O` Anusandhan University	33	30	51	61	14	37
National Institute of Technology Tiruchirappalli	34	80	33	28	32	28
Bharath Institute of Higher Education & Research	35	37	62	48	1	78
Homi Bhabha National Institute	36	2	49	85	79	57
Indian Institute of Technology Mandi	37	15	74	64	29	74
Osmania University	38	69	5	52	78	47
Indian Institute of Management Calcutta	39	12	71	90	31	23
Punjab Agricultural University, Ludhiana	40	5	89	63	93	77

(Continued)

Appendix 3.3 *(Continued)*

HEI	OS	TLR	GO	RPC	OI	PR
Institute of Chemical Technology	41	92	40	19	85	30
Jamia Hamdard	42	56	28	38	81	91
Gauhati University	43	63	7	62	75	87
Indian Institute of Science Education & Research, Kolkata	44	46	88	40	44	65
Bharathiar University	45	77	59	21	65	55
National Institute of Technology Rourkela	46	83	47	24	50	75
Kerala University	47	64	8	65	58	93
Tezpur University	48	61	68	34	61	63
TATA Institute of Social Sciences	49	60	24	87	3	26
Shanmugha Arts Science Technology & Research Academy (SASTRA)	50	86	46	30	55	48
Indian Institute of Management Lucknow	51	28	69	86	6	43
Indian Institute of Science Education & Research, Mohali	52	49	64	58	10	59
Indian Institute of Technology (Indian School of Mines)	53	94	48	23	49	58
Panjab University	54	99	50	17	95	32
S.R.M Institute of Science and Technology	55	75	57	44	13	51
Indian Institute of Space Science and Technology	56	14	95	78	42	41
Mysore University	57	91	4	53	88	81
National Institute of Pharmaceutical Education and Research, Hyderabad	58	35	78	67	26	76
Pondicherry University	59	82	30	42	52	72

HEI	OS	TLR	GO	RPC	OI	PR
Tamil Nadu Veterinary & Animal Sciences University	60	7	73	88	82	96
Sri Ramachandra University	61	19	99	68	34	56
Anand Agricultural University	62	8	37	91	98	85
Indian Institute of Management Udaipur	63	16	83	99	2	69
University of Madras	64	81	70	32	64	50
National Institute of Technology Surathkal	65	89	34	50	63	31
Indian Institute of Technology Bhubaneswar	66	44	96	51	27	86
Indian Institute of Management Tiruchirappalli	67	11	82	100	16	89
Sri Venkateswara University	68	74	43	46	57	90
Andhra University	69	93	19	56	84	29
Indian Institute of Technology (Banaras Hindu University), Varanasi	70	87	32	54	80	25
Indian Institute of Management Kashipur	71	9	81	98	43	94
Sathyabama Institute of Science and Technology	72	88	54	49	17	49
Indian Institute of Engineering Science and Technology, Shibpur	73	78	56	39	87	53
Jagadguru Sri Shivarathreeshwara University	74	50	72	79	21	38
Thapar University	75	95	38	33	92	42
Dr D. Y. Patil Vidyapeeth Pune	76	25	80	93	54	44
North Eastern Hill University	77	53	35	76	72	82
Indian Institute of Technology Gandhinagar	78	38	97	60	59	54
Kalinga Institute of Industrial Technology	79	70	45	73	46	27

(Continued)

Appendix 3.3 *(Continued)*

HEI	OS	TLR	GO	RPC	OI	PR
Sri Sivasubrmaniya Nadar College of Engineering	80	55	58	69	70	40
Guru Angad Dev Veterinary & Animal Sciences University	81	10	90	80	99	98
National Institute of Technology Warangal	82	73	42	59	56	61
Indian Institute of Technology Patna	83	58	92	55	40	84
Dr Y. S. Parmar University of Horticulture & Forestry	84	17	55	95	97	97
Indian Institute of Management Kozhikode	85	43	77	89	39	67
AMITY University	86	97	63	47	69	34
Indian Institute of Crop Processing Technology	87	32	76	97	18	92
PSG College of Technology	88	76	75	66	66	22
Banasthali Vidyapith	89	98	16	81	30	60
Bharati Vidyapeeth	90	67	91	72	68	16
Saveetha Institute of Medical and Technical Sciences	91	62	87	77	22	66
Annamalai University	92	96	44	41	96	79
Calicut University	93	65	31	84	83	70
Mizoram University	94	57	36	92	45	100
Kurukshetra University	95	85	20	71	91	88
Shiv Nadar University	96	39	100	82	33	68
Symbiosis International University	97	79	79	83	11	39
Indian Institute of Science Education & Research, Bhopal	98	72	93	57	41	83
Rajiv Gandhi Indian Institute of Management	99	34	84	96	67	99
KLE Academy of Higher Education and Research	100	26	98	94	53	95

Source: Compiled from the India Ranking Report 2017.

REFERENCES

Gnanam, A. (2014). National ranking system for the universities. *University News*, *52*(49), 15–17.

Konwar, B. K. (2014). Indian higher education and ranking standard. *University News,* 52(49), 18–24.

MHRD (Ministry of Human Resource and Development). (2017). *NIRF ranking report 2017.* MHRD. Retrieved 15 March 2018, from https://www.nirfindia. org/flipbook/2017/index.html#p=1

National Institutional Ranking Framework (NIRF). (n.d.). *India Rankings 2017.* Retrieved 25 July 2917, from National Institutional Ranking Framework: http://www.nirfindia.org

Pahari, S. (2011). World university rankings and Indian universities. *Current Science*, *100*(1), 7.

Qamar, F. (2017). Higher education, low regulation. *The Indian Express*, 2 May. Retrieved 15 March 2018, from http://indianexpress.com/article/opinion/ columns/higher-education-low-regulation-university-grants-commission-quality-of-education-4636106/

The Indian Express. (2016). President Pranab Mukherjee tells India institutions to take global ranking process seriously. *The Indian Express*, 8 December. Retrieved 15 March 2018, from http://indianexpress.com/article/india/ president-tells-india-institutions-to-take-global-ranking-process-seriously-4415935/

Chapter 4

Research on Higher Education in India

N. Jayaram

Since Independence, India has experienced a phenomenal expansion of its system of higher education in terms of the number of institutions, teachers and students as well as the number and variety of courses.[1] With 799 university-level institutions, 39,071 colleges, 11,923 stand-alone (non-university) institutions, 1.35 million teachers (excluding those in stand-alone institutions) and 34.6 million students, the country today has the second-largest system of higher education in the world (MHRD, 2016). With some rare exceptions, this expansion has taken place in an isomorphic fashion based on the model of the University of London inherited and adopted as part of the colonial legacy. Within the first two decades of Independence, the crisis confronting this system was diagnosed. In 1982, J. P. Naik succinctly summarized the nature of this crisis:

> [O]ver-production of 'educated' persons; increasing educated unemployment; weakening of student motivation; increasing unrest and

---

[1] Between 1950–1951 and 2014–2015, there was a 24.7-fold increase in the number of degree-awarding universities/institutions, a 58-fold increase in the number of colleges, a 52-fold increase in the number of teachers and a 67-fold increase in student enrolment.

indiscipline on the campuses; frequent collapse of administration; deterioration of standards; and above all, the demoralizing effect of the irrelevance and purposelessness of most of what is being done. (Naik, 1982, p. 163)

The phenomenal expansion of higher education since then has exacerbated the crisis. The National Knowledge Commission (NKC) reiterated this in its first report to the nation in 2006 (NKC, 2007). There is nothing in scholarly writings, as also reports in newspapers and periodicals, suggesting that the situation has improved since.

The ongoing impasse in higher education has obviously attracted the critical attention of scholars and policy-makers alike, who either individually or through institutions have been engaged in research on higher education. Based on available documentation and literature, this chapter attempts to review state-of-the-art research on higher education in India.[2]

INSTITUTIONS ENGAGED IN RESEARCH ON HIGHER EDUCATION

Higher education as an area of research has attracted the attention of both institutions and individual scholars. The institutions have generally been interested in creating a database for policy formulation and programme evaluation. This is explained by their raison d'être as well as by the objectives of the government or allied bodies which finance their activities. Some of the institutions are autonomous, and others function as intermediaries between the government and the agencies or individuals engaged in research.

The interest of individual scholars, on the other hand, is primarily personal. As postgraduate students, they are interested in obtaining academic credentials, for example, a doctoral degree; at the postdoctoral level, they are often motivated by career opportunities or promotion. Even so, some of them are, no doubt, desirous of influencing policy perspectives. As a part of postgraduate studies, the research is generally self-financed, but some financial subsidy is obtained in a few deserving

---

[2] Also see Jayaram (1997).

cases or as a statutory policy measure meant for the amelioration of the status of indigent sections such as the scheduled castes, scheduled tribes and other backward classes. Institutional subsidy is usually available to individuals for postdoctoral research, provided their projects conform to the agenda of the funding agency.

The National Council of Educational Research and Training (NCERT) is the public institution set up for educational research in India. Established in September 1961 as an autonomous body to deal with the three dimensions of education, namely, research, training and extension services, its programmes are carried out by the following constituent organizations: the Central Institute of Educational Technology, New Delhi; the Regional Institutes of Education at Ajmer, Bhopal, Bhubaneswar, Mysuru and Shillong; and 17 field offices located all over the country. While it has a number of departments, units and cells covering practically all aspects of education, its primary orientation is to primary- and secondary-level education. In fact, the Government of India views NCERT as a national-level body providing leadership in the formulation of policy and implementation of school programmes at these two levels.

Obviously then, NCERT's contribution to research on higher education is not much. Its main contribution in this regard is in the documentation and dissemination of research findings through its journals and other publications. Every four months (February, May, August and November) it publishes the *Journal of Indian Education*, and every six months (January and July) it brings out the *Indian Educational Review*. The seven surveys of research in education sponsored by it are particularly noteworthy. Its projects on national integration and national talent search are also important for higher education.

The National Institute of Educational Planning and Administration (NIEPA) is the second-most important institution engaged in educational research in India. Its origin dates back to 1962 when UNESCO established the Asian Regional Centre for Educational Planners and Administrators, which later became the Asian Institute of Educational Planning and Administration in 1965. In 1969, it was taken over by the Government of India and renamed as the National Staff College for Educational Planners and Administrators. Subsequently, it was renamed as National Institute of Educational Planning and Administration in 1979. In 2006, it was conferred the 'deemed university' status and got its present name. NIEPA is primarily concerned with the management, administration, planning and financing of education at all levels. Its research agenda is oriented to providing feedback to policy-makers, and training educational policy-makers and administrators in India and in other developing countries. It also provides consulting and advisory services. Its official quarterly *Journal of Educational Planning and Administration*[3] carries insightful articles on higher education.

Although all the departments at NIEPA touch upon issues of higher education, at least tangentially, the Department of Higher and Professional Education is specially devoted to studying the various aspects of policy, planning and management of higher education. The issues it researches on higher and professional education include quality, governance, financing and internationalization. The department provides technical and professional advice to policy, planning and implementing agencies of higher and professional education. The World Trade Organization (WTO) cell of this department played an important role in analyzing requests and articulating India's offers at the General Agreement on Tariffs and Trade.

In 2013, the Centre for Policy Research in Higher Education (CPRHE) was established in NIEPA as a specialized centre in the area of higher education policy and planning in the country. Though located in NIEPA for administrative reasons, this centre enjoys autonomy to develop and implement its own research agenda and other programmes, as also to mobilize resources. This centre has set for itself the task of analyzing trends in higher education development, promoting research to generate reliable database for policy and planning, and encouraging policy dialogues involving policy-makers.[4] Its research thrust lies in the following interrelated areas: (a) expanding and improving the provision of higher education ensuring equity and

---

[3] This journal took its present form and title in 1987; earlier, it was published under the title *EPA Bulletin*.

[4] This centre has embarked on the project to bring out an annual report on higher education in the country. The first report has been published (see Varghese & Malik, 2015), and the volume carrying this chapter constitutes the second report.

inclusion; (b) enhancing quality; (c) improving relevance of curriculum and employability of graduates; (d) improving financial efficiency and flows; (e) strengthening teaching–learning process and improving learning outcomes; and (f) increasing efficiency and effectiveness of governance, and management of higher education institutions. The centre is funded by the University Grants Commission (UGC).

While both NCERT and NIEPA are autonomous organizations set up by the Government of India, the Indian Institute of Education (IIE) at Pune is an organization set up entirely through voluntary efforts, though it now gets financial support from the Indian Council of Social Science Research (ICSSR) and the Government of Maharashtra. Its origin goes back to 1948 when a band of dedicated educationalist led by J. P. Naik felt the need for an independent institute of education. It became dormant for some time, but was revived in 1976.[5]

IIE is not exclusively devoted to research on higher education, nor is higher education even one of its priorities. Its orientation is interdisciplinary investigation on the interface between education and society on the one hand, and between education and development on the other. It is also interested in 'action research' on educational problems within and outside formal education. In addition, it conducts doctoral-level training in educational research, with emphasis on social science aspects.

With the firm belief that the quality of educational research in the country must improve, and it can improve only if placed outside the physical precincts of teacher-training colleges, the Zakir Husain Centre for Educational Studies was established in the Jawaharlal Nehru University in 1972. It both undertakes educational research and gives interdisciplinary training in educational research while still retaining its roots within the social sciences.

Yet another organization which is interested in research on higher education is the Association of Indian Universities (AIU; Bhandarkar, 1975). It was established in 1925 as the Inter-University Board of India and Ceylon, but after the withdrawal of the latter in the early 1970s, it adopted its present name in 1973. It originally came into existence

---

[5] IIE was first established in Mumbai on 1 January 1948, but was shifted to Pune on 1 August 1976.

as a result of a realization by the academic community that a coordinating body for universities had become necessary. AIU is concerned exclusively with higher education, but research on higher education is only one of its wide-ranging objectives.

AIU serves as a bureau of information on universities. Its biennial publication, earlier published as *Universities in India*, is now published as *Universities Handbook* (now in its 33rd edition[6] [AIU, 2014]). It has published several handbooks dealing with health sciences education (AIU, 2009), engineering education (AIU, 2016), management education (2012) and distance education (AIU, 2010). Based on the notifications it receives, it periodically publishes on its website a list of doctoral theses accepted by universities. Every week it also issues a periodical called *University News*. It has undertaken or sponsored some research projects on internal assessment, examination, reforms, etc.

The expansion and consolidation of AIU's academic potentialities were in a way blocked by the creation of UGC in 1956 (see Singh, 2004), which took over several of the former's functions.[7] Since UGC is a grant-giving body backed by governmental authority, it is hardly surprising that AIU has lost some of the prestige and effectiveness that it had built up over the three decades of its existence.

UGC has sponsored or undertaken many research projects, on the structure, organization and functioning of higher education on the one hand, and on the pedagogical aspects of higher education on the other. To promote discussion on contemporary higher education problems and policies, as well as scholarly study of higher education, it started the tri-annual *Journal of Higher Education*, which has since been discontinued. Also discontinued is its official organ, earlier published

---

[6] This edition of *Universities Handbook* (AIU, 2014) is a compendium containing the latest information on 402 university-level institutions, including 56 technical, 41 agriculture, 24 health science, 13 law, 3 journalism and 15 open universities. In addition, it includes information on five associate members, namely, Kathmandu University, Nepal; University of Mauritius, Mauritius; Royal University of Bhutan; Middle East University, United Arab Emirates; and Semey State Medical University, Semey.

[7] UGC is headquartered in New Delhi and has six regional centres in Bengaluru, Bhopal, Guwahati, Hyderabad, Kolkata and Pune.

tri-annually as *Bulletin of Higher Education* and later published quarterly as *UGC News*.

The annual reports, review-committee reports and other publications put out by UGC are a valuable source of information on the state of higher education. In 1974, UGC set up panels on various disciplines to advise it on matters relating to the development of teaching and research in those areas. The reports of these panels are perhaps the only systematic documents available on the pedagogical aspects of higher education in India.

In order to promote interdisciplinary research in education, UGC set up several units: sociology of education at the Tata Institute of Social Sciences, Mumbai; economics of education at Mumbai University's School of Economics; social psychology of Education at the Allahabad University; and educational psychology at the Utkal University's Centre for Advanced Studies in Psychology. Not much is known about the present status or research output of these units; higher education was not the primary facet of their research interests anyway.

By and large, research on higher education is left to the independent initiatives of individual scholars spread out in university departments, teacher-training colleges and some research institutes. University departments do not by themselves generally specialize in higher education. Even the Centre of Advanced Study in Education at the Maharaja Sayajirao University, Vadodara (Baroda), set up in 1963 under UGC's scheme of developing some university departments as 'centres of advanced studies', has not been able to promote a comprehensive programme of research on higher education.

In addition to the foregoing, various apex research bodies such as ICSSR, the Council of Scientific and Industrial Research, and the Indian Council of Historical Research have sponsored isolated studies on selected aspects of higher education. They have also sponsored surveys of research undertaken in the subjects falling under their purview. But in none of these councils does higher education *per se* form an independent area of research.

Professional associations in India have as a rule steered clear of research responsibilities; rather, they provide forums for presenting the findings of research through periodical conferences or meetings, and publish those findings in their professional journals. But in all these activities, higher education forms only an incidental research theme. There is not even an informal network of scholars interested in research on higher education, as there are very few scholars who have a sustained interest in this area.

Almost every university in India prepares an annual report compiled from information obtained from various colleges and departments within the jurisdiction of the university. These reports are packed with statistical information and rarely do they contain any critical assessment. In addition, some vice-chancellors have written memoirs of their tenure as the executive heads of universities (Mathur & Arora, 1992; Narain, 1990; Singh, 1984). Subjective and self-righteous as their reminiscences may appear, they do offer valuable—sometimes very critical—insights into the inner dynamics of the university system.

FUNDING OF RESEARCH ON HIGHER EDUCATION

There is no special institutional arrangement in India for funding research on higher education. Only when the government or an allied body is interested in a particular problem in higher education will there be extra grants available specifically for this purpose. The funding of various para-research activities associated with the New Education Policy (MHRD, 1986) and the associated Programme of Action (MHRD, 1992) is a case in point.

Broadly, we can distinguish three types of research projects in higher education in terms of the source of funding: (a) agency-sponsored research projects, (b) agency-funded research projects and (c) self-funded research projects. In the case of the *agency-sponsored* research projects, the objectives and scope of the project are determined by the sponsoring agency, and the individual or the team undertaking the research may have freedom only in the manner of execution of the project.

In the case of the *agency-funded* research projects, an individual or a team makes a formal application to the funding agency seeking financial support for the project. The scope and objectives of the study are determined by the applicants themselves. If the application is in conformity with the norms of the funding agency, and if the agency is satisfied with the relevance and significance of the proposal as well as with the capabilities of the applicants to execute it, funds are sanctioned. The responsibility for the execution of the project and the results of the study are entirely those of the applicants.

In the case of *self-funded* research projects, the researcher bears most, if not all, of the cost. Often the researcher, if he or she is an academic teacher, may be provided leave of absence from work and a small grant to cover contingency expenses. However, since research is an expensive proposition, self-funding is a rare phenomenon. Some agencies extend financial support to enable the researcher to publish the reports of the self-funded or agency-funded research projects. It must be mentioned here that most of the research on higher education in India comprises small-scale projects undertaken by scholars as part of the requirements for a doctoral degree.

The most important agency financial research on higher education in India is the UGC, which, in fact, is the prime governmental agency set up by an Act of the Parliament for funding higher education. Apart from the block grants it gives to universities, centres of advanced study, departments of special assistance and colleges, UGC also directly funds research projects submitted by individual scholars or teams working in university departments or colleges.

ICSSR is another organization which funds research on higher education. Apart from sponsoring its own surveys and research projects, ICSSR entertains applications for research grants from individual scholars or teams working in university departments, colleges or research institutes.

Higher education, as a 'concurrent subject' in the Constitution of India, falls in the direct jurisdiction of the Ministry of Human Resources Development (MHRD). While MHRD generally allocates funds to UGC for disbursing grants to universities and colleges, it often initiates on its own or funds research projects on higher education. Very rarely, some state governments also extend such financial assistance.

Research funds provided by UGC, ICSSR, MHRD and state governments are invariably routed through the universities or institutes in which the research is undertaken. It is observed that university bureaucracies, functioning as they often do with archaic rules and procedures, are a hindrance to the quick and efficient conduct of research. Thus, many scholars are wary of accepting research projects channelled through the universities, as they will have to encounter more non-academic than academic hurdles in executing them. For the same reason, non-governmental funding organizations seem to repose greater faith in research institutes than in universities.

Funds for research on higher education also come from outside the country. The World Bank and UNESCO have shown interest in research on higher education in India. Foreign governments (for instance, the US Department of Education), foundations (such as the Ford Foundation and the United States–India Educational Foundation or USIEF [formerly known as the United States Educational Foundation in India]), and other agencies (the British Council and Alliance Française amongst others) have also funded research on higher education in India. When foreign funds are involved, it is incumbent on the research scholar or the research institute concerned to obtain permission of the Home and External Affairs Ministries of the Government of India.

The existence of a wide range of institutional mechanisms for funding research on higher education does not necessarily imply that funds are readily available. In fact, higher education is not an area of research priority even for organizations directly connected with education, let alone those interested in research in general. And, given the resource crunch which the higher education sector has always experienced, research on higher education has certainly become a casualty.

TRENDS IN RESEARCH ON HIGHER EDUCATION

The survey of educational research in India reveals that higher education has not been a priority area. Introducing the *Fourth Survey of Research in Education*, M. N. Buch, its chief editor, had rightly observed that 'research on higher education, the pedagogy of higher education, has not taken substantial root in Indian Universities' (Buch, 1991, p. 33). The situation does not appear to have changed much in the quarter century since.

A review of the bibliographies on higher education reveals that the topical coverage of research on higher education in India is remarkably extensive. Broadly, two general foci of research emerge: (a) the structure and functioning of higher education and (b) the relationship between higher education and other social institutions in general and the economy in particular.

As far as the first focus is concerned, the issues that are among those which have been investigated are the organization of higher education; the offices of higher education; the problems of administering universities and colleges; the background, role and problems of teachers; unionization among teachers; the background, attitudes and aspirations of students; unrest and activism among students; curriculum development in various subjects; the language question in higher education; the financing of higher education, the process of policy formulation; the process of planning at various levels of education; and the structure and functioning of UGC.

As far as the second focus is concerned, the issues investigated include the inequality of educational opportunities in higher education; the role of higher education as a channel of upward social mobility; the education–employment mismatch; and the role of higher education in economic development and modernization of society.

Buch bemoans the fact that the development of education research in India has been lopsided. The primary motivation of individuals undertaking research in any area of education is to obtain a doctorate or achieve career advancement. The scope, objectives and coverage of such studies are, therefore, extremely limited, and most of them are not even published.

As regards quality, C. L. Anand and Buch note that the 'bulk of this research consists of replication studies adding little either to the fund of knowledge or by way of suggesting solutions to some of the vexed problems in higher education in our country' (Anand & Buch, 1991,

p. 1349). In fact, 'the repetitive nature of the research, on the one hand, and its horizontal spread, on the other, has inflated the apparent value of research' (Anand & Buch, 1991, p. 1349). This assessment is as valid today as it was made a quarter century ago.

The research that is being done in the country is hardly documented efficiently, and it does not get the publicity that it often deserves. Frequently, there is a considerable time lag between the completion of the research report and its becoming available to the interested audience. Even the documentation of research work takes an unduly long time and is never comprehensive. As a consequence, unpublished research work often goes unnoticed.

It is intriguing in this context that with such a large system of higher education, encompassing enormous material and human resources, India did not have a research centre devoted exclusively to higher equation until recently. It is hoped that the CPRHE, established in 2013, will meet this long-felt need. This centre could identify individuals and agencies interested in higher education, and stimulate, sponsor and co-ordinate research on higher education in order to improve its system-level and institutional functioning.

HIGHER EDUCATION: RESEARCH AND POLICY

Higher education as a national enterprise necessitates a policy framework. The exercise of policy formulation and the implementation of a programme of action following it presume a sound and reliable database, a set of critical empirical insights and realistic socio-economic policy-development mechanisms. Similarly, the exercise of reformulation of a given policy necessitates an exhaustive review of its implementation and outcomes. In either case, the importance of research on higher education can hardly be exaggerated.

However, the formulation and reformulation of policy for higher education in India is seldom based on scholarly research on higher education. As in many developing countries, policy-making is predominantly a political exercise and programme implementation is a bureaucratic activity. The politicians and the civil servants have revealed themselves to be generally complacent in the matter of education and, as such, do not value academic research in the area.

It is also true that academic research on higher education is, by and large, so pedestrian and weak as regards both data and insight that it is deservedly rejected by policy-makers. Seldom does a higher education researcher work on a problem which has direct policy implications; in most cases, the policy implications of research work are either tenuous or non-existent. Hence, academic research on higher education is not taken into consideration in policy-making unless it is sponsored by or conducted at the behest of policy-makers.

The history of educational policy-making in India since Independence reveals the mechanical adoption of the time-honoured colonial practice of appointing a committee or commission to study the crisis in the realm of education and to make policy recommendations. The University Education Commission (the Radhakrishnan Commission, 1948–1949) examined the development of higher education and made proposals for its future expansion and improvement (MOE, 1962). A similar inquiry in regard to secondary education was carried out by the Secondary Education Commission (the Mudaliar Commission; MOE 1952–1953).

These two commissions, or for that matter any commission appointed in the pre-Independence period, looked at education in a compartmentalized fashion (higher education *or* secondary education) and totally ignored primary and adult education. The Education Commission (the Kothari Commission; GOI, 1964–1966) was the first commission in India's educational history to look comprehensively at almost all aspects of education and evolve a blueprint for a 'national system of education'.

Having influenced the two statements on the National Policy of Education (1968 [GOI, 1968] and 1986), and through them the policies and programmes adopted in the Fourth, Fifth and Sixth Five-year Plans (1968–1983), the report of the Kothari Commission was in the works for over two decades. However, the educational developments in the country since the report was first published 'show marked variations with those postulated by the Commission' (Naik, 1982, p. 6).

This is partly attributable to the deliberately normative path that the commission chose, as revealed by the eight premises set forth in Chapter III of its report: (a) strong central and state-level governments that would be committed to educational development, (b) stable political conditions, (c) declining birth rate, (d) a growth of national income at 6 per cent per annum, (e) a lessening of social tensions due to effective development, (f) a strengthened and revitalized bureaucracy, (g) a committed and competent body of teachers and (h) a community of students dedicated to the pursuit of learning (Naik, 1982, p. vi). With most of these premises turning out to be wishful thinking, together with socioeconomic and political constraints, the thrust of reform was doomed.

Nevertheless, it looks as though this report was handled in a slipshod manner. The Public Accounts Committee of the Sixth Lok Sabha (the lower house of Parliament) characterized UGC's approach to the recommendations of the Education Commission (1964–1966) as 'perfunctory and insubstantial' (Public Account Committee of the Sixth Lok Sabha, 1977–1978, p. 11). UGC, being only an administrative handmaid of the government, however, cannot be solely held responsible for the pathetic outcome. The then Ministry of Education, which processed the report, totally obliterated it by treating in a piecemeal fashion of what was conceived as a 'package deal' (Naik, 1982, pp. 31–32).

An important strategy of the government for dealing with a report of a committee or a commission has always been to obviate any controversial debate on it by accepting its recommendations in principle. Considering this, the 1985 exercise in policy formulation by the government was unorthodox. In August 1985, the Ministry of Education (since reorganized as MHRD) presented to Parliament a 119-page document (Ministry of Education, 1985). This document was intended to act as a catalyst, and to elicit the views and opinions of those dealing with or interested in the complex task of 'restructuring the system of education' confronted by a crisis.

This document, known popularly as the 'New' Educational Policy, laid the utmost emphasis on higher education, as it 'can provide ideals and means to give shape to the future and also sustain all other levels of education', and is, therefore, 'the single most important indicator of ... [our] country's future' (Ministry of Education, 1985, pp. 6, 45). Among the key policy measures contemplated by the documents were (a) the delinking of degrees from jobs; (b) the diversification and redesigning of courses; (c) placing a moratorium on the expansion of the conventional pattern of colleges and universities, and development of autonomous colleges and departments; (d) selective admission to higher education based on 'scholastic interest and aptitude'; (e) establishment of new centres of excellence; (f) strengthening of research; (g) decentralization of educational planning, administration and monitoring; (h) training teachers; and (i) the depoliticization of the academic issues.

By the time the government could implement its programme of action fully, it was defeated at the general elections held in 1989. The National Front (an ensemble of erstwhile opposition parties) government which came to power set up the Acharya Ramamurti Committee to re-examine the 'new' educational policy. By the time this committee submitted its report in December 1990 (Singh, 1991), this government too had fallen. Thus, the policy perspective on higher education in the country has been characterized more by rhetoric than by purposeful implementation. One would not be surprised if the move for another educational policy contemplated by the current government that came to power in 2014 follows suit.

WHITHER RESEARCH ON HIGHER EDUCATION?

The general lack of linkage between research and policy-making in the realm of higher education does not necessarily mean that research on higher education is redundant. Such research certainly seems to keep the issues alive and remind the policy-makers about lacunae in the policies as well as the challenges and tasks ahead. In any case, systematic research is the only source of continuous feedback on the trends in and problems of higher education.

Research on higher education assumes all the more importance in light of the fact that the impact of changes in the international scenario consequent upon the pervasive forces of globalization. After four decades of experimentation with 'democratic socialism', in 1991,

India embarked on a programme of economic liberalization and free market enterprise. The consequences of this have been felt in the area of education in general, and higher education in particular.

An important fall out of the changes pursued by the Government of India is its gradual distancing itself from the sphere of higher education. Already state and even central grants to universities have been slashed. Under these circumstances, fresh initiatives for the development of higher education only come from the private sector, and pending such initiatives, if any, the existing state-supported system has to fend for itself. This has produced a wide range of problems deserving the attention of researchers on higher education.

Education as private enterprise, financing higher education, linkages between industry and institutions of higher learning, and the predicament of state universities and state-supported institutions should naturally be high on the research agenda. Certain sectors of higher education, hitherto neglected by researchers, seem more responsive to socio-economic changes. Thus, for instance, non-formal education at the tertiary level and formal education offered by professional associations deserve greater attention by the researchers, as to research centres outside the university orbit such as the 'institutions of national importance', the 'institutions deemed to be universities' and the 'research laboratories/institutes' established by the Council of Scientific and Industrial Research.

The demand for new and advanced skills in various fields, as well as the advancements in science and technology, necessitate the reorganization of curricula. The process of curriculum formation in different fields and the restructuring of courses could obviously contribute towards making good candidates for research. Closely associated with these is the language question in higher education.

The human element in higher education is yet another aspect deserving greater attention by the researchers. The background of students, their academic preparation at lower levels of education, and their motivations, aspirations and attitudes need to be documented. Similar documentation also needs to be done for teachers. In addition, the outcome of a variety of programmes for the improvement of quality

of teachers and the amelioration of the conditions of students belonging
to the indigent sections of society needs to be reviewed.

REFERENCES

Anand, C. L., & Buch, M. N. (1991). Research in higher education. In M. N. Buch
(Ed.), *Fourth survey of research in education, 1983–88* (vol. II, pp. 1339–1391).
New Delhi: NCERT.

AIU (Association of Indian Universities. (2009). *Handbook on health sciences education*
(17th ed.). New Delhi: AIU.

———. (2010). *Handbook of distance education*. New Delhi: AIU.

———. (2012). *Handbook of management education* (10th ed.). New Delhi: AIU.

———. (2014). *Universities handbook* (33rd ed.). New Delhi: AIU.

———. (2016). *Handbook of engineering education* (12th ed.). New Delhi: AIU.

Bhandarkar, S. S. (1975). *Association of Indian universities, 1925–1975*. New Delhi:
Association of Indian Universities.

Buch, M. N. (1991). New directions for educational research in India. In M. N.
Buch (Ed.), *Fourth survey of research in education, 1983–88* (vol. I, pp. 1–46).
New Delhi: NCERT.

GOI (Government of India). (1966). *Kothari Commission (1964–66)*. New Delhi:
GOI.

———. (1968). *National policy on education, 1968*. New Delhi: Ministry of
Education, GOI.

Jayaram, N. (1997). Research on higher education in South Asia: Old problems and
new challenges. In J. Sadlak & P. G. Altbach (Eds), *Higher education research at the
turn of the new century: Structures, issues, and trends* (pp. 65–79). Paris/New York,
NY and London: UNESCO Publishing/Garland Publishing.

Mathur, M. V., & Arora, R. K. (1992). *The vice-chancellors remember*. New Delhi:
Associated.

MHRD (Ministry of Human Resource and Development). (2016). *All India
survey on higher education (AISHE) 2015–16*. New Delhi: Ministry of Human
Resource and Development, Government of India.

———. (1986). *National policy on education*. New Delhi: Government of India.

———. (1992). *Program of action*. New Delhi: Government of India.

MOE (Ministry of Education). (1952–1953). *Mudaliar Commission report 1952–53*.
New Delhi: Ministry of Education, Government of India.

———. (1962). *Radhakrishnan Commission 1948–49*. New Delhi: Ministry of
Education, Government of India.

———. (1985). *Challenge of education: A policy perspective*. New Delhi: Ministry of
Education, Government of India.

Naik, J. P. (1982). *Education commission and after*. New Delhi: Allied Publishers.

Narain, I. (1990). *Pages from a vice chancellor's diary*. Delhi: Chanakya.

NCK (National Knowledge Commission). (2007). *Report to the nation—2006*. New Delhi: National Knowledge Commission, Government of India.

Public Accounts Committee of the Sixth Lok Sabha. (1977–1978). *Seventy-third report*. New Delhi: Lok Sabha Secretariat.

Singh, A. (1984). *Asking for trouble: What it means to be a vice-chancellor today*. New Delhi: Vikas.

Singh, Amrik. (1991). Ramamurti report on education in retrospect. *Economic and Political Weekly, 26*(26), 1605–1613.

Singh, Amrik. (2004). *Fifty years of higher education in India: The role of the University Grants Commission*. New Delhi: SAGE.

Varghese, N. V., & Malik, G. (Eds). (2015). *India higher education report, 2015*. London and New Delhi: Routledge.

PART II

Teachers and Teaching–Learning

Chapter 5

Availability and Shortages of Teachers in Higher Education

Chiranjib Sen

Higher education (HE) occupies a central place in India's growth and development. The sector has expanded rapidly, being fuelled by rising demands emanating structurally from India's demographic structure, as millions of new potential job seekers entering college-going age look towards HE as a means to better their opportunities. As the Indian economy has grown more rapidly and has liberalized, the economic role of HE has also evolved. This has led to a greater emphasis on professional and technical education both from students as well as policy-makers. To meet this demand, the higher education institutions (HEIs) have expanded recently in number, size and diversity. To take a longer perspective, the expansion of the Indian HEI system has taken place historically in three waves. This evolutionary process has shaped the institutional composition of HE providers, as well as the nature of demand for teaching faculty.

During the first wave of expansion in the second and third decades of the planning era, central government policy was the main driver of HE expansion. A set of new institutions were established with government funding—the central universities, the Indian Institutes of Technology (IITs), the Indian Institutes of Management (IIMs), the All-India Institute of Medical Sciences (AIIMS) and the regional engineering colleges (RECs). During the mid-1980s, the second wave of expansion brought the emergence of private institutions. These were mainly private-sector-run professional colleges, which were located particularly in some states such as Karnataka, Andhra Pradesh, Maharashtra and Tamil Nadu. During the 1990s, another phase of accelerated expansion began, and this process is still unfolding. Driven by the policy of economic liberalization, as well as the demographic bulge in the college-age population, there has been a sharp expansion in the number of new universities, and technical and professional institutions in both the private and the public sector. The latter includes the recent dramatic increase in the number of new IITs, IIMs and AIIMS across the country. This urgency as well as the institutional composition of intensification of HE reflect the emergence of scientific, technical and professional education as strategic priorities to deal with the economic challenges of globalization. The new international economic system requires such branches of knowledge for industries and professions to remain competitive in the global economy.

This vast expansion of the Indian HE system has necessitated a commensurate demand for appropriately skilled faculty members. For some years now, concern has been growing among HE policymakers and administrators about the adequate availability of faculty resources. There is a general acknowledgement of a 'shortage of faculty', despite the lack of comprehensive and reliable quantitative data. Efforts to cope with the faculty shortage have led to the appointment of ad hoc teaching staff in both public and private universities on a large scale. This development has created tension between the quantity and the quality of HE produced in the country.

The Ministry of Human Resource Development (MHRD), Government of India constituted the Task Force on Faculty Shortage and Design of Performance Appraisal System to examine the matter.[1] The Task Force submitted its report in 2011 in which it observed that

[1] Hereinafter, we shall refer to this committee as the Task Force. Professor Sanjay Dhande was its chairperson. The present author served as a member. This chapter draws on the report of the Task Force, and in particular on the chapter on analytical framework which he contributed. Other members of the

the shortage of faculty in the Indian HE system had already reached a critical level. This opinion was supported by the uniformly expressed views of the vice-chancellors and regulators who met with the Task Force. While noting that this was a 'rough estimate' due to paucity of data, the Task Force stated that the shortage was approximately 380,000 teachers (or 50 per cent of sanctioned positions). It is also observed that the scarcity was likely to worsen further during the coming decade, and reach 1.3 million (MHRD, 2011, Preamble, p. x).[2] Hence, the matter needs urgent policy attention (MHRD, 2011).

Faculty availability had been a source of longstanding concern long before the problem assumed critical dimensions. Prior to the Task Force, several committees commented in passing on the faculty shortage question though they did not study the problem systematically. They tended to view this as a supply-side problem, and suggested ways to increase and/or retain teaching faculty. This included the G. K. Chadha Committee to Review the Pay Scales and Service Conditions of University and College Teachers (for the Sixth Pay Commission). Even as early as 1964, the Kothari Commission had expressed the concern that scholars of high potential might be discouraged from joining the teaching profession because of the unattractive working environment in academic institutions.

GAUGING FACULTY SHORTAGE AND STRUCTURAL ISSUES IDENTIFIED BY EXPERT GROUPS

The Task Force attempted to assess the quantitative extent of faculty shortage. It soon realized that there was a severe paucity of reliable data. The major regulatory bodies did not possess data, and hence were unable to provide much information. The data available with the UGC were dated and highly incomplete. Hence, the Task Force attempted to conduct a survey on its own. Unfortunately, the data that could be collected was limited mainly due to the short time available.

Task Force were Professor Devi Singh, Professor V. Kannan, Professor K. K. Aggarwal, Dr R. K. Chauhan and Dr Niloufer A. Kazmi.

[2] According to the AISHE 2013–2014, the total number of teachers is approximately 1,368,000 in HE.

Nonetheless, the Task Force drew some tentative conclusions from the limited data that it was able to gather. It found that in the central universities, on an average, 35 per cent of faculty positions were vacant. In several cases, the shortage exceeded 50 per cent. The gap was high in some leading universities—for example, Delhi University had a shortage of 53 per cent. However, in a few central universities the situation was comfortable (e.g., Vishwa-Bharati, Assam University, Aligarh Muslim University and Jamia Millia Islamia University). With respect to the state universities, the average shortage in the 77 universities that responded to the Task Force survey was 33 per cent. However, in 25 per cent of the responding universities, the faculty shortage was above 50 per cent, and in another 18 per cent of the responding universities, the figure was above 40 per cent. The situation was alarming in some state universities which had over 70 per cent of unfilled positions (MHRD, 2011, Chapter 3).

Viewing the faculty shortage problem in relation to the size of enrolment, the average student-to-teacher ratio was found to be 20.9. This compares unfavourably with the UGC norms, which is 13.5 (with 15 for undergraduate and 12 for postgraduate programmes). The Task Force thus estimated that the faculty size should be increased by 54 per cent of the existing strength in order to bring it on par with the norm. To fill the data gap, the MHRD has recently launched the All India Survey on Higher Education (AISHE), which provides more recent information on various aspects of HE. According to the AISHE 2013–14 Report, the all-India figure for the pupil-teacher ratio (PTR) for universities and colleges in the regular mode (i.e., excluding distance education) remained at 21 (MHRD, 2015). This confirms and validates the estimate made by the Task Force. The AISHE data shed additional light on the regional variation. There is a very wide variation in the PTR across the states, which implies a corresponding disparity in faculty shortage. Bihar (54) and Jharkhand (55) show very high PTR, followed by Uttar Pradesh (38) and West Bengal (37). The faculty resource position is grave in these states, as they are very far from the UGC norms. On the other side of the spectrum, we have states where the overall faculty availability is comfortable. These are Sikkim (11), Karnataka (13) and Tamil Nadu, Kerala and Andhra Pradesh (14 each) (MHRD, 2015).

To summarize, the available quantitative evidence confirms that there exists an overall shortage of faculty. Precise measurement of its magnitude remains difficult. If it is measured as the proportion of unfilled positions, the average national shortage is about 35 per cent. If, however, it is assessed in terms of the shortfall from UGC norms on PTRs, the average shortage is 54 per cent. There is a large disparity across regions as well as across universities. Many institutions with alarming faculty shortages are state universities. However, perhaps surprisingly, some of the leading central universities also have high faculty shortage. There are significant variations in the faculty shortage in specific academic domains.

For policy-making, these quantitative estimates of faculty shortage need to be complemented with an understanding of how the Indian HE system actually functions. We present such an understanding which is gleaned from the observations of various expert committees, as well as from the insights that senior HE administrators and regulators shared with the Task Force. These judgements and insights convey a sense of the prevailing 'ground realities' and decision-making environment affecting faculty resource availability. We have grouped these observations into three categories—(a) factors affecting the supply motives of faculty resources; (b) demand-side perspectives; and (c) regulatory and policy context.

Supply-side Factors

Given India's population size and long tradition of HE, there exists a large pool of potential teachers. However, the requisite skills are scarce and there are alternative professional options for potential teachers. Hence, the central issue is whether the teaching profession is adequately attractive for qualified and talented professionals. The diagnosis of inadequate supply has generally rested on (a) salaries and (b) academic working environment. The Chadha Committee (UGC, 2008) held that the problem of faculty shortage needs to be addressed by offering adequate pecuniary incentives so that competent individuals are motivated to join the teaching profession. In the early decades following Independence, salaries were perhaps less important. Arguably, many teachers were attracted by the dignity, intellectual freedom and respect associated with the teaching profession. However, after the 1991 market reforms, pecuniary considerations carry more weight in career decisions of skilled professionals. This is particularly true because salaries have skyrocketed in the globalized and/or newly commercialized professions such as information technology, law, management and medicine. The globalization of the skilled labour services market is a relatively recent structural change in the Indian economy, and it is a key driver of income inequality. The desire for some parity between teacher and other professional salaries therefore plays a key role in career choices of potential teachers.

The Goverdhan Mehta Committee (MHRD, 2009), titled The Pay Committee for Faculty and Scientific/Design Staff of Central Technical Institutes, pointed out a different supply-side structural constraint—not enough PhD degree holders are being produced in the country who are qualified to teach in technical and professional institutions. Moreover, very few of even the small numbers who possess the required qualifications are joining the teaching profession. So, motivating new entrants to teaching is an important problem that must be addressed.

What about those who are already in the teaching profession, and their willingness and ability to perform? With regard to the academic working environment for in-service teachers, the Kothari Commission had long ago noted specifically certain features that affect motivation. These go far beyond salaries. This includes the feeling of isolation experienced by 'thinly spread' research-oriented faculty members and hence the lack of stimulating interaction with colleagues, heavy teaching loads, classes of large size with 'unchallenging students', and academic administrators who consciously or unconsciously discourage intellectual vitality and motivation. Citing the 1964 report, the Task Force remarked on the continuing validity of the observations today. These considerations make us realize that, even though economic factors are important, teaching cannot be treated merely as a skilled, commodified service to be bought and sold.

The act of teaching embodies a significant component of individual performance akin to the performing arts. Here skill, inspiration, autonomy, research activity, intellectual renewal and creativity are extremely important. The notion of a good academic work environment includes these subtle but difficult to quantify elements, the significance of which administrators may not fully grasp. The ongoing process of commercialization of HE has tended to further marginalize such aspects. Hence, while adequate physical infrastructure of buildings, IT and library resources are important, these are still not sufficient to produce quality education. If quantity of teaching services is increased at a substantial cost of quality, it would defeat the very social and economic purpose of HE policy.

Finally, maintaining a good working environment over the longer run for in-service teachers also includes having a credible system of performance appraisal and promotion to support the career path of teachers. The Task Force examined this matter in some depth, reviewed the findings of earlier committees, and made detailed recommendations for design of an appraisal system. This system has several components—teaching and learning activities, co-curricular and professional development activities, and research-related activities.

Demand-side Perspective

While acknowledging that supply-side issues constraining the availability of faculty are important, we must recognize the important role of demand. This is an aspect that has not received sufficient attention. Not only has the demand-supply gap for faculty been rising rapidly in recent years, the composition of demand has been changing significantly. Hence the shortage of faculty may be more acute in some programmes and associated disciplines than in others. For example, demand is booming in fields such as engineering and management, whereas it is relatively stagnant in traditional disciplines such as liberal studies and humanities. Moreover, the problem of faculty shortage is not only a matter of assuring sufficient number of teaching hours. The problem of quality is closely intertwined with it, because attempting to stretch the quantity of teachers inevitably affects the quality of education. HE policy-makers and administrators attempting to increase the availability of faculty resources need therefore to keep in mind

the inseparable relationship between quantity and quality of education services. There might arise a situation where HEIs must trade-off
quality vis-à-vis quantity, and this condition should be avoided. The
Task Force observed that the quality of Indian HE is 'patchy' and
'uneven'. In this chapter, we analyze the problem of faculty availability
and shortage within a framework that integrates both the demand and
supply perspectives.

The Task Force adopted an economic analysis approach, which
we follow in this chapter. In our view, the economic motivation has
become crucial to both the demand and supply of faculty resources.
We need to explicitly consider how the HEIs determine their demand
for faculty resources by the HEIs. Failure to account for the underlying
economic pressures can lead to the frustration of well-meaning policy
and regulatory steps. Thus, there is a need to bring the complex and
multidimensional elements that determine the availability and deployment of faculty resources into a simplified and coherent framework.
A chain of economic relations and causation determines the market
demand for faculty. In the first stage, there is a demand for HE itself,
which emanates from the student-age population. This is reflected
in the demand for seats in HEIs. The HEIs in turn respond to this
demand for HE by making operational decisions regarding admissions,
programmes, facilities and faculty resources. The consequent demand
for faculty resources is one element in the operating strategy of HEIs.
As discussed elaborately in the next section, the nature of demand for
faculty resources differs across different types of HEIs. The demand
depends on the sources of their operating funds, and specifically on the
relative importance of tuition fees, government support, endowment
incomes, research grants and so on.

While bringing in this economic behaviour perspective, we
remain conscious that HE is not a commodity in the standard sense.
Nevertheless, we believe that keeping the economic dimension in
mind will lead to a more nuanced formulation of policies. In this way,
the broader social goals can be maintained, and hopefully policies that
curb the possible negative features of 'over-commercialization' can be
pursued.

The Regulatory and Policy Context

Senior functionaries (heads or chairpersons) of a large number of regulatory bodies and universities met with the Task Force to discuss the faculty availability scenario. Their evidence covering a variety of HE domains is summarized further (MHRD, 2011, Chapter 2). It sheds light on the structural changes in the system, and especially the significant effect that the large-scale entry of the private sector institutions is having on the faculty resource scenario across a broad spectrum of HEIs:

(i)   There is an incidence of faculty shortage in both central-government-funded and state-government-funded HEIs. This problem can actually be traced back to a de facto ban on new recruitment, and even on the filling up of existing sanctioned teaching positions. The underlying reason was a resource crunch on government budgets. However, surprisingly, even after the ban was eased, many centrally funded institutions have continued to neglect faculty recruitment. Thus, the perceived faculty shortage is a result of both a policy decision regarding HE funding, as well as an institution-level decisions. These decisions have constrained the demand for faculty by the HEIs. This has manifested as a 'faculty shortage' as student enrolments have risen. In several state–government-funded institutions across the country (e.g., Madhya Pradesh, Rajasthan and Bihar) the situation was allowed to worsen drastically. It is not obvious why exactly the HEIs behaved as they have even after the hiring freeze was withdrawn. Hence, it is all the more important to analyze the determinants of the HEIs' demand for faculty resources.

(ii)   With regard to the faculty-resource creation pipeline, doctoral programmes are weak, partly because there are not sufficient funds for doctoral and postdoctoral fellowships. In government-owned teacher education institutions (TEI) there is a 25 per cent shortfall in faculty resources, and private sector institutions have entered the domain.

(iii)   Both public sector and private sector function in tandem in medical education. However, there are more private sector institutions entering the sector. Faculty shortage is experienced in the older established public sector medical colleges. We may infer that there is competition for faculty resources between the older government medical colleges and the newly emerging private medical colleges, in which government colleges are losing out.

(iv) In the case of dental colleges, the regulator (Dental Council of India or DCI) highlighted the weak and ineffective position of the regulator. The council is apparently short of staff, and has no 'teeth' to regulate either the numbers of students admitted or faculty strength. Over 88 per cent of the dental colleges are in the private sector, and they cannot be effectively regulated. They do not provide up-to-date information on their faculty strength. Indeed, they often provide unreliable and misleading information to the regulator. For example, the name of the same individual might appear on the list of 'full-time faculty' in more than one institution. While on paper, there is no faculty shortage, the DCI estimated the de facto shortage to be between 30 per cent and 35 per cent.

(v) The All India Council on Technical Education (AICTE) stated that the shortage in technical education (covering a wide gamut of disciplines—engineering, management, pharmacy, architecture, hotel management, etc.) was very acute. This was so, especially at the senior faculty level. There were 150,000 teachers in position, against an actual requirement of 300,000 teachers (i.e., a 50 per cent shortfall).

(vi) The situation was less extreme in legal education. There was no overall faculty shortage. However, it was difficult to find 'qualified faculty' as per the prevailing eligibility criteria. To meet the situation, the Bar Council of India (BCI) had relaxed some eligibility criteria in order to expand the pool of available teachers. It did not insist on the LLM degree as an essential qualification for teaching, and practicing advocates were encouraged to teach.

(vii) Several vice-chancellors shared their views and experience with the Task Force. They confirmed that most universities had not recruited faculty 'for decades'. Government funding has been a constraint, and they felt that central government support to supplement the resources of state government might ease the situation. They roughly estimated an overall shortfall of faculty amounting to 35 per cent to 40 per cent, while it was worse at the senior faculty level.

(viii) A recurrent theme on which there was uniform agreement was that recruiting 'quality faculty' was a difficult task. We conclude from this that the problem of faculty shortage as experienced by the HEIs was not that of receiving an inadequate number of applications for a teaching post during a recruitment exercise. The applicants do not have the desired and expected level of quality and competence for the academic task at hand. This confirms the observation made earlier that the doctoral and postdoctoral programmes in the country are extremely weak. Inadequate availability of quality faculty raises a larger question: Are the students graduating from such programmes 'employable' as teachers in standard academic programmes? In many instances, this situation had resulted in 'inbreeding' in faculty appointments—as departments absorbed their own outgoing students. Resorting to temporary and ad hoc appointments had also tended to compromise the quality of teaching as individuals with adequate quality opt for permanent position or to other lucrative professions.

FACULTY AVAILABILITY AND SHORTAGE THROUGH AN ECONOMIC LENS

As noted earlier, faculty shortage is commonly assessed by policy-makers and academic administrators as the proportion of unfilled positions to sanctioned faculty positions. This is useful as a rule of thumb, but it is an imperfect measure of faculty shortage. The 'sanctioned posts' for any institution are administratively set. They remain fixed for relatively long periods of time and serve as an upper limit on recruitment. This measure does not help to understand the actual reasons for the faculty shortage, nor do they indicate whether the institutions intend to fill the 'gap'. Without an analysis based on behavioural functioning of the HEIs, policy response to the problem could go wrong. As part of our contribution to the Task Force, we had developed a simple analytical framework through which we may examine the faculty shortage question using an economic lens. We draw on this framework to present the essential logical structure of this framework, as well as some of the key insights that follow from this perspective (MHRD, 2011, Chapter 4).

From an economic standpoint, HE services constitute an 'output'. This output is demanded by students and supplied by the HEIs. Faculty resource is one among several 'inputs' that are required to produce HE. Hence, to analyze faculty shortage and availability, we need to see first how the demand for faculty resources by the HEIs is derived from the underlying market for HE services. The demand for HE at the aggregate level depends on three broad determinants—(a) the size of the student-age population (demographic structure), (b) tuition fees charged to students and (c) 'desired gross enrolment ratio (GER)' (Sen, 2013). The desired GER is a parameter that summarizes the attractiveness of HE to potential students. This parameter in turn depends on expected economic growth trends, as well as the social status associated with academic qualifications. High economic growth results in more favourable job prospects and high salaries on graduation. This increases the demand for HE from the student-age population, that is, it increases the 'desired GER' in the population. Thus, the demand relationship for HE is described as follows:

$$D_E = f(S; G_d; P_E),$$

where D_E is the demand for HE, S is the proportion of student age population in the total, G_d is the desired GER and P_E is the price of education. If S and G_d rise, D_E would rise. If these parameters remain constant, the demand for HE is inversely related to the tuition fees, as in a normal demand function. While from an economic standpoint, the price of HE (tuition fee) is a crucial determinant of the demand for HE, in actual practice, there may be regulatory constraints on the possible tuition fee. The same logic can be applied at a more disaggregated level to predict the demand for individual postgraduate programmes and academic disciplines. Demand for such programmes would depend on the relevant tuition fees, while the desired enrolment ratio would reflect the job prospects and expected incomes in specific domains (e.g., engineering or management and so on).

Having assessed the demand, the HEIs supply the HE services. Their supply decisions include (a) the quantum and composition of HE that they will provide during the period,[3] and (b) the number of faculty members that would be utilized for delivering the chosen programmes and the number of new faculty members to be recruited. This latter magnitude represents the demand for faculty resources by an HEI. How do the HEIs make these decisions? We postulate that the HEIs behave in an economically rational manner so as to attain their institutional goals. They have two independent goals: (a) maximize net operating income and (b) maximize institutional reputation. These goals reflect their short-term and long-term institutional objectives respectively. HEIs attempt to find an optimum combination of these two objectives, subject to a number of constraints that they face. These constraints include infrastructure constraints, regulatory norms, government policy directives and the size of the operating budget.

Net operating income is the difference between income flows and recurring costs.[4] With economic liberalization, rising costs and stagnant or shrinking grants, generating a net surplus has become an important goal for all categories of HEIs. *Institutional reputation* is difficult to measure directly. It is gradually created over a longer period by sustained performance and expenditures on a number of activities. These include providing high-quality education in widely respected academic programmes, good job market acceptance of graduates, and the recognition of the institution's research and faculty quality. This goal requires investment on infrastructure as well as on maintaining a good academic work environment. There is a very close association between institutional reputation and the *quality* of education that an institution is able to deliver. Institutional reputation pays off in the long run through the ability to attract good students, as well as to

---

[3] The quantum of HE is measured by the size of student intake and, hence, the planned number of students graduating with degrees. Composition refers to the mix of programmes being offered and the size of enrolment in each programme.

[4] Income is obtained from tuition and other fees paid by students, as well as from other sources, such as income from endowment investments, grants, funded research and consulting activities. From this we subtract recurring costs to get the net operating income.

recruit and retain good faculty resources, and to obtain financial grants, earn consultancy income and build endowment funds. It enables the HEIs to fulfil the broader goals of HE, which is difficult to do under conditions of commercialization, where the main focus is on generating profit. High institutional reputation also enables publicly funded HEIs to have a higher degree of operating flexibility and academic autonomy with regard to regulatory treatment. They tend to have greater flexibility in the operating characteristics of HEIs. The relative weights that they assign to each of these goals vary depending on the type of HEI. Moreover, the age of the institution is another important determinant. A new institution may have to devote more attention to reputation-building efforts. In general, there is likely to be a trade-off between the two objectives of net income and institutional reputation given limited operating budget for the HEI.

The Indian HE sector contains a very wide variety of institutional types. According to the AISHE 2013–14 survey report (MHRD, 2015), there are 723 universities, 36,634 colleges and 11,664 stand-alone Institutions.[5] Out of these, 248 are affiliating universities, that is, they provide the degrees for colleges under them, and 219 universities are privately managed. Some of the universities are specialized by discipline—398 of the universities have general programmes, 90 are technical universities, 61 universities offer agriculture and allied courses, 43 are medical, 20 law, 11 Sanskrit, 7 language and 56 'other' universities. The colleges are also quite diverse with respect to their ownership and management—75 per cent of the colleges are privately managed, 60 per cent are private-unaided and 15 per cent are private-aided institutions. The objective functions of each of these types of HEIs would vary depending on their operating context. However, our framework is general, and may be adapted to each context by assigning an appropriate weight to each of these components of the institutional objective function. For example, a commercially oriented, privately managed HEI would assign a very high weight to generating a net operating income, and a very low weight to institutional reputation. This would translate into choice of and/or discrimination in favour of academic programmes where high tuition fees can be charged. By

---

[5] Stand-alone institutions offer only diploma courses.

contrast, a well-endowed public institution with adequate and assured financial support from the government would be less concerned with earning a surplus from teaching activity.

The supply behaviour of the HEIs may be conceptualized in the following terms. Let us first abstract from the quality–quantity trade-off.[6] We assume that the HEI is maintaining its desired quality–quantity balance. It supplies a certain quantity of HE services (measured by the number of students graduating) in accordance with its objective function. As tuition fees rise, the HEI increases the supply of HE. However, the responsiveness of quantity of education supplied depends on a set of underlying conditions. If there are no faculty shortages or infrastructure constraints, the HEI can respond easily to a small increase in tuition fees. In economic jargon, the supply function for HE will be 'elastic'. However, when input constraints exist, the supply response is less flexible. In this manner, different configurations can be analyzed. Apart from input constraints, there may be other factors that can affect the HE market. This includes regulatory or policy-induced requirements. As discussed earlier, there could be a 'ban' on fresh recruitment.

The analytical framework delineated earlier can be represented in simple diagrams representing the HE market. The diagrammatic analysis has been presented more fully elsewhere.[7] We present here some key insights derived using this framework to analyze faculty shortage in a number of different contexts. The appropriate policy response in each of these contexts is very different. In some situations, what may appear as a faculty shortage is not really so. Measuring faculty shortage by the proportion of unfilled to sanctioned posts tends to shift the focus towards increasing the supply of faculty resources. However, this may not be the correct diagnosis of the situation in all cases. Here, we present a set of hypothetical cases to illustrate the need for policy to be based on a careful assessment of the operating context and economic motives of the HEI. While faculty availability is our focus in this

---

[6] We shall discuss the quality–quantity trade-off subsequently in the chapter.

[7] The framework is explained more fully in a paper by the author (Sen, 2013). We shall use it here to convey some of the key insights that are relevant here. The work originated from the author's participation in the Task Force.

chapter, we should keep in mind that the more important policy issue is whether HE is available in adequate quantity and quality.

Case 1: Excess Demand for Higher Education Without Faculty Shortage in Public-funded HEI

Faculty shortage causes concern because it may prevent education services from expanding to meet rising demand. However, consider a situation where there is no shortage of faculty (in a structural sense). Demand and supply of HE both respond to the price (tuition fees). The supply for HE is elastic—that is, the HEI can increase the supply of HE by hiring additional faculty resources if needed. If the HE market functions according to market principles, supply and demand would be equal at a particular equilibrium tuition rate. However, this may not be possible because of an upper limit on tuition fees imposed by government on grounds of economic accessibility. This is the effective tuition fee, and it is lower than the equilibrium rate. This situation will lead to an excess demand for HE—the supply by the HEIs will be less than the demand at the low price. Here, HEIs may claim that they face a faculty shortage, but the real problem is that they have no economic incentive. Under the prevailing conditions, they would recruit more faculty resources only if salaries were lower. In fact, if faculty supplies are increased by policy steps to expand doctoral programmes, there will be a downward pressure on faculty salaries and perhaps on quality as well. There is no reason to suppose that faculty salaries in India are too high, and therefore lowering them may not be the best policy. The correct policy, therefore, would be to increase budgetary support to the HEIs to enable them to expand supply. This is the better way to meet the goals of affordable education together with quality.

Case 2: Excess Demand for Higher Education with Faculty Shortage and Regulatory Constraint

Here, we examine a situation where there are two additional and different types of constraints on the supply of education—there is a structural barrier to expanding faculty size, and a policy-induced 'ban' on faculty recruitment. The structural constraint on faculty supply implies that beyond a point, the supply of education cannot be increased easily. This could be because potential teachers are attracted by alternative job opportunities, and they can only be induced to join the teaching profession by offering higher salaries. Thus, education supply can be increased by the HEIs, but only at a sharply rising cost. The ceiling imposed on tuition fees remains. In this case, the magnitude of excess demand for HE can be shown to depend on which of these three constraints is actually binding. If the faculty supply constraint is binding, then the appropriate policy would be to take steps to increase the supply of faculty resources. If on the other hand, it is the policy-induced freeze on faculty hiring that is the binding constraint, then no other policy intervention would ease the problem until this policy is relaxed. Further, even if both of these constraints (i.e., faculty shortage and hiring freeze) are relaxed, if the upper limit on tuition is binding, then the excess demand for higher will still remain until the HEI receives enhanced funding.

To summarize, our economic framework suggests that policy-makers must (a) carefully identify the different potential constraints on the HE market, (b) establish which *particular constraint is binding* at any given time and (c) decide on the policy step to ameliorate the binding constraint.

We now apply our framework to analyze the market for faculty resources. This market is also subject to three influences—demand, supply and regulatory/policy norms. The demand for faculty resources is determined as follows. Faced with a demand for HE, the HEI decides on faculty utilization so as to maximize net operating income subject to maintain a chosen level of education quality and institutional reputation. The demand for faculty resources can then derived to be a function of the faculty salaries. If salaries fall, they would employ more faculty resources. If there is a rise in the demand for HE, then the demand for faculty resources would also increase correspondingly.

On the supply side, the main determinants are faculty salaries (relative to jobs with comparable qualifications), service conditions (e.g., teaching workload and research opportunities), career advancement prospects (promotion prospects and skill upgradation opportunities), institutional reputation of the HEI, better post-retirement benefits, and attractive fellowship opportunities for PhD and postdoctoral research. These conditions comprise factors that would increase faculty supply over the long term by making academic careers more attractive for new entrants. In the medium and short run, faculty availability can be increased by such steps as relaxation of the age of mandatory retirement, enabling other professionals and practitioners (who are qualified but whose normal jobs do not involve teaching) to teach on a part-time basis, attracting NRIs and international academic personnel. However, given such enabling conditions, the most effective determinant of supply in the short run is the faculty salary. As wages rise, up to a point, faculty supplies would increase readily. However, after a certain level, the availability would run into a limit. Beyond this level, further increases would require significant increase in the salary. However, Indian faculty salaries in public HEIs are traditionally fixed by administrative procedures. So we shall assume that the prevailing salary level (say W) is given. W is less than the market clearing equilibrium wage rate.

Finally, regulatory norms influence the faculty market. These can be of two types—(a) those that set a floor on faculty positions through such norms as PTRs and (b) those that set an upper limit to faculty positions by such mechanisms as freezing fresh hiring, or via rigidity in the number of sanctioned posts.

Applying our framework to the faculty market yields the following insights. The actual faculty shortage is the gap between demand and supply at the administrative fixed salary W. The shortage would disappear if the market salary was permitted to rise. The actual shortage can be shown to be greater than the gap between sanctioned and actual filled posts—that is, *the traditional measure is inaccurate and underestimates the true economic faculty shortage.* The number of actually filled positions is low because the fixed salary level is insufficient to elicit adequate quantity of faculty supply.

If we consider a different hypothetical situation where the supply position of faculty is even more stringent, it is possible that at the given wage rate, the quantity of faculty resources supplied in the market would be *inadequate to meet the norm of a maximum PTR*. The appropriate policy responses in this situation would be a combination of the following—(a) in the short term, allow the faculty wage to rise; (b) take steps to increase the short-term supply of faculty; (c) initiate measures (noted earlier) to improve the long-term attractiveness of academic careers. It is possible, however, that in this situation, HEIs and policy-makers may attempt to take some other actions. One such action is to restrict the size of enrolments by making entry requirements much more stringent. We observe this phenomenon occurring in the case of the popular professional programmes in management, engineering, medicine and law.[8] Such a step would keep the demand for faculty resources down to manageable levels, but at the cost of unmet demand for HE. The HEI might also attempt to lower the effective cost of faculty resources by increasing teaching loads and discouraging research and professional development activity. This strategy would, however, lead to a weakening of institutional reputation. HEIs could also adopt short-term measures to increase faculty supply—such as ad hoc appointments. However, without adequate processes for certification and quality control, this step may lead to lower quality.

The economic competition for faculty resources has important structural consequences for the HE sector. Economic liberalization has led to a sharp rise in the demand for those branches of HE that offer prospects for high-paying jobs. This trend has reinforced the commercialization of HE by making very high tuition fees feasible and acceptable in certain disciplines. Consequently, the salaries that faculty members in these disciplines can command have risen relative to the teachers in other traditional disciplines. Private sector HEIs have entered such segments of the HE market. In some cases, they offer higher salaries to teachers whose skills are in short supply relative to the demand. In large, established Indian public universities it is difficult if not impossible to have differential salaries for different groups of faculties. This process has contributed to the *institutional fragmentation of the HE sector*, and explains the emergence of highly specialized and smaller

---

[8] For example, in the Common Admission Test (CAT) to join the IIMs, the successful candidates represent approximately 1.5 per cent of the total number of applicants.

universities. Moreover, the new private HEIs have a strong incentive to 'poach' senior faculty members away from the older universities. The latter are consequently weakened through such a process. Thus, the intensified commercialization of HE under conditions of excess demand heightens institutional competition. Because the competition does not occur in a level playing field, it has a differentiating impact on the HE system. Private HEIs operate with a much greater degree of economic autonomy—they are able to engage in commercial cherry picking. Consequently, they often offer a narrower range of programmes and courses. The strong reliance on net operating surplus of the commercialized private HEIs keeps them focused on revenue earning. However, this also implies that they do not have the capacity to build institutional reputation. On the other end of the organizational spectrum, the public HEIs have a bigger social mission and less operational flexibility which restricts their ability to commercialize, and pay higher salaries to their faculty resources. Hence, their faculty resource acquisition and retention strategies must rely on non-pecuniary incentives—such as high reputation, better working environment and research opportunities.

Our analysis from an economic perspective, thus, suggests that commercialization would exacerbate the fragmentation and differentiation within the HE system. The commercially oriented institutions would tend to stretch limited faculty resources by focusing on fee-paying courses and high student intakes and heavy teaching loads. The public-funded universities (which typically receive limited funding from government) would be under pressure to increase student intakes, particularly of those students who cannot pay high tuition fees. However, with adverse salary differentials, they would find it difficult to have adequate faculty in the disciplines and programmes that are in high demand. Both these types of institutions would face challenges in maintaining quality. Under such conditions, well-intentioned regulatory norms aimed at maintaining quality (such as PTRs, and adequate infrastructure) might be evaded. As we have seen, many regulatory bodies expressed their inability to adequately implement their decisions, mainly because HEIs have an incentive to evade them while the regulators' resources are limited.

CONCLUSION

The Task Force made a set of comprehensive recommendations which should be adopted. These were grouped under the following heads: (a) administrative reforms, (b) academic reforms, (c) financial reforms and (d) miscellaneous reforms. Among the administrative reforms, it recommended that each HEI should establish a faculty induction and development cell. It also suggested ways to establish procedures and standards for different categories of non-permanent faculty members. These include those who are hired on contract, guest faculty members, adjunct faculty, visiting faculty, distinguished mentor faculty and international adjunct faculty. Under academic reforms, there are suggestions for institutionalizing schemes for inducing younger professionals to academic careers, and award schemes for excellent teachers. Among the financial reforms, the Task Force proposed honorariums for the time that faculty members devote to sponsored research, and establishing externally endowed chair professorships. The miscellaneous category included the setting up of a web portal for greater information dissemination that would help academic career aspirants.

While these recommendations are very useful, we have highlighted here the implications for faculty resources of significant variations in the focus and functioning of different categories of HEIs. It is desirable that the differentiation and fragmentation of the HEI system should be kept within some reasonable limits. Our analysis suggests that while appropriate steps to increase the availability of faculty resources are desirable, a broader policy approach is necessary. In essence, this would entail ensuring mechanisms for enabling (and encouraging) the HEIs to attain a better balance between the two objectives of adequate net income and institutional reputation. At the moment, the different types of HEIs pursue objectives that are highly skewed because their operating environment does not incentivize them to seek a better balance. A better balance between the two goals would narrow the sharp differences in faculty resource strategies. In the case of both private HEIs as well as public HEIs, policy should encourage the creation of some type of endowment fund. Such a fund can be crucial in enabling them to focus on and invest in building institutional reputation. This long-term goal may be relegated under pressures to increase student enrolments and/or to raise financial resources. An important component of institutional reputation is creating and maintaining a good work environment for faculty, and adequate opportunities for research and professional development. Additional regulatory steps and mechanisms such as rewards based on objective performance criteria may be needed to channel competition among HEIs towards building institutional reputation. In the case of public HEIs, it is very important to increase their financial autonomy—by enabling steps that would encourage them to build a strong corpus funds from the savings that they earn. They should be adequately incentivized to fulfil their larger social mandates, without their having to compromise on quality and reputation.

In many ways, such enabling conditions are evident in such institutions as IIMs and IITs. They are publicly funded, have acquired the reputation and also have been allowed the academic autonomy that enables them to have a good faculty management processes. The issue of tuition fees and accessibility remains a cause for concern in such cases, and this needs concurrent attention. They are able to attract and retain faculty resources in the face of stiff domestic and international competition. Among the private HEIs as well, we find exceptional institutions where institutional reputation is accorded importance. Hence, the problem cannot be attributed to a simple private sector–public sector dualism. Indeed some of the great universities of the world are private. There is, however, no easy way out. The faculty availability problem requires calibrated short-term, medium-term and long-term policy responses, as well as adequate financial resources.

REFERENCES

MHRD (Ministry of Human Resource Development). (2009). *The pay committee for faculty and scientific/design staff of central technical institutes* (Goverdhan Mehta Committee Report). New Delhi: Government of India.
———. (2011). *Report of the Task Force on Faculty Shortage and Design of Performance Appraisal System* (S. G. Dhande Committee Report). New Delhi: Government of India.
———. (2015). *All India survey on higher education (AISHE), 2013–14*. New Delhi: Department of Higher Education, Government of India.

Sen, C. (2013). A framework for analysing demand and supply of faculty and the quality of higher education. *Journal of Educational Planning and Administration, 27*(3, July), 281–309.

UGC (University Grants Commission). (2008). *The committee to review pay scales and service conditions of university and college teachers* (G. K. Chaddha Committee Report). New Delhi: Government of India.

Chapter 6

Professional Development of Teachers in Higher Education

Santosh Panda

INTRODUCTION

This chapter examines the continuing professional development (CPD) of higher education (HE) teachers in India. This has been done at the backdrop of a closer look at the scholarship of teaching–learning, and what entails becoming an effective teacher in the changing context of HE pedagogy and technology, and the reforms in HE today, requiring changing and updating roles for HE teachers. The existing schemes and strategies of CPD for HE teachers from general and professional fields have been examined from the viewpoints of a wider contour of professionalism in the teaching profession as well as the existing resource networks and resources to meet the goals. At the end, a CPD framework is articulated, based on the existing provisions and also the emerging requirements of the profession.

SCHOLARSHIP OF TEACHING AND LEARNING

Scholarship of teaching or scholarly teaching involves reflective practice which combines both professional discipline practice with teaching as a profession, and research and knowledge base in the discipline of teaching–learning (Boyer, 1990). Worldwide, there has been considerable stress on disciplinary research at the cost of teaching students (Elton, 2009). Today, in many parts of the globe, HE institutions value research in disciplinary pedagogy/teaching–learning as much as disciplinary study itself. This needs to be taken forward in any CPD programme, which would require (a) inward reflection by university management and academics, (b) autonomy to pursue the formulation that 'research into teaching is as important as research in the disciplines' and (c) shift 'from stressing teaching to stressing learning' (Elton, 2009, p. 3).

While professional development (PD) is considered limited, time-bound and structured, professional learning (PL) takes place throughout the professional life and even later, and contributes much more to the quality of a professional and his or her professional practice than the former. PL entails reflective engagement of teacher-practitioners in their contextualized practice, reflecting on innovative processes and outcomes, linked with standards set by either the HE regulator or the professional association(s). This occurs in many different ways informally and formally, and therefore must be valued in any schema of PD. While a formal PD provision may ensure mundane and essential innovations in curriculum design and teaching–learning (including assessment), a wider PL formulation attempts to bridge research–policy–practice gap. PL happens in many different ways, at various levels of scholarship, and cannot be fully codified for immediate outcomes. This leads to sustained professional growth and increase in the scholarship of teaching and learning. Professional freedom, mentoring and collaboration are the keys to such a process of continuous individual and group critical reflection (which a formal course of PD may not be able to achieve). However, in any case, the institutional goals cannot be submerged to individual scholarship—there must be congruence between the two. In essence, collaboration in the learning community leads to *complementarity* in the collective effort towards qualitative changes in both thinking and action, contextualization of teaching–learning, and therefore learning outcomes.

CONTOURS OF TEACHING IN HIGHER EDUCATION

Traditionally, teaching, research and extension/community work/ social action linked to one's discipline have been the primary work of a teacher in HE (UGC, 1978). Any discipline has its own structure and characterization, and a teacher is required to have grounding in these, besides mastery of the content at a particular level of one's discipline. While teaching entails disseminating and explaining information relating to content and concept, this also presupposes facilitating students to develop insight, and be reflective and critical in what they study. The students also need to be engaged in translating knowledge and information into practice in-context. This could be possible when the skills of questioning, verifying, analyzing, synthesizing, reviewing and creating are developed in the students in the process of the discipline of teaching–learning. A teacher needs to be constrained as a professional in order to represent multiple ideas and actions more faithfully, notwithstanding the freedom to critique an idea and express ideological preference(s). This is how a true professional acknowledges and engages with opposite as well as antagonistic ideas or viewpoints in a community of professionals (Yadav & Panda, 1997).

Within teaching, there are hosts of tasks that a teacher needs to undertake, including communication and language competence, dealing with varied levels of students, and handling individual and collective student questions (Chaurasiya, 2016). Further, evaluation of students' formative and summative performance requires a combination of the competence in assessment and evaluation and the ethical commitment to undertake the task without prejudice. An essential skill required of teachers is to engage as well as assess students' individual and collective construction of social reality. This is what is lacking in teaching in HE today, and this has wider implication for CPD.

Changes in pedagogies and developments in ICT demand from teachers (a) experience in discipline-specific pedagogic innovations and (b) technological pedagogic content knowledge to deal with the complex nature of concepts as also the varied learning styles of learners. Not only has the workload of teachers increased, the teachers also need to undertake, besides innovative learner-centric teaching, a host of extra-curricular and administrative tasks. The introduction of the Academic Performance Indicator (API), Choice Based Credit System (CBCS) and compulsory massive open online courses (MOOCs) has been considered as a game changer by the University Grants Commission (UGC). All HE teachers are expected to be rigorously oriented to these changes. Teachers are not only required to be acquainted with generic pedagogies/andragogies but also need continuous updating in discipline-based pedagogy and inclusive classroom at set time intervals. Today, students also need training in social and life skills, ICT and research skills starting from the undergraduate level upwards. These, in turn, demand from teachers that they are well versed with the theory and practice of these skills.

Any aspiring teacher who, as a student, never witnessed (a) an effective interactive teaching–learning, (b) teachers dealing with varied academic levels of students and bringing in inclusivity to teaching–learning, (c) engagement in collaborative learning and (d) practicing innovative assessment, among others, neither has the awareness and skills nor finds a system which encourages innovation in teaching–learning. This lack of experiential learning and unsupportive system leads to the continuation of poor teaching in a vicious cycle. Even if one assumes that teachers have been committed to their teaching and discipline-research as per their understanding and skills, there are developments today in teaching–learning in HE which necessitate the teachers to go beyond what is being practiced as routine and ensure scholarship in teaching and learning, and greater engagement in PL.

TEACHER PROFESSIONAL DEVELOPMENT

PD of HE teachers is not a new phenomenon. However, the impact of PD programmes on the balance between the quality of the profession, the professional status and the quality of service rendered are to be considered. As is noted by Clegg (2003, p. 38), 'the first peculiarity of CPD in universities is that, while universities are major providers of CPD for other professions, this activity has had relatively little influence on the rhythms of institutional life'. Clegg further argues that academics' pursuance of personal scholarship is not recognized by any formalized CPD schema, nor is informal learning a part of recognized pathways within CPD. The major chunk of professionals is engaged in undergraduate teaching. The larger portion of their professional time is devoted to the major task of teaching. In this scenario, it is imperative that any CPD schema needs to recognize and accommodate these through continuous facilitation. Also, the CPD needs to be accredited. Barnett (2003) contends that there has always been a distinction between teaching and research, between massification of HE (which is focused on teaching) and knowledge generation/innovation (which is focused on research and scholarship). The CPD programmes in universities generally tilt towards teaching–learning. However, in the formation of academic identity, both formal and informal learning through conferences, collaborative projects, faculty exchange, peer review, scholarly publications, and online discussions and communications, among others need to be considered in a comprehensive CPD schema (Clegg, 2003).

Enhancement of status and improvement in the quality of service go hand in hand. Sometimes professionalism is used as rhetoric by an occupation simply to improve professional status and job conditions (Hoyle, 2001). Sachs (2003) notes that three factors have influenced the way teacher professionalism is perceived: (a) external pressures, (b) public discourses and (c) scientific developments. Indian HE has also been similarly influenced by a combination of these factors from time to time. Irrespective of any disciplinary orientation in the teaching profession, public service and autonomy/independence of judgement are two crucial ingredients (David, 2000) that distinguish it from other professions. Arguably, while professionalism is very strong in the teaching profession, the same may not be claimed for professionalization.

Teachers, like any other professional, are required to exhibit certain professional behaviour, including self-control through codes of professional ethics (Barber, 1965). The UGC (2010) highlights teachers and their responsibilities, teachers and students, teachers and colleagues, teachers and authorities, teachers and non-teaching staff, teachers and guardians, and teachers and society as components of the code of professional ethics. These codes, which could be seen as expectations from the teachers, coupled with the established functions of universities such as teaching, research and extension may be juxtaposed as shown in Table 6.1, classifying into old professionalism and new professionalism (Sachs, 2003).

When teaching enters into the framework of new professionalism, what essentially emanates is the public nature of the discourse, self-regulation, individual professional commitment and conscious

Table 6.1 *Old and New Professionalism*

Old Professionalism	New Professionalism
• Exclusive membership	• Inclusive membership
• Conservative practices	• Public ethical code of practice
• Self-interest	• Collaborative and collegial
• External regulation	• Activist orientation
• Slow change	• Flexible and progressive
• Reactive	• Responsive to change
	• Self-regulating
	• Policy-active
	• Enquiry-oriented
	• Knowledge building

Source: Sachs (2003).

engagement with building high order PL. It is a continuous process, evidence/portfolio-based, reflective and responsive. The teachers of those institutions which have gone through the process of NAAC accreditation know the rigour involved in this exercise, as also the professional gain that teachers accrue through this process. This, in a way, is also a PL and PD strategy, since it demands the teachers to be mindful about their professional progress.

The 12th Five-year Plan of 2012–2017 (GOI, 2011), which largely focused on quality and employability for HE, underlined certain expectations which could be useful ingredients to CPD of all HE teachers. These include strategies of skill development, institutional ranking, open and distance education, and multi-disciplinary learning for knowledge-creation and knowledge-sharing, National Vocational Education Qualification Framework (NVEQF)/National Skill Qualification Framework (NSQF), technology-enabled learning, overhaul of academic staff colleges (ASCs), strong accreditation, involvement with intellectual leadership to society, excellence in teaching and research, competitive salary/challenging work environment/greater flexibility and industry–institute interface.

The UGC, besides providing travel grants for conferences and research grants, had in the past initiated a few flagship programmes for PD of college and university teachers such as a faculty recharge programme, encore programme (scholar-in-resident), enhancing faculty resources programme and ASCs, later recast as human resource development centres (HRDCs). The institutionalized and designed staff development programmes in HE are analyzed in the backdrop of a brief analysis on CPD programmes in select countries.

REVIEW OF STAFF DEVELOPMENT PROGRAMMES

The review undertaken in this section focuses largely on India, though a brief tabular mapping has been done on a few countries on which information is available. The section on 'CPD framework' highlights select models and strategies adopted for CPD of teachers of HE, based on which a framework is articulated.

International Examples

Reports or country cases for CPD in HE are rare, and therefore the brief outlined in Table 6.2 may not be construed as that the countries not included do not have any formalized CPD programmes in place.

Table 6.2 *Professional Development of Higher Education Teachers World-wide*

Types of Requirement for Professional Development		Countries
Compulsory	Compulsory 'certificate in teaching–learning'	Sri Lanka, Ethiopia, Denmark, Croatia
Not man-datory but linked to incentives	Legally not compulsory, but is preferred	UK, Netherlands, Sweden, USA, Ireland, Spain
	Indirectly mandatory	UK
	Probation/ promotion	South Africa, Denmark, India
	Incentives for skill development	Spain, Israel, India

Source: Based on ICED (2014).

Through a case study on the PD programmes at eight world class universities, Jacob, Xiong and Ye (2015) distil nine lessons which may enlighten us to consider the factors in any scheme of CPD for HE teachers: (a) the PD should form the part of the portfolio of a top university administrator, at least at the level of a pro-vice-chancellor/provost; (b) the managers of PD must have a deeper understanding of, and leadership abilities in, PL and collaborative engagement; (c) the CPD centres must address faculties on individual basis, one-on-one through the individual PD pathway; (d) small communities of practice with disciplinary affiliation and synergy within and across institutions may form the nucleus for CPD intervention; (e) a strong and seamless linkage is required between CPD centres and institutional and national CPD resource repositories; (f) creation of database on CPD to refer to and address both individual and collective requirements of PD interventions; (g) there is a need to have a wider basket of multiple PD resources and strategies to match individual choices and needs; (h) information and communications technology should be appropriately and optimally used to implement CPD; and (i) there should be an appropriate reward system for staff and mentors to engage in maintaining and leading institutional CPD.

Based on the study by the ICED (2014), the inferences on requirements for PD of HE teachers as compulsory, not compulsory but preferred, indirectly mandatory, requirement for promotion/probation, and incentive-based staff development across selected countries can be drawn as follows.

Compulsory 'Certificate in Teaching-Learning'

In Sri Lanka, since 1997, the newly recruited university faculty are required to earn a Teaching Certificate in HE as part of the 'teaching qualification'. This is accredited by the UGC since 1997. The education and training policy, 1994, in Ethiopia mandates the teachers from school to university level to undergo training qualification so as to gain employment as teachers. Following the National Ministerial Memorandum in 1993, all assistant professors in Denmark have to undergo teacher training in HE. The policy requirements of the University of Osijek in Croatia demand that the candidates applying for the post of assistant professor undergo 'pedagogical-psychological education' before making an application.

Legally Not Compulsory, But Preferred

Even in the absence of a legal requirement for teaching certificate as mandatory/legally required qualification for teachers, there is a trend of preference for such qualification in several countries.

Most universities in the UK have made a PG certificate in teaching compulsory for probation and further progression. In addition, every year, the universities publish data on the number of teachers possessing HE teaching qualification. In the Netherlands, a self-regulated system to implement University Teaching Quality (UTQ) by universities exists, which is not legally tenable. The applied sciences universities had planned to implement teaching qualification for jobs by 2016. The UTQ certificate is encouraged through portfolio assessment. Between 2009 to 2010, in Sweden, it was compulsory for the teachers in HE to have teacher training. Though now the universities have autonomy on this issue, there is a national standard agreed by the Rectors' Association to be respected by all. Consequently, most universities have 5–10 weeks of compulsory training for HE teachers.

There is no national mandate in the USA for teachers training in HE. Usually, the graduate teaching staff undergoes at least a one-day training, but the period of training may be several days in some of the universities. The national framework for PD of teachers developed by the National Forum for Teaching and Learning in Ireland follows CPD pathways for various types of teachers. A few universities do mandatory accredited programmes for newly appointed teachers. In Spain, the in-service staff is encouraged to gain qualification offered by national quality agencies.

Indirectly Mandatory

The UK Professional Standard Framework (UKPSF, 2011) requires staff to apply for recognition against the set standards at various stages of career, including promotion, to show evidence of expertise in teaching–learning. University teaching fellowships and national teaching fellowships encourage staff to join for researching various aspects of teaching–learning in disciplines useful for all colleges and universities.

Probation/Promotion

In South Africa, on-the-job training can count towards promotion. In the Danish system, additional compensation is given in forms of teacher award, headship with added responsibility and pay supplement. The teachers in the Indian HE system are expected to undergo number of orientation programmes (OPs) and refresher courses (RCs), in subject domain, for promotion to next pay grade.

Incentives for Skill Development

Spain provides modest increase in salary every six years for staff who shows evidence of training or engagement in teaching–learning improvement. In Israel, excellence in teaching is rewarded through compensation, and achievements of outstanding staff are made available in public domain for students and other stakeholders to appreciate their achievements and accordingly make decisions. In India, one and three increments in salary are given to MPhil and PhD qualified candidates so as to encourage them to join the teaching profession in colleges and universities. The Indira Gandhi National Open University (IGNOU) provides for one increment when a staff completes a PG diploma in distance education (PGDDE). In the past, completion of PGDDE was mandatory for confirmation of the job at the open university (OU).

The instances of selected countries show that the countries are using the strategies to make it mandatory for staff to maintain evidence-based portfolios. While on one hand, these requirements provide evidences to the institution(s) as well as to professional network(s), they may also facilitate self-critical reflection for further improvement. This is supported by a flexible system of availability of professional standards frameworks and benchmarks.

Indian Case: Historical Developments

CPD and/or training of college and university teachers was never considered as necessary until the early 1960s when the UGC initiated the 'summer institutes' programme in which teachers of various disciplines joined together to learn from senior mentors the further nuances of their disciplines. In continuation to this, the Kothari Education Commission (1964–1966; NCERT, 1971) recommended the organization of regular OPs for a few weeks by each university, and virtually each college to orient new teachers through their interaction with seniors drawn from within and outside the college. The initial suggestion has almost been carried forward by the subsequent education commissions and committees in the country. This led to further initiation of summer or short-term institutes by the UGC in a few universities to orient both fresh and junior teachers on methods of teaching. Universities of Punjab, Indore, Meerut, South Gujarat and Mysore and the Maharaja Sayajirao University of Baroda (MSU) conducted the orientations. The state government of Maharashtra made such orientation compulsory for teachers of junior colleges (Singh, 1980). However, these initial efforts were neither nationwide nor compulsory.

In 1975, the University of Calicut initiated a one-year master of college teaching as a pre-service requirement for college teachers, so also the one-year master of higher education by the Annamalai University in 1977. A diploma in higher education was initiated in 1972 by University of Bombay (now Mumbai) and in 1975 by University of Madras as in-service OP for teachers. Madurai University (later named as Madurai Kamaraj University or MKU) also implemented, in 1976, a certificate course for orientation of lecturers of affiliated colleges. A significant professional OP for training of in-service teachers was instituted by MSU, in 1975, covering all dimensions of teaching, research, discipline knowledge and the teaching profession. Though compulsory for new lecturers for their confirmation, the programme was to open to all teachers of the university (Yadav & Roy, 1984).

Except MSU, the rest of the programmes have since been discontinued. These programmes, however, led to serious national discussions and debates on the nature, duration and weightage to be given to these programmes. Taking cognizance of this, the National Commission on Teachers in Higher Education II (NCT-II; GOI, 1984) recommended orientation courses as well as RCs for in-service teachers. In 1986, the Mehrotra Committee, which considered the pay scales of HE teachers in the country, examined the recommendations of NCT-II and prescribed one orientation course as compulsory for promotion to selection grade/reader. Further, the committee entrusted this national responsibility to IGNOU, which practiced open and distance learning through multiple media, including the teacher contact programme at the study centres. In consideration of the Mehrotra Committee report (GOI, 1987), the UGC formulated the scheme of ASCs in 1987–1988 to regularly organize four-week OPs and three-week RCs all over the country.

Current Professional Development Programmes

Since information/data on PD programmes, especially on various professional education programmes, regulated by respective professional education councils/regulators, is not readily and accurately available, what follows is a discussion on the available information on how such programmes are organized and to what extent they have contributed to enhancing the quality of teaching–learning in HE.

Academic Staff Colleges

There was tripartite arrangement for the implementation of CPD programmes whereby UGC-funded and ASC-implemented CPD, and National Institute of Educational Planning and Administration (NIEPA) was entrusted with professional coordination of the scheme. The director, deputy director and assistant director acted as the core staff (at the level of respectively professor, associate professor and assistant professor) and acted at times as resource persons, besides largely drawing from the host university and other universities in the country. In 1988–1989, NIEPA conducted a need survey to get feedback based on which the orientation and refresher programmes could be re-designed (Sharma, 1995). The results indicated the priority requirements summarized as follows:

(a) *General Awareness:* HE and national development; promoting national integration; developing scientific temper; information on UGC schemes and programmes.

(b) *Learning:* Imparting knowledge and skills; new education technology; developing new restructured courses; subject competency.

(c) *Planning:* Preparing teacher's own academic plan.

(d) *Management:* Managing library; managing financial resources.

(e) *Development of Corporate Life:* Dealing with students; creative work.

The four-week OPs were designed for the newly appointed college and university teachers to understand the significance of HE in the global and Indian contexts, understand the linkage between education and socio-economic–cultural development, acquire basic skills of teaching adults, understand the dynamics of institutional management and the role of the teacher, and develop personality and creativity. Accordingly, the OPs had four components: (a) awareness of linkages among society, environment, development and education; (b) philosophy of education, Indian education system and pedagogy; (c) subject upgradation (vis-à-vis teaching–learning); and (d) management and personality development, personality development of teachers, and monitoring and evaluation.

The full-time, face-to-face programmes were conducted through lectures, panel discussions, group work, workshops and audio-visual technologies. There was a small budget allocated for resource materials, and the participating teachers were paid for travel and for lodging and boarding expenses (Kundu, 1997). The one-year full-time diploma in HE (later named as the postgraduate diploma in higher education or PDGHE) by IGNOU in 1991 (as mandated by the Mehrotra Committee) focused on HE context and linkages, instruction, socio-psychological dimensions, and planning and management of HE. It was offered through a combination of media including self-learning materials, teleconferencing, audio-video programmes, face-to-face counselling and compulsory extended contact programme, theoretical and practical assignments, and a project (Menon & Dash, 1997). Such a programme is much more reformative than the OPs of ASCs in as much as both pre-service and in-service teachers get a wider exposure and hands-on experience in respect of the entire gamut of HE. In the process, they learn the practice of blended teaching–learning towards which the present reform in HE is moving. The PGDHE has subsequently been recognized by UGC as equivalent to two OPs and/or two RCs in education.

Similar to the PGDHE, IGNOU also initiated a diploma in distance education (DDE) programme in 1987 (later renamed as postgraduate diploma in distance education or PGDDE) to train a large number of faculty, technical and professional staff, and administrative staff engaged in mediated teaching through open and distance learning. Meant for faculty, academic counsellors, course writers and editors, and media presenters, among others, the DDE/PGDDE became mandatory for faculty and staff for lifting probation and permanency in job at the OU, with one increment in salary. Since then, many state OUs implemented such an initiative, and the PGDDE subsequently got offered to distance teachers in more than 22 countries, supported by many international agencies including the Commonwealth of Learning and UNESCO (Mullick, 1997). More than 100,000 faculty and staff are involved in distance teaching (Murali Manohar, 1997) in OUs and dual-mode university/distance education institutes. The diploma has been broken down to small capsules in the form of resource-based blended training and ASC-equivalent RCs in curriculum development, instructional design, ICT, learner support, planning and management, and research in distance and online learning.

With reference to an estimated number of teachers trained, it may be highlighted here that most of the ASCs do not maintain data as per the simple format provided to them, nor do they display the number of programmes and participants on their website. Even if the UGC collects and maintains a database of ASCs, it has not displayed any data on its website, nor was it possible to obtain the data. The data for initial years were collected by NIEPA (Sharma, 1995) and was therefore are more reliable. Data collected from ASCs in the recent past shows that 22 ASCs had conducted 91 OPs with 2,968 participants in 2014–2015, and 226 RCs with 6,885 participants the same year.[1] The total programmes listed in Table 6.3 for each year are cumulative. If the data

---

[1] N. Chaurasiya (personal communication, 2017).

Table 6.3 *OPs and RCs (and Participants) Conducted ASCs (1998–2016)*

Year	Orientation Programmes		Refresher Courses		Total	
	Programmes	Participants	Programmes	Participants	Programmes	Participants
1987–1988	158	4,946	26	649	184	5,595
1988–1989	614	18,588	338	9,316	952	27,904
1989–1990	413	12,305	335	8,861	748	21,166
1990–1991	630	18,583	650	17,808	1,280	36,391
1991–1992	722	21,203	941	20,967	1,673	42,160
1992–93	867	24,684	1,225	33,748	2,092	58,432
1993–1994	1,015	28,665	1,567	41,790	2,582	70,455

Source: Sharma (1995).

for 2014–2015 are considered as noted earlier, the total number of OPs per annum could not exceed 330 (with about 10,000 participants) and RCs could be estimated to be 660 (with about 30,000 participants). According to AISHE (2015–2016) there are 1.51 million HE teachers in India (including 112,006 temporary teachers; MHRD, 2016). Considering, if about 168,000 teachers and 336,000 teachers would have attended OPs and RCs respectively, and if each teacher would have taken part in two RCs for promotion to the next grade, (excluding 146,021 professors or equivalent who need not attend OPs and RCs), then around 1.20 million teachers are yet to attend any orientation and refresher programmes.

Technical and Professional Education

Technical and professional education relating to engineering, technology, management, architecture, pharmacy, town planning, and applied arts and crafts is regulated by the government statutory regulator, that is, All India Council for Technical Education (AICTE), established in 1987. Since its 2013 regulation, AICTE (2013) has allowed technical education through a hybrid/blended model. It is imperative that the faculty also develop understanding and skills relating to blended learning. The Career Development Bureau of AICTE financially supports faculty development, research and development, and the larger participation of women in technical education. Such support includes travel grants, seminar grants, career awards for young talented teachers, emeritus fellowships for superannuated professors, faculty development/ induction training through staff colleges, and the scheme of visiting professorship. Staff training facilities are provided for technical colleges or polytechnics through on-the-job and off-the-job training.

The AICTE also funds quality improvement programme (QIP) centres in IITs, IISCs and University of Roorkee, among others. These centres implement short, summer and winter courses for their faculty, and those from other engineering colleges and university departments of engineering and technology. The courses focus on teaching–learning in the discipline and more specifically on educational technology (Kumar & Bhattacharya, 1997). The Indian Society for Technical Education

(ISTE) also offers short courses on educational technology. The MHRD review of QIP in the country suggested willingness by faculty as well as institutional heads for the design and offer of short courses as also PhDs in instructional design, curriculum development, laboratory development, teaching methods, institutional development and subject expertise (Awale & Kumar, 1992). The post-review modified programme includes study skills, presentation skills, multimedia, instructional systems design, simulated teaching, and innovations in assessment and evaluation. Since the AICTE has made participation in short courses a prerequisite to faculty promotion, the IITs have been seriously organizing such programmes, including the latest educational technologies and MOOCs under the National Programme on Technology Enhanced Learning (NPTEL).

Similarly, there are other professional regulatory bodies, which support professional upgrading of teachers in respective domains. For instance, the Indian Council for Agricultural Research (ICAR) is the government statutory regulator for agricultural scientists and college/ university agricultural education. ICAR selects and funds summer institutes for professional upgrading of teachers in various disciplines at agricultural universities and ICAR research institutes, including agriculture engineering, fisheries and animal sciences (Hansra & Adhiguru, 1997).

The Medical Council of India (MCI), since 2009, has approved 20 medical colleges and universities of repute to organize faculty development programmes covering new concepts of teaching and assessment, clinical skills for effective teaching and mentoring, clinical research, communication and behavioural skills, and use of ICT and other technology tools. However, its recent amendment to the 1998 minimum qualifications regulation (MCI, 2017) does not mention any faculty development requirement as mandatory to appointment and promotion.

Health practices differ across states and across locales in the states. Keeping this in view, national institutions such as the All India Institute of Medical Sciences (Delhi), Post Graduate Institute of Medical Sciences (Chandigarh), Jawaharlal Institute of Post Graduate Medical Education and Research (Puducherry) and Institute of Medical Sciences (Varanasi) have been innovating in teaching technologies, instructional delivery, curriculum reforms, ICT, and assessment strategies for quite some time. A few National Teachers' Training Centres (NTTCs) at medical colleges offer faculty development programmes, though these have been inadequate to orient medical teachers at the beginning of their teaching career (Mohapatra & Singh, 1997). Many of the medical colleges and universities have bilateral agreements with universities overseas for improving the quality of faculty, medical practices and the quality of medical education.

The legal education in the country can be thought of comprising mainly two types of professionals, that is, law professors and judges of all courts—from lower judicial magistrates and civil judges to benches in the Supreme Court. Initially a laggard, the PD of law teachers got momentum especially after the establishment of various integrated national law school/universities. The UGC-ASCs and the law universities have been organizing faculty development programmes for the law faculty. While senior judges act as mentors or trainers, they hardly have any background in training, instructional design and use of ICT in training (Oberoi, 2012). As a matter of policy, the RCs are not compulsory.

Critique of the Programmes on Facilitating Teachers for Effective Teaching

A significant number of studies conducted on staff development programmes for college and university teachers (Chalam, 1987; Das, 1990, 2012, 2017; Deshpande & Jantli, 1991; Dhar & Singh, 1990; Passi & Pal, 1991; Patil & Ramalingam, 2009) have appreciated the positive contributions of ASCs to the knowledge, attitude and skills of participating teachers. The scheme of OPs and RCs is the first comprehensive and systematic nationwide attempt to improve the quality of teaching–learning in HE through systematic interventions in both domain knowledge and pedagogy.

The review of staff development programmes prescribed and implemented by various regulators suggests that there is a need for post-induction (discipline-specific) OPs on teaching–learning in HE to be made compulsory for all HE teachers, including those teaching in private institutions/universities. While this could be made compulsory for those recruited on an 'ad hoc' basis, OPs and RCs must be a prerequisite to confirmation of the job. Since the ad hoc teachers may have been teaching for a number of years, the contents of such programmes need to be appropriately designed to make them need-based, refreshing and engaging. As part of self-reflection as well as institutional collaboration, the criteria for evaluation of participants and also the results of such evaluation need to be made available in public domain.

The evaluation and impact of ASCs and other related programmes construe that the single-most contribution by ASCs to the CPD of college and university teachers has been the development of awareness and competencies in teaching–learning and classroom management. In a critical assessment of the functioning of ASCs and implementation of various programmes, Singh and Sansanwal (1997) pointed out that ASCs had constraints in respect of lack of hostel facilities; faculty participant selection, where the participants attend mostly to get the certificate required for promotion; and selection of resource persons, which was based largely on non-academic considerations. While a one-year gap between programmes is prescribed, many participants completed one OP and two RCs within the same year. Furthermore, the prescribed courses did not match with the felt lack of competencies by the participants; lack of training by resource persons resulted in disregard for andragogy and preference for only lecturing. Programmes are decided as per availability of resource persons, wherein evaluation of the programmes and resource persons is ritualistic, without consideration to further redesign of programmes.

The evaluation study by NAAC (2012) rated most of the ASCs (53 out of 66) as functioning below expected performance level and seven ASCs as non-performers, and therefore suggested a significant re-haul of the scheme. Based on a recent study on RCs offered by 14 out of 26 ASCs (Das, 2017), the institutional feedback results may be classified into three main categories: infrastructure, management and methodology. The study revealed that there is lack of standardized resource materials, problem of office and hostel space and participants were not relieved on time from the parent institution(s) to attend the course(s). There was lack of homogeneity in the qualification and experience of the participants, and they lacked sufficient motivation. It was also difficult to get reputed resource persons and the synopsis/handouts from resource persons were not made available to the participants. The remuneration provided to the resource persons was too low. There was lack of freedom to directors of ASCs to independently handle funds and the institutions did not release funds on time. The methodologies used by ASCs were not widely available to institutions, and the resource persons are not guided by the methodologies prescribed by ASCs.

While the UGC National Eligibility Test (NET) initiated in 1986 and its equivalent State Eligibility Test (SET) is made compulsory for recruitment to the post of assistant professor, this by itself, and even a research degree like PhD, does not equip a pre-service aspiring teacher to have proficiency in the art and science of teaching. Therefore, it is important to consider a pre-service programme on teaching–learning and/or a national test on teaching–learning in HE including discipline pedagogy as a prerequisite to enter the teaching profession. This should be followed by an OP before undertaking the job of teaching.

Alongside, a serious limitation of the current CPD programmes is that there is nothing like 'continuing' in the scheme, nor do they provide for any linkage between CPD, research, and personal pursuit for academic excellence. While some disciplines expect interdisciplinarity in the perspectives of teaching and learning, almost all disciplines require transfer of learning to the world of work, and linkage to the community, life and living. One basic flaw in the formulation is the assumption that PL and PD is a one-shot affair.

CONCURRENT REFORMS IN CPD IN HIGHER EDUCATION

The changes and reforms that have generally taken place in HE in the recent past need a closer examination since these do have implications for the existing and prospective teachers, and their PD.

Indian HE has seen significant reforms, especially after formulation of the Five-year Plans. Subsequently, the system has witnessed considerable changes, including massive expansion to reach the 24.5 per cent GER today (MHRD, 2016). There are still unresolved questions relating to access, equity, relevance and quality. These notwithstanding, there are some breakthrough reforms in the recent past which are poised to transform the quality of teaching–learning. We shall be discussing three major reforms that have concomitant implications for teacher CPD.

The first reform is the launch of Pandit Madan Mohan Malaviya National Mission on Teachers and Teaching (PMMMNMTT; GOI, 2015), which directly addresses quality enhancement in teaching–learning and research. Under the Justice Verma Commission on Teacher Education, and in tripartite collaboration of NCTE (National Council for Teacher Education), MHRD and UGC, 11 schools of education have been established in respective central universities to expand the basket and interdisciplinarity of teacher education through multiple departments and centres, and 30 such centres are approved to be established. The other institutional mechanisms include centres of excellence in curriculum and pedagogy, centres of excellence in science and mathematics education, faculty development centres (i.e., HRDCs, in place of ASCs), interuniversity centres for teacher education, subject networks, HE academy, institutes of academic leadership and education management, innovations and awards, and teaching–learning centres (TLCs). It is envisaged that the TLCs, which started functioning in some universities and institutes of higher learning, shall bring in discipline-specific, and interdisciplinary research and innovations, in discipline-specific pedagogy, and should eventually be linked to CPD of college and university teachers.

The second reform was the introduction of CBCS (UGC, 2015), which has been visualized as a game changer. For the first time, a national policy created space for choice-based credit accumulation in skill-based courses from a discipline/department other than one's own, and more interdisciplinary and value-based credit courses.

The UGC regulation on the Study Web of Active Learning by Young and Aspiring Minds (SWAYAM) is the third reform, which introduces statutory provision for online/blended learning into HE by facilitating college and university departments and disciplines to offer students the choice to accumulate up to 20 per cent of total credit hours in subjects through MOOCs. The MOOCs are offered through the comprehensive nationwide platform of SWAYAM (UGC, 2016) dedicated to the nation on 9 July 2017. This new development has brought into fore the need for orientation, training and CPD for teaching–learning and research in the pedagogy of blended learning, both for those who will develop those courses and those who will teach through MOOCs.

GOALS FOR CPD OF TEACHERS IN HIGHER EDUCATION

At the backdrop of the PD vision and activities of the ASCs (now HRDCs), a recent well-articulated but simplified draft document from the National Forum for the Enhancement of Teaching and Learning in Higher Education (NFETLHE, 2016, p. 5) underlines six goals for such activities for HE teachers. First, PD activities should empower staff to create, discover and engage in meaningful, personal and in a variety of ways, which are accredited or credit-based programmes of study; structured but non-accredited courses organized by networks and professional associations; unstructured and non-accredited courses focusing on individual need-based engagement; and collaborative non-accredited programmes based on collaborative research, peer review and conference presentations.

Second, the programmes should encourage staff to engage in peer dialogue and support in their PD activities. Third, staff should be encouraged to engage students in their learning and maintaining their well-being. Fourth, the pedagogy of their discipline should be developed for relevance and authenticity, and they should be encouraged to learn from other disciplines. Assisting staff to reflect on, plan and contribute to evidence-based transformation of their teaching and learning approaches is yet another goal. Finally, the goal of the PD programme should be to assist in the quality enhancement and assurance of the student learning experience.

The goals also subsume the existing disciplinary CPD activities across disciplines, and are flexible enough to accommodate any evidence-based initiatives undertaken by the teachers. The revised CPD formulation needs to consider the stated goals.

A CPD FRAMEWORK

As has been reiterated, CPD for teachers needs to be viewed as a personal process of engaging, experiencing and reflecting on teacher as a professional and teaching as a qualitative professional activity. Therefore, any CPD provision must consider diversity, flexibility, personalization, choices, and a flexible scheme of credit- and resource-based multiple pathways to engage with both the theory and practice of what may be called 'reflective and critical teaching'. Further, such a framework must be inclusive of both professionalism and professionalization dimensions.

Hargreaves (2000) discusses four historical phases of teacher professionalism: pre-professional, autonomous professional, collegial professional and post-professional. It is argued that the last two are crucial in deriving a framework of CPD for teachers. The collegial professional believes in a culture of collaboration and responds positively to the complex and uncertain changes and reforms, and the post-professional strives to resolve the conflict between de-professionalizing and redefining PL in a manner that is flexible, inclusive and diverse. Since teacher professionalism has off late been viewed as social and political strategy to legitimize the status of the teaching profession, the contours of a CPD framework and plan of action need to be sensitive to this aspect.

An overall assessment is that the PD programmes of ASCs/HRDCs still stand as unique in the absence of any comprehensive CPD regime. However, the programmes are found to be generic without much input on significant discipline-specific teaching–learning strategies and use of ICT. Second, they have been mostly theoretical, skewed in the theory-praxis formulation. In addition, there is absence of a continuum, and the choice to proceed through individual pathways. What could be essentially brought to the table is the strategies to engage students, in-practice. This lack of capacity to engage students is a widely held criticism against teaching–learning generally and a major concern for the CPD in HE.

Based on the discussion carried out in this chapter, a generic but representative CPD framework is outlined in Figure 6.1 which needs to be viewed in totality, and which needs to be based on needs of

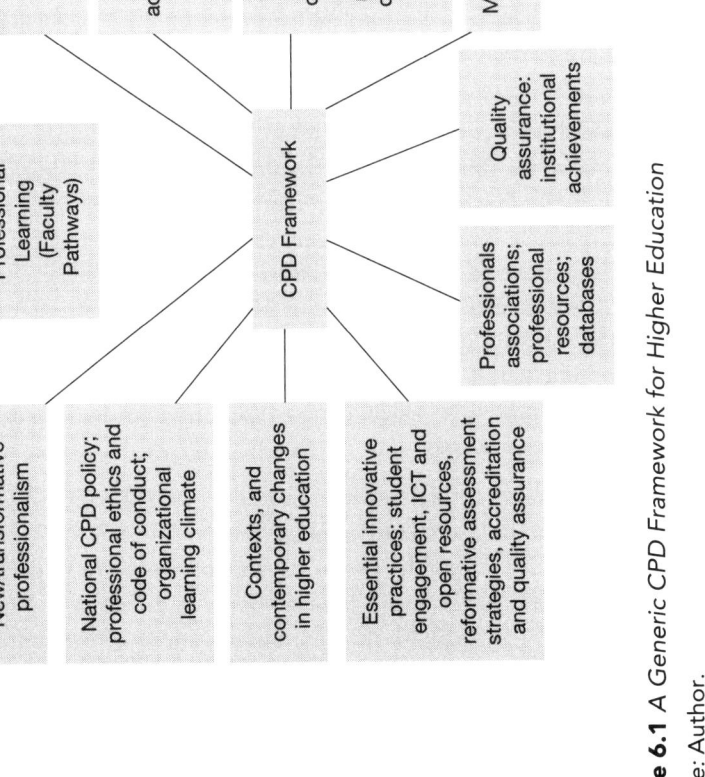

Figure 6.1 *A Generic CPD Framework for Higher Education*

Source: Author.

teachers, flexibility in strategies and institutional willingness to be a learning organization.

The framework outlined in Figure 6.1 is based on the premises that CPD needs to be viewed within a larger formulation of PL. Teaching and research need to be balanced in teacher workload. Discipline-specific teaching as well as scholarship of teaching–learning need to gel well in the working of a professional. Discipline research and publication should be considered as important as research and publication in discipline pedagogy/teaching–learning, and should be equally credited for in the API and reward/tenure/promotion. CPD needs to be a life-long activity of a professional within a flexible, need-based, modular and diverse pathway. Further, the CPD strategies need to be linked to evidence-based teaching, internal organizational quality assurance, and institutional accreditation and ranking.

At the first instance, a CPD scheme, which focuses equally on teaching, research, social action, individual scholarship and professional ethics, needs to be viewed as the primary strategy towards quality teaching–learning. Further, such a CPD scheme must be prioritized in the national policy on education, as also in the policies of various education and training regulators. This also brings to focus the need for a national CPD policy and its linkage to contemporary developments in HE. The proposed practice is credit-based, modular, resource-based, blended, flexible, interdisciplinary and grounded in praxis. The plan for CPD pathways should be based on national and regional surveys identifying actual teacher needs, competencies and professional identity.

The framework is flexible but comprehensive, and also provides for mentored PL through simple to complex pathways in the scholarship of teaching and learning. The process is evidence-based, transparent, context-based and experiential. This also combines the initial compulsory orientation/training with the continuous process of institutional and regulatory PD requirements as well as self-reflective learning, complementing each other within the PD pathways. Finally, the proposed CPD framework does not suggest a performance indicator regime; rather, it is based on the principle of individual choice, and freedom of time and space in the CPD pathway.

Operational Strategies

Though the framework provides for flexibility and autonomy, the strategization requires a systematic, well-linked, collaborative, networked and transparent implementation of a continuous PD and PL provision. First, at the federal level, there is a need for the national CPD policy and its articulation in the national policy on education, and at the institutional level, there is the need for a comprehensive database of individual teachers containing, in a continuum, the needs, competencies and specializations, achievements, research evidences in both the discipline and the scholarship of teaching–learning, and credit accumulation in the CPD pathway.

Second, this pathway is to be linked to evidence-/portfolio-based teaching, research and other achievements, as also to the internal quality assurance database. Besides the internal quality assurance cell (IQAC), which acts as management of information system MIS for the entire institution, the existing TLCs under the PMMNMTT also need to be linked to the individual faculty CPD pathway, API and the IQA.

In current times, teaching–learning has become more blended and flexible, away from the traditional single-strategy delivery. The AICTE, in 2013, issued regulation towards blended teaching–learning in technology and professional education. Blended learning is the requirement of the present times. There have been resistances from respective regulators in so far as blended learning is concerned.

The NCTE, in the recent past, resisted the idea of the practice of blended learning in teacher education, and disallowed distance and online learning for teacher educator programmes. Though in the course curriculum of all teacher education programmes, ICT—theory as well as application in teaching–learning—was made compulsory in its 2014 regulation. However, an innovative step was its proposed—a refresher programme for teacher educators through ASCs/HRDCs, which included a blended strategy in place of a full-time three weeks RC (NCTE, 2014).

More than 5,000 teacher educators are engaged in teaching at about 975 M.Ed. institutions and 60,000 teacher educators in 7,554 B.Ed. institutions. As a reformative step, CPD of teacher educators was proposed to be organized all over the country through a blended approach comprising 108 hours of guided teaching–learning activities equivalent to three weeks as per the UGC norms (see Table 6.4).

This is just one example to show how the existing model of PD through ASCs has lived its life, and that revisions with alternative formulations need to be considered. Besides being blended, an individual choice-based CPD pathway in confirmation to mandatory requirements by the regulators, and individual desirable pursuits is proposed. The CPD pathway for each faculty may be visualized as given in Figure 6.2.

The individual progress in one's own PL pathway is linked to institutional database of faculty progress and achievements, as also to the national database repository. Unlike the ASC scheme, this formulation links together individual progress, action research, quality teaching–learning, and institutional requirement of evidence–based teaching and teacher PD. This could be considered to lead to higher order PL, which the present system lacks. As also proposed by Kennedy (2005) this model

Table 6.4 *Operation Strategy for Teacher Educator Refresher*

Component 1	Component 2	Component 3
• Guided self-study.	• Face-to-face practice workshops.	• Online.
• Hours 24 (22%). • To be undertaken by individual faculty under the supervision of a mentor.	• Hours 60 (56%). • Expert presentation and small group activities supervised by the resource persons.	• Hours 24 (22%). • Guided small group and individual projects. • Online support group. • Online interaction among participants and resource persons.
• Learning achievements shall be assessed.	• Learning achievements shall be assessed.	• Learning achievements shall be assessed.

Source: NCTE (2014).

Note: The programme is based largely on OERs, good practices, cases, research evidences and theory-practice praxis.

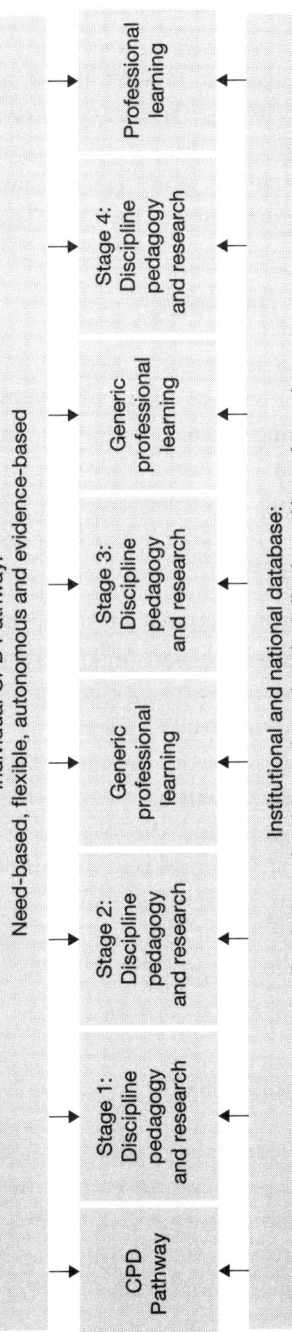

Figure 6.2 *CPD Pathway(s)*
Source: Author.

of CPD goes beyond the transmission model, that is, training, award-bearing, deficit and cascade strategies. The CPD pathway should traverse through the transitional model, comprising standard-based, mentoring and community of practice strategies to the transformative model, based on action research and transformative professional strategies.

Limitations

The scheme outlined earlier is practical, desirable and doable. This requires a systematic and authentic basket of innovative good practices in all aspects of teaching–learning-research, depending on the classroom requirement and individual choice. Contextualization in discipline-specific teaching at various levels of education is also required. Unfortunately, the MOOCs developed for either e-Pathshala or SWAYAM, in their present format, do not meet these requirements.

The major problems in Indian HE have been the lack of (a) inter-disciplinary orientation and training, (b) linking theory to practice and (c) going beyond individualism to collaborative engagement in teaching–learning. The proposed CPD framework assumes inter-disciplinary collaborative engagement, and engagement in-practice. The proposed changes demand political understandings and political will to undertake reforms. Alongside, this requires understanding of international developments, and national contexts and culture, without undue politicization. Wisdom of various professional associations to see value in updating and contextualising teaching–learning, and also their involvement and leadership to sustain CPD in a systematic manner is a must requirement.

CONCLUSION

Any CPD intervention, including the outlined framework requires a tripartite convergence of PL, professional commitments and professional ethics on the part of the professionals, as also its recognition and inclusion by both the professional associations and the regulators. Any profession for that matter is practice in-context. The teaching profession is no exception to this. Further, this strategy could work more effectively in an individually charted flexible PD/PL pathway, with accreditation of accomplishments as and when achieved, while at the same time being organized in a systematic pathway from lower to higher levels of PL. Such a framework subsumes both initial and periodic orientation and refresher interventions.

It also needs to be highlighted that in majority of Indian HE institutions, there is lack of infrastructure, adequate financial support, congenial organizational climate, learning environment, positive attitude and motivation. At the same time, the classrooms are oversized. There are vacant faculty positions and sizeable number of ad hoc teachers, political interference and reduced public funding, which impede institutional functioning. Increasing privatization with suspect quality is also a stark reality.

In conclusion, it may be underlined that a dynamic national CPD policy as well as positive and progressive organizational learning climate are the essential determinants of a successful and transformative PD programme.

REFERENCES

AICTE (All India Council for Technical Education. (2013). *Grants of approvals for technical education in blended learning mode regulations 2013*. New Delhi: All India Council for Technical Education.

Awale, S. D., & Kumar, K. L. (1992). *Redefining quality in engineering education: Quality improvement programme*. New Delhi: Ministry of Human Resource Development.

Barber, B. (1965). Some problems in the sociology of the professions. In Kenneth S. Lynn and editors of Daedalus (Eds), *The professions in America* (pp. 15–34). Boston, MA: Houghton Mifflin.

Barnett, R. (2003). *Beyond all reason: Living with ideology in the university*. Buckingham: SRHE and Open University Press.

Boyer, E. (1990). *Scholarship reconsidered: Priorities of the professoriate*. San Francisco, CA: Jossey-Bass.

Chalam, K. S. (1987). Academic staff orientation scheme—Some critical issues. *University News*, 14 December, pp. 13–19.

Chaurasiya, N. (2016). *Problems faced by entry-level university teachers: Need for a participatory programme*. Paper presented at the national conference, Tezpur Central University, Tezpur.

Clegg, S. (2003). Problematising ourselves: Continuing professional development in higher education. *International Journal for Academic Development*, *8*(1&2), 37–50.

Das, B. C. (1990). *Effectiveness of self-learning material for the orientation of university and college teachers* (PhD Thesis). Banaras Hindu University, Varanasi.

———. (2012). *A critical evaluation of the systems adopted for the management of refresher courses in the academic staff colleges in India.* New Delhi: UGC major research project.

———. (2017). Problems of staff training in the academic staff colleges in India. *Staff & Educational Development International*, *21*(2), 93–104.

David, C. (2000). *Professionalism and ethics in teaching.* London: Taylor & Francis.

Deshpande, S., & Jantli, R. T. (1991). Effect of orientation course on teaching methods in higher education on the attitude of ASC participants towards teaching at the tertiary level. *University News*, *29*(43), 8–11.

Dhar, T. N., & Singh, T. (1990). *Academic staff college—A developing concept.* New Delhi: Sterling Publishers.

Elton, L. (2009). Continuing professional development in higher education: The role of the scholarship of teaching and learning. *International Journal for the Scholarship of Teaching and Learning*, *3*(1), Article 28.

GOI (Government of India). (1984). *Report of the national commission II.* New Delhi: Ministry of Human Resource Development, Government of India.

———. (1987). *Report of the committee for revision of pay scales of teachers in higher education (Mehrotra Committee Report).* New Delhi: Ministry of Human Resource Development, Government of India.

———. (2011). *Faster, sustainable and more inclusive growth: An approach to the twelfth five year Plan (2012–2017).* New Delhi: Planning Commission, Government of India.

———. (2015). *Scheme of Pandit Madan Mohan Malaviya National Mission on Teachers and Teaching: Guidelines.* New Delhi: MHRD, Government of India.

Hansra, B. S., & Adhiguru, P. (1997). Staff development in agricultural sciences. In S. Panda (Ed.), *Staff development in higher and distance education* (pp. 125–130). New Delhi: Aravali Books International.

Hargreaves, A. (2000). Four ages of professionalism and professional learning. *Teachers and Teaching: History and Practice*, *6*(2), 151–182.

Hoyle, E. (2001). Teaching: Prestige, status and esteem. *Educational Management Administration and Leadership*. *29*(2), 139–152.

IECD (International Consortium for Educational Development). (2014). *The preparation of university teachers internationally.* London: International Consortium for Educational Development.

Jacob, W. J., Xiong, W., & Ye, H. (2015). Professional development programmes at world-class universities. *Palgrave Communications*, *1*(2)1–27.

Kennedy, A. (2005). Models of continuing professional development: A framework for analysis. *Journal of In-Service Education*, *31*(2), 235–250.

Kumar, K. L., & Bhattacharya, M. (1997). Staff development in science and technology. In S. Panda (Ed.), *Staff development in higher and distance education* (pp. 87–110). New Delhi: Aravali Books International.

Kundu, C. L. (1997). Academic orientation programmes: development, status and challenges for the future. In S. Panda (Ed.), *Staff development in higher and distance education* (pp. 55–64). New Delhi: Aravali Books International.

MCI (Medical Council of India). (2017). *Amendment notification.* 5 June. New Delhi: Medical Council of India.

Menon, M. B., & Dash, N. K. (1997). Higher education staff development at a distance. In S. Panda (Ed.), *Staff development in higher and distance education* (pp. 183–198). New Delhi: Aravali Books International.

MHRD (Ministry of Human Resource Development). (2016). *All India survey on higher education 2015–16.* New Delhi: Ministry of Human Resource Development, Government of India.

Mohapatra, S. C., & Singh, V. P. (1997). Academic staff training in medical sciences. In S. Panda (Ed.), *Staff development in higher and distance education* (pp. 183–198). New Delhi: Aravali Books International.

Mullick, S. P. (1997). Academic staff development at national open university. In S. Panda (Ed.), *Staff development in higher and distance education* (pp. 199–204). New Delhi: Aravali Books International.

Murali Manohar, K. (1997). Staff development in distance education: A national perspective. In S. Panda (Ed.), *Staff development in higher and distance education* (pp. 205–227). New Delhi: Aravali Books International.

NAAC (National Assessment and Accreditation Council) (2012). *Review of academic staff colleges.* Bengaluru: National Assessment and Accreditation Council.

NCERT (National Council of Educational Research and Training). (1971). *Education and national development: Report of the education commission 1964–66.* New Delhi: National Council of Educational Research and Training.

NCTE (National Council for Teacher Education). (2014). *NCTE guidelines on refresher course for teacher educators.* New Delhi: National Council for Teacher Education.

NFETLHE (National Forum for Teaching and Learning in Higher Education). (2016). *National guidance for the professional development of staff who teach in higher education.* Dublin: National Forum for Teaching and Learning in Higher Education.

Oberoi, G. (2012). The limitation of the training discourse for continuing professional development of judges. *International Journal for Court Administration*, (June), *4*(2)64–74.

Passi, B. K., & Pal, R. (1991). Academic staff colleges: The relevance of their curricula. *New Frontiers in Education*, *21*(3), 11–18.

Patil, V. T., & Ramalingam, P. (2009). *Impact study of academic staff colleges.* New Delhi: Authors Press.

Sachs, J. (2003). *The activist teaching profession.* Buckingham: Open University Press.

Sharma, G. D. (1995). Staff development programmes in higher education. In K. B. Powar & S. K. Panda (Eds), *Higher education in India: In search of quality* (pp. 171–185). New Delhi: Association of Indian Universities.

Singh, L. C., & Sansanwal, D. N. (1997). Academic staff college programmes: A critique. In S. Panda (Ed.), *Staff development in higher and distance education* (pp. 79–86). New Delhi: Aravali Books International.

Singh, S. (1980). *A critical study of the programmes of the pre-service and the in-service education of teachers of higher education in India* (PhD thesis). M. S. University, Baroda.

UGC (University Grants Commission). (1978). *Policy frame for higher education.* New Delhi: University Grants Commission.

———. (2010). *UGC regulations on minimum qualifications—Maintenance of standards in higher education.* New Delhi: University Grants Commission.

———. (2015). *UGC guidelines on choice based credit system.* New Delhi: University Grants Commission.

———. (2016). *UGC (credit framework for online learning courses through SWAYAM) regulations, 2016.* New Delhi: University Grants Commission.

UKPSF (UK Professional Standards Framework). (2011). *The UK professional standards framework for teaching and supporting learning in higher education.* Heslington, York: Higher Education Academy.

Yadav, M. S., & Panda, S. (1997). Higher education and professional development. In S. Panda (Ed.), *Staff development in higher and distance education* (pp. 3–24). New Delhi: Aravali Books International.

Yadav, M. S., & Roy, S. (1984). Professional orientation for university teachers—A programme. In A. K. Gupta (Ed.), *Teacher education: Current and prospects* (pp. 133–150). New Delhi: Sterling Publishers.

Chapter 7

Critical Perspectives of Teaching-Learning in Indian Higher Education*

Sayantan Mandal

INTRODUCTION

Massification of higher education is a recent phenomenon in many developing countries. India too experienced an unprecedented expansion of the sector in this century (Agarwal, 2009). The massification of the sector is also accompanied by the diversification of the sector. More first-generation learners and students from diverse socio-economic educational backgrounds are entering into higher education with varied level of competencies. These also pose challenges for providing quality education to the students, as many of the students are at different levels of subject, lingual and critical competencies. Nevertheless, their development is the key for the success of higher education, and the teaching–learning process is at the core of the reform agenda to

* The chapter is based on a national-level research project, titled 'Teaching and Learning in Indian Higher Education' (2015–2016), conducted by the Centre for Policy Research in Higher Education (CPRHE) of the National Institute of Educational Planning and Administration (NIEPA), New Delhi. The author is the coordinator of the project.

improve the quality of higher education. Hence, the teachers in higher education are challenged to ensure higher levels of learning outcomes, however, very often under difficult teaching–learning conditions. The teachers are also finding it difficult to cope with the multiple challenges of preparing learners for the 21st century, developing relevant skills and competences, imparting values and nurturing active citizenship.

The perception of teaching and learning is changing globally (Altbach et al., 2009) and in India. The shift is from a mere content-oriented teaching to a more contextualized and innovative teaching. With the high expectation from the government, the market, students and society, the profession of teaching has become more demanding than ever.

Surprisingly, while extensive research and development are being carried out to improve teaching in primary and secondary education sectors, there is a dearth of research evidence for evolving strategies for improving teaching in Indian higher education. Despite the priority accorded to quality and excellence in higher education at the national level, the reforms in teaching–learning have experienced limited changes and marginal improvements in India. In most of the major reports and public discussions, teachers and teaching–learning process are criticized for their disconnect with the realities of practical world.

Only recently in India, teaching–learning has started gaining importance, both in policy and practice. While the performance yardsticks, based on readily available resources, are emerging as a sine qua non for teaching excellence in Indian higher education, there is a growing consensus to get a deeper understanding of the actual profession of teaching. This understanding will not only help to identify the shortcomings, but also help improve the quality of the profession to a commendable level. For this, the researches seem to venture into the territory of teaching–learning, which is personalized, especially in the tertiary sector. They are to look into the processes of how teachers teach and how students learn in colleges, universities and other higher educational institutes.

Recognizing that the factors influencing effective teaching–learning are many and context-specific, this chapter, based on the first large-scale national-level study on teaching and learning in Indian higher education (Mandal, 2017),[1] argues that teaching–learning in Indian higher education did not evolve with the changing demands. It follows a rather traditional and mostly unidirectional, non-communicative method of teaching, which is largely ineffective in the contemporary world. Most of the teachers and institutional administration in higher education often do not have a clear perception on what effective teaching means in contemporary time. Some teachers, however, try to teach effectively, but often do not succeed due to the lack of understanding about the modern pedagogies, professional training and support. Although the basic practice is similar, there are subtle differences between various levels (for instance, undergraduate and postgraduate) and disciplines. Therefore, rather than blaming the teachers for their ineffectiveness, it is important to analyze the issues associated with teaching–learning in Indian higher education. For this, it is important to look beyond the available and easily quantifiable performance indicators, and venture into the uncharted territories of context-specific teaching–learning processes to truly comprehend the magnitude and complexities of the issue.

This chapter attempts to comprehend how teaching–learning processes vary among disciplines, levels and institutions, and why there is a need to consider evidence-based policy-making to improve teaching quality in higher education.

To comprehend better and analyze its complexities, the chapter discusses the core issues associated with teaching–learning in Indian higher education processes from different vantage points—that of the teachers', learners' and institutions'. It helps provide a comparable and triangulated base of analysis. However, the chapter does not claim to be representative of the situation of teaching and learning of entire India, as it is more diverse and micro-context specific. Nevertheless, this discussion based on the evidences could certainly highlight some of the salient issues, which are worth discussing.

This chapter lays out issues as follows. It starts with an overview of teaching–learning in Indian higher education, highlighting the issues

---

[1] The national-level study is based on quantitative and qualitative data from around 2,000 students and 400 teachers. Interviews with teachers and students, and classroom observations are some of the major sources of data.

and concerns, and discusses associated policy development. In later sections, the chapter digs deeper into the discussions, especially into the practices of teaching in higher education. The differences of teaching practices in different levels and disciplines are highlighted. It also tries to critically exfoliate the hierarchical power dynamics among teachers and students to explain the unidirectional nature of lecturing. This helps in our understanding, why teaching in Indian higher education, in its present guise, is not student-centric in practice. The chapter attempts to understand the changing dimensions of teaching–learning and tries to provide a critical understanding of it in the Indian higher education.

OVERVIEW OF TEACHING–LEARNING IN INDIAN HIGHER EDUCATION

Teaching in Indian higher education is intertwined with the diversified higher educational landscape of the nation. Hence, making a general observation seems less desirable. However, by analyzing the policies, we may understand the evolution of teaching–learning in Indian higher education.

The Radhakrishnan Commission, the first education commission in independent India in 1948, started with a positive note about reforming the tertiary education system. The report clearly mentions that 'a teacher has to stimulate the spirit of enquiry and of criticism' (GOI, 1949). It puts the highest value for teachers who should not be measured in terms of mere performance. The commission was in fact very concerned when it found that mass lecture is most common in the institutions and not supplemented by any regular work by students in the library, post lecture (Mathew, 2016). The commission went ahead and suggested flexibility in the choice of courses, and stressed on the importance of liberal arts and social sciences. However, not much progress happened in the next 20 years (Mathew, 2016).

Later, the idealistic positions of the Radhakrishnan Commission were hindered by the bureaucratization of expanding Indian higher education in the 1960s. The affiliating university system, the large and complicated university administration, somewhat reduced the academic freedom, which the commission vouched for. In this process, rather similar to the industrial top-down management, the teacher became a mere component of the bigger system, largely following mandates of the higher order. The National Policy on Education (NPE) 1986 (revised Programme of Action in 1992; MHRD 1992) has later pointed out that teachers are not provided adequate freedom and opportunities for professional and career development. There is also lack in proper orientation to the methodologies of teaching and learning or the value of innovative and creative practices.

The role of the institutions, especially the affiliated colleges, was also reduced to mere providers of educating students. These institutions often do not exercise enough freedom in terms of designing or modifying the curricula, course structure, evaluation systems and experiment on teaching–learning practices—which are essential for the timely evolution of teaching–learning in any institution. The universities with more number of affiliated colleges imposed more centralized forms of administration, which made the system more standardized and less flexible (Varghese, 2015). The lack of academic freedom and long chain of command also means that teachers are less prone to take innovative steps and go beyond what is prescribed.

The bureaucratic and restrictive nature of Indian universities point out that the teachers are not given enough freedom and opportunities. Moreover, there is a lack of proper orientation of the methodologies of teaching practices. Expressing concerns about the teachers' qualities and the limitations of the higher education to keep pace with the growing demand of flexible learning approaches, the NPE recommended to introduce stricter norms for teacher selection. As a consequence, the National Eligibility Test (NET) was introduced in 1989 by the UGC, post the recommendations of the Mehrotra Committee.

Since then, the NET has served a useful purpose by ensuring standards for recruiting teachers in higher education. The study by Varghese, Malik and Gautam (2015) shows that the competitive nature of the NET examination works as one of the central-level mechanisms to eliminate the non-eligible candidates to enter into the higher education teaching profession. However, teachers with NET qualification do not always guarantee effective classroom teaching. It depends on the teachers' knowledge of the content, teaching methodologies, pedagogies and his or her adaptability to change. This also means that the institutions should take proactive role in improving the qualities of the teachers through innovative approaches.

The need to change leads the government to introduce several programmes such as the faculty induction programme and establish the academic staff colleges (now human resource development centres) in universities. The committees focused on a range of issues, starting from making the teaching profession more attractive, introducing and improving ICT infrastructure, teacher professional development and so on. To improve both the teachers and the institutions, two major steps were taken. First, the national advisory body for the central and state government on matters related to teacher education was upgraded to the 'National Council for Teacher Education' (NCTE) in 1993. The NCTE was established to achieve planned and co-ordinated develop-ment of the teachers in India with maintenance of norms and standards of teacher education. However, their efforts to train teachers are largely focused on developing teachers and academic leaders for the school (including early childhood education) levels. The second initiative was the establishment of the NAAC in 1994. The Plan of Action (PoA) in 1992 laid the foundation of the NAAC which, as an autonomous body, works to enforce quality in the HEIs through external review processes. Teaching–learning is among the seven criteria for NAAC evaluation, which focuses on admission process and student profile, catering to diverse needs, teaching–learning processes, teacher qual-ity, evaluation processes, and reforms and best practices in teaching–learning and evaluation. However, the NAAC evaluation attempts to evaluate teaching–learning more from the institutional perspective, and somewhat ignores analyzing the personalized teaching–learning process from an individual teacher's or learner's standpoint.

Later, in the post 2000 period, the National Knowledge Commission (NKC) and the national Five-year Plans (10th, 11th and 12th) (GOI, 2007, 2012) criticized the nearly unchanged structure of the Indian higher education. It strongly recommends revising them to meet the changing demands. It also mentioned that teachers should be involved in this process, and more autonomy should be given to the institutions. The Yashpal Committee report on *Renovation and Rejuvenation of Higher*

Education in India (MHRD, 2009) also supported these ideas and stressed on linking education with the world of work (GOI, 2013). However, the lack of consistency and the reluctant follow-up action has limited the success of such recommendations. Without a few notable exceptions, the overall scenario has not evolved towards a greater flexibility.

Concerned by the drawbacks, the government has recently emphasized on both teaching and faculty development in India, as one of the main agendas of the coming NPE. However, the focus on quality in higher education started getting increased importance from the post-2000 period in general and post-2010 in particular. At the national level, a range of recent policy initiatives and high profile national reports have highlighted the importance of teaching (at school and college levels) as the core of education quality challenges facing India. The latest in this line is the scheme of Pandit Madan Mohan Malaviya National Mission on Teachers and Teaching (PMMMNMTT). This umbrella mission is envisaged to address all the issues related to teachers, teaching and teacher preparation, and professional development across all educational sectors (MHRD, 2015).

Nearly all recent committees and commissions (Kakodar Committee, Madhav Menon Committee, UGC Pay Review Committee, Rama Rao Committee and the Planning Commission's subcommittee on faculty issues in higher education are some of them) have emphasized on improving teaching–learning by focusing on the teachers as the first stakeholder and the administration as the next. The issue of the teaching–learning environment and, importantly, changing the approach of teaching and learning are also mentioned, but in a rather sublime fashion. Collectively, these documents and status updates point towards the need for a holistic policy and for implementation plans for preparing and supporting high quality teachers and teaching in the classroom. This chapter, however, argues that for the development of effective teaching, teacher, learner and learning environment (institution and other informal learning environments) should be given equal priority. It will not only represent a more comprehensive picture to understand the teaching–learning process, but also provide a 360-degree dynamic picture to chalk out the roadmap of reform in this area.

Issues of Concern

Based on the reports of the commissions and committees, and the scholarly work of Jayaram (2006, 2009) and Agarwal (2011) the major issues of concern can be drawn. One of them is the shortage of teachers (see also Chapter 5). The issue of teacher recruitment is a serious concern towards the practice of effective teaching. The trend of hiring temporary faculty on minimal salary is rampant, and vacant teaching positions are not filled for years in many institutions. Among the existing faculties, poor ICT skills, lack of adaptability with the new hybrid teaching–learning mode or with the student's demands are some of the important factors hindering the quality. In addition, there is no effective national system and very limited institutional mechanisms to support teachers' development as well. The academic staff colleges, now human resource development centres (established to train teachers) have limited success in improving the situation. Along with these, the lack of quality content and massive growth of private parallel coaching are also resulting adversely in teaching–learning, both in its process and outcomes (British Council, 2014).

Although the earlier discussions and reports have helped to uncover some of the pertinent issues, ranging from faculty shortage to lack of institutional adaptability, and support professional development, it is still important, to analyze what is going on in the institutions and especially in the classrooms, where a majority of teaching–learning takes place under formal educational set-up. Exploring the practices of teaching and learning in Indian colleges and university systems could facilitate to analyze why the process of teaching–learning in higher education has evolved minimally. The following sections make an attempt in this direction.

UNDERSTANDING TEACHING–LEARNING IN INDIAN HIGHER EDUCATION

The section starts by providing a critical understanding of the common method of teaching in Indian colleges and universities. It was observed by the Radhakrishnan Commission that 'lecturing' is the common form of teaching in Indian higher education. The situation after seven decades has not changed much. Defying the changing demands of the dynamic society, the dominant process is still lecturing and, hence, it deserves special attention. Here, it is important to mention that although 'lecturing' is the most common method of teaching, there are certain differences in approach and practices. This can vary between courses, levels and disciplines. The following sections help explaining starting with the discussion of the most common form of teaching, as observed mostly in the undergraduate levels.

Teaching–Learning in Undergraduate Level

The chapter points out that the dominant process of teaching–learning in Indian higher education is still unidirectional and less interactive lecturing. It is information transaction in a rather prescribed form, where students are passive listeners of the information provided by the teacher. With a handful of exceptions, it is mostly the dominance of the teacher, which is widespread in Indian classrooms. However, there is no or less resistance to this mode of teaching, in spite of the understanding that this type of teaching is not engaging or helping the students much in the age of information abundance.

Teaching in Indian higher education, however, has long been synonymous with 'lecturing' and without a doubt; it has been successful in several occasions. Hence, it is a tried and tested method, deep rooted in the practices of the so-called ivory towers of academic excellence—the universities. Either because of the success of 'lecturing' or the lack of adaptability with the changing demands of the society, or both, the practice of 'lecturing' remained almost unchanged over time. That is why a large section of the teachers (63.6%) from all disciplines recognize it as an important mode of 'transmission' of knowledge. About 60.8 per cent of teachers and 41 per cent of students confirmed that traditional lecturing is the most common teaching method followed in both undergraduate and postgraduate levels (Mandal, 2017).

The unidirectional lecturing, however, poses major hurdles for learning, especially for the first-generation learners from disadvantageous backgrounds and with limited vernacular competencies. They find it difficult to understand the subjects during the initial days, and the unavailability of books in vernacular languages adds to their problems. As a result, they are often silent members with minimal confidence level. Such students in a large classroom, which is a common scenario in Indian colleges, often cannot clarify their doubts. The traditional lecturing takes a rather blanket approach to teaching, and there is limited attempt from teachers to critically assess the competency level of the students and plan classroom practices accordingly (Sabharwal & Malish, 2017).

The classroom observations provided a unique opportunity to observe some of the regular classes and follow the lecturing method. Like in most of the Indian schools, the classrooms are positioned in a unidirectional way, so that all the students face the teachers. The benches/desks are all set up in a very typical manner, which does not allow any interactions with other students, except some cross talks. Hence, the focus of the class lecture is always on the teacher and not on the students. Describing one such class session would help understand the issue better.

In undergraduate courses, the teacher, of a social sciences subject, enters the classroom and greets the students. Some students are already prepared with their notebooks, for taking notes based on the lecture. The teacher starts the lecture and focuses on the topic of the day, which he or she pre-selected. There is no/minimal discussion on what students want or what their existing knowledge about the topic is. The students also do not try to make any intervention during the teaching. Only occasionally, during the observations, it is noticed that students ask questions. The questions they ask are mostly descriptive, asking the teacher to reiterate some sections to help them to understand and take more comprehensive notes.

There was not a single incident where students expressed a contradictory view to that of the teacher or challenged the teachers' opinion. The teacher also did not encourage group discussions or one-to-one interactions, and continued to transact information with an occasional pause to check if the students understood him or her properly, before moving on with the lecture. Towards the end of the session, some time was given to the students for asking questions. A student from the first row of desks questioned. It was a question related to the coming exam, as she tried to get a clarification from the teacher about the topics which could be important in the examination. The teacher reiterated and the student noted it down. The class officially concluded.

This is a typical classroom teaching practice in an average Indian college. Clearly, it is a unidirectional process with minimal participation from the learners. The teacher is more focused towards providing the information and making sure that students 'understood' what he or she has said. It also seemed that there are fewer interactions among the students in the class. However, a post-class observation revealed that students did not leave the classroom soon after the teaching ended. They rather started asking questions to each other about the topic. Later, in the focus group discussion (FGD) with the same group of students, they mentioned that they use social networking (e.g., WhatsApp and Facebook messenger) to discuss about their subject(s) and course(s). Although these groups are not officially created and almost none of the groups have all of the students of the class, it points towards something important.

This indicates that even the classroom, as described earlier, which is apparently devoid of any interaction between students, is actually full of communications, although not visible. These interactions, such as sharing of ideas and Internet links about the topics in the groups, show that students have curved their own way of learning and are somewhat using the lecture as a complementary resource. That is why taking notes during the class becomes a common activity, where students often collect the information, and later use them to improve their knowledge base through inter-student communication via contemporary digital technological platforms.

Why are the students looking for alternative ways of interacting and are not interactive enough in the classrooms? The study found that many teachers in Indian colleges and universities are supportive of traditional teaching methods. During the interviews, university teachers expressed that since the students are entering the higher education from the school system, which is information-oriented, students are accustomed to lecturing, 'and it works well' (teacher from a college in West Bengal, India). Although teachers often express that they are open to listen to the students to facilitate learning, this does not reflect much in practice, as observed (Mandal, 2016c). The classroom observations further focused on this type of teaching, where there is a common trend of using reference books or class notes for teaching. The observer of a computer science class of a state university noted that

> The teacher has often depended on the reference books to explain the concepts. So the students were not actively listening to the teacher and lost their attention. But the teacher has not taken any effort to regain the students' attention. (Mandal, 2017)

The main focus then was not to facilitate learning. 'I want to complete the selected topic effectively within a class hour' was the response from the teacher, which depicts that the focus was to transact information and not to focus on making it exiting or thought provoking to the students. The students of the same class reconfirmed that lecture method is 'boring', 'teaching without interaction is not effective' and 'teaching process without questioning is actually not helping them' (FGD, during the CPRHE Study, Mandal, 2017). Clearly, there is a mismatch and miscommunication between the teachers and the students. Why so?

From a pedagogical standpoint, the present form of lecturing is merely a transmission of information. The first-generation learners or the learners from the disadvantaged backgrounds often cannot grasp what the teachers are trying to convey, and among the advanced or today's 'net-generation' learners, this informative lecturing is not attractive enough. However, why is it not interactive and interesting, as informative representation could be interactive as well? Why is there unequal participation in the teaching–learning processes, considering that the learners are adults, and have opinions and abilities to actively participate in the discussions?

Less Interactive Nature of Indian Higher Education

The root of the answer perhaps lies in the very origin of the word, 'lecture', which traditionally means telling or the act of reading from the text. This suggests that lecturing was originated from the very idea of communication, however, with the aim of transferring meanings to others. This also means that the lecturer gets a commanding legitimacy over others (listeners) on the topic of the lecture (Chasi, 2016). However, on the other hand, knowledge emerges from collective or individual reflection in which faculty recognize, critique, and develop theories and practices about their teaching (Zeichner, 1993), which are largely missing in the higher education teaching in India. Professors are less engaged in critical and reflective practices of teaching and, hence, less open to learn and adapt to the collaborative construction of knowledge.

Felder (1993) and Stitt-Gohdes, Grews and McCannon (1999) explain that lecturers often favour their own learning style, and often instinctively teach the way they were taught. Since nearly all the teachers in higher education have experienced academic success in an instructor-oriented learning set-up, it is understandable why teachers intend to teach in a particular style. Chasi (2016) adds to this by saying that lecturers think that they know more than the learners, and that they have a duty to transfer the information them in order to change how the learners perceive the world. The students usually accept this commanding role of the teacher and become passive participants of the process.

The Power Relations

Brookfield (1995) argues that to understand why students accepted the imposed view, or the predominance of the professor's authority, it is important to look at the power relations. Traditionally, since the age of the 'gurus' in ancient India, students were taught to consider the teacher or guru as an unquestionable authority (Jayaram, 2002). The guru is the one who knows everything and knows the best. The tradition and its underlying principals, clearly, have not changed much. The teacher is usually called as 'sir'/'madam' or 'master', a practice inherited from the colonial era. This connotation of superiority (and inferiority of the students) translates into the conceptualization of 'lecture' and, hence, even though a teacher in higher educational institute opens the floor for questions and counter opinions, students prefer to be silent. Perhaps that is why the teachers also, most of the time, quickly asks the students if they have any questions, before moving on to the next discussion.

This power relation around knowledge is visible in the context of Indian higher education in general. The common foundation of the teacher-student relationship also explains why, in general, classrooms are not interactive enough. Looking at this issue from the institutional or from the context of the learning environment, a new dimension emerges. An example can perhaps highlight the issue. From the physical arrangement of the classrooms, it is observed that the lecturer is the centre of focus and his or her 'voice is privileged' (Marcela, Gutiérrez & Aldana, 2014). This unidirectional set-up is less oriented to facilitate interactions amongst the students and the teacher without the hierarchy. It is rather designed so that the lecturer is audible and visible to all for a monologue. The students also form a subtle hierarchical formation, where the 'brilliant' students take the front rows and the others occupy the following ones. This acceptance of hierarchy results in even less interaction in the classrooms, as not only the teachers but also the students form an environment which is less free and encouraging for all. Even if the teacher wants to change the classroom set-up, in Indian higher education, with rigid top-down management, he or she has limited authority.

The university administrations are also unaware about the necessity of infrastructure and its set-up which can facilitate interactive learning. It seems important for the higher education management to realize that the use of 'interactive teaching–learning' as a mere buzzword in reports (found while evaluating the self-evaluation reports prepared by the institutions for NAAC review) is not going to solve the problem, which they often fail to recognize.

Ignorance on the one hand and lack of action on the other to promote learner-centric teaching seem also to encourage students to opt for private coaching classes for additional support, or expect that their teachers would eventually suggest the important questions and provide ready answers for the coming exam(s). A large section of lecturers think that the transmission of information and using ready-to-use answers (usually prepared or compiled by the teacher) is essential for the students, as 'they (students) want them just to pass the exam easily' or 'these (ready answers) are actually helping the students to get an overview' (common response from many teachers interviewed). This ill practice is so deep rooted that 44.7 per cent of undergraduate and 36.6 per cent postgraduate students think that it is essential for their success, and that the teachers should continue to provide the ready-to-use answers or study notes. Here, rather than blaming the students for wanting easy ways to pass the exams, it seems important to reckon that in the process, the learning goals become secondary, and this in turn limits the participation in the construction of knowledge.

Quite expectedly, it is seen that these content-driven lectures have less impact on changing learners' perceptions or impart learning skills, and remain as a mechanism to transfer information. Dewey (1933) called it 'out-of-context' learning, which may work only in the classroom, governed by series of rules and preconditions. It assumes that the teacher will teach and the students will absorb what was taught. These rules, in fact, make it difficult for the teacher and the students to engage in authentic learning experiences that transform their beliefs and change them (Parra, Gutierrez & Aldana, 2015). Ramsden (2003) terms it as *teaching as telling or transmission* where the main task of teaching is the transmission of information, in a rather 'authoritative' way. This rather traditional lecture method represents a perspective on teaching taken from the point of view of the teacher, where the teacher is the source of knowledge (Ramsden, 2003). Students in this situation are often passive recipients of the information. Biggs (1999) termed this as 'blame the student' theory of teaching where teacher often categorize them as 'good' or 'bad' students. This is because a lecturer who practices a unidirectional teaching, perceives it as an unproblematic one. Hence, if any or some of the students cannot comprehend the meaning out of it, it is not seen as the fault of the teacher, but the inability of the students. An interview with a teacher of a renowned state university of India helps explaining the teachers' attitude further.

> Both under-graduate and post graduate students learn here. I basically teach both of them and follow the same strategy. However, the quality of students is poor, because M.Tech [s]tudents come from different institutes. B.Tech students learn computer science but M.Tech students come from different streams, such as B.Sc. Computer Science, B.Sc. Physics, Mathematics, Statistics…. So, some of the students know about computer science but not everyone. It is a heterogeneous class or group.

In my class, I start from the beginning of the study and sometimes I face problems and try to help students to improve it and help to solve it. Some students are not interested to take the classes and they bunk their classes (A teacher of a central university). (Mandal, 2017)

The focus on the fundamentals of a subject in a heterogeneous group cannot be contested. However, the teacher used simply lecturing, and when it yields limited success, the teacher cannot solve the issue and rather pushes the 'blame' towards the limited subject knowledge of the students. Different teaching–learning methods, such as peer-to-peer teaching and group work, could have retained the interest of the students, including the ones who have prior knowledge of the fundamentals of the discipline.

TEACHING–LEARNING IN POSTGRADUATE AND HIGHER LEVELS

There are instances which highlight considerable variations in teaching–learning, especially across levels (undergraduate and postgraduate levels). Although unidirectional lecturing dominates the practice, there are considerable variations as well. There are efforts from the teachers to understand the demands of the students, especially in the postgraduate or senior level and in laboratory-based subjects. Teachers spend some more time asking questions to the students to get an overview of their understanding of the subject before lecturing. A few teachers also ask the students their opinion on where exactly they want the teacher to focus more. Interestingly, sometimes it is the same teacher who has different perspectives of teaching in undergraduate and postgraduate classes.

The teaching approach while I teach in M.Com, that is the PG (postgraduate) class in commerce, I always keep things in my mind that these are the students who has completed their B.Com [Bachelors in Commerce] will seek for employment or higher studies. So, little changes should be there. When I teach in the B.Com first semester there is more emphasis on the discipline part, clarity and encouraging, so I focus on the syllabus… there [is] more writing etc. At the UG [undergraduate] level, the learning habit should be developed as per me, but in PG classes, I don't bother about the discipline, whether they are recording lectures or maintaining notebook, it is not about completing syllabus alone. There should be a pragmatic approach in PG classes and self activation; there should be goal oriented approach among the students and the teacher.

—A teacher from a Public University, India (CPRHE Study). (Mandal, 2017)

The teacher of the postgraduate level, thus, perceives the learning as 'a complex process' than just transmitting information. As a consequence, the teacher puts additional effort to know the requirement of the students and modify his or her lectures accordingly. Looking through the pedagogic lenses, teaching here is moving towards a cognitive model, where it has started gaining the acceptance of a mutual process of knowledge processing. Although it is at its nascent state and only a limited section of the teacher practices it, this is perhaps a move from the 'surface approach' to the 'deep approach' of learning, although in its prefatory stage in Indian higher education. Marton and Säljö (1976) concluded that in the deep approach, there is a strong intention to learn the meaning, which encourages students to attempt to relate concepts and find new meanings of existing understandings. Teachers who take student-focused approaches, usually encourages students towards a deep approach to study (Prosser & Tringwell, 1999). Teachers who believe in this approach put more effort to analytically perceive the need so that their teaching helps reconstruct the meaning.

The teaching practices described earlier have not yet followed the deep approach. Nevertheless, even with this slightest change from the surface approach, there is a remarkable shift in the perceptions of the learners. They are more vocal. They not only ask questions, clarify doubts in the classrooms, but also proactively discuss the subjects among themselves and with the teachers (Mandal, 2016a, 2016b). It is observed that students in their postgraduate level are more confident about what they want from the teacher and shared that they feel comfortable if the teacher(s) is/are open to new ideas and discussions. This openness may not have any positive or negative correlation with the experience of the teacher. During the study, it is found through classroom observations and students FGDs that some teachers, both newly recruited and experienced (over 10 years), are trying to 'listen to them [the students] to know what they want'-a teacher said (Mandal, 2017).

Ramsden (2003) explains this as '*teaching as organizing student activity*'. Teachers, who practice this also urge to try different set methods to enable learning. This view of teaching indicates that there are certain conditions that guarantee learning, and one of them is certainly openness and interactivity. Students' view of teaching indicates that there are certain conditions that are desired for learning, and the most important of them are knowledge and encouragement. Perhaps that is why factors such as 'knowledgeable' and 'motivating' come out as two of the most preferred characteristics of an effective teacher, in responses from both the students and teachers (Table 7.1). However, as the students, especially that of the undergraduate level, are not exposed to new kinds of teaching and are mostly accustomed to traditional lecture methods, they are not fully able to indicate what kind of teaching they want and what methods work best.

How to make teaching interactive and effective depend on the teacher and planners of teacher training (Cornelius-Shite, 2007), and asking this to students would be naïve as they are not acquainted with different forms of teaching and hence, cannot compare or suggest. Therefore, it is important to find out the clues from the opinion of the students and modify the practices or teacher training accordingly to address the problems. In essence, we have seen that the students focus on many attitudinal competences, which indicates a need of innovative teachers and teaching.

Table 7.1 *Desired Characteristics of an Effective Teacher: Students' and Teachers' Opinions*

Rank	Students' Opinion	Teachers' Opinion
1	Knowledgeable	Knowledgeable
2	Motivating	Motivating
3	Friendly	Up-to-date
4	Open minded	Approachable
5	Interactive	Interactive

Source: CPRHE study (2015–2017), Mandal (2017).

Table 7.1 shows that both students and teachers prefer a teacher who has adequate knowledge about the subject and who can motivate the students. In addition, students also want a 'friendly' and 'open minded' teacher where most of their teachers are said to be focused more on the subject and knowledge–domain-specific competencies (such as being up-to-date). However, a teacher who is more interactive is seen to have a widespread preference.

Looking beyond the top five characteristics of an effective teacher, the trend becomes clearer, on one hand, where being creative, confident and enthusiastic has been considered to be important traits for a teacher among the students. On the other, the teachers themselves prefer to be confident, stimulating and open minded. It is also evident that the teachers who interact and are open to the students are considered effective. Even with the lack of exposure to new forms of teaching, students are able to point out what are the lacks in the present teaching practices. Students' opinion, therefore, holds great value also and can provide insights while devising new forms of teaching–learning practices based on the their needs.

The view of the students' about effective teaching, implies that the teachers' role is largely to understand the problem areas and address them interactively to organize student activity, and thereby to facilitate effective and collaborative learning. In practice, however, many of these teachers' attributes are not visible. During the interview, the teachers mentioned another important aspect when we asked them about the reasons for the lack of innovative approach in teaching in Indian higher education. The teachers, who mostly teach undergraduate courses, mentioned about the pressure of completing the syllabus, lack of student attention and large class sizes. All these pose hindrances in practicing newer teaching approaches, which essentially demands smaller class sizes for better attention as well as interaction. Nonetheless, in contract to such realization, during the quantitative survey, 61.8 per cent of teachers are seen to be opined that the main focus of teaching is to complete the syllabus. This is the practice that currently dominates the Indian higher education.

TOWARDS EFFECTIVE TEACHING

A small step towards interactivity has a leap of impact in promoting effective teaching–learning in any educational context, and especially so in higher education. Indian teachers, largely overwhelmed by the task of completing the syllabi, burdened by non-academic works, managing large size classrooms (sometimes up to 150 students in a classroom, as found in the study) and lack of understanding about higher education pedagogy, often follow a method which is ineffective in today's world of information abundance. However, in spite of the drawbacks and limitations, such as poor infrastructures and poor maintenance of infrastructure, lack of ICT facilities and ineffective trainings, delay in administrative process or poor coordination between supply and demands of recurring materials (e.g., chemicals in laboratories), only a handful of teachers in Indian colleges and universities try to teach effectively. These constrains can become detrimental for creating facilitative conditions for teaching–learning.

Teachers, in these circumstances, allow their personal time to talk to students. They take laboratory sessions without the required chemicals, with the hope that they can get them someday, and then take the class once again, even though that particular test will no longer be a part of the following semesters. The study found that there are teachers who borrow time from other departments to teach certain computer-based courses as the concerned department has not been allotted computers and/or the software required. In an interview, a teacher from an Indian university said,

> There is no computer lab here, so we can't even teach the students Tally, e-filing, e-return, etc. We try to make them [students] understand through diagram[s], or go to other departments, but they often don't have the software [required for the course].

> —Interview with a teacher of a central university, India (November 2015)

These remarkable initiatives to overcome the constraints and facilitate learning, although not always effective, can be considered as 'efforts towards' *making learning possible*. According to Ramsden (2003),

Biggs (1999) and Biggs and Tang (2007), 'making learning possible' is more complex than the previous two approaches (*teaching as telling or transmission and teaching as organizing student activity*). Teachers who use this approach focus on the critical issues of student learning and try to address them. Therefore, the traditional role of the teacher differs substantially. However, this is not so in the Indian scenario. The teachers, sometimes without any idea of what works best for effective teaching–learning, try to help the students as much as they can. These efforts could also emerge from the sheer frustration of not being able to teach properly, because of the lack of infrastructure as a part of learning environment, and may not be a conscious decision towards 'applying and modifying one's own ideas', as suggested by Ramsden (2003). This is why the 'out of the box' teaching as observed in the Indian higher education cannot be termed as 'making learning possible' (after Ramsden, 2003), but rather an 'effort' towards it.

Here, rather than the ineffectiveness of the teacher, the role of an institution to build not just the classrooms but the learning environment becomes important. Providing necessary infrastructure and support is the key in effective teaching–learning process. Otherwise, teachers with limited facilities, no matter how hard they try, will not be able to make learning possible.

In the study, it is observed that even in the top institutions, there are problems constrains of resources. Both in central and state universities, there are shortages of classrooms (especially for humanities and social sciences disciplines), discussion rooms (other than classrooms), computer laboratories, laboratories or practicum facilities for departments other than sciences (such as language lab) and ICT infrastructure (not mere availability of computers or Internet connections, but more access to academic journals, resources, and providing open access to the students and academics). Even basic modern infrastructures, such as projectors, Internet connection and so on, are not optimally used in many institutions (Varghese & Mandal, 2016). There are also problems in purchasing recurring materials, such as laboratory equipment, chemicals and other utilities. It is observed that in some institutions there is more bureaucratic red-tapism for girl students in the name of 'security'. For instance, the girl students of a central university are not permitted to stay outside their hostels, even in the libraries, after 6 PM, or sometimes they are not even allowed to visit other girls' hostels situated in the premises for study or other purposes.

Here, it is important to mention that the institutions (the administrators, academic heads and other decision-making bodies) need to understand that learning does not only happen inside the walls of a classroom. Building a flexible yet robust environment is essential for learning to thrive. Limiting the resources or putting gender-based restrictions will further narrow down the higher studies into a bookish, more theoretical knowledge reproduction and will not help to develop the learners as complete, critical and competent human beings. Introducing more teacher trainings or more restrictive practices without solving these issues related to learning environment building is not going to improve the teaching outcome substantially.

THE WAY FORWARD

The aspiration of the students, the efforts of the teachers or the reform initiatives of the government have not yielded much success in making teaching–learning more effective or learner-centric, or bringing it out of its traditional cocoon. Why so? Is it the limitations of the efforts or the approach, with which we try to understand and improve teaching–learning? These trigger one more intriguing question: How should we consider or perceive 'teaching–learning'? The current trend is to focus on the input and outcome in the form of the gross enrolment ratio (GER) and the number of students completing the course successfully. In addition, easily quantifiable achievements, such as number of publications and hours of teaching, are also considered as benchmarks of teaching. However, learning and teaching is best conceived as a process, and not in terms of outcomes (Kolb & Kolb, 2005). To improve teaching in higher education, the focus should therefore be on the process that enables learning. The process of learning is, however, holistic, and it should not be seen in isolation. That is why it is essential to give equal importance to teachers, learners and the learning environment. Theories and practical examples may also help in explaining that learning is a dialectic process of assimilating new experiences into the existing one to form new perspectives about the world through a synergic transaction between the person (teacher and students) and the environment (institutions). In this process, all the components play very significant roles in synergy to help in relearning the teaching–learning.

In Indian higher education, this synergy is somewhat missing, and this could be the reason why Indian teachers are not being able to fully transact effective teaching into practices. We cannot perhaps *blame the teachers* for this. The teachers are also in a flux on how to teach a large size class/cohort with wide lingual, critical, socio-economic and educational diversity and disparity. The teachers lacks ideas and methodologies on what is effective and feasible in this circumstances, as they are deprived of proper training to make teaching–learning a successful process of collaborative knowledge construction.[2] They are not trained in higher education learning theory and principles. The existing teacher trainings (e.g., B.Ed. and M.Ed.) are designed to develop school teachers and leaders. The faculty development courses in the universities have not being able to address this issue effectively either. Therefore, it seems important to adopt new approaches and strengthen teacher training in higher education, as studies show that the teachers who are skilled in theories and practices of adult learning, are more likely to adopt student-centred model of teaching (Stitt-Gohdes et al., 1999), even if it is not the way they have learned (Brown, 2003).

This systematic change, however, requires proper planning and training of not only the teachers but also the educational administrators where students should also be included (High Level Group on the Modernisation of Higher Education, 2013). Through transmission of knowledge, development of complex understanding about the learning processes, engaging in dialogic processes, nurturing the interpersonal elements of student learning and through social reforms (Pratt, 2002), the synergy can be achieved.

It is important to reckon that the higher educational landscape in India is immensely diverse and complex. To change the long haul culture would therefore not be an easy task. It requires proper planning

---

[2] Further discussion on teacher professional discussion is in Chapter 6.

and sustainable strategies. Addressing the lack of physical and other supportive infrastructures, the recruitment of tenured teachers or introducing internships are some of the important aspects which are at the surface of reform agendas. The core is more intricate, which deals with age-old traditions of lecturing and unidirectional teaching in the midst of changing ambitions of the learners. The aspects of inclusion and empowerment of the fragile, oppressed sections of the society is also an important factor, where the power dynamics plays havoc in and outside the classrooms. The challenges are faced by both students and teachers on effective learning and teaching. Changing these would require a truly robust policy and institutional mechanism(s) based on rigorous research. This is why the chapter started with an argument that it is important to understand the process of teaching–learning in Indian higher education with its peculiarities, to avoid making reforms which are not grounded.

Based on the discussion, which is not extensive but rather exploratory in nature, it seems that the reform agendas also need to recognize the changes that have occurred in recent times and plan accordingly. One of them is certainly the increasing demands of the more informed and aspiring students, many of whom are first-generation learners and from disadvantageous socio-economic and educational backgrounds. They are entering into the higher education not for the pleasure of learning but to utilize it to improve their life situation. The existing colleges and universities in India, with some exceptions, somewhat failed to recognize these and make necessary changes in their teaching practices and extend effective administrative supports for the same. As a result, learners of the net-generation are stuck with an outdated system, and learners from the disadvantageous sections and first-generation learners are lagging behind. It is important to note that this system is also creating future teachers, and the loop of ineffective teaching–learning continues, with fewer concerns and limited understandings of learners and learning.

The solution to this problem is not easy, and to spread the small-scale successful efforts of teaching reforms to the entire nation is a colossal task. Nevertheless, it is of utmost important.

REFERENCES

Agarwal, P. (2009). *Higher education in India: The need for change.* New Delhi: Indian Council for Research on International Economic Relations.

Agarwal, P. (2011). *Indian higher education: Envisioning the Future.* New Delhi: SAGE.

Altbach, P. G., Reisberg, L., & Rumbley, L. (2009). *Trends in global higher education: Tracking an academic revolution.* Paris: UNESCO.

Biggs, J. (1999). *Teaching for quality learning at university.* Buckingham: SHRE and Open University Press.

Biggs, J., & Tang, C. (2007). *Teaching for quality learning at university,* 3rd ed. Berkshire: Open University Press and McGraw-Hill Education.

British Council. (2014). *Understanding India: The future of higher education and opportunities for international cooperation.* London and New Delhi: British Council.

Brookfield, S. D. (1995). *Becoming a critically reflective teacher.* San Francisco, CA: Jossey Bass.

Brown, B. L. (2003). *Teaching style vs. learning style: Myths and realities.* Washington, DC: ERIC.

Chasi, C. (2016). A philosophy for teaching in this strange place. *Africa Education Review, 12*(4), 618–631.

Cornelius-Shite, J. (2007). Learner-centered teacher-student relationships are effective: A meta-analysis. *Review of Educational Research, 77*(1), 113–143.

Dewey, J. (1933). *How we think: A restatement of the relation of reflective thinking to the educative process.* Boston, MA: D.C. Heath and Company.

Felder, R. (1993). Reaching the second tier: Learning and teaching styles in college science education. *College Science Teaching, 22*(5), 286–290.

GOI (Government of India). (1949). *The report of the University Education Commission.* New Delhi: Ministry of Education, Government of India.

———. (2007). *XIth plan 2007–2012.* New Delhi: Planning Commission, Government of India.

———. (2012). *XIIth plan (education) 2012–2017.* New Delhi: Planning Commission, Government of India.

———. (2013). *Report on employment and unemployment survey 2012–2013.* New Delhi: Ministry of Labour and Employment, Government of India.

High Level Group on the Modernisation of Higher Education. (2013). *Report to the European Commission on improving the quality of teaching and learning in Europe's higher education institutions.* Brussels: European Union.

Jayaram, N. (2002). The fall of the Guru: The decline of the academic profession in India. In P. G. Altbach (Ed.), *The decline of the Guru: The academic profession in developing and middle income countries* (pp. 207–239). Boston, MA: Centre for International Higher Education, Boston College.

———. (2006). India. In J. J. Forest & P. G. Altbach, *International handbook of higher education* (pp. 747–767). Dordrechi: Springer.

Jayaram, N. (2009). Higher education in India: The challenges of change. In D. Palfrcyman & T. Tapper (Eds), *Structuring mass higher education: The role of elite institutions* (pp. 95–112). New York, NY and London: Routledge.

Kolb, A., & Kolb, D. (2005). Learning styles and learning spaces: Enhancing experiential learning in higher education. *Academy of Management Learning & Education, 4*(2), 193–212.

Labour Bureau of India. (2013). *Report on youth employment-unemployment scenario 2012–13.* Chandigarh: Ministry of Labour & Employment, Government of India.

Mandal, S. (2016a). Developing best teachers in Indian higher education: What can we learn from others? *Indian Journal of Educational Research,* 5 (March), 73–85.

———. (2016b, August). Development of education and skills of rural youth in India. Kurukshetra: Ministry of Rural Development, Government of India, *64*(10), 14–19.

———. (2016c, July). Teaching-learning process. *Economic and Political Weekly,* 79–81.

———. (2017). *Teaching and learning in Indian higher education: A national level study by CPRHE-NUEPA.* New Delhi: CPRHE-NIEPA.

Marcela, O. P., Gutiérrez, R., & Aldana, M. F. (2014). Engaging in critically reflective teaching: From theory to practice in pursuit of transformative learning. *Reflective Practice, 16*(1), 16–30.

Marton, F., & Säljö, R. (1976). On the qualitative difference in learning I: Outcome and process. *British Journal of Educational Psychology, 46*(1), 4–11.

Mathew, A. (2016). Reforms in higher education in India: A review of recommendations of commissions and committees on Education. *CPRHE Research Paper* Series (Research Paper No. 2). New Delhi: CPRHE-NIEPA.

MHRD (Ministry of Human Resource Development). (1992). *National policy on education 1986 (revised POA in 1992).* New Delhi: Government of India.

———. (2009). *Yashpal Committee report on renovation and rejuvenation of higher education in India.* New Delhi: Government of India.

———. (2015). *Scheme of Pandit Madan Mohan Malaviya National Mission on Teachers and Teaching (PMMMNMTT).* New Delhi: Government of India.

Parra, M. O., Gutierrez, R., & Aldana, M. F. (2015). Engaging in critically reflective teaching: From theory to practice in pursuit of transformative learning. *Reflective Practice, 16*(1), 16–30.

Pratt, D. (2002). Good teaching: One size fits all? In *An update on teaching theory. New Direction for Adult and Continuing Education,* (93), 5–16.

Prosser, M., & Tringwell, K. (1999). *Understanding learning and teaching: The experience in higher education.* Buckingham: The Society for Research into Higher Education and Open University Press.

Ramsden, P. (2003). *Learning to teach in higher education.* London: Routledge Flamer.

Sabharwal, N., & Malish, C. (2017). *Achieving academic integration in higher education in India* (CPRHE Policy Brief No. 2). New Delhi: CPRHE-NIEPA.

Stitt-Gohdes, Wanda. L., Crews, T. B., & McCannon, M. (1999). Business teachers learning and instructional styles. *Delta Pi Epsilon Journal, 41*(2), 71–88.

Varghese, N. V. (2015). Challenges of massification of higher education in India. *CPRHE Research Papers Series* (Research Paper No. 1), pp. 1–46. New Delhi: CPRHE-NIEPA.

Varghese, N. V., & Mandal, S. (2016). *Report on the international seminar on teaching-learning and new technologies in higher education.* New Delhi: NIEPA.

Varghese, N. V., Malik, G., & Gautam, D. R. (2015). *National eligibility test (NET)—An analysis of the examination results (Report submitted to the University Grants Commission).* New Delhi: Centre for Policy Research in Higher Education (CPRHE-NIEPA).

Zeichner, K. M. (1993). *Maestro como profesional reflexivo.* Retrieved from www.practicareflexiva

Chapter 8

Developing e-Content for Massive Open Online Courses (MOOCs)
An Experience of Teaching-Learning Centre

Vimal Rarh

INTRODUCTION

The expansion of higher education system in India has been chaotic. The drive to make higher education socially inclusive has led to a sudden and dramatic increase in the number of institutions without a proportionate increase in material and intellectual resources. As a result, academic standards have been jeopardized (Béteille, 2005).

India has the third-largest system of higher education in the world, next only to USA and China, with a gross enrolment ratio (GER) of 24.5 per cent (MHRD, 2016). However, there is a big question mark on the access to quality higher education in the massifying system. There is not only the shortage of teachers in Indian higher education institutions (HEIs) but also the lack of ability of traditional teaching–learning methodologies to nurture innovation and creativity amongst the students (Agarwal, 2009). In addition, there is a dearth of good learning resources available to all the students. Higher education in India needs to be improved in terms of both quality and quantity.

ICT can help overcome the challenges of accessibility and teaching–learning quality in Indian higher education. Traditional classroom teaching through 'talk and chalk' method, howsoever bright a teacher may be, does have certain limitations in the sense that many a times concepts cannot be well explained just on the board, and one does feel that had there been some technological aids, learning could have been more effective. Besides this, the paucity of time also creates pressure on the teacher to finish the course on time and, therefore, even though a teacher wants his or her pupil to achieve an in-depth understanding of the subject, it cannot be accomplished. ICT can help overcome these problems. ICT-enabled education is not only an answer to the growing demands for enrolment in higher education but is also in tune with the mindset of the present-day students. If used creatively, it can make a big difference in the way teachers teach and students learn, and can help students acquire 21st century skills such as digital literacy, innovative thinking, creativity, sound reasoning and effective communication (Bakhshi & Rarh, 2012). To create a holistic learning environment focusing on quality, innovation, expansion, excellence and inclusion, integration of ICT with education is deemed essential.

Conceptually, ICT-enabled education or e-learning has the potential to address many of the ills afflicting higher education, but introducing such a mode of education in a country like India is a challenging task. To introduce ICT-enabled education in such a large and evolving education system as India, several efforts are essential. These involve (a) development of high quality multimedia enriched and interactive e-learning material (e-content) and its multi-lingual conversion; (b) capacity building of all stakeholders (staff, faculty and students) in ICT skills; and (c) state-of-the-art infrastructure, along with networking and Internet connectivity via virtual private networks (VPNs)/broadband connectivity, for disseminating the content, and affordable access devices so that it reaches the doorsteps of the learners.

DEVELOPMENT OF MULTIMEDIA ENRICHED
E-CONTENT AND CHALLENGES

The launch of the National Mission on Education Through ICT (NMEICT) in 2009, during the 11th Five-year Plan was a major initiative of the Government of India whereby 392 universities and 18,374 colleges were provided broadband connectivity. The ongoing institutional initiatives as well as new initiatives were encouraged for creating of e-content. The aim of NMEICT was to leverage the potential of ICT in providing high quality personalized and interactive content, free of cost, to all the learners in HEIs in *anytime anywhere* mode. Another intention was to strengthen the teachers in higher education in enhancing learning (NMEICT, 2009). Recently, various other schemes have been initiated for e-content and online courses development in a more structured manner—web-portals to host the e-content and online courses, and for capacity building of teachers for enhancing the quality of education by integrating ICT.

The content is the basic element of e-learning to be blended with suitable technological tools using appropriate pedagogies. Quality e-content, which are interactive and multimedia-enriched, facilitate in-depth understanding of the subject, encourage thinking on the subject, and promote creativity and innovation (Alonso et al., 2006). The e-content may have copyright with the creator/content developer. Alternatively, the content may be made open to customization or allowed to be used as such. In India, most of the public-funded institutions/projects developing the e-content are making it available as an open educational resource (OER),[1] which can be freely used by entire educational community.

---

[1] The term OER was first coined at UNESCO's 2002 Forum on Open Courseware. OER can be defined as:

> [T]eaching, learning, and research resources that reside in the public domain or have been released under an intellectual property license that permits their free use and re-purposing by others. Open educational resources include full courses, course materials, modules, textbooks, streaming videos, tests, software, and any other tools, materials, or techniques used to support access to knowledge. (William & Flora, 2008)

The OERs are licensed under the Creative Commons, which host an OERs policy registry and list various existing and proposed open education policies from around the world. Creative Commons and multiple other open organizations launched the Open Policy Network to foster the creation, adoption and implementation of open policies and practices (William and Flora Hewlett Foundation, 2008). They help in advancing the public good by supporting open policy advocates, organizations and policy-makers; connecting open policy opportunities with assistance; and sharing open policy information. India subscribes to a similar OER policy for its e-content development and dissemination by the public institutions.

In view of globalization, English as a medium of instruction in higher education has increased in demand in India. However, the capacities of the learners as well as the standards of the instruction are diverse. This calls for the need to introspect on the nature of interventions and facilitation, which can be provided for both onsite and online courses. In addition, the arguments for the resources made available in local languages need to be weighed. Considering the diverse and massifying higher education scenario, the scale of efforts, while developing content, has to be large and has to be drawn from the available repertoire of resources.

Many course contents are available on the Internet, but the quality of the contents remains a major concern. Indian learners struggle to find content as per their course requirements, in their own language and in a comprehendible English accent. Experts find it difficult to link the course contents with appropriate technical specifications, especially in vernaculars. There are a number of measures to be ensured whilst developing the context-specific e-contents. Of them, the most significant ones relate to conceptual clarity, which ought to be vetted minutely through a separate body of experts. In addition, specification of learning outcomes coupled with questions requiring cognitive operations at the levels of knowledge, understanding, application, analysis, synthesis and evaluation are of paramount significance (Clark & Mayer, 2011). Other issues such as modularization of the contents, the intellectual property rights (IPR), gender bias in contents, multimedia enrichment, easy navigation and disabled-friendly formatting are some of the aspects of quality e-material. Besides, all elements such as text, audio, video, simulations, assessments and weblinks may be so sequenced that they create adequate interest among learners (Bakhshi & Rarh, 2011).

Content compatibility with various platforms and access devices is a technical requirement, such as quality of graphics and visuals on the learning management system (LMS). It must be easy to navigate and interact. The mobile-learning or M-learning is an extension of e-learning relying on mobile devices. In India, the smart mobile devices are more commonly utilized in rural areas than the laptops or tablets. Mobile-device-based learning can be used as a cost-effective and pedagogically accessible educational tool in the country. As India is the second-largest player in the global telecom market, there is a potential for developing mobile applications (Apps) and resources in higher education.

Four Quadrant e-Learning Model

The NMEICT has adopted the Four Quadrant model, which defines the features of the content and also the type of interactions that are to be included for producing an engaging experience for the learners. The Four Quadrant model (Figure 8.1) suggests the content development features that are to be included at each stage. Amongst the four stages, the first stage involves 'basic learning', characterized by self-learning by the learners and includes basic learning materials in the form of web-based notes, presentations and video lectures. Demonstrative learning, which is the second stage, involves learning through demonstrations with the help of animations, visuals, interactive simulations and so on. The third stage is supplementary learning, which refers to learning through consulting resources, where learners are expected to do some theoretical reading. Interactive learning is the fourth stage, comprising of learning through active interactions between the learners and the content developers/instructors through discussion forums, online quizzes and chats, among other mediums. Good quality e-content must contain maximum number of these elements (NMEICT, 2009).

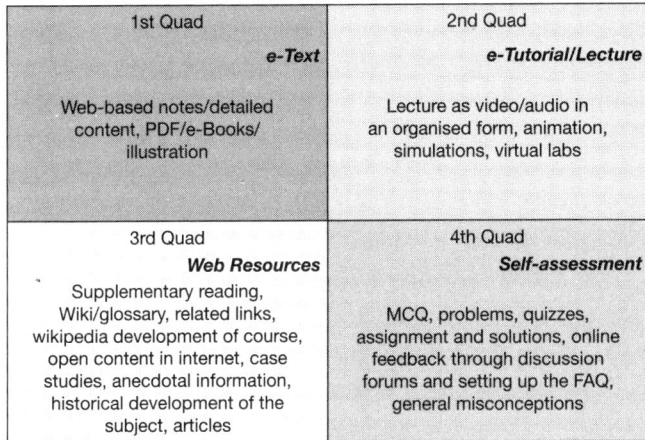

1st Quad	2nd Quad
e-Text	*e-Tutorial/Lecture*
Web-based notes/detailed content, PDF/e-Books/ illustration	Lecture as video/audio in an organised form, animation, simulations, virtual labs
3rd Quad	4th Quad
Web Resources	*Self-assessment*
Supplementary reading, Wiki/glossary, related links, wikipedia development of course, open content in internet, case studies, anecdotal information, historical development of the subject, articles	MCQ, problems, quizzes, assignment and solutions, online feedback through discussion forums and setting up the FAQ, general misconceptions

Figure 8.1 *Four Quadrants e-Learning Model*
Source: NMEICT (2009).

THE E-CONTENT DEVELOPMENT PROCESS

In India, the methodology for generation of e-learning content addresses the scalability, availability in a short span of time and relevance in view of ever-expanding disciplinary boundaries. This is achieved through involvement of large teams, so that the generated content retains its relevance when made available to learners. The generation of high quality e-content requires proper coordination between subject matter experts (SMEs) and technical experts (Rarh & Goel, 2011). The development of quality content is divided into two broad stages—Stage 1: Static content production involves development of content in document and presentation format by SMEs. Stage 2: Repurposing content into technically compatible modules, its uploading and testing by technical experts. The static content developed in Stage 1 is converted into a multimedia enriched and interactive form (Figure 8.2). In Stage 1, the SMEs develop the static content, which is then converted to e-content as per the desired output technical format compatible with the LMS by technical experts in the Stage 2.

A rigorous process of authoring, reviewing, editing is undertaken in Stage 1 before technically changing its form in Stage 2 to ensure

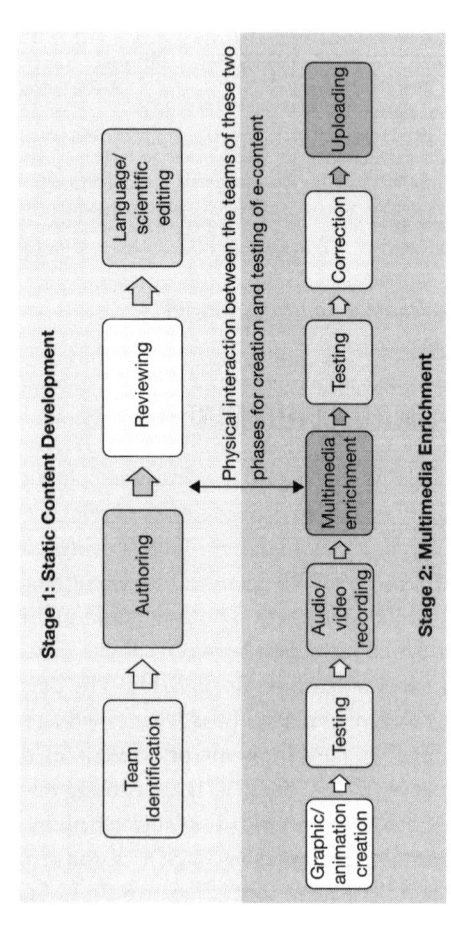

Figure 8.2 *The Important Stages of e-Content Development*

Source: Author.

the quality of e-content. Both the stages work in coordination and for the development of a large amount of e-content, where the role of coordinators at each level is significant. A prototype is developed to ensure that all the features of the content related to subject as well as technicalities to a minimum desired level have been included.

The development of a prototype is important at the initial stage, which is done by a team of experts not only having knowledge in the field of ICT and e-learning but also having a strong educational background. The experts are able to judiciously blend the suitable technologies with the needs of the learner/project. Based on the prototype, which eventually forms the output template, the input templates are evolved using instructional designing. Considering the Indian context, it is essential that the input templates are teacher-friendly, also for those teachers who may not be proficient in the use of ICTs. A recent project on the teaching–learning centres (TLCs) funded through the Pandit Madan Mohan Malaviya National Mission on Teachers and Teaching (PMMMNMTT) scheme of the Ministry of Human Resource Development (MHRD) at the SGBT Khalsa College of Delhi University has involved renowned teachers, also from remote rural areas, who may not be tech-savvy in the process of e-content development.

In the templates, all the learning elements, the heading, sub-headings, value additions as boxes and references are clearly earmarked so that at the time of re-purposing, the least amount of interaction is required between the teachers and the technical team. The input template is made synchronous with the output template so that the technical team, repurposing the content, requires minimum interactions with SMEs to ensure quick process (Bakhshi & Rarh, 2013). The TLC project at the SGBT Khalsa college has shown that the teachers can be facilitated and trained, while at the same time the system can be augmented to develop context-specific e-content.

THE CHANGING FACE OF TEACHING–LEARNING THROUGH ONLINE COURSES AND MOOCS IN INDIA

In India, *Massive Open Online Courses* (MOOCs) have immense potential for all types of learners. MOOCs with a basic philosophy of

4A's (anytime, anyone, anywhere and any number of times) have the potential to enhance the quality of education and increase the GER by providing the best quality e-learning resources to learners across country. The students from the conventional universities can use them in several ways, such as supplementary material for self-learning, as blended learning where conventional and online learning takes place in hybrid mode, and for earning credits through an entirely online mode. For students of open and distance education (ODE) universities, it has potential, as it provides them with a better alternative as compared to present day self-learning printed material.

We may observe that learners earning academic qualifications based on fully online programmes through Indian MOOCs. In addition to the regular learners, learners from geographically remote locations, physically disadvantaged learners, working professionals and learners in various challenging circumstances across the country can have the opportunity to enroll in MOOCs. The grades earned can be transferred to their parent university, if required. MOOCs also empower the teachers by providing them good content for ready reference.

Development of MOOCs in India

As a part of the Digital India initiative of the Government of India, e-content and MOOCs are being developed for various courses by different national coordinators (NC) namely, NPTEL, a group of seven Indian Institutes of Technology (IITs) and Indian Institutes of Science (IIScs) for engineering discipline courses; UGC, for non-technical postgraduate (PG) courses in 77 disciplines; Consortium for Educational Communication (CEC) for undergraduate courses in 87 disciplines; IGNOU for diploma and certificate courses, CBSE/NCERT/NIOS for Grades 9 to 12 CBSE and open education courses; IIM Bangalore for management courses and NITTR Chennai for teacher training course. These NCs overall guide, identify and invite reputed academicians of various institutions as principle investigators (PIs) as per MHRD guidelines for the development and running of MOOCs in a project mode.

MHRD, Government of India, has launched MOOCs under the NMEICT on SWAYAM platform. SWAYAM is an acronym for *Study*

Webs of Active and Young Aspiring Minds (MHRD, 2017). Technically, it has been developed as an LMS having the functionality of uploading and hosting e-content in weekly format along with online self-graded quizzes, discussion forums and so on for each MOOC (UGC, 2016b).

The MOOCs on SWAYAM to be utilized for credit transfer are being developed with some uniformity in terms of duration as per MOOCs guidelines by MHRD. A course with one to four credits is expected to be covered in 4–12 weeks' duration including the assessment component. According to the guideline, 40 hours engagement time must be provided to the learner for a three (3) credit course; it shall be around 90 hours for a six (6) credit course of learning from e-content, reading reference material, discussion forum posting and assignments.

MOOCs can be developed from scratch by adopting the requisite syllabi to meet specific learning outcomes followed by the development of e-content. As e-content production requires dedicated effort and time; it is suggested that wherever e-content is available, it can be modified/enhanced in terms of quality and can be repurposed into MOOCs. Existing high–quality e-content in modular format can be easily mapped as per syllabi requirement, the missing content can be added and it can be restructured to be delivered in weekly format. Interactive elements such as online quizzes, discussion forums and online assignments can be added to MOOCs.

For example, for PG-level MOOCs to be used for credit transfer, the e-content developed under e-PG Pathshala project of UGC are being repurposed. A conventional one-semester paper/course can be developed into one MOOC for 4–6 credits. Here, each semester paper has 35–40 modules. Each module has four components, namely, (a) e-Text, containing detailed text; (b) Self-learn, containing video-audio lectures having text, graphics and animations; (c) Self-assessment, containing self-graded e-quizzes with feedback; and (d) Know More, containing suggested readings, web-links and value additions. These four components facilitate self-learning and self-assessment of a virtual learner. In these PG MOOCs, the e-content in the modular format are arranged in 15 weeks (Figure 8.3), and in addition to these components, there are course-specific activities and discussion forums.

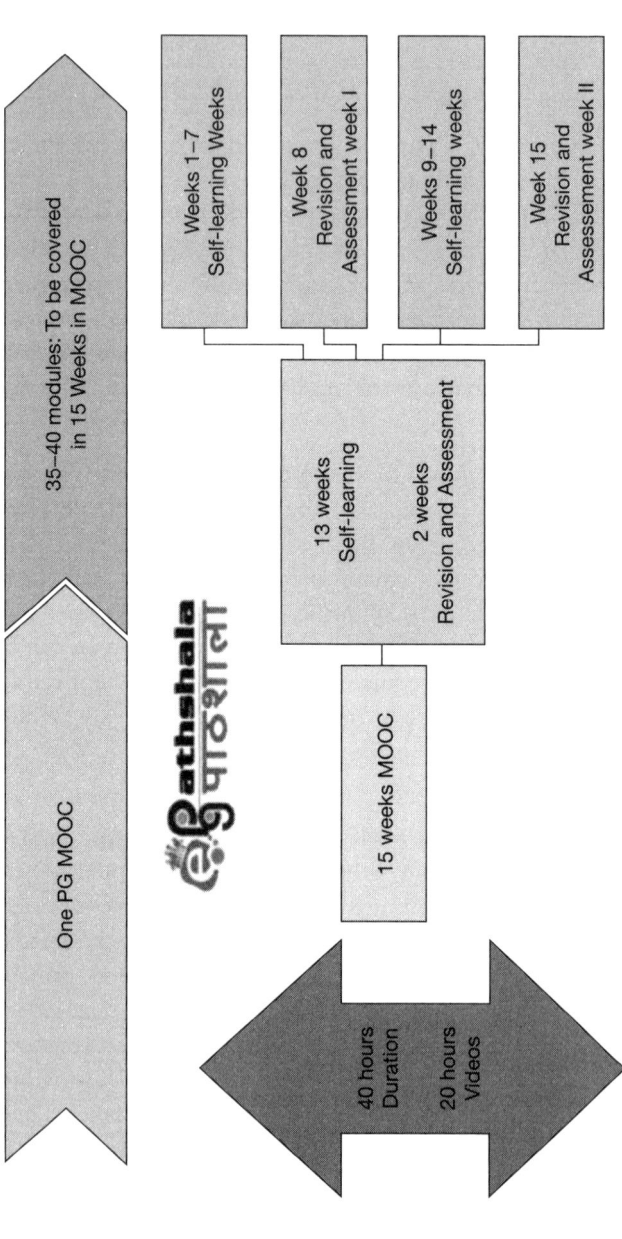

Figure 8.3 *Structure of e-PG Pathshala Postgraduate MOOCs*

Source: Author.

Of these 15 weeks, 2 weeks are for a revision and a self-study week, where the student is required to submit assignments. At the end, there is proctored examination.

UGC e-PG Pathshala Projects for e-Content and MOOCs at the Centre for e-Learning

The Centre for e-Learning (CfeL) at SGTB Khalsa College of the University of Delhi, where the author is a member of the core team, is contributing in the development of e-content and MOOCs at the national level. The main purpose of the e-PG Pathshala project is to develop high quality interactive and multimedia-enriched e-content for PG courses. Out of the all the total 77 subjects to be covered under this project, six subjects (chemistry, commerce, economics, psychology, forensic science and business economics) are being handled by the CfeL. It is for the first time that e-content for PG level is being developed for non-technical courses. For each subject, e-content for 13–16 papers, and in all, e-content for 89 papers in six subjects is being developed. These papers are then being repurposed into MOOCs (one MOOC per one semester paper). Under this massive national project, the development of nearly 3,000 videos, 35,000 pages of e-text, 40,000 questions and 15,000 value additions is nearing completion at CfeL. Value additions are the additional content under the heads 'some common misconceptions', 'did you know', 'points to ponder' and 'timelines'. The end-to-end production of the content including audio-video recording and editing are done in-house. The team at CfeL has the technical know-how on various ICT tools and educational technologies to develop and deliver online courses through LMSs. 42 MOOCs have already been created and are available on SWAYAM portal of MHRD, Government of India. The e-content in these MOOCs is developed to be learner-friendly.

MOOCs have gone through a rigorous process of quality check. The stages in the development of e-content include development of static content, its reviewing, and then multimedia enrichment with videos, animations, graphics and simulations, all of which have been done at CfeL. In each MOOC, there are weekly quizzes having MCQs with feedback to facilitate self-learning and self-assessment. Besides, there are various assignments and activities for the virtual learner in each MOOC. There is also a provision for discussion forums to answer the queries of the learners. The discussion forums are managed by teachers. Learners being the main stakeholders are also given opportunity to give feedback to further enhance the quality of the MOOCs. Nearly 1,000 academicians from across the country and about 60 full-time staff (both administrative and technical) have been involved in the development of e-content and MOOCs at CfeL. All the content creation has been done as per a unique methodology of a judicious combination of subject, technology and pedagogy for the virtual learner. Out of the UGC's 72 MOOCs ready to be offered in July 2017, at PG level from entire the nation, 42 MOOCs have been contributed by CfeL.

DEVELOPMENT OF E-CONTENT FOR ONLINE COURSES AND MOOCS

The backbone of online courses and MOOCs is the quality of e-content. A major challenge in development of e-content is in terms of quality in a timely manner. Most of the times, there are contradicting parameters. The e-content production must be done in a time-bound manner with the aim to provide students a multimedia–enriched and interactive content to enable self-learning and self-assessment. Undoubtedly, the entire e-content production process is time con-suming. The development of e-content requires proper financial management as well as coordination amongst large number of academic and technical experts, for which there are many challenges in terms of administrative, institutional and pedagogical. The generation of high quality e-learning content must be done by teachers who are SMEs in their respective knowledge areas, also referred to as *e-authors* (Angelo, 2007).

In India, in order to incentivise teachers contributing towards e-content development and delivery process, contribution towards one module has been recognised equivalent to 10 API to be counted for their academic growth (UGC, 2016a). In spite of this, the e-content production is yet to take off in a speedy manner. Many contribute towards e-content development just for the sake of earning APIs, due to which quality may suffer. There are many other challenges depending upon the methodology adopted out of the following two methodologies for static content development stage:

By Single SME: Here, only one teacher develops the entire e-content for the online course or MOOC. This methodology, although provides a renowned senior academician to develop the e-content and provide MOOCs in his or her name, has many challenges. It often takes longer to develop such courses due to research and other commitments of the senior academician. In India, not many senior academicians are forthcoming in this endeavour. They prioritize research and other commitments over this work. Majority of such content produced consist of video recordings of either class or simulation of the classroom lecture in front of a video camera. Many academicians may be excellent teachers in classroom scenario, but when they come in front of camera, they are not so effective. Most of the time, this type of e-content is devoid of animations and graphics as the senior teacher may not have the technical know-how and time to do this. Further, the review mechanism is either not required or if done, it is of not much significance.

By a Team of SMEs: Here, a team of teachers (retired, senior and junior teachers) develop the e-content of the online course or MOOC. The senior teacher keeps a track of quality and uniformity of the content being developed in modular format with 4–5 teachers simultaneously working on different modules. This process ensures timely completion, but one needs to be careful in choosing the correct team as per the expertise required for the topic(s). Further, the content generated in this manner must be subjected to plagiarism check, language editing and review before the audio/video recording. The text is converted into audio/video script by utilizing instructional designing and storyboard creation. As a result, the addition of graphics, animations and other multimedia enrichments is easier to be carried out by teachers without the involvement of the teacher supervisor. To have a better outcome for this methodology, rather than speaker videos, it is suggested to have more visuals, graphics and animations along with audio.

For both the given methodologies, rather than long videos, either interactive modules or interactive videos, or videos of small duration are better options for learner. The LMS hosting the online course/ MOOC must support it technically.

The next challenge lies in the customization of the existing e-content as per different learners' needs. In India, due to diverse regional and social backgrounds, a learner often requires bilingual content and local case studies for better understanding. The transcript of videos can be translated to other languages and provided to learner as either dubbed video or with subtitles.

Another challenge involved in the development of e-content and MOOCs is the initial and recurring cost. There is no doubt that an initial investment is required to develop a good quality e-content, but as it shall be utilized by large number of students, it will prove to be highly cost-effective. In the long run, the online courses shall over- come the economic cost required for analogous physical infrastructure, coupled with need for good teachers especially in remote areas. Online courses/MOOCs have the potential to provide quality education to every learner despite the urban-rural as well as socio-economic divides. There can be economically sustainable models of MOOCs. The fee structure could be differential for students belonging to private and public-funded institutions. Alternatively, there can be a PPP model to create skills courses as per different industry needs. In addition to academic knowledge, the technical expertise and adequate hardware is also required for creating good e-contents.

Yet another challenge is to continuously update the online course or MOOC. The MOOCs development must not be considered as a one-time activity; rather, it is a continuous process. Many of the topics are dynamic in nature, which need continuous upgradation. The MOOCs content should be revised regularly based on the feedback of learners and experts, to incorporate new knowledge in the content for development/delivery process. The teacher must track the progress of the learner, and engage the learners in activities and discussion forums as per the specified learning outcomes of the course. There must be a mechanism to handle the grievances and changes in the processes, if any, as well as other problems that learners face.

Many modern web-based systems provide a 'responsive' design that allows material and services to be accessed on mobile and desktop devices, with the aim of providing *ubiquitous access*. Besides offering access to learning materials such as podcasts and videos across multiple locations, mobile and other wearable technologies have some additional affordances that may enable new forms of learning on MOOCs. However, with the newer technologies coming so fast, there is a challenge for educational institutions and teachers to be aware of these technologies for utilizing them to the maximum and evolve better online courses with more interactivity. Interestingly, sometimes the guidelines of the funding agency or the technical limitation of the LMS are such that teachers cannot work on innovative ways to introduce interactivity as per different needs of different type of learners.

A national centre or facility and several regional centres are required to be created where teachers can be given the requisite technical support and training to develop and manage online courses or MOOCs. Teachers across the country can be awarded fellowships or avail their study leaves or come on deputation basis to learn and contribute towards the development and management of e-content, online courses and MOOCs. When the teachers go back to their parent institutions, they not only themselves adapt these tools but also motivate other teachers and students.

IMPLEMENTATION OF MOOCs

All over the world, for MOOCs and other similar platforms, although the enrolment rate is high, the completion rate is abysmally low. For the first time in the history of higher education in India, MOOCs have been introduced as a part of the formal education system to earn credits, wherein a student can earn up to 20 per cent of credits per semester through these online courses called as UGC (Credit Framework for Online Learning Courses through SWAYAM) Regulation, 2016 (UGC, 2016b).

Moreover, in the Indian context, there is considerable amount of dichotomy on how the online courses are to be assessed for their quality and equivalence, or how to assess the learning obtained through online/blended sources (learning assessment) objectively. Recently, the debate has intensified, as there are many cases of cheating in the online examinations. Thus, the problems are several-fold; one at the conceptual level and another in the implementation and methodological level. Looking at the scalability of the MOOCs, a huge challenge in terms of its implementation, especially the assessment of students, is to be planned and executed well. A major component of the assessment of MOOCs can be managed through online assessments. Online testing initially requires large infrastructural investment, but is cost-effective in the long run and can meet the challenges of a growing number of enrolments.

For successful implementation of MOOCs, MHRD envisages for the active participation of the universities to offer and/or adopt these courses. A university may act as host university or parent university, having one or both the following roles—(a) As host university: To manage and transfer credits/provide certifications for a MOOC developed and offered by PI belonging to this university/affiliated college; (b) As parent university: To offer the available MOOCs on SWAYAM platform to its students for earning credits. For both the host and the parent universities, it is important to evolve coordination centres for examination and learning to provide requisite facilities and adequate manpower for students' authentication, monitoring and smooth conduct of examinations. Such centres shall be helpful for advising, counselling, providing interface between the teachers and the learners, and rendering any academic and any other related service and assistance required by the learners.

For the proctored examination at the end of the MOOC, it is important that all the learners should be tested in a fair and transparent manner. There should be a technology-enabled interface for the management of the online as well as paper-mode examination and its evaluation to cater to the massive number of students enrolled in MOOCs. Along with the software and portal for uploading and evaluating the scripts online, these must have features where the evaluation of any test can be done by multiple examiners independently. It is recommended that the HEIs conduct the proctored online examination under the supervision of a team of observers, examiners, coordinators and/or invigilators, and at the approved centres or in collaboration with parent university on cluster basis for the students seeking credit transfer. There must be proper biometric or an alternate secure learner authentication facility and proper seating arrangement for candidates appearing for proctored examination. The uniform testing must be ensured if the examination is being conducted in more than one batch by designing questions as tagged questions (topic, level of difficulty, type) for randomized testing. Secured technical and human environment and processes must be utilized for conducting proctored examination.

CAPACITY BUILDING OF TEACHERS IN ICT SKILLS: PREPARING MODERN AGE TEACHERS

With the advent of ICT in the 21st century, the education system throughout the world is undergoing a metamorphic change in respect to the way teachers teach and the way students learn. For success in their new roles in imparting digital education to the learners, the teachers no doubt will need domain knowledge and pedagogical skills, but they will also need to be proficient in ICT skills, which can help them in both teaching and research. In imparting digital education to the learners through MOOCs, ICT skills can indeed be very helpful, especially in regard to managing discussion forums in virtual classrooms and in assessing the students online. With the MOOCs being implemented in the formal education system in India for credit transfer, there is a need to train teachers in ICT skills at a fast pace.

The Pandit Madan Mohan Malaviya National Mission on Teachers and Teaching (PMMMNMTT) of the MHRD is a mission envisaged to comprehensively address all issues related to teachers, teaching, teacher preparation and professional development. Many centres have been envisaged under the PMMMNMTT scheme such as TLCs, Faculty Development Centres (FDC), Centres for Innovations in Mathematics and Science, among others (MHRD, 2015). The TLCs aim to train teachers to build and upgrade their skills in developing discipline-specific curricula; pedagogy for conventional and virtual learner; development of learning materials (teacher material and student material) (including e-content); and subject-specific assessments and technological interventions. The following section briefly discusses the initiatives funded through PMMMNMTT scheme at several institutions.

The recently set up Guru Angad Dev TLC of MHRD at SGTB Khalsa College, University of Delhi, is focusing to meet the challenges of e-content and MOOCs development at the national level by training teachers in ICT skills and pedagogy as per their domain requirements. The objectives of the TLC are *to prepare modern-age teachers* who are proficient in the practice of ICTs, can develop e-content on their own to disseminate it to the students and perform many other digital activities to enhance the quality of education. Teachers are being trained in various levels of ICT competencies from basic level to management of MOOCS in addition to pedagogy and curriculum development. Under this TLC, many national-level workshops at both basic and advanced level are being conducted to empower the teachers in ICT skills, develop teaching kits/teacher's tools and pedagogy to enhance teaching–learning process. This centre is also developing OERs for the teaching fraternity. For OER, a unique e-Teacher's Kit has been innovated, which is being developed by the teachers getting trained through the centre and shall be made available to all the teachers. These kits are being developed for theory- and practical-based papers to provide pedagogy for transformation of conventional classrooms into blended mode by integrating domain knowledge with ICT tools.

Similarly, the Indian Institute of Science Education and Research (IISER) Bhopal, Madhya Pradesh, has established the Centre for Research in Advanced Technology for education in science (CREATES), as a TLC under the PMMMNMTT Scheme. The central theme of the CREATES is to use the technology to make education accessible to masses and to improve pedagogy. To achieve this, the centre is developing a core technology and a framework for development and deployment of e-content in science and mathematics. About five hundred micro e-content in the form of MCQs has been created in the areas of physics, chemistry and mathematics. Currently, the authors can add micro-content in the form of dynamical MCQ and fill in the blanks, with support for basic editing features. All micro-content questions support 'hint' and 'explanation' feature for systematic inquisitive guided learning. The core technology and the framework is envisaged on the principal of ease of access for content developer and learners, content development through crowd sourcing, scalability through cloud-based distribution sources and big data-friendly databases. The centre has developed a cloud-based language called Mingo, for dynamical mathematical content that gives output in MathML format, which can be accesses through most of the browsers. Mingo empowers content developers and educators to create content that can help in assessment and learning. Methods to curb plagiarisms during assessment through online quiz and exams are planned to be weaved into the framework.

Although the mentioned initiatives have focused on aspects such as interactive e-content and videos, due to low bandwidth in many parts of India, especially remote and sparsely populated areas, users find it difficult to access video-based content. The MOOC platform—'mooKIT' developed at IIT-Kanpur, Uttar Pradesh—can deliver the audio part of the lecture over a telephone. Integration with telephone exchange has enabled the facility whereby the system will call the user and play the audio.

The diversity of languages in India demands creation/availability of e-content in languages other than English. The TLC for Hindi studies at the Mahatma Gandhi Antarrashtriya Hindi Vishwavidyalaya (MGAHV), Wardha, Maharashtra have developed course material and e-content in Hindi for the Bachelors in Education (B.Ed.) and Masters in Social Work (MSW) courses. In addition, Hindi word frequency counters—'Ganak'; Hindi text standardizer 'Shodhak' and context-free Hindi POS tagger-'Hintai'; and morphological form analyzer 'Roopvishleshak'—have been made available as part of the project funded through PMMMNMTT scheme. To the well-developed international MOOC systems, these might seem basic. However, availability of these facilities in Indian languages is an important step towards increasing accessibility to the content among diverse lingual population.

CONCLUSIONS

ICTs, if properly integrated with education can change the face of higher education in India. However, with the advent of newer technologies every day, there are many challenges in adopting ICTs. The need of the hour is the judicious selection and integration of ICT tools with educational pedagogies to enhance the quality of entire education system. These must be able to provide individual customized solutions to the learners, right from guiding them in selection of course, admission, learning, examination and result, as well as helping them to find job and to pursue another related course in later part of their career.

The quality of ICT-enabled education shall ultimately depend upon the quality of interactive multimedia enriched e-content constituting MOOCs. It is imperative that this high quality e-content is developed in different languages by top experts in a time-bound manner and be made available. All this will help in enhancing not only the GER but also the quality of education imparted to the students.

With the use of ICTs, the boundaries between the regular students and ODE students shall diffuse as more and more learners opt for ODE system to enhance their knowledge and skills through flexible-time mode. The boundaries between the urban and rural students, as well as between different regions would also diffuse. But in order to make this successful, in addition to improving infrastructure, we must also empower our faculty, non-teaching staff and students in basic ICT skills so that they are able to use these technologies easily. TLCs and FDCs of MHRD created under PMMMNMTT can work towards these goals by adopting a unified approach.

REFERENCES

Agarwal, P. (2009). *Higher education in India: The need for change*. Indian Council for Research on International Economic Relations (ICRIER). Retrieved 4 June 2017, from http://dspace.cigilibrary.org/jspui/handle/123456789/20971

Alonso, F., Couchet. J., Manrique, D., & Soriano, F. J. (2006, November). *Learning objectives for e-learning instruction*. Paper at the 4th International Conference on Multimedia and Information and Communication Technologies in Education, November 2006, Spain.

Angelo, G. D. (2007, September). *E-authoring-didactic methodologies and models of e-learning content development*. International Conference on ICT for Language Learning, September 2007, Italy.

Bakhshi, A. K., & Rarh, V. (2012). Chemistry education in the 21st century. *NISCAIR-CSIR, India*, 38–42.

Bakhshi, A. K., & Rarh, V. (2013). ICT for enhancing the quality of open and distance education through e-learning. In A. Chaturvedi & K. V. Singh (Eds), *Open and distance learning in India: Challenges and prospect* (pp. 13–35). New Delhi: IGNOU.

Béteille, A. (2005, July). Universities as public institutions. *Economic and Political Weekly, 40*(31), 3377–3381.

Clark, Ruth C., & Mayer, Richard E. (2011). *E-learning and the science of instruction: Proven guidelines for consumers and designers of multimedia learning.* NJ: John Wiley & Sons.

MHRD (Ministry of Human Resource Development). (2015). *Scheme of Pandit Madan Mohan Malaviya National Mission on Teachers and Teaching (PMMMNMTT).* New Delhi: Government of India.

———. (2016). *All India survey of higher education 2015–16.* New Delhi: Ministry of Human Resource Development, Government of India.

———. (2017). *SWAYAM portal.* New Delhi: MHRD, Government of India. Retrieved 10 June 2017, from SWAYAM: https://swayam.gov.in/

NMEICT (National Mission on Education Through ICT) Mission Document. (2009). *National Mission on Education through ICT. New Delhi:* MHRD, GOI. Retrieved 1 June 2017, from http://www.sakshat.ac.in/

Rarh, V., & Goel, A. (2011). *A methodology for e-quiz content production for e-learning.* Second International Conference on Emerging Applications of Information Technology, 145–148, 19–20 February 2011.

The William and Flora Hewlett Foundation (2008). *Open educational resources.* Retrieved 1 June 2017, from http://www.hewlett.org/strategy/open-educational-resources/

UGC (University Grants Commission). (2016a). *UGC (minimum qualifications for appointment of teachers and other academic staff in universities and colleges and measures for the maintenance of standards in higher education) (4th Amendment), regulations, 2016.* New Delhi: UGC.

———. (2016b). *The Gazette of India—Part III, Section 4.* 20 July. Retrieved September 2017, from UGC: https://www.ugc.ac.in/pdfnews/0272836_moocs.pdf

Chapter 9

Student Assessments in Higher Education

K. Pushpanadham

INTRODUCTION

The role of higher education (HE) as a major driver of economic development is well established, and this role will increase with further changes in technology, globalization and demographic impact. Today, higher education institutions (HEIs) are more diversified and are characterized by (a) massive expansion and wider participation; (b) privatization; (c) interdisciplinary and multi-disciplinary academic programmes; (d) broader adoption and more integrated use of disruptive technologies; (e) greater internationalization; and (f) new modes and roles of governance, including increasing demand for outcomes, quality and accountability. All these call for a new landscape for learning in HE. One must realize that teaching, learning and assessment constitute the integrated and indissoluble components of any education system. The objectives of education can only be achieved adequately and satisfactorily if this cohesion is accepted and appreciated.

Assessment has been defined in the educational literature as a systematic process of collecting information about the students' progress towards the learning goals (OECD, 2008). Students' performance can be measured in various ways, including traditional paper and pencil tests, extended responses (essays), performance of authentic task, teacher observation and student self-reports. Tests are for measuring students' performance on a specific task(s). Measurement is the process of obtaining a numerical description of the degree to which an individual possesses a particular characteristic (Linn & Miller, 2005, p. 26). Several research studies have revealed that assessment influences the teaching–learning process, accountability and learning outcomes on the part of the learner and teacher as well as the institution (Birenbaum & Feldman, 1998; Gordon, 2008; Shepard, 2000).

Assessment in education is probably the outcome of the last century and there is a growing demand for systematic and thoughtful student learning assessment across all levels of education. The student assessment system in the HE sector comprises of all policies and practices related to student assessment and evaluations. This includes assessment and examination policies, examination structures and practices, national assessments, national standards, classroom assessments and certification. Effective functioning of a student assessment system is determined by its 'backwash effect' (Biggs, 1995), which means the impact of assessment on students learning, teaching, curriculum and instruction, and educational goals.

Assessment plays many roles in education. From a learner's perspective, there are three main roles for assessments: choose, learn and qualify. Assessment data help learners to choose the particular course or programme, identify the learners' progress and difficulties and also help in identifying whether the learners can be certified or qualify to be awarded degrees and diplomas (Black & Wiliam, 1998). From the organizational perspective, there are three critical functions of assessment: select, monitor and hold accountable. The assessment data helps the organizations to determine which learners are allowed to proceed to the next level of education, monitor the learning path of students and track the effective functioning of other different sub-systems, and to hold people accountable to their tasks.

Among the academia, there is a great deal of dissatisfaction regarding the recent assessment approaches in HE, and it raised several questions with respect to what is essential to teach in HE and how such teaching–learning should be organized and assessed. The question remains whether students are taught so that they can excel on a test or whether they are taught to construct meaning that will sustain in the long term and evoke curiosity to learn further.

TEACHING, LEARNING AND ASSESSMENT

Teaching and learning in HE is the great concern today as the heart of any academic institution lies with the learning outcomes and transformative learning of students. Learning at HE is essentially constructive, cumulative, self-regulated, goal-oriented, situated, collaborative and individually different (De Corte, 1996). The engagement of the learner in the process of learning, teaching and assessment is important, through which learners select, perceive, interpret and integrate new information to form a coherent and meaningful whole by integrating prior knowledge and former experiences (Dochy, Segers & Buehl, 1999). These changes in learning require innovation in teaching as well as assessment practices. With the rapid changes in teaching and learning processes in HE, assessment of students has become a point of concern. This is because the existing assessment evaluates the memorizing capacities and information accumulated by the student(s) rather than critical thinking and other competencies relevant to the contemporary society.

Teaching aims at learning of students, and to know about students' learning, assessment is required. There are many forms of learner assessment in HE, and all of them involve students' work, which could be written or oral, individual or group/collaborative, and project-based and/or by demonstration. This process helps to understand the learning outcomes of students in a specific course or in the overall programme. Student work empowers learners to chart their own journey of learning. It is worth noting that outcome-based education (OBE) clearly describes learning objectives. To the learner, the learning outcomes describe what is learnt, including the competencies. To the teacher, they describe how successful the methodology of teaching is and deciding what teaching–learning activities can lead to learning what should have been learnt. To the regulatory agencies and government, they provide indicators for audit, accreditation and further funding (Biggs, 1996; Davis, Pool & Mits-Cash, 2000).

The initial task of the teachers in a formal education system is to define and state precisely the learning outcomes at a particular level. Logically, the next move is to plan learning experiences appropriate for enabling students to attain them. Such learning experiences vary with the kind of programme and also the level of students. Now it is obviously necessary to know how far the learning experiences have actually resulted into to learning outcomes in terms of the defined objectives. This evaluation process will certainly identify the effectiveness of the teaching and learning process that is conceived and also experienced.

The main goal of assessment is to determine the effectiveness of the institution in transforming students as self-learners. Assessment involves

> [M]aking our expectations explicit and public; setting appropriate criteria and expectations for learning quality; systematically gathering, analyzing, and interpreting evidence to determine how well performance matches those expectations and standards; and using the resulting information to document, explain, and improve performance. (Angelo, 1995, p. 7)

This also includes the assessment of both skills and competencies of the learner acquired over the course of studies, and continuously assessed using scaffolding approach through formative assessment and feedback (Fry, Ketteridge & Marshall, 2009).

ASSESSMENT AND LEARNING OUTCOMES

Assessments are a vital component of an education system. Assessment is defined as 'the process of obtaining information that is used to make educational decisions about students, to give feedback to the students about their progress, strengths and weaknesses, to judge instructional effectiveness and curricular adequacy and to inform policy' (AFT, NCME, NEA, 1990). Appropriate assessment in HE is an ongoing debate across the academic community. Particularly, the emergence of formative and summative assessment as two different formats has attracted educators' attention in the current literature. Formative assessment is introduced as an ongoing process of evaluating students' learning, providing feedback to adjust instruction and learning, and improving the curriculum, whereas the summative assessment, on the other hand, is bound to administrative decisions and assigning grades to the tests.

Bloom (1969) asserts that when assessment is aligned with the process of teaching and learning, it will have 'a positive effect on students' learning and their motivation'. Assessment in general accounts for supporting learning (formative), certifying the achievement or potential of individuals (summative), and evaluating the quality of educational institutions or programmes (evaluative). A distinction is made between 'assessments *for* learning' and 'assessment *of* learning'. While the former describes the process of assessment as a support for learning, the latter describes the nature of assessment or the product (Black & William, 1998; Wiliam & Thompson, 2008). Because assessment significantly affects students' approach to learning, assessment paradigms have shifted from 'testing learning of students to assessing for students learning' (Birenbaum & Feidman, 1998, p. 92).

Assessment of student work serves a number of different purposes including structuring, guiding and enhancing student learning, certifying student achievement and admitting students to subsequent learning opportunities. A comprehensive student assessment is an indicator of quality in HE, and its efficiency is greatly influenced by the quality and timing of the feedback given to students. Good feedback occurs soon after the task is completed by the student, provides clear indications of the strengths and weaknesses of the student's work, gives clear guidance on how to perform better on future tasks of a similar nature, and helps to motivate the student to put further effort into learning. Assessment should take into account the university's teaching and learning plan and expected graduate profile, that is, the descriptors of attributes, or knowledge, skills and attitudes.

ICT AS TOOLS FOR STUDENT ASSESSMENT

Information and communication technologies (ICT) have the potential to make the assessment process more authentic, flexible and user-friendly. Teachers use computers to construct their assessment tasks, to deliver these tasks to the relevant students, and to record and provide feedback and grades to these students. ICT resources can be programmed to critically analyze the students' performance and provide feedback to the students with respect to their strengths and weaknesses, and also help teachers to understand the student learning difficulties. The e-assessment basically uses digital devices to assist in the construction, delivery, storage or reporting of student assessment tasks, responses, grades or feedback. With the help of technology, e-assessments can use a multitude of formats, including text documents or portable document formats, and multimedia formats such as sound, video or images. It can also involve complex simulations or games. E-assessment can be undertaken by students in groups or individually, and can be organized with large numbers of students in a synchronous or asynchronous manner. E-assessments can be used to test many different capabilities and skills that are developed by students.

Many universities in India have adopted online examinations for entrance tests or university examinations, which are assessment of prior learning. Symbiosis Centre for Distance Learning (SCDL) has more than 200,000 active students from all states of India, and over 40 different countries conducts over 60,000 examinations each month and approximately 800,000 examinations each year with the help of a computerized examination system, which is world class. Various internationally recognized large-scale examinations such as GRE, GMAT and TOEFL have long been following this approach.

PROFESSIONAL ETHICS IN ASSESSMENT PRACTICES

Assessment results have a great value to the learner and also in the society as these grades will help the students to access several employment opportunities and also further education. Therefore assessment practices in the university must be based on sound ethical standards on the part of the institution as well as the teachers who conduct assessment. Authentic assessment is very much essential in the system of HE. Plagiarism software is already in use in several universities to check the originality of the research work done by the students at postgraduate and doctoral levels. However, the malpractices in the examination and assessment, such as copying, fraudulent entry of assessment data, forging of mark sheets and certificates and plagiarism, are indicative of the fear of assessments and outcomes. This fear is the result of lack of teaching and learning environment, which deprives the learners in developing capacities and competencies and building confidence. Lack of institutional resources, in terms of infrastructure and faculty, leads to a degraded teaching–learning environment. Thus, one solution of addressing malpractices and fraudulent events in examinations and assessments is to create resource-rich teaching–learning conditions, enabling teachers to be accountable to teaching and developing critical analytical skills amongst learners. In addition, a much necessitated change is required to bring about examination reforms, which focus on assessing critical and analytical abilities of the learners, rather than information memorizing capacities. These reforms should also revise the existing pattern of assessment questions, including the multiple choice questions (MCQ), which, in the current format do not assess the subject-specific critical abilities of the learners.

Professional conduct and responsibilities of teachers in use of assessments can be ordered within three levels: (a) legal issues, (b) ethical issues and (c) professional issues. The practices and behaviours within these three levels are certainly interrelated. Legal, ethical and professional issues form a continuum of standards for professional conduct wherein laws and government regulations are legal mandates that affect all individuals to protect their rights and equal educational opportunities. Ethical codes may range from enforceable, to exemplary to educational principles that guide the professional behaviour and conduct of members of any profession. Professional ethics is the code of conduct and self-regulation. In addition, institutions can provide an environment conducive to the teachers to successfully operationalize professional ethics and code of conduct without any fear or restraint.

STUDENT ASSESSMENT IN INDIAN HIGHER EDUCATION

The word 'examination' has a high emotional tone in the education system right from kindergarten to HE. Anxiety, fear and phobic reactions in students are generally seen during the examinations. These expressions are even seen in parents as well. However, there is no education system without assessment, which may or may not be in the form of examination. Assessments help in evaluating students' performance and also provide feedback to the educators on the effectiveness of their instructional designs and strategies.

A chorus of criticism is repeatedly heard from academia and society about the deteriorating quality of HE. It is well known that one of the important components of HE is the manner in which students' learning outcomes and academic performance is assessed. A great degree of diversity has been observed in terms of assessment and grading of the students in the university system at present (UGC, 2003).

In this regard, RUSA (2013) has recommended a semester system for determining the quantum of work to be completed by the students in different programmes, choice-based credit system (CBCS) to enhance learning opportunity and making inter-institutional transferability of students possible. The University Grants Commission (UGC) has introduced flexibility for working students to complete programmes over an extended period of time by making use of digital learning platforms and the thrust on issues related to employability. Streamlining admission process, and continuous internal evaluation in addition to end of semester evaluation and mandatory accreditation of HEIs are the efforts of the government to make HE relevant.

University graduate students who have secured first division or top performers in various public examinations sometimes find it difficult clear national and international examinations such as CAT, NET, NEET, Banking Services, UPSC and GRE to name a few. The statistics reveal that the employability of the graduates in India is very low (FICCI, 2014). Nationally, 300,000 graduates appear for the UGC-NET examination every session and the success rate is less than 5 per cent (MHRD, 2014). These data inform the system to reflect on two aspects: one is on the quality of teaching–learning and other is on the reliability and quality of the assessment of the students.

POLICY INITIATIVES TO ADDRESS ISSUES IN STUDENT ASSESSMENT IN HIGHER EDUCATION

The UGC (2012) has made recommendations to improve the standards of student assessment in HE. The key recommendations with respect to the assessment for learning include change from the annual system to semester system in teaching and evaluation. Continuous internal assessment is recommended to formatively assess students' learning outcomes. A 10-point grading system and its equivalence in terms of percentage of marks are suggested to be followed uniformly across universities and disciplines. However, the evaluation methodology may vary across disciplines/institutions. The commission also recommends that the examination process be made transparent in terms of properly documenting the pattern of papers, evaluation methodology and disciplinary rules, and communicated to students well in advance. Use of ICTs can ensure appropriate and effective feedback mechanism.

Similarly, UGC (2012) has provided the guidelines for the successful implementation of the CBCS with semester breakups and grading pattern. The key facets of the new semester system include two semesters each of five to six months in duration per academic year. The teaching workload is revised in correspondence with credits with 15 teaching hours leading to one credit point. One semester must include a minimum of 90 teaching days spread over 18 weeks, with clear definitions on the duration of instruction, assessment and end-of-semester examinations for evaluation. Instruction is to be divided into three components: lecture, tutorial and practical (lab, fieldwork and case studies), with credits weighted for each component based on hourly contact per week. With the introduction of continuous and comprehensive assessment (CCA), new assessment protocols have been suggested, based on grades rather than marks, and the use of cumulative grade point scores to define overall achievement. Assessment protocol would include both internal and external evaluation. Internal evaluation would include essays, tutorial presentations, lab work and term papers. End-of-semester evaluation would seek to assess the skills and knowledge of students on cumulative grade points.

With respect to CBCS, recommendations were made to promote flexible learning patterns with increased course choices and provision to transfer credits between institutions. The RUSA (2013) policy document is outlining a process of curriculum stocktaking and revision every three years. Credits under the CBCS calculated in terms of classroom contact hours and volume of content studied. A semester credit is measured as one lecture (one hour) per week over the course of the semester, a minimum of two hours of tutorials a week, or one practical session per week. Most courses of study are weighted at three or four credits. The specific credit make-up of a course will vary from subject to subject and from institution to institution, based on curriculum design and desired learning outcomes.

All the institutions of higher learning in India have incorporated the changes in their student assessment system based on the guidelines. It is interesting to understand the current practices of student assessment in Indian universities.

CURRENT PRACTICES OF STUDENT ASSESSMENT IN INDIAN UNIVERSITIES

With the recommendations of the UGC, universities in India have moved away from marks and division system in student assessment and introduced grading and CBCS. Here are some of the cases for broad understanding of student assessment in Indian universities.

An instance of the Maharaja Sayajirao University of Baroda, Gujarat, is discussed here. The university has introduced semester system and CBCS, and a new pattern of grading in 2013–2014. Each course is of some credits, and each credit requires 15 hours of teaching in a semester. The students' academic performance in each course offered during a semester is evaluated on a 10-point scale. With regard to pattern of assessment, a student's academic performance in a particular course is evaluated through a mid-semester examination having weightage of 30 per cent, which is an internal assessment (IA) at the faculty/department where the concerned teacher will evaluate the student performance. The end of semester examination is an external assessment conducted by the university (UA) with a weightage of 70 per cent where the subject experts from outside the university are appointed. Passing shall be decided on the combined result of mid-semester and end-semester examination in the respective courses, and a minimum of 40 per cent is required for passing the examination. For each semester, a semester grade point average (SGPA) is recorded, which is averaged out over the course of a programme as a cumulative grade point average (CGPA). In the Faculty of Family and Community Sciences, the undergraduate (UG (hons.)) courses have 144 credits, where as general UG courses have 120 credits. The postgraduate courses have 60 credits. In the Faculty of Social work, postgraduate course have 104 credits and in the Faculty of Commerce the UG courses have 120 credits.[1]

As evident from the earlier discussion, even within the university system, the credits attached to the courses are different across the disciples and also across the levels of the study. There are universities in India where there is a provision of earning more credits and get qualified to be bachelors with a 'major with emphasis' and still more credits will lead to 'double major'. And also students who are unable to complete the full credits required of a UG programme will be considered for the awards of certificate and diploma.

Indian Institute of Management Ahmedabad (IIM-A), is another instance which offers two-year postgraduate programme and four types of courses spread across two years: foundational, tools and techniques oriented, and functional and perspective-building courses. IIM-A also provides opportunities for project courses and courses of independent study during the second year. The summer internship is a powerful source of practical managerial insights, validation of management concepts, and valuable market knowledge.

The elective courses, which are offered in the second year of the programme, allow students to choose a bouquet of courses that interest them and develop proficiency in the areas of their choice. The elective courses consist of in-class courses, often with project components, offered by different areas, courses of independent study, exchange programmes and intensive field courses. Several learning opportunities are provided to the students.

Regular courses help students to learn tools, techniques, skills and concepts primarily through classroom discussion, and seminar courses provide specified number of class sessions and time for research to explore the frontiers of knowledge. Projects are designed to suit individual learning needs. The course of independent study (CIS) allows

---

[1] MSU Baroda. Website. *MSU Baroda Home.* Retrieved 26 July 2017, from www.msubaroda.ac.in

exploration of a topic in the student's area of interest. It makes possible the integration of several fields of study in searching for the solution to a single problem. It provides valuable experience in the research process such as definition of the problem, search for relevant data, analysis of the data and drawing conclusions. Thus CIS allows for individual initiative, judgment and resourcefulness with a problem-based learning framework, well beyond what is possible in the regular curriculum.

Different assessment techniques such as quizzes, midterm exams, seminar presentations, oral exams, project work and end-term exams are effectively used to assess the student learning outcomes as well the programme potential. The comprehensive project (CP) provides an opportunity to learn in a real world context. This provides a vehicle for integration of learning across functions and disciplines. The assessment criteria include that the project must be organization-based and not entirely on secondary data or library work. Furthermore, the project must be multifunctional and multidisciplinary in nature.

The proportionate relative weightage of the other components for a specific course is at the discretion of the instructor. The evaluation scheme for each course is conveyed to the students at the beginning of the course along with the course outline by the course instructor. This information about the expected outcomes helps the learners to focus on the utility of the learning activities/tasks.

The results of individual learning are also reflected in the percentile grade of the group of learners. About 30 per cent students may be given 'A' grade g (including A+, A and A-), grading will be done by the faculty themselves and they decide the percentage of 'B' or 'C' grades depending upon the number of students and their class performance. This enables learners to understand their relative learning in correspondence with their peers. The grades submitted by the faculty are discussed in the moderation committee along with the course faculty and postgraduate programme committee members. This exercise records and improves consistency in learners' assessments. Every student is required to achieve the minimum prescribed standards for the programmes, which may vary according the programmes and the institutions. These standards also describe scores required for qualifying the course, placement support and merit award.[2]

The practice of the Indian Institute of Technology, Mumbai (IIT-M), is somewhat different than that of the previous institutions. IIT-M offers graduate and postgraduate programmes in engineering and technology. The institute follows a specialized credit-based semester system. There are three semesters in a year. The semester that begins in July (July to November, Semester I) is known as the autumn semester, and the semester that begins in January (January to April, Semester II) is known as the spring semester. During the summer vacation, that is (May and June), there is one additional semester for summer courses known as Semester III. The institute runs summer courses: self-study courses (subject to availability and consent of the faculty) to provide an opportunity to clear backlog course/s, if any.

In general, a certain quantum of work, measured in terms of credits, is laid down as the requirement for a particular degree. The student acquires credits by passing courses every semester, the amount of credit associated with a course being dependent upon the number of hours of instruction per week in that course. There are mainly two types of courses: lecture courses and laboratory courses. Lecture courses consist of lecture and tutorial hours, but may have attached practical hours in special cases. Laboratory courses consist of practical hours, but may have attached tutorial hours in special cases.

The various modes of assessment used for rating students' performance in a lecture course include quizzes, class tests (open or closed book), home assignments, group assignments, viva-voce, and the mid-semester test and semester-end examination. The distribution of weightage for the assessment through the various modes is normally as follows. There is one mid-semester test of two hours duration for each course, held as per the schedule fixed in the academic calendar. In addition, two quizzes (or one quiz and one test) and/or assignments or viva-voce make up the rest of the in-semester assignment. The relative weightage is approximately 30 per cent for the mid-semester test, and 20 per cent for the two quizzes/tests/assignments/viva-voce and active participation

---

[2] IIM-A (n.d.) *Post Graduate Programme in Management*. Retrieved 15 May 2018, from https://www.iima.ac.in/web/pgp/programme

in discussions in class room. For active participation, the instructor may set aside up to a maximum of 10 per cent of the total marks. The relative weightage for the semester-end examination is 50 per cent. The semester-end examination covers the full syllabus of the course. The end-semester examination is compulsory for all students. The assessment in laboratory course is based on supervision of the student's work, their performance in viva-voce examinations and group discussions, the quality of their work as prescribed through laboratory journals, and an end-semester test that contains an experiment or a written exam.

The performance of the students in a semester is assessed on a 10-point scale and is indicated by a number called Semester Performance Index (SPI). The SPI is the weighted average of the grade points obtained in all the courses registered by the student during the semester. An up-to-date assessment of the overall performance of a student from the beginning of the course is obtained by calculating Cumulative Performance Index (CPI). The CPI is the weighted average of the grade points obtained in all the courses registered by the student since their entry to the institute. At the end of each semester, the grade report, which reflects the performance of students in that semester, is sent to the faculty advisors, students and parents. The purpose is to share the learners' progress with the major stakeholders, that is, learner, faculty and parents.

The Medical Council of India (MCI), a statutory body with the responsibility of establishing and maintaining high standards of medical education and recognition of medical qualifications in India, established the norms related to student assessment consisting of day-to-day assessment and evaluation of student assignment, preparation for seminar, and clinical case presentation (MCI, 1997). Regular periodical examinations are conducted throughout the course. Day-to-day progress records are given importance during internal assessment, where the weightage for the internal assessment is 20 per cent of the total marks in each subject. The minimum eligibility to appear in final university examination is set at 50 per cent of the total marks for prescribed for internal assessment.

Internal assessment relates to different ways in which students participate in learning process during the semester. This includes the assessment on the preparation of subject for students seminar, preparation of a clinical case for discussion, clinical case study/problem solving exercise, participation in project for health care in the community (planning stage to evaluation), proficiency in carrying out a practical or a skill in small research project and an MCQ test after completion of a semester teaching. Each item tested shall be objectively assessed and recorded. Some of the items can be assigned as homework/vacation work. The pattern of examination for formative evaluation (internal assessment) for the first semester will have one periodical short test each carrying 25 marks each in theory and practical. There will be a terminal examination before the completion of each semester, and it includes one theory paper of 60 marks, practical of 40 marks and viva-voce of 20 marks. Viva-voce/oral includes evaluation of management approach and handling of emergencies. Candidate's skill in interpretation of common investigative data, x-rays, identification of specimens and electrocardiography (ECG) is evaluated. Internship of the medical students is also assessed.

The earlier cases explain the different types of student assessment practices across disciplines and also across different levels of education. The common practices of student assessment in HEIs are achievement tests, viva-voce/oral examination, project work and seminar presentation. Portfolios, quizzes, open book examinations, reflective journals, simulations, self-assessments and peer assessments are some other assessment practices which are not as common but are gaining currency. The element of external and internal assessment that is weaved into the assessment system builds trust into academic quality.

Managing large-scale assessment systems are resource intensive, besides requiring good management practices. In resource-starved HEIs, especially the state-funded ones, planning and management of assessment practices as described earlier is challenging. However, good assessment practices build trust on the quality of HEIs. Conversely, poor assessment practices have de-motivating and regressive impact on teaching–learning due to lack of accountability measures.

TEACHER COMPETENCE IN EDUCATIONAL ASSESSMENT

In order to make assessment more meaningful and purposeful in the process of teaching and learning, there is need to evolve standards for teacher competencies in educational assessment of students, which currently are not existent in Indian HE. The HE professional associations in India can play an important role in evolving the standards. Internationally, the recommended teacher competencies include selection of appropriate assessment methods for instructional planning; design and development of relevant assessment methods; grading and interpretation of results; competencies for using assessment results when making decisions about individual students; planning, teaching and developing curriculum; and improving the quality of the institution and communicating assessment results. However, to put standards in place and to develop the competencies in HE professionals, appropriate professional support and development is required. Currently, Indian professionals learn about the assessment competencies on job and mostly delinked from the learning goals.

GENERAL PERCEPTIONS ABOUT STUDENT ASSESSMENT IN HIGHER EDUCATION

Studying the perception of teachers and students of HE on the existing practices of student assessment could help in building trust, getting feedback to review the assessment system and understanding how teachers and learners link assessment with learning goals and future expectations, such as employability. A study was undertaken under the aegis of the Centre for Policy Research in Higher Education (CPRHE) of the National Institute of Educational Planning and Administration (NIEPA) to understand aspects of teaching–learning in Indian HE. 'Assessment practices' at the university and college level was amongst the themes covered through the study. The data was collected from 500 graduate students of a public university.

The data with respect to the perceptions of the students on the current assessment practices revealed that, students consider assessment a powerful motivator, and a major vehicle for learning and facing the examinations. Current assessment practices are directing students towards 'surface approaches' to learning, that describe an intention to complete the learning task with little personal engagement, exclusively suitable to the pattern of examination with very restricted conceptual understanding. With respect to the students' preference and assessment expectations, the study revealed that multiple-choice format was preferred along with essay type pattern. This preference was perhaps due to the popular national and international examination patterns for further occupation or education. There was only one dimension of which students thought that essay exams were more appropriate and thus more favourable than the multiple choice type, namely, for the purpose of representing one's knowledge in the subject. Majority of the students perceived traditional assessment tasks as arbitrary and irrelevant as they do not reflect effective learning. In addition, the pattern of questioning in the examinations was perceived as not challenging and not testing the higher cognitive abilities. Thus, the students perceived the assessment practices as routine and stressful. They also opined that the way in which semester system is conducted has resulted into continuous written examinations and the time for learning and teaching has drastically reduced. The students wanted the feedback on the assessment to be more informative and without much delay.

CONCLUSION

One of the important components of HE is the manner in which students' academic performance is evaluated. A great degree of diversity across universities and disciplines has been observed in terms of assessment and grading of the students in the university system at present. UGC and other higher and professional education regulatory bodies in India have been designing new guidelines for student assessment and making a sincere effort in standardizing the examination system in India. However, there are still functional challenges embracing the educators in the HE. Teacher autonomy and accountability issues in student assessment are always a matter of discussion. Judicious combinations of variety of alternative assessment techniques need to be employed to carefully assess the student performance.

India is one of the largest HE systems in the world, having one of the highest numbers of student enrolment in HE. Student assessment in HE is the matter of concern today in the context of massifying the HE system. India needs to create a globally relevant and competitive HE system focusing on student learning goals and outcomes. The important component of HE is the manner in which students learn and perform on assessments. In this regard, assessment reforms focused on competence-based learning outcomes need to be undertaken. Professional competencies of teachers for student assessments should be defined, and support should be provided to develop those competencies. Management practices should be streamlined and refined to reduce the fear factors of students, build their confidence in the assessment practices, and to support learning and address the assessment of data management requirements of a masifying HE system. Clear guidelines should be developed by the regulatory bodies in this regard. The guideline should also allow autonomy to the institutions and faculty to undertake context-specific assessment reforms. At the decision-making level, the evaluation pattern and methods should be reviewed and revised in view of feedback from students, faculty and other stakeholders to make evaluation supporting of learning goals and more robust. Research in assessment practices, and their impacts on student learning and outcomes should be encouraged to feed into evidence-based policy-making on assessment. All these measures would require resource enriched learning environments, including teachers, infrastructures and technologies.

REFERENCES

(AFT, NCME AND NEA). American Federation of Teachers, National Council of Measurement in Education and National Education Association. (1990), Standards for teacher competence in educational assessment of students. *Educational Measurement: Issues and Practice*, *9*(4), 30–32.

Angelo, T. A. (1995). Improving classroom assessment to improve learning: Guidelines from research and practice. *Assessment Update*, 7, 1–2. doi:10.1002/au.3650070602

Birenbaum, M., & Feldman, R. A. (1998). Relationships between learning patterns and attitudes towards two assessment formats. *Educational Research*, *40*(1), 90–97.

Biggs, J. B. (1995). Assumptions underlying new approaches to assessment. Curriculum Forum, 4*(2)*, 1–22.

———. (1996). Enhancing teaching through constructive alignment. *Higher Education*, *32*(3), 347–364. doi:10.1007/BF00138871

Black, P., & Wiliam, D. (1998). Inside the black box: Raising standards through classroom assessment. *Phi Delta Kappan, 80*(2), 139–148.

Bloom, B. S. (1969). Some theoretical issues relating to educational evaluation. In R. W. Tyler (Ed.), *Educational evaluation: New roles, new means* (National Society for the Study of Education Yearbook, Vol. 68, Part 2, pp. 26–50). Chicago, IL: University of Chicago Press.

Davis, D. R., Pool, J. E., & Mits-Cash, M. (2000). Issues in implementing a new teacher assessment system in a large urban school district: Results of a qualitative field study. *Journal of Personnel Evaluation in Education, 14*(4), 285–306. doi:10.1023/A:1011139203370

De Corte, E. (1996). Active learning within powerful learning environments/Actief leren binnen krachtige leeromgevingen. *Impuls, 26*(4), 145–156.

Dochy, F., Segers, M., & Buehl, M. M. (1999). The relation between assessment practices and outcomes of studies: The case of research on prior knowledge. *Review of Educational Research, 69*(2), 147–188.

FICCI. (2014). *Higher education in India: Moving towards global relevance and competitiveness.* Kolkata: Ernst & Young LLP.

Fry, H., Ketteridge, S., & Marshall, S. (2009). *A handbook for teaching and learning in higher education,* 3rd ed. Oxon: Routledge.

Gordon, S. (2008). *Testing times: The uses and abuses of assessment.* London: Routledge.

Linn, R. L., & Miller, M. D. (2005). *Measurement and assessment in teaching.* Upper Saddle River, NJ: Prentice Hall.

MCI (Medical Council of India). (1997). *Regulations on graduate medical education.* New Delhi: MCI.

Messick, S. (1995). Standards of validity and the validity of standards in performance assessment. *Educational Measurement: Issues and Practice, 14*, 5–8. doi:10.1111/j.1745-3992.1995.tb00881.x

MHRD (Ministry of Human Resource Development). (2014). *Annual report 2013–2014.* New Delhi: MHRD.

OECD (Organisation for Economic Cooperation and Development). (2008). *Tertiary education for the knowledge society.* Paris: OECD Publishing. Retrieved 26 July 2017, from www.oecd.org/edu/tertiary/review

RUSA (Rashtriya Uchchatar Shiksha Abhiyan). (2013). *Rashtriya Uchchatar Shiksha Abhiyan: National Higher Education Mission.* Ministry of Human Resource and Development, in collaboration with Tata Institute of Social Sciences. New Delhi: Government of India.

Shepard, L. (2000). The role of assessment in a learning culture. *Educational Researcher, 29*(7), 4–14.

UGC (University Grants Commission). (2012). *Higher education in India at a glance.* New Delhi: University Grants Commission/Government of India.

———. (2003). *Higher education in India: Issues, concerns and new directions.* New Delhi: University Grants Commission.

Wiliam, D., & Thompson, M. (2008). Integrating assessment with learning: What will it take to make it work? In C. A. Dwyer (Ed.). *The future of assessment: Shaping teaching and learning* (pp. 53–82). New York, NY: Lawrence Erlbaum Associates.

Chapter 10

Choice-based Credit System (CBCS) and Semester System in Indian Higher Education

M. Rajivlochan and
Meeta Rajivlochan

INTRODUCTION

This chapter discusses two recent academic reforms introduced in the Indian higher education (HE) sector, that is, the choice-based credit system (CBCS) and the semester system in colleges and universities. The CBCS and semester system have been introduced alongside changes in the admission procedures, curriculum revision, and development and examination reforms in order to raise the standards and quality at the institutional level. Besides raising standards, another reason for the introduction of reforms is to address the ambition of the policy-makers and various stakeholders in making Indian HE institutions globally competitive, linked to international HE arena and become important players in the knowledge economy. To that effect, it becomes imperative to introduce certain reforms which have been internationally introduced and pave way for more in the future.

THE UGC IMPLEMENTS THE CBCS

The University Grants Commission (UGC, 2015) expressed its concerns over the rigid structure of Indian HE. It clearly mentions the need and direction to change:

> Majority of Indian higher education institutions have been following the system which obstructs the flexibility for the students to study the subjects/courses of their choice and their mobility to different institutions. There is need to allow the flexibility in education system, so that students depending upon their interests can choose inter-disciplinary, intra-disciplinary and skill-based courses. This can only be possible when choice based credit system (CBCS), an internationally acknowledged system, is adopted. The choice based credit system not only offers opportunities and avenues to learn core subjects but also explore additional avenues of learning beyond the core subjects for holistic development of an individual. (UGC, 2015, p. 2)

Since then the UGC began to influence universities in India to switch over to the CBCS by the next academic session. The transformation was approved by the ministers of human resource development (HRD) from different states in January 2015.[1] After a little bit of hand-holding,[2] the universities were asked to implement the CBCS by the academic session 2016–2017.

CBCS aims to bring a 'paradigm change' (UGC, 2015) and bridge the gap between an undergraduate degree and employability by targeting a curriculum change and overhauling the institutional governance to a large extent. The CBCS, at least conceptually, provides freedom to the students to select courses of their choice, and by creating a core 'holistic syllabus' (UGC, 2015), it attempts to build the base for all students, irrespective of their discipline. Similar to the design

---

[1] Press Release #8 of 6 January 2015 for the MHRD by the Press Information Bureau. Also see, Lok Sabha, Starred Question No. 124, answered on 4 March 2015, answered by the Union Minister for Human Resource Development, Ms Smriti Zubin Irani.

[2] Here is the address of the web-page of the UGC that carries links that would be of help in creating a CBCS compliant syllabus: Retrieved 29 July 2017, from http://www.ugc.ac.in/ugc_notices.aspx?id=1077

mechanism, it offers a uniform model of evaluation and grading system, which is claimed to be better than the varied existing practices. This 'uniformity' and transferability will help students to move from one institution to another, and even internationally, as the mechanism will be comparable. Universities, on the other hand, are allowed to design and review the syllabi (except of the core papers). Even in the core papers, the universities can modify 30 per cent of the content, based on the template designed by the UGC.

In the next three years, that is, by July 2019, as the previous batches of students graduate from the university system, one could hope that the entire university system of India would have switched to the CBCS. This chapter then focuses on the thinking that underlay the introduction of the CBCS and the concerns that have been expressed about it.

RATIONALE FOR INTRODUCING CBCS

The thoughts that underlay the CBCS had been in the making for at least a decade. They also echoed a lasting concern, from the time of at least the national movement from before 1947, that students should be sensitized to the dignity of labour lest they presume that those who labour are of a lower social and moral order (e.g., Gandhi, 1953). There was also this concern, sotto voce, that Indian universities were not doing enough research either in quantity or in quality. The policies of Indian education, since 1947, have criticized the rigid nature of HE. The Radhakrishnan Commission report (1948) expressed great concerns over the traditional non–adaptive nature of Indian HE, and urged it to become more dynamic and responsive to the changes and demands. Later, the Educational Policy of 1986 (revised in 1992) introduced the idea of HRD, thus giving education a utilitarian, more pragmatic outlook. The economic restructuring, widespread globalization and development of modern information communication technologies (ICT) further strengthened the notion that Indian HE needs to change and become more flexible. Therefore, several changes have been suggested at various levels; however, since education is a joint responsibility of the centre and the states, the changes have not been uniform nationwide. Nevertheless, some of the policy endeavours stand out in the midst of plethora of recommendations and reform guidelines, which are somewhat 'controversial' yet noteworthy to mention. This section discusses some of them, to get an overview of the policy progression.

OPENING UP HE

The Ambani-Birla report on education in India noticed the almost complete divorce between education that was being imparted and practical skills of a higher order (Ambani & Birla, 2000). It castigated India's education system without any ambiguity for having created a society that was 'non-competitive and labour-oriented', one that merely produced industrial workers rather than a society that fostered knowledge resources, for no one at the higher end of the education system seemed to be interested in doing things with their hands. 'The world of education in India encompasses different "worlds" that live side by side. One world includes only a fortunate few with access to modern institutions computers, Internet access and expensive overseas education' (2000, p. 840), it said, and went on to identify the majority of the education system as 'a second world [that] wants to maintain status quo—teachers, administrators, textbook publishers, students—all have reasons to prefer things to remain as they are or change only gradually' (2000, p. 840). It also noticed the existence of a 'third world' that 'struggles with fundamental issues such as no books, wrong books, teachers desperately in need of training, teachers with poor commitment, rote learning of irrelevant material, classrooms with hundred students, dirty floors and no toilets'. Correspondingly, of the various recommendations that the Ambani-Birla report made for improving HE, one was to enable an easier movement of students '*from one institution to another based on a system of transfer of professional credits*' (2000, p. 844, emphasis added). It also recommended the introduction of students to research right from the undergraduate level in all fields.

FREEDOM FOR STUDENTS

The Ambani-Birla report was not much discussed within the university system, except to castigate it for its recommendations about inviting private investment for education. However, many of its ideas found a new life in the report of the National Knowledge Commission (NKC) that was set up in 2005, and worked from 2006 through 2009 (Pitroda, 2009). The NKC too talked of allowing students the freedom of movement from one institution to another, and of the importance of them learning to work with their hands.

Sam Pitroda's Report to the nation of the NKC was of the view that '*it (was) essential to provide students with choices instead of keeping them captive*' (NKC, 2009, p. 68, emphasis added). Correspondingly, it suggested that in order to obtain a degree, while students earn a minimum number of credits in their chosen discipline, they also should be provided the freedom to earn the remaining credits from courses in other disciplines. The idea was to free students from the tyranny of being tied down to just one set of subjects for study merely because they had chosen a particular stream of education on leaving school.

'The NKC proposes a transition to a course credit system where degrees are granted on the basis of completing a requisite number of credits from different courses, which provides students with choices', it said (NKC, 2009 p. 64). One of the benefits of such an education, it hoped, was that it would remove the pressure on students leaving school to think of only medicine and engineering as two meaningful options for the future—both of which were options that had to be chosen during school, and once chosen could be changed only after suffering a loss of years. Moreover, the report said that the students should have the freedom to choose the subjects they could study while obtaining a degree. It would put pressure on the institutions of HE to create courses that the students would find meaningful.

The present system of education, it pointed out, was characterized by too many rigidities and too few choices for students. In its opinion, universities that were smaller or had a semester-based system were more flexible. However, that simply meant that, in the opinion of the NKC, the larger universities—the site of education for most students in India—would also have to transform themselves, especially in order, the NKC hoped, to 'introduce greater diversity and more flexibility in the course structures'. Providing choices to students, in other words, would also enhance 'competition between institutions and correspondingly enhance accountability' (NKC, 2009, p. 64).

ISSUES WITH SEMESTER AND CREDITS

The idea that universities should teach their courses through the semester system using a system of credits to give relative value to courses and grades to evaluate the students had been floating around for many decades. However, with the exception of a handful of relatively resource rich universities such as the JNU (founded in 1969) or the Hyderabad Central University (founded in 1974), where teaching was always based on the semester system and which typically had less than 10,000 students, the majority of the general universities had avoided converting their teaching from an annual system to the semester system. Some universities like the Panjab University (PU), with over 160,000 students being examined in over 400 examinations, could not seem to decide which system of teaching to follow.[3] One of the problems before the universities such as PU was the tremendous diversity of the student body. Some 18,000 regular students were on campus, distributed in over 78 departments/centres, while the majority of students (not counting the humongous mass of students in the distance education mode) taking the exams of PU were distributed among 188 affiliated colleges. Some of their courses were always taught in the semester format, while others were in the format of the annual system. Some of the courses that were taught in the format of the semester system were even converted back to the annual system citing local exigencies. While some courses of study, when taught in the colleges, were in the format of the annual system, when taught in the university teaching department, the same courses were in the format of the semester system.

In 2008, the university ordered every course to be converted into the semester format. From the following semester, without a single formal murmur of protest, the entire university shifted to the semester system. Since then, all the teaching in the university was done in the semester format. Delhi University too changed from the annual format to the semester format by the session of 2011–2012 but, only after considerable public criticism prior to the change, suggesting that there was a large body of teachers that was resistant to change and quite vocal about sharing their reasons for resistance, most of which

---

[3] Data from the AISHE Report 2015–16. Retrieved 2 August 2016, from http://aishe.nic.in/aishe/dataUserReportHome

revolved around two sentiments: (a) institutional and faculty autonomy is being compromised and (b) there are not enough resources. That is another matter that once the semester system was introduced, it was met with reports of approval (Thilak, 2011), and no particular shortfall was reported as compared to the previous annual format.

Apart from advocating the semester format for teaching, the NKC repeated some of the other, by now well-known, points of criticism of the system of HE in India. The NKC criticized the universities for creating unemployable graduates without any skills. Creativity was wanting in these graduates of India's HE sector. For such lacunae too, the NKC held the availability of choice to be the appropriate solution. It was the system of HE that, the NKC suggested, made the graduates not have any skills.

Left to them, it was possible that students would take courses that would make them employable. The onus of espousing creativity, though, was left by the NKC to the teachers when it was said that all teaching in HE should be designed to foster creativity. The courses should be 'relevant' and should be application-oriented, with a judicious mix of projects that attract the theoretical researcher and those interested in general abstraction. Even the social science courses and humanities, the NKC recommended, should have a component that required either desk-based or field research (Pitroda, 2009, p. 115). Clearly, according to the recommendations of the NKC, the freedom to students to choose what courses they wished to pursue was the key to transforming HE in India.

Autonomy for the Learner

A further boost to this idea was received through the recommendations of a coeval committee that had been giving some thought to the matter of improving the quality of HE in India. This was the Yashpal Committee that was set up in 2008. In its report submitted in 2009, the Yashpal Committee suggested a number of transformative ideas for the universities and colleges of India. Not only did these ideas give greater credence to the recommendations of the NKC, they also laid out a much more detailed philosophical basis for them, thus distinguishing these new ideas from many of the ideas to reform education that had been floating in India for past many decades (Yashpal, 2009).

Yashpal had been tasked the year before with making certain recommendations, in the light of the recommendations that had been flowing from the NKC, on improving the performance of India's institutions of HE. Instead, Yashpal redefined his task completely. He transformed what otherwise would have been yet another re-examination of the ills that plague India's HE into a grand 'report to the nation' on the state of HE, and he called for significant changes in the basic thinking underlying HE.[4] He called his report as one providing ideas on the *Renovation and Rejuvenation of Higher Education in India* that addressed some of the 'basic aberrations' that had developed within the system of education.

One of the key issues that Yashpal identified as being problematic in the HE sector in India was the almost complete absence of autonomy for the learner. The university system had hitherto recognized the importance of autonomy for the faculty in framing their syllabus and pedagogic style. The committee says, 'that autonomy should also be available to the students who should be allowed to take courses of their choice in a relaxed manner from different universities and then be awarded a degree on the basis of the credits they have earned' (Yashpal, 2009, p. 46).

The report noticed that right from school age, our education restrained and restricted our young people and continued that way into the college and university stage. In a severe indictment of the education system, the report noted that the intense focus on merely collecting information mindlessly and rewarding its regurgitation had resulted in creating a system of education that was highly restrictive of the mind. The report observed that 'most instrumentalities of our education harm the potentiality of human mind for constructing and creating new knowledge' while adding that this was particularly vile at the university level because 'one of the requirements of a good university should be to engage in knowledge creation—not just for the learner but also for society as a whole' (Yashpal, 2009, p. 76).

---

[4] Yashpal in a letter to Arjun Singh, the Minister, HRD, India, on 21 September 2008 (Yashpal, 2009, p. 2).

Water-tight Institutional Boundaries, Low Quality and Restricted Student Mobility

What leant special credence to the pleas put forth by the NKC and the Yashpal Committee was the successes achieved in the field of education during the period of the 11th Five-year Plan (plan period, 2007–2012). As the 12th Five-year Plan (plan period, 2012–2017) document noted, the reach of education had expanded considerably during the 11th Plan. A lot of investment in civil works and the creation of an institutional framework of rules and regulations had been made (Varghese, 2015). However, the dramatic expansion of education had posed the problem of quality. The expansion had not been accompanied with any improvement in quality. The water-tight compartments in which institutions, and departments within institutions existed, ensured that cross-seeding of good ideas was difficult and students were imprisoned within the compartments.

The absence of focus on quality was especially problematic, the 12th Plan noted, because the inevitable economic expansion of the world economy meant that by the year 2020, there would be a projected requirement for 40 million workers who had higher order skills. A slide in the quality in HE was noticed with some concern while recognizing the centrality of HE as 'the principal site at which our national goals, developmental priorities and civic values could be examined and refined' (Planning Commission, 2013, p. 89). HE was important because, it 'creates an intellectual repository of human capital to meet the country's needs and shapes its future'.

What was needed, therefore, was to shift focus away from a handful of great institutions that existed in the country and try to improve the quality of the 'average' institution. For it was such institutions that enrolled the majority of students. Moreover, despite the tremendous growth of technical HE, over half of the students were projected to enrol in general undergraduate programmes as much as they were reported to have done in the past years. Even two years into the plan, for the reporting year 2015–2016, more than half of the students from the institutions of HE, were graduating with an 'arts' degree/certificate (Table 10.1 and Figure 10.1).

Table 10.1 *Showing the Number of Students Who Graduated from Different Streams*

Stream	Number of Graduated Students 2015–2016	Kind of Education (while classifying Science, Laws and Management as 'Technical')
Agriculture	51,222	Technical
Arts	3,937,577	General
Commerce	981,960	General
Engineering	1,261,118	Technical
Laws	82,637	Technical
Management	384,372	Technical
Medical	336,167	Technical
Science	1,491,479	Technical
Veterinary	7,009	Technical
Grand Total	8,533,541	

Source: All India Survey of Higher Education (2015–2016), Out Turn Report # 55 A, MHRD (2016).

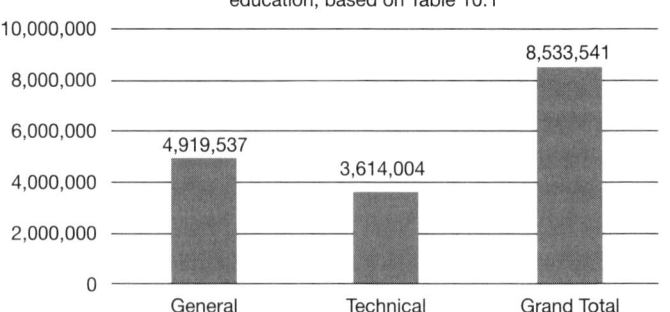

2015–2016: Number of students who passed out from 'general' education comprising of a BA degree/certificate and all other who have a 'technical' education, based on Table 10.1

Figure 10.1 *Showing Total Number of Students Who Passed from Different Streams*

Source: All India Survey of Higher Education (2015–2016), Out Turn Report # 55 A, MHRD (2016).

The 12th Plan emphasized, much like the NKC and the Yashpal Committee had done earlier, on the need to bring in radical pedagogical transformations in HE. The input-centric and credential-based pedagogy that characterized education had to be transformed into one that was learner-centric and learning–outcome based. Towards this end, it suggested the need to improve the general education system of India, for it was from here that the majority of the students were slated to come for an undergraduate degree in arts, science or commerce. The knowledge that these students acquired whilst in college had to be such as to equip them with the capability to be able to re-skill themselves as many times as was required by changing economic circumstances in the future. The economies of the future, it was predicted, would require people to change jobs and careers several times (Planning Commission, 2013).

CBCS AS A POTENTIAL SOLUTION

Towards this end, it was suggested that the universities and colleges needed to, inter alia, switch to the CBCS. Having a CBCS, with its possibility of students choosing courses from across departments and universities, the 12th Plan felt, may also force the faculty to interface more actively in other areas such as research and go in for more cross-institutional collaborations. This was almost entirely missing at that moment, despite everyone within the university system agreeing that collaborative researches, across departments and universities, were the most fruitful strategy for producing meaningful researches of a high quality. These reforms would 'create an active learning environment in colleges and universities'. An amount of ₹120 million was earmarked for the purpose of Research Innovation and Quality Improvement during the 12th Plan for creating research hubs/parks, incubation centres, innovation hubs, etc. and for the creation of facilities for attracting top-rated faculty and researchers to India.[5] The government also put in place a new institutional mechanism, the Rashtriya Uchchatar Shiksha Abhiyan (RUSA), launched in 2013, to disburse these funds, and others that were needed to make the system of HE better and to

---

[5] Lok Sabha, Unstarred question 557, 26 November 2014.

ensure that funds for the centrally sponsored schemes were disbursed in consonance with local requirements through the state HE councils.

Primarily, the focus of the reforms was to be on the undergraduate programme. It had to be such as to provide, among other things, the experience of hands-on research, job skilling, experiential learning, creative thinking, leadership, ethics and community service. Since it would be beyond the capacity of any one existing institution to be able to serve all these objectives adequately, the idea of a 'meta university' was promoted. This, it was hoped, would enable several universities to come together and offer courses across disciplines, treat faculty and students from all institutions alike, and provide all network members access to content, teaching and the research support they required.

Meanwhile, there was much hesitation in most of the institutions and academia about the latest transformation in Indian education. In the next section, we shall look at the issues that formed the basis of hesitation and the challenges that may rise in making the transformation to CBCS a fruitful endeavour.

'FLAILING STATE' AND HESITATIONS ABOUT CBCS

The CBCS had been introduced in universities of Kerala in 2010. Guru Nanak Dev University, Mumbai University and the Himachal Pradesh University quickly followed suit for some of their courses. Other universities remained in various stages of introducing the CBCS. It was only with the academic session of 2016, that all the public universities of India implemented the CBCS. Correspondingly, it would be 2019 when country-wide there will be university graduates who will have completed their course of study under CBCS.

As of today, too little a time has elapsed, and too small is the number of graduates, to make a strong evaluation of those who obtained their degree under the new dispensation. Though a variety of subjective views have come forth till now, mostly expressing fears and hesitation about the CBCS even while agreeing that the CBCS is a good idea whose time had come. A view from Kerala, for example, said that the CBCS, six years after it was introduced in all the universities of

Kerala, had 'proved to be a complete success'. The Kerala experience, it was said, showed that 'higher education should strive to be more student-centred than it is now. Students must be given sufficient and qualitatively varied choice in the selection of subjects, courses and credits. Ensuring facilities for inter-institutional mobility is also the need of the times. Interdisciplinary synergy is to be ensured at any cost' (Padmanabhan, 2016).

The most, all pervasive hesitation about the CBCS and allied reforms in the HE sector came from the understanding that all these reforms emanated from some directive from the World Bank. These reforms were part of some larger transformation of HE worldwide into one where mobility between institutions was easily achievable because of the possibility of credit transfers and easily defined equivalences between courses. It was considered to imply that the accountability of HE would be judged in managerial terms such as were used in private businesses. This was a set of fears that seemed to be intercontinental in dimension and to be based on a general belief that there was always something more than meets the eye with recommendations about integrating with a globalized world (Cardak, 2004; Ensor, 2004; Mason, Arnove & Sutton, 2001; Quyen, 2009; Wellman, 2005). A rare statement appreciative of such globalization, and one which identified a dialectical link between the transformation of the country to the globalization of its education, came with respect to the transformations in the HE sector in South Korea—and there too a lot of emphasis was placed on having rooted the transformations into the local cultural template (Shin, 2012).

Institutional Concerns and Inertia

At the same time, the concerns about the CBCS were considerable. Especially damning were the fears that there would be an increase in tuition, reduction in public funding and, worse, the emergence of a market for trade in HE (Sharma, 2010). Another practical concern was based on having experienced, institutional lethargy in India even in some of the best institutions. One critic, for example, pointed out the discomfort at the pace of change 'at JNU, attempts to revamp an entire MA course has at times taken ten years', while warning that bringing about too many changes too fast, such as was being done through introducing the CBCS, may cause problems (Kumar, 2013).

There was also a fear that many of the ideas that underlay the present set of reforms—such as encouraging interdisciplinarity—might only create problems since even in JNU 'after more than 40 years of existence and many attempts to be true to the original mandate, inter-disciplinarity remains a distant goal' (Kumar, 2013, 2015). These concerns regarding lack of interdisciplinarity mirrors the larger reality in other state-run as well as central universities.

Such criticism needed to be understood in the context of institutional failure of universities that had a vocal body of faculty, some among whom practiced interdisciplinarity in their own researches. However, these practices at individual levels could not promote interdisciplinarity at the institutional level or make it the basis for the generality of research that was being done at the institution. Fifty years of paying homage at the altar of interdisciplinarity whilst all the while creating narrower and narrower disciplinary turfs was bound to create a sense of discomfort when faced with the prospect of being forced by the CBCS to work within a new set of rules that were hostile to disciplinary boundaries. Institutional inertia would remain the most important source of hesitation regarding any transformation that would be envisaged in the system of HE (Agelasto, 1996).

Impact of Student Choice on Faculty Demand

Any restructuring exercise at the institutional level impacts the organization of courses, which leads to changes in the student intake. In traditional university system, student enrolments are used as benchmark for calculating faculty demand. However, a fluctuating student intake and mobility due to the reorganization of course as in CBCS could pose a challenge for calculating permanent faculty demand. The fact the students could choose from a basket of courses in the CBCS was problematic insofar as it would imply that there would be a fluctuation in student demand for courses and would result in the possible redundancy of teachers whose courses did not attract enough students (Padmanabhan, 2016).

For instance, till now, the 'humanities and social science subjects accounted for over half the total student strength in Indian universities (see Table 10.1). Introduction of CBCS could substantially change the faculty profile and strength across disciplines. These anxieties are more substantial for traditional disciplines in social sciences, arts and humanities, than those in the applied fields.

Institutional Preparedness

Scaling up of the CBCS also posed concern for the institutions. The freedom to choose courses across disciplines could create unforeseen chaos. For instance, not every university in the country is equipped to implement the CBCS successfully. Forcing universities to adopt it because of a fiat from the UGC represented a serious threat to the university autonomy.

The issues of inadequately equipped libraries and other learning resources, and serious faculty shortages played upon the minds of all. The inability of HE institutions to address these long-standing structural lacunae till now would only create greater problems for the institutions to make provisions for the successful implementation of CBCS. At least one critic warned that such reforms were 'potentially disastrous' and might 'aggravate the problems of higher education' (Kumar, 2013). The success of the CBCS in Kerala was attributed to the universities, and their faculty, being left free to determine the way the teaching would be structured and the content of the course (Padmanabhan, 2016).

Of course, there was a problem associated with the idea of autonomy and wide-spread consultations: the existing institutional structures within institutions of HE already provided for the faculty to have autonomy in determining the courses. So why was there this consistent and vocal complaint about not having academic autonomy? Could there be something other than autonomy at play?

Vocationalization and Privatization

The element of vocalization inherent in the CBCS too evoked concerns. The changing nature of market, and therefore required skills, could mean wastage in training for skill sets, if they become obsolete for the market (Roy, 2015).

Similarly, the open invitation for public universities to collaborate with private universities too evoked discomfort. Some even saw the CBCS as an open invitation for private universities to attract students who had originally sought admission to public universities, but which were unable to offer adequate number of skill-oriented courses as stipulated under the CBCS. The governance structure of a public university and introduction of new courses including faculty hiring could pose a challenge to flexibility as demanded by the CBCS. The private universities, because of their flexible governance structure, could bring in changes in terms of course structures, hiring of faculty more swiftly than that in the public system. This flexibility enables them to offer courses and attract students who had originally enrolled in the public universities (Sharma, 2010; Thakur, 2016).

Student Diversity and Local Relevance

Students in an Indian university come from diverse backgrounds. There is a great diversity among them in terms of prior knowledge of the subject and their learning abilities. Tying the students down to a strict pedagogic timetable, such as was presumed in the successful working of the semester system, also evoked discomfort. 'How would it be possible, within a single semester, to reach out to all students, given their different learning abilities' was one kind of question that was asked (Gupta, 2010).

Since the CBCS was proposed to be implemented through the semester system, the tight academic schedule for students leaving little space for extracurricular activity was another concern. The uniformity of syllabus and the possibility of students being taught subjects that have little relevance to the needs of the locality in which the university was based, attracted adverse comments too, forgetting that at the undergraduate level in India, for most courses, there already existed a considerable degree of uniformity across the country (Kumar, 2013; Padmanabhan, 2016; Roy, 2015).

The UGC had initially suggested that universities be free to localize 20 per cent of the syllabus. Following initial criticisms, this limit was raised to 30 per cent. Chances are that as the CBCS gets operationalized across the country and local adjustments are made in the coming sessions, it would become possible for every university to determine the quantum of diversity from the model syllabus to suit its local conditions.

In practice, each university determines its own syllabus based on the recommendations made by its own faculty and respective Boards of Study. Neither the UGC nor the National Assessment and Accreditation Council (NAAC) have any mechanism to evaluate the details within a syllabus. Also, since the early 1990s, the UGC has been providing 'model' syllabi for different subjects for the universities to use as a guide in framing university-specific syllabi. The greatest possibility is that even in the case of the CBCS, the UGC-ordained syllabi too would provide a model rather than be a restrictive prescription.

The problems as discussed minimally indicated great apprehensions on the part of teachers and institutions in HE regarding the ability of the system to cope with the new demands that the CBCS would pose.

EXPERIENCE OF IMPLEMENTATION: A CASE STUDY OF PANJAB UNIVERSITY

The universities that did implement the CBCS in the academic session, beginning in 2016, immediately discovered that some of their academic, administrative, and infrastructural set-ups became over-stretched. Even in a rather well-equipped university such as the Panjab University at Chandigarh, many newly established interdisciplinary departments found that they simply did not have enough laboratory space and faculty to accommodate the sudden increase in the number of students in the much sought after interdisciplinary courses.

The traditional departments, such as physics, chemistry, botany, and zoology, basking in the reputation of their teachers and researchers, had a larger number of faculty and large laboratories. They welcomed the demand from a larger number of students who now chose to study in these departments that had high ranking in the academic world and offered better placement opportunities after graduation. Both students and faculty reported apprehensions in the use of Gaussian distribution for grading students. The fear was that five years later this would create a problem for graduating students, since all subsequent academic opportunities were based heavily on absolute marks obtained.

The faculty also reported the inability of existing data management strategies within the university to support the relative fluidity in choosing courses that CBCS allowed students. Senior faculty members also felt that switching to the CBCS had effectively diluted the learning standards that the departments had been following under a tried and tested honours school system that Panjab University had been following for many decades.

BY WAY OF CONCLUSION

Since Independence, the society and government in India have had multiple aspirations about HE. That HE would transform the country and its people in some dramatic ways remains the most important hope.

Over the years, we have witnessed multiple layers of expectations being imposed on the system of HE. Thus, the university was supposed to be the key institution to foster equality, equity, justice, cultural change, economic growth of the country, economic transformation of the region, nationalism, humanism and many other things. Under these layers of expectations, those involved in the practise of HE—law-makers, politicians, policy-makers, the faculty and even the students—seemed to have forgotten that the core purpose of the university is to foster the creation of new knowledge and its effective distribution in society.

Perhaps with the introduction of the CBCS, giving students a choice to study what they please without the restriction of disciplinary boundaries, there may be a possibility for HE in India to really transform itself. However, to make the CBCS successful, it is imperative that there be the requisite upgradation of administrative and academic infrastructure. Also, that there is the immediate need to ensure that the rules and regulations governing studies and work after graduation were changed adequately to accommodate the students who would emerge as graduates from the CBCS system in the summer of 2019.

REFERENCES

Agelasto, M. (1996, March). Educational transfer of sorts: The American credit system with Chinese characteristics. *Comparative Education, 32*(1), 69–93.

Ambani, M., & Birla, K. (2000, October–December). *Report on a policy frame work for reforms in education.* Special subject group on policy framework for private investment in education, health and rural development, Prime Minister's Council on Trade and Industry, pp. 840–845. New Delhi: Government of India.

Cardak, B. A. (2004, October). Education choice, neoclassical growth, and class structure. *Oxford Economic Papers, 56*(4), 643–666.

Ensor, P. (2004, October). Contesting discourses in higher education curriculum restructuring in South Africa. *Higher Education, 48*(3), 339–359.

Gandhi, M. K. (1953). *Towards new education.* Bharatan Kumarappa (Ed). Navajivan Trust, Ahmedabad.

Gupta, V. (2010, February 27). Semester system for undergraduates: A critique. *Economic and Political Weekly, XLV*(9), 18–20.

Kumar, A. (2013, June 15). Delhi University and the crisis in India's higher education. *Economic and Political Weekly* web-exclusive. Retrieved 29 July 2017, from http://www.epw.in/journal/2013/24/debating-du-web-exclusives/delhi-university-and-crisis-indias-higher-education.html

———. (2015, December 26). Challenges facing new education policy in India. *Economic and Political Weekly, L*(52), 14–16.

Landry, E. (2012, March 11). *The flip side: IIT vs. Rice University.* Retrieved 29 July 2017, from *Insight: The Third Eye,* Student Media Body of IIT Bombay: http://www.insightiitb.org/2012/the-flip-side-iit-vs-rice-university/

Mason, T. C., Arnove, R. F., & Sutton, M. (2001, July). Credits, curriculum, and control in higher education: Cross-national perspectives. *Higher Education, 42*(1), 107–137.

MHRD (Ministry of Human Resource and Development). (2016). *All India survey on higher education (AISHE) 2015–16.* New Delhi: Ministry of Human Resource and Development, Government of India.

Padmanabhan, C. (2016, January 30). Endangering academic autonomy. *Economic and Political Weekly, LI*(5), 20–22.

Pitroda, S. (2009). *National knowledge commission: Report to the nation, 2006–2009.* Advisory Report, Government of India. New Delhi: Ministry of Human Resource Development (Department of Higher Education), GOI.

Planning Commission. (2013). *Twelfth five year plan (2012–2017): Social sectors* (Vol. III). New Delhi: SAGE.

Quyen, D. T. (2009, June). Contact hours in Dutch and Vietnamese higher e-education: A comparison. *Higher Education, 57*(6), 757–767.

Radhakrishnan, S. (1948). *The Report of the University Education Commission.* New Delhi: Government of India.

Roy, K. (2015, May 19). Decoding 'new education policy'. *Economic and Political Weekly* web-exclusive. Retrieved 29 July 2017, from http://www.epw.in/journal/2015/19/web-exclusives/decoding-new-education-policy.html.

Sharma, V. (2010, September-December). UPA's agenda of academic 'reforms' facilitating trade in higher education. *Social Scientist, 38* (9/12), 91–127.

Shin, J. C. (2012, July). Higher education development in Korea: Western university ideas, Confucian tradition, and economic development. *Higher Education, 64*(1), 59–72.

Thakur, N. (2016, February 27). De facto privatisation in Indian public higher education: A transition from FYUP to CBCS. *Economic and Political Weekly, LI*(9), 20–21.

Thilak, N. (2011). Winds of change sweep Delhi University. *Indian Express,* 23 December. Retrieved 29 July 2017, from http://indianexpress.com/article/india/india-others/winds-of-change-sweep-delhi-university/

UGC (2015). *Instructional template for facilitating implementation of choice based credit system (CBCS).* Retrieved 29 July 2017, from http://www.ugc.ac.in/pdfnews/4426331_Instructional-Template.pdf

Varghese, N. V. (2015). Challenges of massification of higher education in India. *CPRHE Research Paper Series* (Research Paper 1). New Delhi: CPRHE-NIEPA.

Wellman, J. (2005, July–August). The student credit hour: Counting what counts. *Change, 37*(4), 18–23.

Yashpal. (2009). *Report of the Committee to advise on 'The renovation and rejuvenation of higher education'.* Advise, Government of India, Ministry of Human Resource Development (Department of Higher Education). New Delhi: GOI.

PART III

Quality Management

Chapter 11

Quality and Accountability in Higher Education

Mariamma Varghese

INTRODUCTION

India witnessed tremendous expansion in terms of higher education institutions in the post-Independence era. The most important challenge before us is not just to guarantee the expansion of education, but also to improve the quality and link education to societal needs and development goals. This chapter highlights the concept of quality in higher education, qualitative aspects of higher education in India, indicators of quality, quality assurance (QA), accountability for QA, factors facilitating quality and accountability, and the key performance measures for quality and accountability.

AIMS AND OBJECTIVES OF HIGHER EDUCATION

Higher education signifies a level of intellectual attainment. It is an *outcome* concept as well as a *process* concept. It has an enduring character and requires effort from all stakeholders. Nevertheless, it also implies attaining some kind of standard in the outcome.

In the present context, *first*, we expect higher education to train students to become qualified manpower. The emphasis is on the processes by which the graduates become product/outputs having economic value in the job market. The quality tends to be the ability of the students to succeed in the world of work, as measured by their employment rates and more specifically by their career earnings.

Second, higher education aims to train students for a research career. The achievement of student is not the focus of quality. The relative input and output measures, such as the amount of research outcome and publications, are the indicators of educational quality. The research and academic culture is achieved by only a few groups of students compared to the other types of education. The formal entry into this section is also important, and the low student–staff ratio is a very important quality performance indicator for this aspect of education.

Third, higher education is seen as the efficient management of teaching–learning. This conceptualization has to be seen in the context where the number of students has gone up and there is change in the social class composition as well as age composition of students. Institutions are considered doing well if their management process is good to accommodate the student clientele, given the resources. Their efficiency determines the number of students that they can accommodate and graduate. The indicators of performance that can capture this sense of efficiency are sought by the institutions and the regulators. Completion rate, number of degrees awarded and number of students who found placements are important, as are the unit costs, student–staff ratios and financial data.

Fourth, higher education is seen as a matter of extending life chances to all types of students. The concept of higher education is valued for its ability to offer opportunities to participate in the institution of repute and to enjoy the benefits of modern society. The student demand is very important indicator in this situation.

A common mission is the driving force for the programmes and activities, and it includes clear goals, leadership, shared values and beliefs. Emphasis on learning is another important function of the educational institutions, which is the process of enabling the students to achieve what one wants to achieve even in view of multiple goals. This is manifested through instruction and experiential focus with a learner-centred approach. In the process of imparting education, whether it is teacher-centred or participative, frequent monitoring and feedback of student progress is important to assess the status, review and further identify the required instructional or learning experiences. All these learning outcomes are possible only if there is a climate conducive to learning, and the students are actively involved in learning.

These days, with the advancement of information technology, it is possible to facilitate the learning environment through educational technology and library resources for effective learning. In order to provide motivation for staff and students, measures have to be evolved for recognition and incentives. This sustains their interests and encourages competition among themselves, which ultimately results in better performance. In this process, positive student behaviours are expected which enthuse the learners and the providers to do their best. The level of aspirations of students has to be at a higher level so that the whole system will gear around to achieve the desired results. Staff collegiality and development is another media by which quality of teachers are maintained and enhanced. This can happen only when there are mutual high expectations between staff and students, and amongst the staff themselves.

Due to the expansion of educational system in the country and the variety of educational providers, there is a need to assure the clientèle of the quality of the system as well as the finance-granting institutions about the quality of the higher education institutions in the country. From the perspective of the clientèle group, there is a variety of expectations and needs to be met. The composition of the student community is so diverse, consisting of the elite group, economically or socially disadvantaged students, the gifted learners, more of women students, students with varying aspirations, students with vocational interest, and others with different aptitudes and challenges.

The whole system caters to the needs of all the diverse groups in a standardized way, which ultimately results in a sub-optimum development of human resources. This complex package has to be unpacked to revamp the system through systemic changes, policy changes and probably a technology aided academic environment. To top it all, we have to cater to the burgeoning labour market with their dynamic requirements, and also to the continuing education students who are required to upgrade their skills/competence according to the changing requirements of the economy and the labour market. The task is not easy, and the journey is too arduous for the universities and colleges, which are at different stages of development. There are elite institutions, mediocre institutions and low quality institutions, and institutions located in rural and tribal areas with poor infrastructure and learning resources. Each institution needs to draw up a quality map and plan for the value additions that can be made to the institutions in their curricular offerings depending on the context.

QA in higher education has thus become a focus of attention as universities have become mega institutions in the education system, with more and more affiliated colleges adding on to the already over-burdened system. The advent of information technology can serve as an enabling tool for coping with numbers and establishing effective administrative structures, thus assuring quality in a globalized educational market. In any case, there needs to be some decentralization and formation of optimum-sized institutions for effective management.

CONCEPT OF QUALITY IN HIGHER EDUCATION

Quality in the context of higher education can be defined as judgement about the level of goal achievement and the value and worth of that achievement. It has a philosophical and pragmatic aspect. A key measure of quality is the satisfaction of users. The definition of quality used in ISO 14000 and ISO 9000 is 'the totality of features and characteristics of a product or service that bear on its ability to satisfy stated or implied needs' (BIS, 1988). This definition of quality is quite relevant to higher education as well. It is more pertinent to fitness of purpose (Green, 1993). Many will argue that the education provided by the institutions should facilitate them to acquire the knowledge, and the professional skills and training that will establish them in the employment market. However, along with the employability of graduates and benefits to the society, the student becoming a responsible citizen is equally important.

Many stakeholders such as parents would also identify quality with the value for money. Thus, quality in higher education refers to highest standards, serves the purpose adequately, is consistent, provides value for money and is transformative in its functions.

We cannot develop a system of QA without conceptual clarity regarding what we are looking for in higher education. That means there is a logical connection between the concepts of higher education and the different approaches to QA. For example, if we conceive of higher education as a process of enabling graduates to find employment, as the pragmatists think, then obviously, placement of students in the job market and also a match between their knowledge and skills become important indicators of quality. Here we might look at the economic returns of the graduates in terms of opportunity costs and costs of their education. We consider the 'value added' to the student through the process of education. On the other hand, some firmly believe that the aim of higher education is for the intellectual development of the students, and the capacity of the students to acquire knowledge that enables them to apply the knowledge and understanding in varying life experiences. In such construction of quality, the focus will be on the educational processes provided by faculty and institutions.

Most of the ideas about quality are value-related and judgemental. Here the focus is on the type of education, which the student experiences in their educational environment. In Indian higher education set-up, both are important. We need to think of an effective system with the appropriate input, processes and output with a focus on efficiency and effectiveness, measuring outputs against inputs to make sure that one gets the value for money. In addition, it should be about the transformation process of the student from the time they enter the portals of the university/college and their continued growth, further after they graduate.

Different stakeholders perceive quality through different lenses. Some at the macro level, some at the meso level and others at the micro level. Each one of these layers has sub-layers, all of which constitute the total quality of higher education. We need to focus on the micro or educational delivery level operations, which directly impact students. This alone can make a basis for continuous improvement.

Numerous measures by which to judge quality in a generalized way have been developed quantitatively and qualitatively. At the organizational level, the structures are changing from static to dynamic forms as knowledge expands and becomes unbounded. There may be need for policy changes at the macro level and changes at the implementation/delivery level, which will have impact on the quality of education. To support these changes, the management needs to become insightful and participative rather than strictly bureaucratic. Moreover, universities and colleges, especially autonomous colleges, have the freedom to design and deliver academic programmes at various levels and set standards for themselves. However, they need to assure acceptable quality according to the national and international standards.

CRITERIA FOR QUALITY ASSURANCE

We need to identify 'educational criteria' for basing the institutional assessment, whether self-assessment or external quality assessment by peers. The formulation of criteria helps to assess where, what and how to improve institutional practices, capabilities and outcomes. This formulation will facilitate communication and sharing of best practices and information amongst all institutions. Eventually, the 'criteria' or the 'yardsticks' should serve as a tool for assessing, reviewing and managing performance, and guiding organizational planning and opportunities for learning. The formulation of educational criteria is rather very complex, since it deals with the dynamic aspects of human resource development.

Analyzing the strengths and weaknesses itself will give an opportunity to further enhance the strengths and reduce the weaknesses in the system. By accepting the ownership of the system, one can improve the quality of education imparted by the institution. According to the recent trends in ICT-enabled education, a number of aspects in terms of quality can be captured through web-based interaction. That is mainly the quantitative parameters in relation to the organization through the institutional profile, staff profile, resource profile, organization structure, infrastructure profile, student's profile and research profile.

In education, the focus is on the *students and stakeholders* who are the key beneficiaries of educational programmes. Therefore, education organizations should respond to a variety of *student (clientele) requirements*, probably the present students and the future students. Since education is considered as a 'continuous process' with multi-skill development, many career options can be envisaged by the students not only for 'being employed' but also to 'become employers'. Therefore, consideration has to be given to address the variety of requirements of the institution's educational services and the requirements of the stakeholders themselves, which will be reflected all through the institutional assessment criteria.

ICT-enabled academic and administrative management runs through all the criteria. A balance of the *input*, strategic *planning and management*, and the *outcomes* are characteristics of the pool of indicators. An integrated system perspective is evolved in assessing the institutional performance during the process of fine-tuning. In order to make the assessment more objective, reliable and valid, considerations have to be given *to quantify the quality parameters by capturing quantitative data* wherever possible, and *quantifying quality through measurement scales* and *validating the qualitative data by peer assessment*. The core indicators are identified under each criterion, and they are operationalized into sub-indicators and then translated into questions that will capture the appropriate responses related to the sub-indicators.

DIFFERENT PERSPECTIVES OF QUALITY ASSURANCE

There are essentially two types of quality assessment and accreditation. One is institutional QA and the other is QA with reference to programmes. The supply of programmes and resources in relation to the demand is only a fraction, which accentuates the problem. Additional programmes with inadequate facilities and teaching faculty do not create the right ambience for effective teaching–learning and do not result in optimum quality.

QUALITY STATUS OF HIGHER EDUCATION INSTITUTIONS IN INDIA

The present state of education in our country is at low ebb, except for some pockets of excellence. This is evident from the applications received by many higher education institutions for the post of teachers at various levels. One can diagnose the quality of graduates when interviewing the candidates. In fact, these graduates are among the 50 per cent of the eligible candidates from Class 12 who enter the portals of higher education. The drop out ratio among the Scheduled Castes (SCs), Scheduled Tribes (STs) and Other Backward Castes (OBCs) are in alarming proportions in higher education institutions.

According to the Effective Education for Employment (EEE) study by Edexcel (2009), there is a remarkable mismatch between what is being taught in universities and colleges, and the skills and behaviour that the businesses and organizations are looking for in new recruits. The study revealed that many employers felt that the present day education failed to effectively prepare individuals for the workplace. Even students felt that their education lacked relevance to the jobs they were hoping to apply for in the future. On one hand, we have high number of unemployable graduates, and on the other, we have many positions vacant.

According to the National Assessment and Accreditation Council (NAAC) accreditation records of October 2013, the number of colleges accredited through the first cycle figure is 5,224, the second cycle is 1,327 and third cycle is 55. The first-time accredited universities are 179, those accredited through second cycle are 75 and there are only 3 universities in the third cycle. The grade break ups shows that 11 per cent colleges have 'A' grade, 71 per cent 'B' grade and 18 per cent got 'C' grade. For the universities, 39 per cent are in the 'A' grade category, 58 per cent in 'B' and only 3 per cent are in the 'C' grade.

The fundamental questions we need to ask ourselves are: Are we performing as per the aims and objectives of higher education? Have we made any changes as per the changing context of the environment? Are we improving our standards of higher education and making corrective actions as and when required? Should we expect excellence of performance among diverse range of institutional missions? Do we depend on QA as main guarantors of quality in education or is there a place for moral or ethical engagement as well? Another important challenge for us is to ascertain how well we are performing compared to other institutions.

QA should be a venture in *decision and discovery* that leads to renewal of programmes, policies and persons, and a diagnostic exercise that challenges our understanding of purpose and the nature of collegiate enterprise. We need to diagnose the quality gaps existing in our higher education system. While identifying the quality gaps through assessment and accreditation, institutions need to be encouraged to examine their functioning, evaluate them and promote accountability in higher education.

QUALITY, AUTONOMY AND ACCOUNTABILITY IN HIGHER EDUCATION

Quality, autonomy and accountability are concomitant. There is a strong perception that the quality of higher education and research can be assured only if institutions are granted *autonomy* in academics and possibly in administrative matters as well. Autonomy is the power to act without external control. It should be viewed as an administrative or managerial requirement for fulfilling the functions according to the educational objectives and quality requirements. An organization cannot be held responsible for the lack of performance in teaching or preparing the students for life and career, or research advancements or innovation unless it is given the freedom to do so. Policy decisions such as not filling up vacant positions, disbursal of funds/grants by the regulatory agencies, and restrictions regarding curriculum content or programmes act as hindrance to enhance quality performance. National Policy of Education (NPE) 1986 (GOI, 1986) proposed to provide universities with a structure and management with self-correcting mechanisms which will allow them to be simultaneously innovative, autonomous and accountable. The policy expectations have not been realized. Now recently, the pronouncement of the MHRD to experiment with complete autonomy to the selected institutions could be another chance to implement in letter and spirit the improvement in quality and accountability of institutions to the satisfaction of all stakeholders.

Concept of Accountability

Accountability, according to Berdahl (1990), is the requirement to demonstrate reasonable actions to some external constituencies. In the case of universities and other institutions of higher learning, this external constituency is broadly speaking, the community, and more specifically the government. Accountability has two aspects: moral, and legal or contractual (Wagner, 1989). Moral accountability is based upon the sense of responsibility—a feeling that one is responsible to one's own clients (students and parents), to colleagues and to oneself. Legal accountability is being responsible to one's own employer, only in terms of fulfilment of the terms of employment. It is possible to satisfy the legal responsibility, yet not live up to the moral responsibility. For the maintenance of quality, it is necessary to devise an accountability system that shifts the emphasis from legal accountability to moral accountability.

Accountability is the assignment of responsibility for conducting activities in a certain way or producing specific results. A meaningful system of accountability for education should do three things. First, it should set educationally meaningful and defensible standards for what the stakeholders can rightfully expect of an educational system. Second, it should establish reasonable and feasible means by which these standards can be implemented and upheld. And third, it should provide an avenue for redress or correction in practice when these standards are not met so that, ultimately, students benefit.

A primary motivation for increased accountability is to improve the system or aspects of it. To have a workable accountability system, there must be a desired goal compliance with legal requirements, improved performance and ways to measure progress towards goal. There is a close relationship between quality and accountability in higher education. The responsibility for the curriculum design, training, content and implementation needs to be accounted for according to each of the parameters of quality. The quality of education imparted by an academic institution is greatly dependent upon the performance of its teachers. For this to be operational, the freedom of individual academic to study, teach, research and publish without being subject to or causing undue interference is essential. Academic freedom is a privilege that carries with it the responsibility of ensuring that it is used primarily for the improvement of the quality of education, the good of the institution, and for the welfare of the academic community and society.

At the institutional level, both autonomy and accountability are important for quality enhancement in the teaching–learning process. Teachers and departments function more cohesively and effectively when they are given the freedom to choose the courses to be taught and to formulate the contents of the curriculum. The freedom allows them to diversify and innovate for processes that often lead to quality enhancement. In the innovative experiment of establishing autonomous colleges, there is certainly enhancement of quality in terms of curriculum development; teaching–learning and evaluation procedures; research, consultancy and extension; adequate infrastructure; student progression and support; governance and leadership including management functions; and, finally, innovations in educational inputs, processes, and use of technology in academics as well as administrative processes and governance.

The search for quality should affirm faculty members as well as the administration as being responsible for their individual impact on campus life, and students and for the collective impact on the community and culture that they help to create. For this, we need to link all stakeholders with a common commitment.

Accountability System

An accountability system has to be established at the individual level in terms of job specifications, and at the institutional level to meet the aims and objectives of higher education considering the core values and criteria for quality education to satisfy all the stakeholders. We need to have a system with its structure and functions and the expected outcomes. We should be able to implement accountability by setting goals and objectives for institution and stakeholders, and periodically assessing the programmes towards the set goals and objectives using predetermined criteria. There are different approaches commonly used for measuring programmes and processes towards the achievement of goals and objectives.

Internal quality assurance cell (IQAC): Accountability has been introduced into the higher education through internal systems at the institutional level. NAAC has introduced the concept of

IQAC in each and every institution and a State Council of Higher Education (SCHE) at the state level. IQAC act as the catalytic agent for improving the academic and administrative performance of the institution. The voluntary adherence to the assessment indicators, and the accrediting process by the institutions as well as teachers and the community of stakeholders reflects the acceptance of academic accountability.

External quality assurance (EQA): This is done by external agencies such as NAAC, NBA etc. to validate the internal assessment by the institution regarding fulfilling their responsibilities and establishing accountability systems in higher education at the institutional level.

Approaches to Measure Accountability

There can be four types of approaches to measure account-ability at the institutional level. The first approach is based on an input-process-outcome model. Another approach for assessing account-ability could be looking at the resource efficiency and effectiveness at the institutional level. Return on investments is another way of meas-uring accountability at the macro level. Stakeholders needs combined with returns on investments can be used as the measure of the impact of higher education in meeting the needs of the individual.

All of these are implied in the measurement of quality education in terms of the parameters outlined for measuring quality of higher education as well. The basic purpose of performance indicators is to evaluate the performance of a system, an institution or an organizational structure. In the case of academic institutions, it is to be used internally for enhancing the quality of teaching, research or extension services provided by the institution. For the other external stakeholders, it provides important evidence regarding the functioning of the institu-tion in terms of the performance of resource planning, allocation, and the processes and methods used in academics and administration, and political accountability and funding decisions. Within the framework of the functions, the performance indicators/criteria may be used as a measure of accountability and also for comparison of the performance of similar institutions or of individuals performing similar functions, for staff development, for improving effectiveness of management, for image building, for marketing of programmes, and for influencing government policy for allocating funds.

The process of demonstrating or judging accountability is complex and difficult, and the main purpose of an accountability system is to not only scrutinize institutional aspects in a mechanical manner, but also facilitate the process of improvement of performance. The key performance issues are whether we have made incremental growth from year to year, or if there is any progress in the status of quality performance in each of the parameters of quality in higher education.

QUALITY ASSURANCE AND ACCOUNTABILITY MATRIX IN HIGHER EDUCATION

Accountability can be classified into different types depending on whether we are dealing with public administration, health care or education. In education, we can categorize accountability into organizational/system accountability, professional accountability, legal accountability and social accountability.

In the *organizational/system accountability,* the educational system as a whole is responsible for achieving the goals. *Legal accountability* is attributed to one of the subsystems dealing with the legal matters as well as the board of management/executive council, which comply with the rules and regulations stipulated by the regulatory bodies such as UGC, ICAR, AICTE, NCTE, MCI and DCI, among others. The organization with its subsystems such as the Board of Studies (BoS), Academic Council (AC) and the Board of Management (BoM) are primarily responsible for curriculum development, restructuring, and following the guidelines and the policy by MHRD as well as UGC.

In *professional accountability*, it is the duty of a teacher to think of ways and means to help the students in acquiring knowledge and skills, and shaping their future. The teacher becomes a friend, guide, adviser and facilitator *for the holistic development of the students.* At the same time, the teacher as professional is also responsible for their professional development and undertaking research for the progress of knowledge.

In *legal accountability*, the institution has to comply with the legal requirements in performing the various functions. The legal aspects may also be included in financial auditing. Students and other stakeholders might also have to get their complaints redressed.

In *social accountability*, the institution and faculties are accountable towards the community. The role of the universities goes beyond degree-awarding institutions to establishing the linkages between the institutional knowledge and community needs. At the same time, the institutions are responsible for breaking the hegemony of certain knowledge systems by acknowledging and bringing in indigenous knowledge system to the mainstream through participative university community development projects. The faculty should be aware of the civic responsibilities, and should co-ordinate the activities of the community to reach out the socially economically and educationally marginalized sections of the society.

At the institutional level, various structures have been created to ensure the responsibility for quality across the QA parameters. The legal, professional and social frameworks govern the QA structures and processes for accountability. The following section presents the 'quality assurance and accountability matrix in higher education in India' (Table 11.1), through an analysis of the QA parameters as part of the NAAC assessment and accreditation system in India, and the accountability types. The NAAC parameters discussed are curricular aspects; teaching, learning evaluation; research, consultancy and extension; infrastructure and learning resources; student support and progression; governance, leadership and management; and innovations and best practices.

Curricular Aspects

Curriculum design and development, academic flexibility, curriculum enrichment and feedback system are the four indicators covered in the QA assessments. The BoS, AC and BoM are the structures at the institutional level that are accountable for the first three of the key indicators, and they are classified within the legal and professional framework of accountability. The feedback system, like the other three indicators,

Quality Assurance Parameters	Accountability Types and Classification		
	Type	Who Is Accountable?	Accountability Classification
Curricular Aspects			
Curricular design and development	System	BoS, AC, BoM	Legal and professional
Academic flexibility	System	BoS, AC, BoM	Legal and professional
Curriculum enrichment	System	BoS, AC, BoM	Legal and professional
Feedback system	System	IQAC	Professional
Teaching–Learning Evaluation			
Student enrolment and profile	System	Governance and management	
Catering to student diversity	System	Governance and management	
Teaching learning process	System	Faculty, students	
Teacher quality	System	Governance and management	Legal and professional
Evaluation process and reform	System	IQAC	Professional
Student performance and learning outcomes	System	Exam board	Legal and professional
Research, Consultancy and Extension			
Promotion of research	System	Institutional governance	Professional
Resource mobilization for research	System	Faculty, institution, students	Professional
Research facilities	System	Institution, faculty	Professional
Consultancy		Management, faculty	Professional
Extension activities and social responsibility	System	Governance, faculty	Social accountability
Collaborations	System	System, governance and faculty	Professional

Figure 11.1 *(Continued)*

Infrastructure and Learning Resources			
Physical facilities		Governance and management	Legal and professional accountability
Library as learning resources	Management system	Governance and management	Legal and professional accountability
IT infrastructure		Governance and management	Legal and professional accountability
Maintenance of campus facilities		Governance and management	Legal and professional accountability
Student Support and Progression			
Student mentoring and support		Faculty, student welfare department, system	Professional
Student progression		Faculty, parents and students	Professional
	Management	Student welfare department, faculty	Professional
Governance, Leadership and Management			
Institutional Vision and Leadership	Governance	System, management and faculty	Professional
Strategy Development and Deployment	Governance	System, management and faculty	Professional
Faculty Empowerment Strategies	Governance	Management, leadership	Professional
Financial Management and Resource Mobilization	Governance	Management and leadership system	Professional
Internal Quality Assurance System	System		
Innovations and Best Practices			
Environment consciousness	System	Management, Governance system	Professional
Innovations	System	Management, Governance system	Professional
Best practices	System	Management, Faculty	Professional

Figure 11.1 *Quality Assurance and Accountability Matrix in Higher Education in India*

Source: Author.

is also a part of the system-level accountability, but is covered under the framework of professional accountability through IQACs.

Teaching, Learning and Evaluation

The second QA parameter is teaching, learning and evaluation. Student enrolment and profile, catering to student diversity, teaching–learning process, teacher quality, evaluation process and reform, and student performance and learning outcomes are the six key indicators to reflect accountability in teaching, learning and evaluation. The institutional governance and management system is responsible for keeping data on student enrolment and profile, catering to student diversity and ensuring teacher quality. Faculty and students are accountable for the teaching–learning process. Whilst the IQACs are deemed accountable for the evaluation processes and reforms initiatives, the examination board of the higher education institutions is accountable for student performance and learning outcomes.

Teacher quality is ensured through the legal and professional framework of accountability as also the student performance and learning outcomes. However, evaluation processes and reforms are led by the professional framework. Arguably, student enrolment and profile, and catering to student diversity are governed by the legal framework, but they also come under the framework of social accountability.

Research, Consultancy and Extension

Promotion of research, resource mobilization for research, research facilities, consultancy, extension activities and social responsibilities, and collaborations are the six key indicators on which NAAC assesses institutions for the quality of research, consultancy and extension.

Institutional governance holds the professional responsibility for the promotion of research. Similarly, the institution and faculty are responsible for resource mobilization for research as well as research facilities. Professional expertise of the faculty and support from the management facilitate the consultancy activities at the institutions. Thus, professional accountability framework guides consultancy as well as collaborations for research amongst institutions. The institutional governance and faculty are guided through the social accountability to ensure research extension activities and social responsibilities.

At the level of governance and management of research, the Board of Research Studies at the institutional level, and expert groups and review committees at the departmental level ensure the quality of research. These structures are constituted for reviewing faculty-led researches and projects as well as researches by students towards the fulfilment of requirements for award of specific degrees, such as MPhil, PhD and postdoctoral research. Within the framework of professional accountability, the quality of researches depends on the proficiency and expertise of the identified experts as members of the group.

Infrastructure and Learning Resources

Physical facilities, library as learning resources, IT infrastructure and maintenance of campus facilities are the four indicators for the assessment of quality of infrastructure and learning resources. To reiterate, every higher education institution is set up according to the rules stipulated by the associated regulator, such as UGC, AICTE and MCI, amongst others. These rules place conditions regarding the minimum infrastructure and learning resources that must be made available while setting up the institution. The governance and management structure of the institution, such as the purchase committee and financial audit system, are accountable for ensuring that these minimum conditions are met. Primarily, these forms of accountability can be classified as legal accountability. However, in terms of the quality of reading material available in the library, or the decision regarding availability of software and hardware according to the user requirement and technological advancement is a matter of professional accountability.

Student Support and Progression

Student mentoring and support and student progression are the two indicators on which NAAC assesses institutions for the quality of support provided to the students and its impact on scholastic progression.

Although led by the professional accountability framework, whereby student welfare department at the institution and faculty are primarily responsible, this form of accountability cannot be realized without active involvement from parents and students.

Governance, Leadership and Management

The system, management, leadership and faculty that can be classified under professional accountability are responsible to ensure the realization of the quality of governance, leadership and management in the institutions. NAAC assesses the quality of this aspect based on five indicators: institutional vision and leadership, strategy development and deployment, faculty empowerment strategies, financial management and resource mobilization, and the internal QA system. Needless to mention, the governance, leadership and management accountability is intricately intertwined with all other QA parameters of the system.

Innovations and Best Practices

Innovations, best practices and environment consciousness are the three indicators of system accountability, guided by the professional accountability framework. The governance and management system of the institution and faculty are responsible to ensure that these parameters are met.

To cite the case of SNDT Women's University, Mumbai, the accountability was a built-in factor since its inception in 1916. The first women's university in India as well as in South East Asia, it was established by Maharshi Karve and was modelled after the Japanese Women's University. Karve's noble mission was about rehabilitating young widows, and empowering them to live with dignity and honour. The university is autonomous and has some special privileges to expand its activities across the globe. The strong institutional commitment formed the basis of accountability. The university has grown gradually from a single discipline of home science to multi-faculty departments, that is, social sciences, the sciences, nursing, fine arts, performing arts, humanities, business management, education management, law, technology, computer science, women's studies, a strong vocational-oriented polytechnic, and continuing and adult education, which offer many courses with an emphasis on vocational education.

The university's interaction with industries is worth mentioning. Realizing the uniqueness of the university in its contribution to the society and ultimately for the national development, the industries came forward to collaborate. Because of the accountability and transparency in running the organization, a trust was created. The collaborators recognized the effectiveness and the operational efficiency of the programmes compared to similar programmes at other institutions. The key was in the details of planning and implementing programmes, and also the efforts of the faculty in mentoring each student. The faculty's commitment has been remarkable in achieving the incremental growth for each student so that they aspire to be excellent in their own specialization. The organizational, professional and social accountability based on commitment were the factors contributing to the quality and excellence at SNDT Women's University.

CONCLUSION

Quality and accountability are two sides of the same coin. QA is the outcome of the expected functions and responsibilities of different stakeholders as per the aims and objectives of higher education. The criteria for assessing the quality of different institutions are well laid out since 1994. Even though the mechanism of operation for IQAC is in order, the accountability measures have to be well-defined for different stakeholders.

Improved accountability is vital to ensure the success of all other institutional reforms. Colleges and universities must become more transparent about cost, price, and student success and outcomes, and must willingly share this information with students, parents and the public. Student achievement, which is inextricably connected to institutional success, must be measured by every institution on a value added basis that takes into account the student's academic baseline while assessing the results. Higher education is accountable in the broadest sense to the society, of which it is a part, creating access to the broad base of the marginalized sections.

The future of the higher education system should focus on a performance-based accountability system. Every one of our goals from improving access and affordability to enhancing quality and innovation, we should take responsibility both individually and collectively in an organization. At the same time, all institutions shall implement the accountability system based on the aims and goals of higher education as well as the criteria for quality education.

REFERENCES

Berdahl, R. (1990). Academic freedom, autonomy and accountability in British universities. *Studies in Higher Education 15*(2), 169–180.

BIS (Bureau of Indian Standards). (1988). *Quality systems guidelines for selection and use of standards on quality systems.* New Delhi: BIS.

GOI (Government of India). (1986). *National policy on education, 1986.* New Delhi: Government of India.

Green, D. (1993). Quality assurance in Western Europe: Trends, practices and issues. *Quality Assurance in Education, 1*(3), 4–14.

Playfoot, J., & Hall, R. (2009). *Effective education for employment: A global perspective.* Retrieved 5 December 2014, from http://eee-edexcel.com/xstandard/docs/effective_education_for_employment_web_version.pdf

Wagner, R. B. (1989). *Accountability in education: A philosophical enquiry.* London: Routledge.

Chapter 12

Managing Quality at Institutional Level

B. S. Madhukar

INTRODUCTION

The concept of defining and assuring quality in a diverse higher education system as in India is very complex. A major attempt in this direction
is made through the accreditation process as envisaged by the National
Assessment and Accreditation Council (NAAC) and National Board of
Accreditation (NBA), and practiced for nearly two decades in the country.

The purpose of assessment exercise the world over is to ensure that
all institutions across the board continuously focus on improving the
quality of education they deliver to the students, and discharge their
accountability to other stakeholders. For example, when we look
at the outcome of the NAACs assessment exercise for colleges and
analyze the results, it can be seen that amongst the colleges that have
gone through the assessment process (about 6,500 as on 11 July 2016),
around 20 per cent fall in grade 'A' (highest level), 65 per cent in Grade
'B' and the rest in Grade 'C'. Only a handful are categorized as not
accredited and fall under Grade 'D'.[1]

---

[1] Retrieved from National Assessment and Accreditation Council (NAAC)
website: www.naac.gov.in

A brief look at the data, without going into the merits/demerits of the grading systems, reveals that these institutions need to evolve systems and processes to deal with refining their administrative, teaching–learning, evaluation, student support and other related activities. They also need to maximize their internal potential, and further integrate with the requirements of the affiliating universities, statutory bodies and central/state governments. A minor research project titled 'Quality Audit (QAu) Effective tool for IQAC' conducted recently to understand the quality improvement mechanism in place amongst the top-graded (by NAAC) colleges in Mumbai and Pune region indicates the lack of any clear and structured approach to address the issue of quality management at the institutional level (UGC WRO, n.d.). This seems to be the trend in other regions as well.

In view of this, it becomes necessary that a structured approach to 'managing for quality at the Institutional level' is envisaged and disseminated across institutions. This aspect is very significant, particularly in the Indian context, as only a periodic external assessment process is not likely to yield substantial results in the long run noting that quality assurance (QA) is a continuous activity and process. Over the years, NAAC has come up with the idea of establishing an Internal Quality Assurance Cell (IQAC) in every institution to take the QA process as a continuous activity. However, the feedback from the ground level shows that there is no clarity in the working of IQAC, wherever it is operational, and it may also not be carrying out activities focused on continuous improvement. The proposed and the expected structure of IQAC can flourish in an institution with a decentralized management culture. However, institutions with rigid structures are unable to practice flexibility and futuristic orientation in the governance system as well as establish credibility of the educational outcome. The requirement for change and flexibility demands autonomy to the institutions.

AUTONOMY FOR QUALITY

The decentralized management culture in the institution is at the heart of the concept of autonomy for quality. The four areas of university management, where autonomy for quality can be analyzed, are organization, finance, staffing and academic. A democratic set-up acknowledges that strict control and regulation stifle the creativity, innovation and entrepreneurial spirit of organizations, thus impacting their journey towards quality. However, there could be differences in perspectives and objectives between the government and institutional view points with regard to autonomy. The government—being the funder of the HEIs—and the HEIs are assumed to be in a principal–agent relationship. However, HEIs may not be only looking forward to implement government policies but may desire to have freedom to design their academic agendas, and develop academic network and alliances at different levels, ranging from national to international (Reilly, Turcan & Bugaian, 2016). In addition, though the HEIs may not be considering ways of generating revenue/funds, they are definitely keen on having financial independence, in terms of fund utilization which they view as pertinent to quality maintenance.

In India, prior to the setting up of Calcutta, Bombay and Madras universities, which were the first universities in India, there were several colleges, which functioned with full autonomy. This implies that these colleges had ultimate freedom in academic and administrative matters, including the selection of students, design of curricula, generating and utilizing funds, and devising their own quality assessment/audit measures.

Later, in 1857, when the first universities came into being, the existing autonomous colleges were affiliated to them, adopting common rules for admission, courses, examination and results. Post 1947, various committees and commissions discussed and emphasized autonomy for educational institutions in the backdrop of concern for quality in an expanding system. The education commission of 1964–1966, also known as the Kothari Commission, made the first formal and specific recommendations on college autonomy. The affiliating system, though initially envisaged as bringing standards and quality to the institutions, has long been reduced to a normative and bureaucratic system. The distortion and consequences of the affiliating system due to rigidity in the structure of higher education and lack of academic autonomy have been highlighted in the University Grants Commission (UGC) guidelines (2003) document.

The 1986 National Policy on Education (GOI, 1986) recommended the selection of students, appointment and promotion of teachers, determination of courses of study and methods of teaching, and choice of areas for research and their promotion as the aspects of autonomy to be given to the colleges. The policy recommended the establishment of 500 autonomous colleges and autonomous departments within selected universities in the seventh plan period (GOI, 1986, Para. 5.28, p. 43). This was further endorsed by the Programme of Action (PoA) 1992.

Autonomy of the institutions combined with academic quality is crucial to the demand for flexibility ingrained in the concept of student choice in curriculum. The tenth plan document proposed to implement the choice-based and open-choice approach at the undergraduate and postgraduate levels through autonomous colleges as well as colleges and universities with potential for excellence. The UGC document on the XI plan profile of higher education in India clearly states, 'the only safe and better way to improve the quality of undergraduate education is to delink most of the colleges from the affiliating structure. Colleges with academic and operative freedom are doing better and have more credibility' (UGC, 2013, p. 2). It is proposed to increase the number of autonomous colleges, that is, to make at least 10 per cent of eligible colleges autonomous by the end of the plan period.

An autonomous college will have the freedom to determine and prescribe its own courses of study and syllabi; restructure and redesign the courses to suit local needs; prescribe rules for admission in consonance with the reservation policy of the state government; evolve methods of assessment of students performance, the conduct of examinations and notification of results; use modern tools of educational technology to achieve higher standards and greater creativity; and promote healthy practices such as community service, extension activities, projects for the benefit of the society at large and neighbourhood programmes (UGC, 2013).

Many accredited/eligible colleges are reluctant to take up 'autonomy' in the present scenario, for which the reason can largely be attributed as 'resistance to change' and lack of information flow. However, the situation is gradually changing with more and more institutions, particularly in Tamil Nadu, Maharashtra and Karnataka, taking the lead in applying for autonomy.

ENSURING QUALITY

To reiterate, the concept of defining and assuring quality in a diverse higher education system as in India is very complex. A major attempt to define and assure quality is made through the accreditation process as envisaged by NAAC and NBA. The NAAC and NBA in general look at the various aspects of functioning of institutions/programmes through a prism of pre-defined parameters/criteria and the responses of the institutions as explained under these parameters in the form of self-study report combined with a peer team review visit. The outcome of these exercises is the granting of accreditation for a fixed period of five years along with a letter grade as practiced by NAAC, and in case of NBA, the accreditation status is conferred by varying the timelines of accreditation. NAAC has also recently incorporated the model of varying timeline vis-à-vis grades in the accreditation process. The grade level at which an institution is placed (NAAC) or the time span for which a programme is accredited (NBA) is taken as an index of the 'quality level' of the institution/programme.

NAAC has assessed and accredited more than 6,000 institutions as on July 2016, so far largely covering colleges across all the states of India. These assessment exercises carried out by NAAC over the years, has created a positive thought process in the higher education system vis-à-vis quality as an ingredient for change. Efforts are also on in many institutions to improve delivery for better quality of education. The NAAC has proposed the establishment of an IQAC in each and every institution in the country as a platform to improve quality. The concept of IQAC has been propagated since the last two decades.

BRIEF ANALYSIS OF NAAC PEER TEAM REPORTS UNIVERSITY AND COLLEGES

The NAAC peer team, as a culmination of the team-visit to a university/college, submits a report in which the overall analysis of the institution is enumerated under the categories Institutional Strengths, Institutional Weaknesses, Institutional Opportunities and Institutional Challenges, followed by Recommendations for Quality Enhancement of the institution. This analysis and the following recommendations can be perceived as an insight of the team on the present functioning of the institution and its view on the future action that can be initiated by the institution. An examination of the overall analysis and recommendations part of the reports of the institutions, which have undergone two or more cycles of assessment, reveals that the team has largely enumerated different aspects of functioning of the institutions under each head in each cycle of visit. This can possibly be explained because each visit takes place at different points in time with different constitution of team members, and all this while, the functioning of the institution also changes. In view of this, it may not be feasible to decipher from the peer team reports whether a systematic process is in place in the institution for continuous improvement in the delivery of quality education in all aspects of its functioning.

IQAC AT INSTITUTIONAL LEVEL

The work of the IQAC is the first step towards internalization and institutionalization of quality enhancement initiatives. Its success depends upon the sense of belongingness and participation it can inculcate in all the constituents of the institution. The IQAC should not be perceived as yet another hierarchical structure or a record-keeping body in the institution but as a facilitative and participative voluntary system/unit/organ of the institution. It has the potential to become a vehicle for quality enhancement by working out planned interventionist strategies to remove deficiencies and improve quality culture (NAAC & COL, 2006).

STATUS OF IQAC: A PROJECT ANALYSIS

A minor research project financially supported by the UGC was undertaken by a college in Mumbai to study the functioning of IQAC in institutions accredited as Grade 'A' under the jurisdiction of Mumbai and Pune universities. The response rate to the questionnaire distributed among the institutions about the functioning of the IQAC was poor. In view of the low response rate, and to know why the questionnaires were not filled in by many colleges, the project functionaries organized in-depth discussions with the IQAC coordinators of a few colleges.

As per the NAAC (2007) guidelines, conducting academic audits is considered one of the activities of the IQAC, even though not explicitly indicated as mandatory by NAAC. However, discussions with the IQAC coordinators reveal that institutions generally understand that it is not necessary to conduct academic audit. In reality, the IQACs are working merely as record-keeping agencies and, based on the collected reports, prepare an annual quality assurance report (AQAR) to submit to NAAC for accreditation and assessment purposes. In the experience of the coordinators, giving suggestions to institutional higher authorities for improvement of procedures and functions for quality enhancement may lead to controversies at the institutional level. The IQAC's suggestions may not be appreciated by all in the college/institution.

Mostly, IQACs end up conducting only the activities that are mandatory in nature. A hectic college schedule also poses a hurdle. However, the coordinators voiced that if NAAC advises to conduct an audit and guide the institutions regarding the pathway to follow, the institutions will act accordingly. Proper training/workshop for IQAC members can be arranged by NAAC, so that the audit is unbiased and not subjective. It was an interesting revelation that despite many workshops and seminars conducted by different colleges, the functions of IQAC, including duties and responsibilities of the cell and the coordinators, are not clear to many institutions.

Coordinators have also suggested preparing manual explaining functions of IQAC, which could serve as guidelines. These observations imply that institutions and the coordinators view themselves in a principal–agent relationship with the government and the regulatory bodies. The point of analysis could be that to what extent the institutions can take the quality initiatives forward and improve IQAC functioning if given autonomous status.

A large chunk of the HEIs in the country comes under the affiliation system particularly in state universities. Thus, there is a perennial top-down approach in their functioning. In addition, they are accustomed to receiving instructions from the government, UGC and other regulatory bodies, which further inhibit efforts to change from within. This explains the lack of initiative on part of the institutions to formulate guidelines and implement those beyond what is explicitly mandated by NAAC or any other regulatory authority.

ROAD MAP FOR THE IQAC

IQAC is envisaged to be the 'think tank' of the college/university/institution. The experiences worldwide show that the roadmap for quality is to be created internally within the institutions. Hence, institutions need to strengthen IQAC and make it effective.

The experience so far in the field indicates a lack of clarity on (a) what signifies the role of IQAC and (b) what is it expected to do. During many NAAC assessment visits to the institutions, in the course of presentation to the peer team, it is not unusual to see that all activities that occur in the institution are classified under IQAC. Further discussion on the functioning of the IQAC during the peer team visit or otherwise gets diffused with interplay of various aspects of functioning of the institution. A conclusion emerges that various constraints within and outside the institution delimit efforts to improve the system. In view of the ground-level situation and the thinking process in the institutions, it is a challenge to motivate institutions to initiate steps to maximize their existing potential and promote a culture of quality in the institutions.

The following sections draw from the international experiences in QA and steps towards promoting quality culture through supporting IQACs at the institutional level.

INTERNATIONAL EXPERIENCE ON HIGHER EDUCATION QUALITY

The development of QA in European higher education has been closely linked to the Bologna Process and the creation of the European Higher Education Area (EHEA). From the statement in the 2003 Berlin Communique that 'consistent with the principle of institutional autonomy, the primary responsibility for QA in higher education lies with each institution itself' (Berlin Communique, 2003, p. 3) to the adoption of the *Standards and Guidelines for Quality Assurance in the European Higher Education Area* (ESG) in 2005 and the establishment of the European Quality Assurance Register for Higher Education (EQAR) in 2008, the Bologna Process has supported a number of measures aimed at developing and promoting QA.

The *Trends 2015* study identified QA as the most important 'change driver' in European higher education in the past 15 years (Sursock, 2015, p. 11). While the initial emphasis lay primarily on system-level changes and the introduction of external QA, the past decade has seen a gradual shift towards internal QA (IQA). To effect change, the IQA has to be supported through regulatory bodies, accreditation agencies and associations.

Empowering Universities

The European Union Association (EUA) has a long record of working on QA in Europe and supporting its members in developing internal quality systems through a variety of activities. The project 'Empowering Universities to Fulfill their Responsibility for Quality Assurance' (EUREQA) was launched in the autumn of 2012. The aim of this capacity-building project was to support participating institutions in developing their IQA systems, thereby facilitating the enhancement of quality and strengthening institutional quality cultures (Gover & Loukkola, 2015). Few key conclusions drawn from the EUREQA project are noted as follows.

The first step in developing an IQA system is to define its roles and responsibilities. Its goals and purposes may differ greatly from one institution to another. However, a consensus prevails in European higher education that the goals are expected to (a) be context sensitive and in line with the institution's strategic priorities; (b) aim at enhancing quality, not only assuring it; and (c) support quality culture.

As mentioned earlier, the goals, purposes and design of any IQA system will depend on the institution's context and specificities. Issues such as strategic priorities of the institution, its existing organizational and decision-making structures and processes, size, disciplines and current state of development in its approach to quality, all influence the fit-for-purpose IQA system.

Table 12.1 depicts various development phases of quality that can exist within an organization (Bollaert, 2014). These phases can be interpreted as factors that influence the design of a system as well as those which describe its maturity. Bollaert concluded that when 'the understanding of quality is still on (a) personal and non-systemic level, it is not worth even considering the setting up of a heavy system' (Bollaert, 2014, p. 287).

The question about the role of QA processes in creating quality is often asked, particularly in higher education, which traditionally relies heavily on individual members of academic staff relaying their expertise to the next generation. Table 12.1 can also be understood as a response to this question. It seeks to demonstrate that by establishing and implementing a more organized approach, the likelihood of quality improvement is enhanced.

Table 12.1 *Short Descriptions of Simplified Development Phases*

Phase #	Management and Organization Processes	Results
Phase 1	Quality is the result of purely individual commitment	Quality is variable
Phase 2	There is a beginning of thinking in processes	Quality is the result of a beginning systematic approach
Phase 3	The organization is managed professionally	Quality is guaranteed
Phase 4	The organization as well as its management is systematically renewed	Quality is continuously improved with innovation
Phase 5	The organization is outward-oriented and strives for excellence	Quality is recognised by externals as excellent, and thus an international example

Source: Bollaert (2014, p. 87).

Examining Quality Culture

A project under the aegis of the European University Association, examining quality culture (EQC) in HEIs, aimed to provide an overview of IQA processes in place within the institutions across Europe. The report, published in 2010, showed that great progress has been made in the institutions in developing QA mechanisms. Institutional autonomy, responsibility and accountability are recognized as the components essential to IQA processes.

The notion of quality culture is understood here as comprising of two distinct sets of elements: 'shared values, beliefs, expectations and commitments towards quality' and a 'structural/managerial element with defined processes that enhance quality and aim at coordinating efforts' (EUA, 2006, p. 10).

The report highlights five conditions that lead to an effective quality culture. First, it is important not to rely on a single QA instrument such as student questionnaires, particularly if they shape staffing decisions, for example, promotions. There must be a mix of several instruments to ensure good intelligence. Second, the most effective IQA arrangements are those that derive from effective internal decision-making processes and structures. Third, it was recognized that leadership is essential to give the initial steer and broad frameworks of QA mechanisms. Leadership should facilitate internal debate—and tolerate dissent—in order to make sure that QA processes do not end up being imposed and simply bolted on.

The more academic and less managerial QA is, the more likely it is to make in-roads in the institution. Fourth, it is essential to invest in people through staff development to avoid IQA arrangements becoming punitive. Fifth, both institutional autonomy and self-confidence are key factors in the capacity of institutions—to define quality and the purposes of their IQA processes, and to ensure that these are in line with their specific profiles, strategies and organizational cultures. In doing so, these institutions are sometimes confronted with their external QA agencies' processes, which might be at cross-purposes. It is essential that the internal and external processes are viewed together, and that the higher education community—the institutions and the agencies—negotiate the articulation between the two sets of processes in order to ensure true accountability, and avoid duplication of evaluations and QA fatigue.

Finally, the report concludes that the factors that promote effective quality cultures are- an 'open' environment of the institution, which is not overly regulated and enjoys a high level of public trust; the institution is self-confident and does not limit itself to the definitions of quality processes set by its national QA agency; the institutional culture stresses democracy and debate; the institution equally values the voices of students and staff; the definition of academic professional roles stresses effective teaching rather than only academic expertise and research strength; and QA processes are grounded in academic values while giving due attention to the necessary administrative processes.

Future Directions

The report on the Quality Culture Project 2002–2003 observes that 'the "quality movement" in Europe started, as it were, from the wrong end, with the rush of establishing external quality procedures rather than building them internally' (EUA, 2005, p. 37). The project has served to highlight the importance of IQA processes.

The internal quality is primarily the responsibility of the institution, whereas how this responsibility is carried out can be reviewed through accountability measures set by external QA systems. The aim should be to gradually attain best possible equilibrium between institutional autonomy and accountability. The action plans developed and implemented by the institutions are thus evaluated for their robustness by EQA.

MANAGING FOR QUALITY AT THE INSTITUTIONAL LEVEL: CHALLENGES IN INDIAN CONTEXT

Managing for quality at the institutional level in India is still at an experimental and exploratory phase. Institutions look up to external inputs to drive change in their internal operations. Reiterating that setting up heavy systems in absence of institutional culture is not worth considering as it will lead to management failure of QA at the institutional level, the following issues need to be addressed to build a robust IQA culture in the institution.

First, it can be inferred from the observations from the minor research project, referred to earlier, that a receptive management and leadership will be a prerequisite to effect any change. It is necessary for the regulatory bodies, associations and/or external QA agencies to exclusively conduct seminars/workshops for the management and leadership of institutions to enable them to imbibe the concepts of quality and its management.

At the institutional level, the IQAC should not be an ad hoc arrangement put in place, just before a visit by an external assessment team as widely practised. Rather, a well-defined entity with clear roles and responsibilities, and empowered by the management and the leadership of the institution should be set up. This initiative needs to be supported by trained manpower, resources and necessary infrastructure. The role and the objectives of the IQAC may be set in motion by each of the institutions (university and colleges) by reflecting on the following suggestive aspects and, accordingly, creating an implementation strategy.

To begin with, the institutions need to identify the cultural and psychological aspects such as shared values, beliefs, expectations and commitment towards quality. Alongside, the institutional structures that define pathways and processes to enhance quality need to be reviewed and/or put in place. Both aspects are necessary to co-ordinate and consolidate individual/unit-level efforts towards quality. To achieve this, the institutions need to identify the barriers to quality at the cultural/psychological levels as well as the structural/managerial levels. This is to be followed by developing a gradual roadmap to address those challenges.

There is a prominence of top-down leadership style in higher education in India, mostly because of how the Indian higher education system is structured. However, for creating shared vision, values and mutual trust, a top-down approach may not be suited. A distributive leadership style, which can restructure conflicts and contradictions between assigned and perceived roles and envisaged responsibilities, may be more suited for implementing quality strategies. A more decentralized, dialogic and democratic style of management is essential to achieve quality culture at the institutional level. However, the affiliated colleges, affiliating institutions, that is, universities, and autonomous/stand-alone institutions will have different pathways to put this style of management into practice due to their structural/organizational specificities. They will have to think of ways in which a sense of ownership can be generated among the staff so that they are motivated to align themselves to institutional goals. Mechanisms of institutional accountability and self-assessment have to be integrated for all processes, systems and sub-systems of the institution.

Any entity assigned the role of developing mechanisms of institutional accountability and influencing quality culture at the institutional level will have a limited role if it does not have a statutory status. The collection and management of data regarding institutional processes, systems and sub-systems should be used for institutional research to generate discussions and informed decision-making regarding institutional goals and practices. The learning about quality should not only be confined to the intra-institutional dialogue, but may also include inter-institutional sharing. In addition, context-specific resources and trainings are required to establish/strengthen decentralized quality management culture.

Whilst the Indian institutions endeavour to maximize their existing internal potential towards quality sustenance and enhancement, the university/UGC/governments should create a positive environment for institutional growth by providing seamless integration of requisite policy support through enhanced and continuous funding, the freedom to appoint suitable faculty and granting of autonomy. These are not linear processes that would unfold in a chronological sequence. There has to be simultaneity of efforts, which can be effective only when embedded in institutional culture. Support from the government and other stakeholders plays an important role in creating frameworks of autonomy and accountability, thus strengthening institutional culture.

CONCLUSION

As evident from the international experiences, capacity building of institutions in developing IQA systems facilitates the enhancement of quality and strengthens institutional culture. The goals, purposes and design of any IQA system depend on the institutions' context and specificity. When the understanding of quality is still on (a) personal and non-systemic level, considerable efforts are required to be made before envisaging setting up of a heavy system. Mapping the observations on the functioning of IQACs in Indian institutions on to the depiction in the Bollaert's (2014) development phases of organizational management and processes (Table 12.1), it can be inferred that that most HEIs in India are either in Phase 1 or Phase 2 of the development process of quality. Interventions at various levels, both internal and external to the institution, will be required to create an optimal meeting point between a top-down-approach and a bottom-up-approach, and reach a fit-for-purpose equilibrium while setting up robust IQA system.

As many of the educational institutions in India are largely used to a top-down approach, it is crucial for the authorities in the higher education space to push for functional autonomy to the institutions, particularly colleges. It may also be worthwhile for UGC/NAAC to identify few universities and colleges, and nurture a model IQAC unit by learning from Indian experience so far and suitably adopting international practices. These institutions can act as prime movers, and help transfer the practices so developed to other institutions that are willing to take ownership; imbibe suitable practices in the context of functioning of their institutions; and graduate themselves to share the experiences with others. Initiatives towards quality through institutional capacity building is a long drawn process, but invaluable for enhancement and sustenance of institutional quality. Further, as observed in the chapter, external accountability procedures should take the form of an institutional audit that could evaluate the robustness and the embeddedness of internal quality monitoring processes. In addition to setting up of QA systems, we need to understand the contours of quality at a personal and non-systemic level. Adequate research facilities should be created in the country to generate evidences for supporting quality enhancement initiatives and emerging issues.

REFERENCES

Bollaert, L. (2014). *A manual for internal quality assurance in higher education with special focus on professional higher education.* Brussels: European Association of Institutions in Higher Education.

Berlin Communiqué. (2013). *Realising the European higher education area.* Communiqué of the conference of ministers responsible for higher education, Berlin, 19 September 2003. Retrieved 13 September 2017, from http://www.enqa.eu/wp-content/uploads/2013/03/BerlinCommunique1.pdf

EUA (European Union Association). (2005). *Developing an internal quality culture in European universities.* Report on the quality culture project, 2002–2003. Belgium: European University Association. Retrieved 7 November 2016, http://www.eua.be/eua/jsp/en/upload/QC_report_final.1076424814595.pdf

———. (2006). *Quality culture in European universities: A bottom-up approach.* Report on the three rounds of the quality culture project 2002–2006. European University Association.

GOI (Government of India). (1986). *National Policy on Education 1986.* New Delhi: Government of India, para 5.28, p. 43. Retrieved 20 march 2018, from http://mhrd.gov.in/sites/upload_files/mhrd/files/upload_document/npe.pdf

Gover, A., & Loukkola, T. (2015). *Eureqa moments! Top tips for internal quality assurance.* Belgium: European University Association. Retrieved 7 November 2016, from http://www.eua.be/Libraries/publications-homepage-list/eua_eureqa_moments_web_highq

NAAC (National Assessment and Accreditation Council). (2007). *Guidelines for the creation of the internal quality assurance cell (IQAC) in accredited institutions.* Bengaluru: NAAC.

NAAC & COL (Commonwealth of Learning). (2006). *Quality assurance in higher education—An introduction.* Bangalore/Vancouver, Canada: NAAC/Commonwealth of Learning.

Reilly, J. E., Turcan, R. V., & Bugaian, L. (2016). The challenge of university autonomy. In J. E. Reilly, R. V. Turcan, & L. Bugaian. (Eds). *[Re]discovering university autonomy: The global market paradox of stakeholder and educational values in higher education* (pp. 3–24). New York, NY: Palgrave-Macmillan.

Sursock, A. (2015). *Trends 2015: Learning and teaching in European universities.* Brussels: EUA. Retrieved 7 November 2016, from http://www.eua.be/publications

UGC (University Grants Commission). (2013). *Guidelines for autonomous colleges during the eleventh plan period (2007–2012)* (As modified up to 8 January 2013). New Delhi: University Grants Commission. Retrieved 7 November 2016, from http://www.ugc.ac.in/pdfnews/9986207_revisedautonomouscollege-jan13.pdf

UGC WRO (Western Regional Office). (n.d.). *Quality audit (QA) effective tool for IQAC* (Minor Research Project Report. File No.#23-685/12(WRO)), p. 19. Pune: University Grants Commission Western Regional Office.

Chapter 13

Effects of External and Internal Quality Assurance on Indian Higher Education Institutions

Anupam Pachauri

INTRODUCTION

The role of higher education (HE) in furthering economic growth, personal income and social development has been increasingly acknowledged across the globe. This century has witnessed the revival and an unprecedented global growth of the HE sector. The trend is particularly visible in emerging economies where growth of GDP and increase in enrolment rates has been observed. Thus, the sector is no longer a domain of the elite and the privileged but is considered must for all the eligible youths across the social, economic, geographical and cultural backgrounds implying the diversity of the HE participants. This change in approach to HE is reflected in the massification of HE with demands for equality of opportunity to diverse groups.

Traditionally, the expectation from education was emancipation of the individual and society; now the universities are expected to address the educated labour and economic demands of the society (Lyotard, 1984). The universities are therefore being propelled to transform their traditional ivory tower image to institutions that are more responsive to societal demands. They are being increasingly challenged to maintain quality and remain competitive because of increased student enrolments, socio-economic dynamics, calls for public accountability and international competition.

Most of the countries across the globe are facing the challenge of maintaining and enhancing the quality of education in an expanding system impacted by economic constraints due to phases of economic recession and cuts in public funds for the HE sector. Traditional quality maintenance and enhancement functions were governed by the internal mechanisms of the institutions, but the mechanisms including the governance structures, rules and examinations at the institutions have been ineffective and are deemed out of sync with the pace of developments in the global HE scenario (Dill, 2010). This was then taken over by private entities. Since last decade there has been a shift where alongside the external private entities the governments are also taking control of the quality assurance (QA) of the system and the higher education institutions (HEIs) through external quality assurance (EQA) arrangements.

Across the world, there is surge in QA initiatives at the level of institutions, systems, policies and schemes. The expanding and diverse system, the pressures of globalization, changing relationship between HE and the state, decreasing public financial resources with increasing demand for better public services driven by new public management approach and internationalization are some of the key drivers for this surge (Brenan & Shah, 2000; Huisman & Currie, 2004; Morley, 2003).

This chapter discusses the effects of external and internal QA on the HEIs in India. The first section describes the development of HE in terms of numbers and diversity and the concerns for quality in India. The second section reviews the literature on effects of national QA systems on institutions. The third section reviews the literature on internal QA cells (IQACs). The fourth section analyses the shifts in the QA of HE. The fifth section is focused on QA in India. Through analysis of empirical data from the CPRHE-NIEPA Research Project on quality, the sixth section analyses the structure and practice of internal QA. The effects of external and internal QA are discussed in the seventh section. This is followed by a discussion on metrics for accreditation. The final section concludes by arguing that effects of QA in the institutions can be sustained through funding support by the regulatory bodies and participation of all stakeholders.

DEVELOPMENT OF HIGHER EDUCATION AND CONCERNS FOR QUALITY IN INDIA

In 1947, there were less than 20 universities with student enrolment not even reaching 200,000 (Tilak, 2013). The university system in general, but particularly so in India, has been termed as elitist. There was general neglect of science and technical education. Moreover, the HE system did not have expanse for addressing the educational needs of the mass population.

The scenario gradually started changing in 1948 alongside the setting up of the first University Education Commission. Headed by Dr Radhakrishnan, the commission had the mandate to suggest improvements in the system in view of the prevailing requirements and the future of the country. Since those were the initial years of making of new India and there were immense gaps of leadership in all walks of the country's life, the commission called for developing universities of high standards. The University Grants Commission (UGC) was also set up at the behest of the University Education Commission's recommendations. This was followed by several other committees and commission that have impacted the growth of HE system in India. The prominent ones of these are the Education Commission of 1964–1966, also popularly known as the Kothari Commission.

The national policy texts and programmes of action also set down the recommendations for the development of HE. However, there have been changes contrary to the recommendations. An example that can be cited here is that of the 1986 policy's recommendation on strengthening existing institutions and increasing the facilities. However, there was explosive rise in the number of HEIs without regulation in that period (Mathew, 2016).

Provision of HE had been the responsibility of the state, but since the recommendations of several government committees, in the post 1990s, it has become clear that the role of the private sector in education is being encouraged with policies of deregulation in HE. At the same time, considering the vast population still left out from the altars of the HEIs, the need for expansion of the sector has been underscored (GOI, 2006). Managing a large number of universities is a policy planner's nightmare. The colleges in India are affiliated to the universities in their region. Quite often, a state university has hundreds of affiliated colleges and is responsible for maintenance of quality of the institutions affiliated to it. At one point of time, the Osmania University was the largest affiliating university in the Asian region with around 1,000 affiliated colleges. In addition, the large size institutions have been found to be poor in quality and difficult to manage by the institutional leaders. The Rashtriya Uchchatar Shiksha Abhiyan (RUSA) launched in 2013 has worked on both these challenges to quality. RUSA has recommended the bifurcation of universities into small size universities, setting up new universities in the underserved locations and transferring the affiliation of colleges to the new universities so as to have a reasonably managed number of colleges with the existing universities (RUSA, 2013).

In a massifying system with caste and class differences such as India, universities are also seen by the policy planners and various actors as spaces of democratization, and social as well as economic mobility (Mathew, 2016). Recently, the ambition of becoming world class and the figuring in world ranking has been added to the list of visions for HE in India. These multiple and often contradictory visions, however, have one thing in common, that is, concern over the quality of education. The definition of what quality is, however, means different things to different people. This is one theme that we will discuss in a later section.

The archaic teaching methods such as delivering lectures like religious discourse have been critiqued the world over and have found mention in concerns over quality of teaching in Indian HEIs. The Radhakrishnan Commission recommended the use of a combination of a variety of approaches including library work and tutorials to supplement lectures (GOI, 1962). Introduction to research methods for research in the postgraduate (PG) programmes was recommended by the commission with a vision to raise standards of PG education. 'Reorganization' of undergraduate curricula, introducing subject

'choices' and 'flexibility', redesigning courses to that effect and introduction of multi-disciplinary curriculum have been recommended
by various committees and commissions (Mathew, 2016, pp. 19–21).
Recently, the role of universities in skill development has been added
to the long list of expectations from the universities.

Concerns about the quality of HE, institutions, curricula, teachers
and graduates have resulted in recommendations on standards of HE
at the institutional level. The call of standards has also been accompanied with the need for autonomy of the institutions and the faculty
(Aggarwal, 2009; GOI, 1949; Malik, 2017). Conditionality of following
the standards and becoming eligible under the UGC Section 12 (f) and
12 (b) in order to receive grants from the public funds were laid out.
Linking fulfilment of standards to eligibility for funding are mechanisms
of ensuring accountability of the HEIs.

UGC was set up on the recommendations of the University
Education Commission and was assigned the task to oversee the cases
of the grants-in-aid colleges. Established by an act of parliament, the
UGC is a statutory body that serves as the main regulatory body for
tertiary-level education, coordinating between the centre and states,
enforcing standards and advising the government.

Since the 1990s, the QA system has been formally introduced in
India. Globally, QA is one of the aspects of governance of HEIs. In
India, there are around 13 (as of March 2017) regulatory and statutory bodies which lay down guidelines, assessment and accreditation
criteria for the institutions within their purview. The central regulator
for higher and technical education is the Ministry of Human Resource
and Development, National Assessment and Accreditation Council
(NAAC) for universities and colleges, and the National Board of
Accreditation (NBA) for technical education. Professional education
is under their respective councils.

The decade of the 1990s also denotes the initial period of liberalization policies in India. Setting up of QA agencies in the 1990s is not
only in response to the national concerns about quality of HE but also
a major initiative to shape HE and compete with international markets
through regulation of the sector. QA bodies set in the 1990s clearly

reflect this focus. We shall discuss in a later section how QA attempted to serve as a tool for preparing Indian HEIs to respond to the pressures, demands and various outcomes of liberalization. We will discuss more on this aspect with reference to the NAAC set up in 1994 in the section on EQA. Besides setting up structures and agencies, academic staff colleges (to reorient HE faculty) and the National Eligibility Test (NET) conducted by the UGC was also put in place to ensure standards of teaching in HEIs (Mishra, 2006; Varghese, Malik & Gautam, 2017). RUSA, with its focus on expansion, equity and quality, aims to bring about transformative reforms in the system and ensure 'conformity to prescribed norms and standards and adopt accreditation as a mandatory QA framework'. Recent introduction of National Institutional Rankings Framework (NIRF; see Chapter 2), also reflects the concern of the government for assessing quality of HEIs.

EFFECTS OF NATIONAL QA SYSTEMS ON INSTITUTIONS

Analyzing the relationship between EQA and its impacts on the HE system and HEIs over three decades in the USA, Ewell (2007) argues that determining the dynamics and impacts of QA is challenging because of the complexities of the system and processes. The choice of policy variables such as directness, that is, whether market-led, state-led or third-party autonomous review; institutional discretion in the QA exercise; quality domain (conceptions of quality such as 'fitness of purpose or value for money'); bases for judgement (objective measures or subjective evaluation); consequentiality (funding, reputation or no consequences); and burden on the institutions impinge upon the 'state goals' such as implementation of diversity policies at the institutional level or 'promoting positive institutional engagement' (Table 13.1).

The studies on impacts of EQA on institutions are diverse in methodology to measure the impact and the nature of the empirical data involved (Harvey & Williams, 2010; Leiber, Stensaker, & Harvey, 2015; Shah, 2012, 2013; Liu, 2016; Stensaker, 2003, 2008). Askling's study considered the impact of EQA on academic leadership (1997). The design of EQA and how it was conducted are the process features that are focused in some studies (Frederiks, Westerheijden & Weusthof, 1994; Harvey & Knight, 1996). How do the institutions 'utilize' the

Table 13.1 *Dimensions of Policy Variables and Institutional Impact*

Directness	Quality Decided by Market Place	Third-party Quality Review	State-run Quality Review
Institutional discretion	Uniform precisely defined statistical indicators	Market (can be influenced by institutions) i) Institutions allowed choice of indicators ii) Institutions allowed to choose what is to be reviewed and how the review should be conducted	Self-accreditation
Quality domain	List of 'qualities'; different conceptions of quality; efficiency/productivity, equity of access, and effectiveness with respect to outcomes (especially including the quality of student learning)		
Basis of judgement	Objective approaches: Empirical indicators Defined standards of performance	Marketplace (aggregate choices of consumers)	Professional judgement of colleagues and experts
Consequentiality (performance funding; performance reporting)	Consequences i) Funding ii) Reputation	Markets (varied influence depending on institution's current reputation and resource base)	No consequences
Burden (costs to the institutional engagement in QA process)	i) Direct costs (personnel time, assembling data, producing performance measures, constructing internal review mechanisms, for example, assessing student learning; expenses of visiting review team ii) Opportunity costs: Diversion of attention and institutional resources to EQA than for own purposes		

Source: Developed by author on the basis of discussion by Ewell (2007).

evaluations and site visits has been considered as one of the impacts of EQA. The quantitative estimation of utilization in a study by Hulpiau and Waeytens (2003) indicates that no follow-up was taken on almost half of the issues found out by the external review. This included not only action but also consideration of intention to follow up recommendations of the external review, as recorded on paper. What was not documented was not included in drawing estimations.

Staff involvement in the QA process and their perceptions about EQA are also studied as the impact of EQA (Barandiaran-Galdós, Barrenetxea Ayesta, Cardona-Rodríguez, Mijangos del Campo & Olaskoaga-Larrauri, 2012; Newton, 2000). Another set of studies considered the establishment of 'internal systems of reporting' and 'quality management' as the structural effects of EQA (Pratasavitskaya & Stensaker, 2010; Shah & Nair, 2013). Organizational learning, development of resources, power systems and undesired consequences have been reported as impacts of quality evaluation by Minelli et al. (2006). Aspects related to organizational learning are 'professional practices' at the institutional level, 'policies' of the institutions, institutional 'culture' and 'attention to evaluation'. University 'funding', development of 'technical infrastructure', 'reputation' of the institution and 'human resource management' are the aspects of development of resources. Power systems imply 'institutional relationships', 'organizational structure', 'management operating systems', the 'evaluation system and bodies in charge of it, and variation in decision-making capabilities and leadership'. The undesired consequences were reported as 'increased paperwork', 'overriding of institutional purposes', 'standardization and flattening of processes', and 'behaviour aimed at maximizing evaluation results' (Liu, 2016).

The studies on effects show that the QA exercise brings changes in HEIs. The changes could be the decision-making becoming more centralized, as also the procedures at the institutional level (Brenan & Shah, 2000; Stensaker, 2003), and the internal quality management at the institutions becoming more systematized (Stensaker, 2007). Also, teaching-learning begins receiving concerted attention (Stensaker, 2003). At the same time, scholars have pointed out that QA exercises do not result in improvement in quality of teaching-learning because the evaluations do not focus on the processes involving teaching and learning, for example, how teaching takes place and how learners learn, which in itself is an under-researched area in HE (Mandal, 2017; Shah, 2013). The effects of institutional initiatives for governance and management, quality initiatives by the government and the EQA need to be considered together in order to evaluate the effects of EQA (Carr, Hamilton & Meade, 2005).

INTERNAL QUALITY ASSURANCE AT THE INSTITUTIONAL LEVEL

The internal quality assurance (IQA) mechanisms are evolved at the institutional level for compliance to the EQA, and also to serve the internal purposes of quality monitoring and evaluation through generating and organizing relevant information (Señal et al., 2008). EQA agencies also expect institutions to set up IQA mechanisms. The organization of IQA mechanisms, however, varies according to the context (Harvey, 1995). Since the current policy discussions stress upon the learning outcomes and the quality of students learning, IQA systems are expected to evolve mechanisms so as to enhance the learning environment at the institutional level and improve the experience of students learning (Srikanthan & Dalrymple, 2005).

The effectiveness of the EQA depends particularly on the organization and management of the IQA system with clearly spelt out objects, plans, strategies and action pathways (Kristensen, 2010). There can be two broad purposes of IQA system. The first is compliance or accountability to the stakeholders both within the institution and outside the institution. The second is to support the institution change. In newly established IQA systems where the institutions are in the initial stages of EQA, the pressure on IQA is likely to be more to fulfil both the purposes. The organization and approaches of IQA could be centred around 'academic', 'managerial', 'pedagogic' and 'employment' aspects of institutional workings and curricula (Brenan & Shah, 2000). Approaches to IQA may be influenced by the disciplinary background of the participants at the institutions. Institutional participants from the domain of disciplines, which are more data-based and quantitative, focus on 'quantification' and 'technical aspects' of IQA, while those from the social sciences, arts and humanities follow qualitative approach with focus on 'procedural elements' (Vukasovic, 2014).

The IQA system at the institutional level comprises of several institutional mechanisms that work to translate the quality policy of the institution. Therefore, the primary challenge of the universities is to evolve an IQA system that is integrated to the institutional planning and management. Since the EQA affects the institutions by shifting the tilt towards centralized governance, another challenge for IQA is find an equilibrium between centralized and decentralized structures and governance. The institutions generate lot of varied data related to faculty, staff, students, governance, and management structures and processes. Some of this data is sought for EQA as per the QA agency indicators. IQAs are deemed to collect data relevant for the purpose of EQA compliance. However, institutional data management are quite often not organized and managed with equal rigour at the level of decentralized as well as centralized units. Thus, the third challenge for IQA is to not only retrieve data but also use it both for external as well as internal purposes. In the resource challenged contexts, with reference to funding, technical expertise, governance and management, and technological advancement, organizing IQA is a major challenge for the HEIs (Mhlanga, 2013).

SHIFTS IN QA OF HIGHER EDUCATION

Internationally, there has been a gradual shift in the trends in QA in HE. The focus from EQA has now moved to also include IQA. In other words alongside the institutional/organizational quality, the quality of teaching-learning is also becoming an intended focus of QA in HE. The mechanisms of QA though important for QA are not anymore considered enough for the quality of HE. There is shift from an instrumentalist approach looking at mechanisms to a more comprehensive and systemic approach (Table 13.2).

The discussions on QA are now not limited to ensuring accountability of the institutions, but also there is an increasing debate on using QA systems to improve or enhance the quality of the HE systems. In addition, the QA literature, agencies and frameworks now increasingly focus on student learning outcomes and student engagement as against the previous focus on accountability and benchmarking. The EQA mechanisms with quality audits derived from the programme evaluation

Table 13.2 *Shift in Global Trends in QA of Higher Education*

From	To
External quality assurance	Internal quality assurance
Quality assurance	Quality enhancement
Mechanisms	Systems
Accountability and benchmarking	Student learning outcomes, student engagement
Programme evaluation	Quality culture
Local/national QA	Greater internationalization in QA

Source: Author.

framework has changed to debates of encouraging quality cultures at the institutional level, challenging the 'one-size-fits-all' approach of earlier models of QA.

In some countries, collaborative models of QA have emerged, for example, the Swiss model. In Switzerland, the government and the university constituency have come together to a establish joint accreditation and quality enhancement board (Schenker-Wicki, 2002). The discussion in the European Higher Education Area is now including internationalization in QA. Whether the national governments trust the QA and accreditation agencies of other countries to accredit their institutions and how that trust can develop is a major discussion (EACEA-P9-Eurydice, 2012).

Students are the major stakeholders of the HE system. The whole set of activities in the universities are primarily organized around teaching-learning. Also, there are research universities where the spectrum of stakeholders is different than a teaching university. The universities are rapidly changing from the times of traditional classrooms in HE which were only lecture-based and teacher-dominated. Student satisfaction about the teaching-learning, courses and curricula, training in soft skills, capacity building for future employment, and support services have become important aspects to be considered in quality evaluations (Harvey, 2003; Hill, 1995; Ratcliff, 1996). However, teachers are not enthusiastic about student feedback (Douglas & Douglas, 2006; Fourie

& Alt, 2000; Prasad & Patil, 2007). Researchers have highlighted issues with the use of student feedback. The first issue is that for the purpose of QA enhancement or improvement, the student feedback data should be analyzed immediately, and the feedback should be routed to the faculty members and relevant administrators. If this is not done soon enough, the feedback becomes redundant. In routine practices of the universities, the student feedback is organized at the end of courses in the stipulated academic calendar. This renders the outgoing cohorts of students deprived from the benefit of actions taken based on their feedback (Narasimhan, 2001).

QUALITY ASSURANCE IN INDIA

The EQA agencies were established in India in the 1990s (Stella, 2002). NAAC was established in 1994 by the UGC and NBA was set up by the All India Council for Technical Education (AICTE) in 1994, although the recommendation for setting up a QA mechanism was made in 1986 (MHRD, 1986). The UGC is the statutory body which serves as the main regulatory body for tertiary-level education, coordinating between the Centre and states, enforcing standards and advising the government. For the major milestones in QA of Indian HE, refer to Table 13.3.

Besides setting up structures and agencies, academic staff colleges (to reorient HE faculty) and the NE) conducted by the UGC was also put in place to ensure standards of teaching in HEIs (Mishra, 2006; Varghese et al., 2017). RUSA, with its focus on expansion, equity and quality, aims to bring about transformative reforms in the system and ensure 'conformity to prescribed norms and standards and adopt accreditation as a mandatory QA framework'.

NATIONAL ASSESSMENT AND ACCREDITATION COUNCIL

Self-study reports (SSRs) and peer review using well-defined criteria forms the basis of quality assessment by the National Assessment and Accreditation Council (NAAC), which follows a four-stage process for accreditation and assessment.

Table 13.3 *Milestones in Quality Assurance of Indian Higher Education*

What	When	Aspects/Outcome
Establishment of Medical Council of India (MCI)	1934	The first regulatory body established in India: Medical Council of India (MCI) to lay down norms and standards, recognize and derecognize courses and institutions
Establishment of the University Grants Commission (UGC)	1953/1956	Establishment of UGC as a statutory body by the parliament 'for coordination and determination of standards un universities'
		Minimum framework of quality: Clause 12(f) for temporarily affiliated colleges and 12(b) for colleges with permanent affiliation
Establishment of the All India Council for Technical Education	1987	
Establishment of National Assessment and Accreditation Council (NAAC) and Establishment of National Board of Accreditation (NBA)	1994	Assessment of quality and accreditation of universities and colleges by NAAC based on seven criteria; and accreditation of technical programmes in technical education by NBA
		External quality assurance
Internal Quality Assurance Cell (IQAC)	2004	Introduction of IQAC requirement for NAAC accreditation for second and subsequent cycles
		Internal quality assurance
Rashtriya Uchchatar Shiksha Abhiyan (RUSA)	2013	NAAC accreditation made mandatory requirement by the UGC for the institutions applying for RUSA funds

Source: CABE (2005), Thorat (2008) and Varghese (2015).

The first stage involves developing the national criteria of assessment. The criteria vary according to the institution type. Institutions vary in terms of college affiliations and jurisdictions (affiliating vs. unitary), their funding (state vs. central) and their specializations (deemed universities and institutes of national importance). There is also great variety within the college system where schools can exist as affiliated, constituent and autonomous institutions. The institutions opting to go for accreditation have to submit a letter of intent (LOI) to NAAC.

The second stage is characterized by the preparation and submission of a SSR by the institution. The institutional assessment process is fundamentally anchored in the SSR and peer team validation. NAAC has prepared and disseminated manuals for various categories of HEIs with detailed guidelines on preparation of the SSR, and the specifications of the assessment and accreditation process. An analysis of their strengths, weaknesses, opportunities and challenges by the institutions in the SSR allows the institutions and the participants to be reflexive about their practice and notions of quality. The report is to be submitted to the NAAC within six months of submitting the LOI.

The third stage entails institutional on-site visits by an external peer team, which includes the validation of the SSR and the drafting of recommendations for the assessment outcome. The peer team review report is shared with the head of the institution at the end of visit and is reported to the NAAC along with a confidential recommendation on grading.

The final decision on institutional grading is taken in the fourth stage by the Executive Committee of the NAAC. The EQA through NAAC considers seven criteria, namely, curricular Aspects; teaching, learning and evaluation; research, consultancy and extension; infrastructure and learning resources; student support and progression; governance, leadership and management; and innovations and best practices. The key aspects under each criterion have their own weightages according to the relative importance of the said key aspect in the context of the type of institution. These weightages are used to calculate the cumulative grade point average (CGPA) score at the institutional level according to the institution type (Table 13.4).

Table 13.4 *NAAC Criterion and Weightage for the Assessment and Accreditation*

		Weightage According to the Institution Type		
S. No.	Criterion and Key Aspects	Universities	Autonomous Institutions	Affiliated Colleges
1.	Curricular Aspects Curriculum Design and Development Academic Flexibility Curriculum Enrichment Feedback System	150	150	100
2.	Teaching–Learning and Evaluation Student Enrolment and Profile Catering to Student Diversity Teaching–Learning Process Teacher Quality Evaluation Process and Reforms Student Performance and Learning Outcomes	200	300	350
3.	Research Consultancy and Extension Promotion of Research Resource Mobilization for Research Research Facilities Research Publications and Awards Consultancy Extension Activities and Institutional Social Responsibility Collaboration	250	150	150

No.	Criteria			
4.	Infrastructure and Learning Resources Physical Facilities Library as a Learning Resource IT Infrastructure Maintenance of Campus Facilities	100	100	100
5.	Student Support and Progression Student Mentoring and Support Student Progression Student Participation and Activities	100	100	100
6.	Governance Leadership and Management Institutional Vision and Leadership Strategy Development and Deployment Faculty Empowerment Strategies Financial Management and Resource Mobilization Internal Quality Assurance System	100	100	100
7.	Innovations and Best Practices Environment Consciousness Innovations Best Practices	100	100	100

Source: http://naac.gov.in/assesment_accreditation.asp, accessed on 16 March 2018.

Over the years, NAAC's grading system has undergone several transformations (Pillai & Patil, 2016). Though NAAC does not rank institutions based on their CGPA score, the scores or grades given to the institutions or earned by them have been cause of grievances when institutions begin to compare themselves with other institutions in their region (Pillai & Patil, 2016). Starting from an initial 10-point scoring scale to grading with A-stars to revised grading from A to C has again been revised in July 2017.

The entire endeavour of accreditation visits and institutional assessments is managed through identified experts and senior faculty members of universities and colleges from all over India. Since 2010, NAAC has been conducting workshops for the assessors, for example, peer review team members, appraising and orienting them about the NAAC philosophy and process of undertaking institutional visits, validation of information and developing accreditation reports.

Although NAAC is responsible for setting standards of HEIs in India, not many institutions have approached NAAC for accreditation till recently. NAAC has maintained a non-coercive mode of allowing voluntarily applications for accreditation and assessment on the part of the institutions. This is to encourage institutions to take ownership of QA at the institutional level (NAAC, 2003). The progress of institutions volunteering for assessment and accreditation has been very slow, but the situation has been changing faster with the NAAC accreditation made mandatory for the institutions applying for RUSA funding. Around 266 universities and 6,316 colleges have been accredited till 25 May 2016 (for details of NAAC accredited institution in January 2017, see Table 13.5). Of the affiliated colleges, 929 colleges have C grade, 4,161 have B grade and 1,226 have 'A'. Amongst those that have approached NAAC, we do not have enough empirical evidence to say what has been the effect of NAAC on the quality of the institutions.

Of the 487 universities accredited till January 2017, only 47 are in the third cycle, while 143 are in the second cycle and 297 are in the first cycle of NAAC accreditation.

There are differences between quality of institutions, rural-urban, and from one state to another. Amongst the seven indicators, the first

Table 13.5 *Status of NAAC Accreditation (23 January 2017)*

	First Cycle	Second Cycle	Third Cycle	Total
Universities	297	143	47	487
Colleges	6,772	2,954	373	10,099
Total	7,069	3,097	420	10,586

Source: NAAC.

set of three indicators relate to academic aspects. The following set of four indicators relate to infrastructure and support aspects. Although, it is possible for institutes to show the best of the infrastructure to gain good scores in NAAC assessments, the quality of academic aspects is not necessarily assured (Gurukkal, 2017). There have been instances of malpractices where institutions applying for NAAC accreditation engage private consultants to develop SSRs. This defeats the whole purpose of introducing the notion of reflexivity about quality systems at the institutional level. Such malpractices have been noticed by NAAC, and the institutions applying for accreditation are warned not to indulge in such malpractices.

Although there have been several anecdotal records, and some articles by NAAC faculty discuss issues and concerns of the institutions that have undergone the accreditation process with reference to the institutional grading, there is not enough empirical evidence that can inform us on the experience of the institutions going through the process of NAAC accreditation and re-accreditation. Related questions are: What value do the institutions see in the re-accreditation process? What do the institutions find unique about developing the SSRs? How do they envisage QA at institutional level to enhance student experience and learning? What feedback does the peer review visit give to the institutions? How is it incorporated in the quality improvement cycle at the institutional level?

NAAC accreditation mandates the institutions to have an IQA cell (IQAC) in place when applying for the second and subsequent cycles of accreditation. Though NAAC has considered role of student feedback very important in the pursuit of enhancement of quality of HEIs, there is again no empirical evidence to show how it unfolds in reality at the institutional level.

A national research project initiated at the CPRHE carried out the analysis of structure and function of IQA and its relationship with the EQA (Pachauri, 2017). The research followed a mixed methods approach. The primary data set included a survey with 2,330 students and 286 teachers; interviews with the key institutional leaders including vice-chancellors, finance officers, registrars, college principals, head accountants, head of the departments, IQAC directors and coordinators, and NAAC assessors and NAAC faculty; and focus group discussions with teachers and students across 10 HEIs. Five universities with Grade A in the latest NAAC accreditation cycle which have been through at least two cycles were selected. One affiliated college with each of the five universities spread across five states was also selected. At least one faculty member from each of the selected institutions was invited as a member of the research team.

Government Initiated Reforms and NAAC

The governments roll out policy changes with purpose of reforming institutions (HEIs). NAAC had been established for the purpose of QA and enhancement in HE through assessment and accreditation. There is presupposition of causality due to purpose, and to some degree also its predictability. Nonetheless, the cause and effect relationships are not linked to the structures in a straightjacket fashion. Rather, there are mechanisms of the operation of effect. Powers and properties, and complex linkages with structures are the outcome of mechanisms. Hence, causation cannot be reduced to a single factor (Bhaskar, 2008). This is the critical realist position which proposes the transformational model of society-person linkage as people reproduce and/or transform the existing structures, practices and conventions.

There have been series of reform initiatives at the behest of the UGC. Introduction of the semester system and choice-based credit transfer system in all the HEIs, academic performance indicators for the HE faculty members, revision of teacher/faculty eligibility criteria and introduction of four-year undergraduate programme (reverted later) are some of the reforms introduced in recent years. The review of the NAAC indicators and analysis of the recommendations to the institutions made by the peer team, since the early years of accreditation shows that EQA exercise in India tends to measure/assess institutions for the extent to which the institutions have started reforms as desired by the government. This is alongside the fact that NAAC envisages quality maintenance, improvement and enhancement as the goals of EQA.

The general observations made by NAAC on the accreditation outcomes across the states of Karnataka, Kerala, Tamil Nadu and Haryana (NAAC, n.d.) reveal that institutions that have scored high in the NAAC assessment and accreditation exercise enjoy autonomy in the form of academic and administrative freedom. Ad hoc appointments are a barrier in quality input to the institutions and have implications for institutional quality. The infrastructural facilities remain underutilized in the institutions. Institutions with clarity of purpose generally updated curricula and made relevant changes. The launch of job-oriented courses was stated as an example of clarity of institutional objective in the NAAC document. In the area of research consultancy and extension, NAAC recommended that institutions and faculty mobilize resources for research, faculty take up more consultancies for revenue generation and extension activities be enhanced by most of the institutions.

While urging the government to keep students' learning and institutional functioning in focus, NAAC recommended several policy measures to be initiated by the government. In addition, NAAC highlighted the policy requirement so as to address the issue of (a) the continuity of funding with opportunities of project funding for both aided and unaided HEIs, and 'outstanding' faculty for the institutions; (b) encouraging collaborations and partnership with private sector; (c) internationalization and commercialization of education, in view of General Agreement on Tariffs and Trade (GATT); (d) performance-based funding, credit transfer and fee for student exchange programmes; and (e) amendment in *acts/statutes/ordinances* of universities in view of globalization, internationalization and national needs. NAAC also recommended policies specific to 'quality issues' in four areas: (a) curricular aspects; (b) restructuring; (c) teaching, learning and evaluation; and (d) research, consultancy and extension. The need to move from mostly traditional courses across disciplines to innovative and interdisciplinary courses was implored upon the institutions.

Our review of around 11 state-wise analysis of accreditation reports[1] by NAAC which have been published between 2003 and 2008, shows NAAC's role as an extended arm of the HE regulatory body, for example, UGC and serving its focus. Even though the reports are written by various authors over a period of time, there is coherence and similarity in the recommendations made for the colleges and the universities from different states. For the purpose of example, we take three aspects here: curricular, teaching–learning and evaluation, and management.

In the area of curricular aspects, NAAC advised the colleges to adopt a semester system and CBCS, and focus on the development of a perspective plan. The colleges were also asked to define their mission and vision. Recommendations were made to open up curricular options for students through the launch of vocational, certificate, PG diploma courses and other add-on courses. The colleges were asked to start self-financing courses and postgraduate courses. The universities were similarly asked to implement semester system and CBCS, revise and upgrade courses, colleges running self-financing courses were recommended to provide feedback on the courses to their affiliating universities, introduce online/distance education programmes mediated by technology, and establish collaborative linkages with universities/industry and other institutions. One can infer that the universities and colleges were being asked to change as per the UGC regulations and also to address the mass transition of students completing schooling to enter HE. The scholars have argued that these changes are in the response to the GATT agreements (Gurukkal, 2017).

In the domain of teaching, learning and evaluation, recommendations were made to the government colleges to 'sort out' frequent transfers of teachers, and regarding professional development of teachers. Universities were asked to fill up positions with qualified faculty, set up an IQAC, implement self-evaluation by teachers, focus on results

---

[1] See NAAC accreditation reports between 2003 and 2008 for the states of Andhra Pradesh, Haryana, Karnataka, Kerala, Madhya Pradesh, North East, Punjab, Tamil Nadu and West Bengal.

and accountability aspects of affiliated colleges, and include student feedback.

Selected colleges were encouraged to move towards an autonomous status with reference to the management related aspects. The recommendations for encouraging colleges for autonomy gelled with asking colleges to mobilize resources and become more self-sufficient. In Maharashtra, granting autonomy to colleges was reasoned so as to ease out the administrative burden of the universities. It is noteworthy that Maharashtra has the largest number of private colleges. Also, recently, a large number of public-funded colleges have been encouraged to generate resources and were granted autonomous status. This development has been seen as linked to cuts in federal funding and the generated concern over the governments retracting from funding the education sector. If we assume that the institutions have followed NAAC recommendations and implemented the same, we can infer that by asking the universities to raise tuition fee, starting more self-financing courses and mobilize resources from various other sources to cover the financial deficit, NAAC has been instrumental in steering the accredited institutions towards increasingly incorporating elements of privatization.

With institutions willingly or grudgingly striving towards state-led reforms, the NAAC accreditation and assessment rating is now being linked by the regulators and funders to the eligibility of the institution to apply for designated funds under various schemes and programmes such as RUSA. Thus EQA, which had started as a voluntary exercise with the inception of NAAC, has recently become 'voluntarily mandatory'.

In the following section, we discuss the empirical evidence generated from our research study on institutional experiences. The focus is to understand the structure and function of EQA and IQA, their interrelationship and involvement of the participants in the QA at the institutional level.

INTERNAL QUALITY ASSURANCE CELL STRUCTURE AND PRACTICE

The IQA at the institutional level is organized as the IQAC. They have been envisaged as an essential component of HEIs for the maintenance, enhancement and improvement of quality. The IQAC is expected to be the link between the EQA agency, in this case, NAAC, and the institutions. The structure and function of IQAC has been broadly suggested by NAAC.

NAAC brought out the first set of guidelines for the establishment of IQAC in 2007 (NAAC, 2007) and revised in 2013 (NAAC, 2013). According to the documents, IQAC's are envisaged as a post-accreditation QA measure, akin to Quality Circles in industries. The UGC has also issued the XII Plan guidelines for the establishment and monitoring of the IQACs in universities (UGC, n.d.; also see Table 13.6). Whilst NAAC expects that '[i]t will not be yet another hierarchical structure or a record-keeping exercise in the institution' (NAAC, 2013, p. 4), almost all the universities and colleges have assigned the task of record-keeping to the IQAC citing, 'In terms of UGC Regulation 2010, IQAC shall act as the Documentation and Record-Keeping Cell, including assistance in the development of the API criteria-based Performance Based Appraisal System (PBAS) proforma using the indicative template separately developed by the UGC'.

Table 13.6 *Guidelines for IQAC Composition*

NAAC	UGC
1. Chairperson: Head of the institution	1. Vice-chancellor of the university—Chairperson
2. A few senior administrative officers	2. Eight senior teachers and one senior administrative official—Members
3. Three to eight teachers	3. Three external experts on quality management/industry/local community—Members
4. One member from the management	
5. One/two nominees from local society, students and alumni	4. Director of IQAC—Member secretary
6. One/two nominees from employers/Industrialists/stakeholders	
7. One of the senior teachers as the coordinator/director of the IQAC	

Sources: NAAC (2013); UGC (n.d.).

The IQACs are supposed to be established according to the NAAC and UGC guidelines. As per the UGC guidelines, amongst the IQAC members, eight senior teachers and one senior administrative official, and three external experts on quality management/industry/local community are nominated by the vice-chancellor in consultation with the academic council of the university. The membership of such nominated members is for a period of two years. The IQAC are expected to meet at least once in a quarter (UGC). However, in reality, the IQACs are not as operational as expected. The structure and staffing of the IQAC differs across the institutions, based on their size and complexity, both at the university level and college level. Many institutions still do not have awareness about the role of IQAC, and those who have set up IQAC according to the NAAC guidelines have been unable to formally involve or integrate IQAC in the institutional functioning and the ongoing internal QA processes at the department or programme level (see Chapter 12).

The responses regarding motivation and reasons to participate in the NAAC accreditation and assessment vary according to the history, type and size of the institution. The well-established institutions are able to garner support from professionals and experts in guiding them to prepare for the peer team visit. Such institutions are also able to prepare well in advance, and are likely to have support from dedicated faculty members. However, in institutions neglected in terms of proper institutional management, the prospects of visits by experts to make judgment on the institutions evokes fear. The lack of preparedness for assessment and absence of trust that institutions can benefit from the advice of the peer team underlies uncertainty and fear. Just optimally functioning management structures and unavailability of critical mass of committed institutional participants (faculty and administration) to support the corporate life of the institution causes institutions to set up ad hoc mechanisms for the peer team visit. This does not give real picture of institutions' capabilities and quality.

In the absence of proper maintenance of institutional data, IQACs end up in the role of data collection centres, and the IQAC coordinators have a tough task of chasing other institutional leaders for data for the purpose of SSR (Pachauri, 2015). Even when institutional data is available, the amount of data and the sorting of data as per the requirement of the NAAC indicators has been reported as a challenge by the coordinators. The lack of cooperation and coordination amongst departments and the IQAC in the institutions shows that SSR is actually not a well-studied reflection of the participants on the institutional workings with a purpose of quality maintenance or improvement. It is, rather, reporting to the authority/regulatory body as per their demand. Evidence suggests that for the institutions going for the first grading cycle, even till the day of the NAAC visit, most of the faculty members were not aware of the existence and significance of a SSR.

Unsurprisingly, in such a scenario, the institutions engage private consultants to write reports for them, which could involve cooking-up data or claiming aspects of institutional functioning and QA mechanisms that, in reality, do not exist, in the SSR of the institution. At least two large universities in our research reported constituting a team of mentors one year before applying for re-accreditation and running a mock exercise similar to NAAC visit involving all university departments for almost seven—eight months. Another university reported that the vice-chancellor held several meeting over one year including developing SSR and preparing for the peer team visit. However, after the successful award of 'A' grade, the frequency of faculty meetings, both at the department and institutional levels, declined. The IQACs tend to go low profile after the accreditation exercise.

In the assessment and accreditation framework operational till March 2017, the duration for institutional cycle to apply for re-accreditation was five years. Institutions are expected to undertake institutional improvement activities for quality enhancement in this period of five years based upon the feedback from the peer-team, and IQACs are to develop annual action taken reports. The situation is far different in the universities and colleges. The NAAC faculty shared many instances when the annual quality assurance reports (AQARs) which should have been submitted annually are required to be asked from the institutions close to the visit of the peer teams, The IQAC have been reported to become active mostly closer to the time of applying for re-accreditation. The faculty members felt that there should also be a mechanism to monitor the IQAC's role. Since IQAC were envisaged more as nodal centres to institutionalize quality culture, monitoring of an institutional unit by an outside agency may not be desirable. Rather, the institutional participants need to demand an active participation of the IQAC. IQAC, in its present form, does not have any statutory status either at the university level or the college level. Unless the structure and function of IQAC is integrated with the institutional/departmental structures, it would be unreasonable to even imagine that IQAC could make contribution beyond data collection at the institutional level.

According to the institutional leaders, the IQACs have played an important role in these transformations by encouraging university departments to implement UGC guidelines. However, perceptions of the faculty members differ on the role and impact of IQAC on institutional quality improvement. These perceptions impact the coordination and interaction between the departments and the IQAC. Majority of the department heads viewed the role of IQACs as that of data collection and management. The institutional leadership therefore needs to affect this perception about IQACs, and increase interaction and collaboration amongst departments through institutionalizing dialogues on quality improvement, collective reporting and sharing of progress reports of the departments.

Conceptually, IQAC is the nodal centre at the institutional level through which the impact of EQA on the institutional workings can be captured. In the institutions going for the second and subsequent cycles of accreditation, the IQACs follow up the suggestions of the peer review team for requisite action and report on the action taken in the AQARs. The experience from the field study shows that several administrative constraints pose a hurdle to the achievement of IQAC's mandate. The major constraint cited by the IQAC coordinators is academic and non–academic/administrative staff vacancies at the institutional level. In the case of the state universities, the delay in decision for recruitment by the state governments affects institutional quality. Another functional constraint is the lack of dedicated staff and office infrastructure available for the IQAC. This also reflects that IQAC are not yet perceived as having continuous role on day-to-day basis by the institutional participants.

EFFECTS OF EQA AND IQA ON QUALITY OF INSTITUTIONS

Evaluating how the EQA has affected the institutions/universities and colleges in India is a challenging and complex task. The complexity arises first because of the fact that the national system of regulation of institutions in India expects institutions to follow certain guidelines and devise the ways of working accordingly. At the same time, state-level institutions are governed by the state HE departments. The organization of EQA in India though develops institutional assessment and accreditation indicators in tandem with the national focus and global developments, the EQA also claims to have certain goals, that is, maintenance, improvement and enhancement of quality. Hence, distinction between changes at the institutional level because of EQA or as affected by the governmental regulations through UGC becomes blurred. In addition, the old universities and colleges have had established mechanisms of academic audit. Besides NAAC, which focuses on institutional QA, there are other professional bodies such as NBA and MCI, among others, which expect institutions to follow QA at the programme level. Better adherence to QA at the programme level indicates that individually the departments may be able to contribute to the overall institutional quality.

As reflected in the NAAC's mandate, IQACs at the universities have an important role to play in creating awareness on quality concerns and assessment indicators for the university departments and amongst the affiliated colleges of the university. The impact of IQACs can be assessed in terms of the compliance of assessment indicators. Implementation of the CBCS, introduction of the semester system, academic reforms including upgrading curricula, launch of new courses, student evaluation reforms and student feedback are some of the changes that we observed in the universities and colleges. These changes are more clearly observable in universities than in colleges. The colleges in our study are still in the process of moving from the annual system to the semester system. The institutional capacity in terms of governance structures and design of management, and deployment of faculty and staff impacts the pace of reforms. The pattern of decentralized governance through sub-committees and several non-statutory bodies not only widens the participation but also enables swift and efficient decisions.

However, these mechanisms are found in the universities which have comparatively more autonomy than the government colleges. In one of the states in our research project, the state government has reverted to the previous pattern of annual system in the government colleges in the state contrary to the NAAC's advice to the institutions to convert from annual system to semester system. Thus, whilst the university-run courses follow the semester system, the government college affiliated to the same university follows the annual system.

Systematization of Norms, Procedures and Structures

Systematization of, norms, procedures and structures for carrying out various functions at the university and college level—such as faculty and staff recruitment, delineating the details of the programmes of study offered by the institutions, and conduct of course evaluations, student assessments and examinations—constitute the bureaucratic dimension of the impact of QA. A regular undergraduate programme of study in India takes three years to complete, while a regular postgraduate programme is of two years. The examinations in some state universities in India, in the past, are reported to be delayed by several months to a couple of years, causing delays in degree completion. Citing examples of some universities in the state of Bihar, the NAAC faculty shared that the institutions undergoing assessment have addressed these delays over the period of two accreditation cycles. Course guidelines and handbooks for students, and learning formats outlining learning outcomes for the students are some of the changes that have been reported by the institutions in our study. Course revisions were also reported as an impact of requirement from external QA agency.

Although teaching and evaluation of students, and timetable-related records are maintained at the department/faculty level, there are many routine yet crucial activities that go undocumented such as organizing academic events for the students, participation of faculty on organizational, academic, research and corporate activities of the institutions. Since, establishment of IQACs at the universities and colleges, the departments are expected to systematically report the activities organized at the department level and those undertaken by individual faculty members. Departments are becoming more aware/mindful of the activities that they organize. Systematization of documentation and reporting serves as a tool for ensuring accountability, and building trust and reputation of the departments and the institution. At the same time, the freight of documentation at the departmental and institutional levels was also reported to have increased the workload.

The curriculum development/course revision is organized at the university level, and members/experts drawn from university departments as well as teachers from colleges who are invited to be member of the team based on their expertise in their respective discipline. The teachers who reported that they are members of course teams expressed their discontentment with the process of course development/revision exercise and reported it as being carried out mostly in haste. Quite often, the committee meetings are organized at short notice, and the duration of the meetings is also not long enough to allow space for the members to have substantial discussions as part of the revision process. The college teachers felt that the course revision meetings are just 'for the sake of formality' because the university was to go for NAAC accreditation.

Inclusion of Diverse Voices and Perspectives

This dimension in the universities and colleges relates to the reorganization of power and student voice in the institutional working. This also includes representation of diversity in various institutional positions. The exercise of going for NAAC accreditation, developing SSRs, and devising rules and regulations (if not existent) about various aspects of institutional functioning assessed by NAAC leads not only to the emergence of new power equations in the institutional set up but also to redistribution of power. Centralized ways of institutional functioning do not gel with the demands of EQA through NAAC. The IQAC coordinator emerges as an institutional leader with skills of persistence and persuasion while approaching departments for the reports and data.

Student feedback is an essential aspect of NAAC institutional assessment. The phrase 'for the sake of formality' came up very often when discussing theoretically democratic arrangements of functioning at the institutional level. Student feedback is also one such aspect where students expressed that the feedback is organized just 'for the sake of formality'.

Although institutions have developed formats of feedback from various stakeholders including students and alumni, it was found that large chunk of the feedback data remains unanalysed and, hence, not used for improving the quality of the course/teacher/department or institution. In addition, the feedback and action on student feedback requires an attitudinal shift amongst the faculty members regarding the utility of the student feedback. Although both students and faculty reported that the teachers take feedback on teaching-learning and courses, they did not report that this has led to changes in the re-organization of teaching-learning in the institutions.

According to the students, faculty behaviour and interpersonal dealings with faculty are very important for building an environment for student learning and defining their institutional experience. Access to productive internship, and practical experience in addition to theoretical understanding were also reported as concerns determining the quality of the learning experience. Post-HE challenges include competition for jobs through examination and acquisition of requisite skills. The students are very much aware of the challenges, and they expect institutions to support them in meeting these challenges. However, much depends on in what ways the institutions and faculty are able to develop a dialogue with the students in addressing those challenges. The absence of dialogue and the anxiety of students related to jobs and competition amongst other factors has resulted in the problem of absenteeism across colleges and universities especially students in arts, humanities and social sciences courses where the students attend coaching for competitive examinations for jobs.

Financial Gains to the Institutions

Recently, funding the institutions through various public sources has been linked to the NAAC accreditation grades. The funding conditionality has been a major trigger for public HEIs applying for NAAC accreditation. NAAC assessors shared that many times institutions which are not yet ready for accreditation apply to be assessed so that even if they get C grade, their public funds are not fully stopped. The institutions gained allocation of finances under various categories such as 'university with potential for excellence' (UPE), 'centre for potential for excellence' (CPE) grants, UGC plan grants, RUSA, Department of Science and Technology (DST) and so on. A RUSA grant of 0.2 billion is given to universities with Grade A from NAAC. Granting institutions the status of Institute of Potential for Excellence (IPE) that makes them eligible for certain grants is also an outcome of NAAC accreditation. However, there is a need to make a distinction between the funding for which the institutions become eligible to apply for and the routine grants for the maintenance of ongoing institutional activities.

IQACs do not have any say in the financial and administrative matters of the institution. Therefore, any quality benchmark that the IQAC may develop for the institution may have limitations if it has administrative and financial implications. The IQAC directors in our study demanded some provision of fund control for certain activities at the departmental level through IQACs.

Human Resources Improvement

The appointment of faculty members and administrative and other professional and support staff is another dimension which is useful to understand the effect of EQA on institutional quality. A large number of regular positions have been reported vacant at the teaching and non-teaching staff level. In one of the state universities in our study, 75 per cent posts of administrative staff are vacant. The vacancies in regular teaching positions as against sanctioned positions range approximately between 40 per cent and 60 per cent. At the same time, a backlog of appointments against reserved positions has also been reported. Institutions appoint contract and guest faculty to manage the teaching workload in the institutions. The focus group discussions with the faculty members reveal that the major teaching workload is shouldered by contract teachers. Lack of administrative staff at the department level combined with decentralization of several activities such as student evaluation and declaration of results has encroached upon the academic time of the regular faculty members, making them take on the administrative and clerical roles.

The quality of administrative staff is seldom discussed in the literature on quality in HE. The universities have undergone a lot of transformation in recent years due to the government-led reforms, advancement of technology, and also its usage for administrative purposes, increased intake of students and changes in student evaluation. All of these changes demand better data management services at the universities and colleges. Although the faculty members in the universities are appointed by the university after seeking permission from the state government, the regular administrative staff is appointed through the state services staff selection commission. Re-training/professional development of administrative staff who are attuned to the recent demands of running the institution and have understanding of the rules and regulations of the institution is a challenge faced by key institutional leaders. The challenges range from the know-how about working with digital technology to the ability of drafting letters and noting on the files. Shortage of administrative staff and limitations of skills leads to delays in several administrative processes, causing management issues and grievances from faculty as well as students and causing extreme workload on key institutional leaders such as the registrar.

NEW MATRICES OF ACCREDITATION

Most of the respondents in this research pointed out that NAAC grading to any institution is not objective and does not reflect the quality of teaching-learning, which is core of any educational institution. The subjective element in the assessment of the peer review team has been confirmed by several NAAC assessors. When the assessors are new to the context or new to the NAAC visit exercise, they tend to be more rigid. In the experience of some of the institutions, the assessors behaved as if they are on a supervision and monitoring visit, and without discussing or trying to understand the context of the institutions, made constant comparisons with foreign universities, facilities and practices. Thus understanding of the assessors is a huge determinant of what institution could get as assessment grade. This subjectivity could also result in institutions getting more than the grade they deserve based on the presence of a world-renowned faculty member on the faculty list or the high reputation of old institutions. Besides, since the grades are cumulating indicators spread across seven key aspects, there could be uneven and non-comparable scores across each of the individual aspects but the same overall cumulative score. The quantitative data provided by the institution could be considered subjective if institutions deliberately manipulate the figures. A debate between subjectivity and objectivity with reference to institutional evaluation thus continues, and the point to ponder is whether external evaluation is subjective or objective, and the extent to which self-evaluation and self-reporting is objective.

In the new Quality Indicator Framework (QIF) of NAAC, the overall weightage of 1,000 spread across seven criteria in NAAC's assessment framework remains the same as earlier. Similarly, the criterion-wise weightage across the seven criteria remains unchanged. There has been revision in the matrices and relative weightages with reference to the peer team visit and objective data supplied by the institutions in the SSR. Criteria III and VII have been changed. From Research, Consultancy and Extension; the Criterion III is now changed to Research, Extension and Innovation and Criterion VII, which was earlier Innovation and Best Practices, is now Institutional Values and Best Practices.

In the previous version of the NAAC assessment, there were 220 measures of key aspects. The key aspects are now known as key indicators and are 34 in number, and the measures are called metrics. In addition, the number of metrics has been reduced to 130 (for grades as per CGPA scored by institutions, see Table 13.7). The metrics are of two types: qualitative (Q^lM) and quantitative (Q^nM). The role of the peer team visit has been rendered very limited to Q^lM in the revised accreditation framework. In addition, NAAC has added pre-qualifiers for peer team visits and grade qualifiers for HEIs (NAAC, 2017).

A grade qualifier for university will include criteria 1, 2 and 3; for autonomous college will include criteria 1 and 2; and for affiliated/constituent college will include criteria 2 and 5 (Table 13.8). The institutions are expected to score a minimum of 30 per cent of the

Table 13.7 *Institutional Grading*

Range of Institutional CGPA	Letter Grade (Accredited-A; Non-Accredited-NA)
3.76–4.00	A++ (A)
3.51–3.75	A+ (A)
3.01–3.50	A (A)
2.76–3.00	B++ (A)
2.51–2.75	B+ (A)
2.01–2.50	B (A)
1.51–2.00	C (A)
Less than or equal to 1.50	D (NA)

Source: NAAC (2016).

Table 13.8 *Calculation of Grade Qualifier Across Types of HEIs*

Type of HEI	Criterion Considered for Calculating Grade Qualifier	Minimum Criterion-wise Grade Point Averages (CrGPA) Score
University	Criterion 1, 2, 3	3.01 for A, A+, A++ 2.01 for B, B+, B++ 1.51 for C
Autonomous college	Criterion 1, 2	3.01 for A, A+, A++ 2.01 for B, B+, B++ 1.51 for C
Affiliated/ constituent college	Criterion 2, 5	3.01 for A, A+, A++ 2.01 for B, B+, B++ 1.51 for C

Source: NAAC (2017).

system–generated score (SGS) based on the quantitative information and qualitative score in each criterion.

Another set of three significant changes may be highlighted here. The first change is the 70 per cent weightage to the quantitative data and the rest 30 per cent weightage comprising of peer team review score and student survey. The second change is the introduction of the student survey figuring in the institutional assessment. The third change is the off-site accreditation, based on the SSR and data provided, to the institutions in the fourth cycle of accreditation.

The validity of accreditation has been extended from five years to seven years for the institutions getting a high score in the third accreditation cycle if they have consistently earned very high grades in the previous two cycles. The institutions achieving low score/grade will have a shorter cycle of accreditation. Whether the new system of accreditation and scores only ends up bringing more institutions under the tally tables of accredited institutions, or would it result in a broader systemic impact on quality, is something which we need to scrutinize in future.

CONCLUSION

The institutions have experienced significant changes in terms of curricular reforms, revision of syllabi, introduction of CBCS and semester system, frequent student evaluation and feedback from students, involvement of alumni and industry, and increase in reported publications from the faculty as an effect of EQA and IQA. These changes have led to an improvement in accreditation scores of the institutions over the two cycles of NAAC accreditation spanning around 10 years. Since the improved scores are linked with conditionality for funding, the institutions have reported access to or promise of grants.

With the inputs to the system including funding and faculty recruitment remaining constant or declining while the student diversity and numbers are increasing, an assessment and accreditation exercise can simply highlight the areas for improvement. However, actual improvement and inputs required to facilitate the institutional functioning reside with the funding and regulatory authorities such as UGC and the institutional participants, that is, students, teachers and institutional leader/administrators. In the era of fast-paced reforms, NAAC is trying to stay afoot in aligning the QA framework with the government demands as well as the international developments.

At the moment, the QA exercise in India has not very much reflected on the issue of motivation for change, and the impact of forced change and institutional workings as the subject of organization behaviour. One might argue that linking grades with RUSA funding is an incentive to adapt change and changed practices. However, this is not enough, because the practice of 'for the sake of formality' will continue and the perceived change will not be sustainable and substantial with regard to quality. What does this 'for the sake of formality' treatment to core processes and outcomes say about institutional workings and institutional culture, and what implications does it carry for the reforms/institutional change and institutionalization of quality initiatives? How can institutions address 'for the sake of formality' way of doing things?

Institutionalization of changes, reforms and quality initiatives is a long process which can unfold over a period of time with the wilful involvement of stakeholders. The drivers for wilful involvement are situated in creating conditions for positive experience. Whatsoever pattern of grading or CGPA score is developed and may appear increasingly objective on paper, the fact remains that the accreditation and the institutional data for the assessment exercise, till now in India, has not been used for the purpose of institutional consumption. The grades and scores create a league-table kind of situation where institution might take pride in moving forward by certain points in comparison to some other institutions in their neighbourhood, but the overall experience of students learning may not actually change. The IQAC role does not need to limit itself to preparing reports but can also look into various aspects of institutional workings/functioning. The HEIs have to seriously check 'for the sake of formality' operations and focus on mechanisms that create a collegial environment for the students, teachers, administrators and assessors to reflect on the practices and develop a plan to move ahead.

REFERENCES

Agarwal, P. (2009). *Higher education in India: Envisioning the future*. New Delhi: SAGE Publications.

Barandiaran-Galdós, M., Barrenetxea Ayesta, M., Cardona-Rodríguez, A., José Mijangos del Campo, J., & Olaskoaga-Larrauri, J. (2012). What do teachers think about quality in the Spanish university? *Quality Assurance in Education*, *20*(2), 91–109.

Bhaskar, R. (2008). *A realist theory of science.* London and New York, NY: Routledge.

Brennan, J., & Shah, T. (2000). *Managing quality in higher education: An international perspective on institutional assessment and change.* Buckingham: OECD, SRHE and Open University Press.

Carr, S., Hamilton, E., & Meade, P. (2005). Is it possible? Investigating the influence of external quality audit on university performance. *Quality in Higher Education, 11*(3), 195–211. Retrieved 20 September 2017, from https://www. tandfonline.com/doi/abs/10.1080/13538320500329665

CABE (Central Advisory Board of Education). (2005). *Report of the Central Advisory Board of Education (CABE) committee on autonomy of higher education institutions.* New Delhi: Ministry of Human Resource and Development, Department of Secondary and Higher Education, Government of India.

Dill, D. D. (2010). We can't go home again: Insights from a quarter century of experiments in external academic quality assurance. *Quality in Higher Education, 16*(2), 159–161.

Douglas, J., & Douglas, A. (2006). Evaluating teaching quality. *Quality in Higher Education, 12*(1), 3–13.

EACEA-P9-Eurydice. (2012). *The European higher education area in 2012: Bologna process implementation report.* Brussels: Education, Audiovisual and Culture Executive Agency.

Ewell, P. (2007). The 'quality game: External review and institutional reaction over three decades In the United States'. In D. F. Westerheijden, B. Stensaker, & M. J. Rosa (Eds), *Quality assurance in higher education higher education: Trends in regulation, translation and transformation.* Dordrecht: Springer.

Fourie, M., & Alt, H. (2000). Challenges to sustaining and enhancing quality of teaching and learning in South African universities. *Quality in Higher Education, 6*(2), 115–124.

Frederiks, M. M. H., Westerheijden, D. F., & Weusthof, P. J. M. (1994). Effects of quality assessment in Dutch higher education. *European Journal of Education, 29*(2), 181–200.

GOI (Government of India). (1949). *The report of the University Education Commission.* New Delhi: Ministry of Education, Government of India.

———. (1962). *The report of the University Education Commission (December 1948– August 1949).* New Delhi: Ministry of Education, Government of India.

———. (2006). *National Knowledge Commission: Report to the nation (2006–2009).* New Delhi: Government of India.

Gurukkal, R. (2017). The state, markets, equity and quality in higher education. In N. S. N. V. Varghese (Ed.), *India higher education report 2016: Higher education in India—equity.* New Delhi: SAGE.

Harvey, L. (1995). Editorial. *Quality in Higher Education, 1*(1), 5–12.

———. (2003). Student feedback. *Quality in Higher Education, 9*(1), 3–20.

Harvey, L., & Knight, P. (1996). *Transforming higher education.* Buckingham: Open University Press and Society for Research into Higher Education.

Harvey, L., & Williams, J. (2010). Editorial: Fifteen years of quality in higher education (Part two). *Quality in Higher Education, 16*(1), 81–113.

Hill, R. (1995). A European student perspective on quality. *Quality in Higher Education, 1*(1), 67–75.

Huisman, J., & Currie, J. (2004). Accountability in higher education: Bridge over troubled water? *Higher Education, 48*(4), 529–551.

Hulpiau, V., & Waeytens, K. (2003). Improving quality of education: What makes it actually work? A case study. In C. Prichard & P. R. Trowler (Eds), *Realizing qualitative research into higher education* (pp. 145–169). Aldershot: Ashgate Publishing.

Kristensen, B. (2010). Has external quality assurance actually improved quality in higher education over the course of 20 years of the 'quality revolution'? *Quality in Higher Education, 16*(2), 153–157. doi:10.1080/13538322.2010.485732

Leiber, T., Stensaker, B., & Harvey, L. (2015). Impact evaluation of quality assurance in higher education: Methodology and causal designs. *Quality in Higher Education, 21*(3), 288–311. doi:10.1080/13538322.2015.1111009

Liu, S. (2016). *Quality assurance and institutional transformation: The Chinese experience*. Singapore: Springer.

Lyotard, J.-F. (1984). *The postmodern condition: A report on knowledge*. Manchester: Manchester University Press.

Malik, G. (2017). Governance and management of higher education institutions in India. *CPRHE Research Papers*, No.5. New Delhi: NIEPA.

Mandal, S. (2017). *Teaching learning in Indian higher education. National synthesis report of the CPRHE research project*. New Delhi: NIEPA.

Mathew, A. (2016). Reforms in higher education in India: A review of recommendations of commissions and committees on education. *CPRHE Research Paper Series* (Research Paper No. 2). New Delhi: CPRHE-NIEPA.

Mhlanga, E. (2013). *Quality assurance in higher education in southern Africa: Challenges and opportunities*. Bern: Peter Lang AG, International Academic Publishers.

MHRD (Ministry of Human Resource and Development). (1986). *National policy on education*. New Delhi: Government of India.

Minelli, E., Rebora, G., Turri, M., & Huisman, J. (2006). The impact of research and teaching evaluation at universities: Comparing an Italian and a Dutch case. *Quality in Higher Education, 12*(2), 109–124.

Mishra, S. (2006). *Quality assurance in higher education: An introduction*. Bengaluru: NAAC and Commonwealth of Learning.

Morley, L. (2003). *Quality and power in higher education*. Berkshire: SRHE and Open University Press.

Narasimhan, K. (2001). Improving the climate of teaching sessions: The use of evaluations by students and instructors. *Quality in Higher Education, 7*(3), 179–190.

NAAC (National Assessment and Accreditation Council). (2003). *Analysis of the accreditation reports of the universities and colleges in the state of Tamil Nadu*. Bengaluru: NAAC.

NAAC (National Assessment and Accreditation Council). (2007). *Guidelines for the creation of internal quality assurance cells (IQACs) in the accredited institutions: A post-accreditation quality sustenance activity.* Bengaluru: NAAC.

———. (2013). *Guidelines for the creation of the internal quality assurance cell (IQAC) and submission of annual quality assurance report (AQAR) in accredited institutions.* Bengaluru: NAAC.

———. (2016). *NAAC brochure.* Bengaluru: NAAC.

———. (2017). *Institutional accreditation: Manual for affiliated/constituent colleges.* Bengaluru: NAAC.

———. (2017). *Revised accreditation framework.* Bengaluru: NAAC.

Newton, J. (2000). Feeding the beast or improving quality? Academics' perceptions of quality assurance and quality monitoring. *Quality in Higher Education, 6*(2), 153–163.

Pachauri, A. (2015). *Internal and external quality assurance at the institutional level: Report of the pilot study.* Unpublished. New Delhi: CPRHE-NIEPA.

———. (2017). *Quality in higher education in India: A study of external and internal quality assurance at the institutional level—A research synthesis report.* New Delhi: CPRHE-NIEPA.

Pillai, L., & Patil, J. (2016). Quality assurance in Indian higher education: Role of NAAC and future directions. In N. V. Varghese & Garima, Malik (Eds), *India higher education report 2015* (pp. 137–162). London and New York, NY: Routledge.

Prasad, V. S., & Patil, J. (Eds). (2007). *Proceedings of the International Conference on Student Participation in Quality Enhancement (SPQE) Bangalore.* Bengaluru: NAAC.

Pratasavitskaya, H., & Stensaker, B. (2010). Quality management in higher education: Towards a better understanding of an emerging field. *Quality in Higher Education, 16*(1), 37–50.

Rashtriya Uchchatar Shiksha Abhiyan (RUSA). (2013). *Rashtriya uchchatar shiksha abhiyan: National higher education mission.* Ministry of Human Resource and Development, in collaboration with Tata Institute of Social Sciences. New Delhi: Government of India.

Schenker-Wicki, A. (2002). Accreditation and quality assurance. *Higher Education Management and Policy, 14*(2), 27–38.

Señal, N. C., de la Rosa González, C., Fischer, F. P., Hansen, S. P., & Ponds, H. (2008). Internal Quality Assurance and the European Standards and Guidelines. *ENQA Workshop Report* No. 7. Helsinki: ENQA.

Shah, M. (2012). Ten years of external quality audit in Australia: Evaluating its effectiveness and success. *Assessment and Evaluation in Higher Education, 37*(6), 761–772. doi:10.1080/13538322.2013.852300

———. (2013). The effectiveness of external quality audits: A study of Australian universities. *Quality in Higher Education, 19*(3), 358–375.

Shah, M., & Nair, C. S. (2013). *External quality audit: Has it improved quality assurance in universities?* Oxford: Chandos.

Stella, A. (2002). *External quality assurance in Indian higher education: Case study of the National Assessment and Accreditation Council (NAAC).* Paris: UNESCO/IIEP.

Stensaker, B. (2003). Trance, transparency and transformation: The impact of external quality monitoring on higher education. *Quality in Higher Education,* 9(2), 151–159.

———. (2008). Outcomes of quality assurance: A discussion on knowledge, methodology and validity. *Quality in Higher Education, 14*(1), 3–13.

Stensaker, B., & Leiber, T. (2015). Assessing the organizational impact of external quality assurance: Hypothesising key dimensions and mechanisms. *Quality in Higher Education, 21*(3), 328–342.

Srikanthan, G., & Dalrymple, J. (2005). Implementation of a holistic model for quality in higher education. *Quality in Higher Education, 11*(2), 68–81.

Tilak, J. B. G. (2013). *Higher education in India: In search of equality, quality and quantity.* New Delhi: Orient Blackswan.

Thorat, S. (2008). Higher education in India: Emerging issues related to access, inclusiveness and quality. In UGC (Ed.), *Higher education in India: Issues related to expansion, inclusiveness, quality and finance* (pp. 1–26). New Delhi: University Grants Commission.

UGC (University Grants Commission). (n.d.). *XII plan guidelines for establishment and monitoring of the internal quality assurance cells (IQACS) in universities (2012–2017).* New Delhi: UGC.

———. (1994). Towards a general model of quality assessment in higher education. *Higher Education,* 28, 355–371.

Varghese, N. (2015). Challenges of massification of higher education in India. *CPRHE Research Paper Series* (Research Paper No. 1). New Delhi: CPRHE-NIEPA.

Varghese, N. V., Malik, G., & Rakshit, G. D. (2017). Teacher recruitment in higher education in India: An analysis of NET results. *CPRHE Research Paper Series* (Research Paper No. 8). New Delhi: CPRHE-NIEPA.

Vukasovic, M. (2014). Institutionalisation of internal quality assurance: Focusing on institutional work and the significance of disciplinary differences. *Quality in Higher Education, 20*(1), 44–63. http://doi.org/10.1080/13538322.2014.889430

Chapter 14

Finance and Quality
The Reshaping of Higher Education

Aarti Srivastava

INTRODUCTION

The social demand for higher education in India has been increasing, while the public provisions for pursuing higher studies cannot not keep pace with the demand. Individuals and households look for alternatives to public provision and seek admissions in private institutions. In the process, higher education is losing its public good character and is becoming more of a private good. This transformation of higher education into a private good has implications for its accessibility and affordability.

The withdrawal of public subsidy has gradually but steadily shifted the financial burden of pursuing higher education from the state to the households. The recent market-friendly reforms in higher education follow from a neo-liberal approach to development in general, and education in particular. The role of the state is redefined in terms of facilitating efficient functioning of markets. The manifestation of this approach is seen in terms of promotion of private institutions and privatization of public institutions. The market operations in this sector consider commercialization and profitability as desirable objectives of educational processes. The burden of financing higher studies is increasingly on the students' shoulders.

The change in the modes and sources of financing has implication for the quality of higher education. Whenever there is a financial squeeze, the quality-enhancing activities are more adversely affected than the salary component of the budgetary provisions. If quality in higher education is non-negotiable, prioritization in financing also needs to reflect it. This chapter discusses issues related to financing of higher education in general, and financing of quality of higher education in particular. The empirical basis for the arguments comes from a case study carried out in one of premier universities in India, namely, Jawaharlal Nehru University (JNU), New Delhi.

FINANCING OF HIGHER EDUCATION IN INDIA

India at Independence adopted a strategy of state funding and control in education in general, and higher education in particular. Consequently, student enrolments were mostly in public-funded and managed institutions. India invested heavily on good quality institutions in the immediate period following Independence. The setting up of the Indian Institutes of Technology (IIT), Indian Institutes of Management (IIM) and regional engineering colleges were examples of investing in good quality higher education institutions.

One of the commonly used indicators to measure priority in allocation of resources to any sector is the expenditure on education as a share of GDP. As can be seen from Table 14.1, the expenditure on education as a share of GDP has been increasing in India from 0.64 in 1950–1951 to 3.85 per cent in 2010 (GOI, 2013a). Public expenditure on education increased from ₹170 million in 1950–1951 to ₹60,677 million in 2001–2002 and further to ₹2,250,545 million in 2011–2012. The public expenditure on education in constant prices (after adjusting for inflation) was also growing, certainly, though at a lower rate than that in current prices. However, this growth in expenditure was inadequate to keep pace with the demand of an expanding higher education sector.

India has not yet reached the goal of 6 per cent of the GDP (Table 14.1) to be invested in education that was recommended by the Kothari Commission in 1966, and later re-iterated by almost all committees and commissions in India. Despite the inadequate state financing in

Table 14.1 *Public Expenditure on Education as a Share of GDP*

Year	Expenditure on Education as % of GDP
1951–1952	0.64
1960–1961	1.48
1970–1971	2.11
1980–1981	2.98
1990–1991	3.84
2000–2001	4.28
2005–2006	3.34
2009–2010	3.85

Source: GOI (2013a).

higher education, no effort was made by state or the non-state actors to fill the fissures accruing from paucity of public financing. This also contributed to the emergence and expansion of the private sector in higher education in India.

A major share of the public expenditure on education has been going to primary education. This is justifiable, given the priority to universalize elementary education and the continued dominance of public financing of elementary education. In 2009–2010, nearly 42 per cent of the public expenditure on education was allocated to elementary education, 25.4 per cent to secondary education and 23.4 per cent to higher education. Some of the recent policy suggestions indicate that the share of higher education will be increased to 2 per cent of the GDP by 2020. Another important trend is that a major share of the expenditure on education is accounted for by the state governments. In 2009–2010, nearly 75 per cent of the public expenditure on education was accounted for by the states while the contribution by the centre was only 25 per cent.

The expenditure on higher education by the centre increased substantially in the past decade, especially during the 11th Five-year Plan period (GOI, 2008). In fact, the share of higher education in the state budgets remained at around 16–17 per cent in the past decade.

A major share of the central government expenditure is allocated to central universities and institutions of national importance as grants. Similarly, a major share of grants from the technical education budget goes to institutions such as the IITs.

It is not only the paucity of public funding but also the priorities in allocation that affect uneven development of higher education. For example, the public funds disbursed by the UGC bring out the asymmetry between central universities and the rest of the institutions of higher education in India. While more than 90 per cent of the students are enrolled in state universities and colleges, a predominantly major share of UGC funding is directed to central institutions. The quality is higher and better, in general, in the centrally funded institutions. In the national institutional ranking framework (NIRF), the centrally funded institutions appear at the top of the list. This may be an example of selective approach to finance quality in higher education.

India is experiencing another phenomenon which is equally important from the quality concerns in the market sector of higher education, especially in the area of technical higher education. Many private technical institutions have been closed down in the past years for lack of adequate student enrolment, and many more are on the verge of closing down due to lack of demand for the courses offered by them. The report published in *The Times of India* (New Delhi, 23 June 2012) states that with more colleges and less students, engineering colleges and universities have requested the All India Council of Technical Education (AICTE) to stop granting clearance to new colleges. This is an important lesson for all market-driven policies that paved the way for mindless quantitative expansion without any quality control. This phenomenon shows that households are willing to invest in quality, and poor quality of services will lead to weak demand, less resources, and low or no profits and going out of business for the providers. This chapter analyzes the approach to financing quality of education in India.

Table 14.2 shows that only 0.82 to 0.89 per cent of the GDP is being spent on higher education, out of the 4.18 to 4.29 per cent of the total spending on education. If the quality of higher education has to improve, then more investment is required for education in general, and higher education in particular. Even the percentage expenditure

Table 14.2 *Public Expenditure on Education and Higher Education*

Year	Sector	Expenditure (₹ in Crores)	Percentage of Higher Education in Total Expenditure on Education (In %)	Expenditure on Higher Education (As % of GDP)
2010–2011	University and higher education	62,654.18	21.3	0.86
	Total (education)	293,478.25		4.05
2011–2012	University and higher education	69,054.66	19.7	0.82
	Total (education)	351,145.78		4.18
2012–2013	University and higher education	83,559.23	20.7	0.89
	Total (education)	403,236.50		4.29

Source: Analysis of Budgeted Expenditure (GOI, 2014).

on higher education in the total expenditure on education is ranging between 19.7 per cent and 21.3 per cent. Despite a certain consistency, the percentage continues to be only one-fifth of the total expenditure on education. This reflects a certain marginalization in terms of spending as well as prioritizing higher education.

The opening lines of the Education Commission 1964–1966 report again emphasizes the value of education: 'The destiny of India is now being shaped in our classrooms. This, we believe, is no mere rhetoric. In a world based on science and technology, it is education that determines the level of prosperity, welfare and security of the people' (GOI, 1964). Teaching is not merely a life work, a profession, but a passion which can be judged by the quality of students. On the quality of education, a policy perspective (GOI, 1985) entitled *Challenge of Education,* highlights that it is difficult to define quality, particularly with reference to educational process. However, it could be stated that a quality-conscious system could produce people who have the attributes of functional and social relevance; mental ability and physical dexterity; efficacy and reliability; and, above all, the confidence and the capability to communicate effectively, and exercise initiative and make innovation and experimentation with new situations. To these personal attributes, one could add the dimension of a value system that is conducive to harmony, integration and the welfare of the weak and the disadvantaged.

Of the total expenditure on higher education, the share of university and higher education is above 70 per cent of the total expenditure, and that of technical education is only the remaining 30 per cent. Actually, the share of university and higher education declined from 80 per cent in 2000–2001 to 72 per cent by 2012–2013. During this period, the expenditure on university and higher education in real price, expenditure on technical education increased by 3.2 times, thus increasing the share of technical education to nearly 30 per cent from 20 per cent in 2000–2001. This decline is not the first one in the history of financing of higher education. In 1950–1951, when the country's first five-year plan was launched, there were 27 universities serving 174,000 students. By 2006 there were 348 universities, 17,625 colleges and 10.5 million students.

Most of the allocated money favoured the 'temples of learning', that is, central universities and technological institutions such as IIT, NITs etc., leaving very little for social sciences, humanities and liberal education. This shows that the central government in its resource allocation policies followed a selective approach to favour the good quality and elite institutions. However, the overall per capita allocation has not risen proportionately, albeit the 'cost disease theory' (Paulson, 2016) which clearly states that the cost of higher education is rising because technology has not been able substitute good teachers, despite the impetus given to information communication technology.

A report presented by the prime minister's task force on education (created in 2000) recommended among other measures full cost recovery in higher education, and that the central and state governments should only fund those disciplines that have no market orientation. In May 2000, the Human Resource Development (HRD) ministry decided that higher education institutions should raise 7 per cent in the current academic session, with 1 per cent cumulative increase in the subsequent years. In order to offset the increase in fees, the Government of India announced a new education loan programme in April 2001. With financing higher education sliding in priority of the welfare state, the quality seems to be even more slippery and elusive. The recent suggestions by the NITI Aayog indicate that each university needs to mobilize 30 per cent of its resources from internal sources.

INVESTING IN QUALITY OF HIGHER EDUCATION

One of the challenges in Indian higher education is to finance quality interventions in an expanding higher education system. This is more so if one moves away from a selective approach to a common approach to improve overall quality of the system.

Now let us try and understand how quality initiatives in higher education can be financed. An approach to improve quality should need high quality teachers, and to attract high quality teachers, the system should have a good remuneration package which needs more liberal public funding of the sector. Further, attracting the teachers to the system will not be sufficient; they need to be engaged in research and teaching, good library, laboratory, residential campus, etc. Investment in all these elements are needed to attract good scholars, keep them active in teaching and research. It may be interesting to discuss some of the quality improving initiatives introduced by the public authorities in India.

Creating Accreditation Agencies

India's higher education system is the second largest in the world, next to China. India has a multiplicity of regulatory bodies in higher education. The main regulatory body for universities and general higher education is the University Grants Commission (UGC). UGC was set up immediately after the country attained Independence with the objective of maintaining quality and standards in higher education, giving advice to the government, and co-ordinating between the centre and the state.

In order to address the quality issue in India, following the National Policy on Education (NPE) (GOI, 1986, 1998) and the Programme of Action (PoA) 1992, the government established accreditation bodies. The National Assessment and Accreditation Council (NAAC) for general higher education, National Board of Accreditation (NBA) by the AICTE for technical education and the Accreditation Board (AB) of Indian Council of Agriculture Research (ICAR) for accrediting agricultural institutions are examples of quality interventions in higher education. Among these, NAAC is considered as a major quality assurance (QA) body in India as it covers all categories of higher education institutions, unlike other bodies focusing on specialized areas in higher education. With two decades of existence, NAAC has also evolved and progressed well. It has a rigorous methodology in place and seven well-defined domains of assessment that are designed and accepted by a large number of specialists in higher education. These seven domains are curricular aspects, teaching–learning and evaluation, research, consultancy and extension, infrastructure and learning resources, student support and progression, leadership and management, and innovation and best practices. Setting up such bodies is a heavy investment for quality in higher education.

QAC: An Intervention for Quality

In pursuance of its action plan for performance evaluation, assessment and accreditation and quality upgradation of institutions of higher education, the NAAC proposed that every accredited institution should establish an internal quality assurance cell (IQAC) as a post-accreditation quality sustenance measure. Since quality enhancement is a continuous process, the IQAC will become a part of the institution's system and work towards realization of the goals of quality enhancement and sustenance.

The prime task of the IQAC is to develop a system for conscious, consistent and catalytic improvement in the overall performance of institutions. For this, during the post-accreditation period, it will channelize all efforts and measures of the institution towards promoting its holistic academic excellence. The setting of IQAC in institutions of higher learning in India is the accelerators of change in quality of higher education. Since quality is not a static but rather a continuous dynamic process, it needs to be fathomed constantly. Currently most IQACs in most institutions are understaffed, leading to additional work for the faculty without additional remuneration. If more investment is made on such cells, then the quality of institutions will drastically improve. Each college and university having IQAC will definitely enhance quality in myriad ways in Indian higher education. The setting of such cells needs twin investment of both physical and human, and they can be acquired by appropriate financing only. As of today, there is under-investment in IQACs and, therefore, there is a need to improved allocations to strengthen the IQACs.

Focus on Teachers for Quality

No education system can excel and sustain without quality teachers. The Indian higher education system suffers because it is unable to recruit and retain the best in the system despite the lofty ideals of the Radhakrishnan Commission in 1948. Even the first policy talks about the organic link among the sectors with a focus on teachers. In fact, the 1986 policy clearly enunciates the setting-up of academic staff colleges now rechristened as human resource development centres to orient and refresh the young teachers in their respective professional journeys.

In order to attract good professionals towards teaching, one has to look at remuneration/salaries which were one of the lowest at the dawn of Independence. The Mehrotra Committee (GOI, 1986) recommend that the teacher's salary, post the fourth pay commission, for university and college teachers, was not able to bring parity in salary with other competitive professions. It was the Rastogi Committee (GOI, 1997), in the post fifth pay commission period that recommended parity in salary scales between teacher's in higher education and other respectable professions, notably civil service. It was on the recommendation of the Chaddha Committee (GOI, 2008) that the salary of a young academic was more at the entry level in comparison with other jobs available in the government sector.

At the recommendation of the Mehrotra Committee, a National Eligibility Test (NET)[1] was introduced to enter the teaching profession. The nature of the test is such that it was designed at par with other public exams, and therefore, students preparing for other public exam benefit due to the spin-offs, while students with critical minds with a singular aim of becoming a teacher are not at disadvantage. The NET has succeeded in selecting better candidates to the teaching profession. The NET is conducted twice a year, and millions of candidates appear for the test. It is also a highly selective test, and less than 5 per cent of the candidates who appear qualify in the test (Varghese, Malik & Gautam, 2017).

The other problem faced by the sector is the large number of unfilled vacancies in many universities and colleges in India. This results in a surge in the number of non-permanent and ad hoc teachers in higher education, adversely impacting teacher motivation and quality of higher education. The All-India Survey on Higher Education, which is the only all India data source on higher education, shows year after year that a large number of teaching positions remain vacant. These vacancies are being substituted by ad hoc and temporary teachers who are

---

[1] I acknowledge with gratitude the assistance of Soumini Ghosh, doctoral scholar at Centre for Political Studies, JNU, New Delhi.

then exploited by the system by offering them short-term employment which may not be considered as 'experience' for full-time employment. Moreover, expenditure on teachers' salaries gives little scope for investment on other activities related to teacher development and research. This is a strategy to save money in higher education, leading to severe compromise to enhance quality. Investment on research plays an important contributory role to improving the quality of higher education. Most of the faculty members in the university departments are research degree holders, while those in the colleges are not. This may be an important factor for the higher quality of education provided in the university departments when compared with that provided in the colleges. Research is a resource intensive activity and depends hugely on the budgetary allocation. The research culture can only be created and optimized through grants and endowments, and academic-cultural characteristics. Due to scarce and competitive grants available for research, it becomes very difficult for college teachers to undertake research. In fact, access to these grants is also selective and, thereby, its outreach is restricted to the hinterland which limits the quality further.

The progress and development of a nation depends on the standard of excellence set by its institutions of higher learning. This is especially true because centres of academic excellence generate creative talents. The Zakir Hussain Centre for Educational Studies in JNU was set up to examine educational issues from a social science perspective. It is a measure of human development and it speeds up national growth. However, excellence is not democratic, but democracies thrive on excellence; democratizing excellence through adopting best practices brings out quality enhancement, and thereby advancement of the society. In our quest for the best practices in research, the age-old 'vaccination theory of education' will not work. Paradigm shifts of globalization, liberalization and privatization have now made many inventions celebrated mothers of new necessities for which massive investment is required for quality improvement.

INVESTING IN INFRASTRUCTURE FOR QUALITY IMPROVEMENT

The infrastructure is the sum total of the utility of space, structure, equipment, learning resources, infrastructural aids, information stock and knowledge-sharing devices. These by themselves may lie unutilized if an effective exploitation of their utility is not made by planned economic, purposeful management and maintenance of these resources. The Rashtriya Uchchatar Shiksha Abhiyan (RUSA) (GOI, 2013), a centrally sponsored programme, aims to work with *300-plus* state universities and its affiliated colleges to raise the bar of campus life. Launched in 2013, the RUSA aims at providing strategic funding to eligible state higher education institutions. The central funding (in the ratio of 60:40 for general category states, 90:10 for special category states and 100 per cent for union territories) is based on norms and is outcome dependent. Funds flow from the central ministry through the state governments/union territories to the state higher education councils before reaching the identified institutions. Funding to states would be made on the basis of the critical appraisal of state higher education plans, which would enlist each state's strategy to address issues of equity, access and excellence in higher education. RUSA places greater emphasis on the improvement of the quality of teaching–learning processes in order to produce employable and competitive graduates, postgraduates and PhDs. Spread across two plan periods (XII and XIII), (GOI, 2013) the programme focuses on state higher education institutions, and draws upon the best practices from colleges and universities across the nation. RUSA also creates space for institution under the state universities to seek central funds. These additional funds will help in improving the quality of such institutions. The process of seeking RUSA grants is cumbersome, but the exercise itself is enriching and leads to increased awareness and accountability towards quality in higher education.

ICT Revolution: The Beginning of a New Era

India has innumerable challenges in terms of infrastructure, and socio-economic, linguistic and physical barriers for people who wish to access education. However, it is hoped that ICT can transform the educational scenario in the country. The emancipatory and transformative potentials of ICT in higher education in India have helped increase the country's requirement of higher education through part-time and distance-learning schemes. It can be used as a tool to overcome the issues of cost, less number of teachers, and poor quality of education,

344 | Aarti Srivastava

as well as to overcome time and distance barriers. While the world is moving rapidly towards digital media, the role of ICT in education has become increasingly important. It has transformed the way knowledge is disseminated today in terms of how teachers interact and communicate with the students, and vice-versa. Moreover, most of the online courses are opted by professionals and lifelong learners who strengthen their knowledge and skills, thereby adding quality to themselves and the system at large. Through ICT, quality is reinforced without much additional investment, provided the basic infrastructure is in place to support MOOCs. Besides, it can provide networking structures, transcending borders, and foster empowerment amongst students. This change can only be actualized by higher financial allocation given to higher education. The MOOCs-SWAYAM portal, in Indian higher education aims at access, equality and quality. However, ICT can only be a successful tool, when the basic infrastructure is developed in order to reach all stakeholders. The initial investment needed is substantial, although the recurring expenditure needed in the subsequent years may be far less.

BUDGETARY PRIORITIES IN A RESEARCH UNIVERSITY

JNU was established in 1969 by an act of Parliament. Due to autonomy of critical thinking and reasoning, JNU has been rated as the best by NAAC, with a grade point of 3.91 on a scale of 4.0. In 2017, JNU was ranked as India's top ranking university (after the Indian Institute of Science Bangalore) as per the Ministry of Human Resource Development's (MHRD) NIRF (GOI, 2017). JNU also won the Hon. President's Award for Best University in 2017. A study on the NET undertaken by NIEPA, New Delhi, also reveals that JNU stood first consistently for 10 NET examinations (Varghese et al., 2017). This observation also reflects the quality of scholarship of the enrolled students.

In an attempt to examine the link between quality and financing, a few tables from the JNU finance department are being analyzed to establish that quality does have financial underpinnings.

Table 14.3 *Jawaharlal Nehru University Income for the Year 2015–2016*

	Income for Current Year (2015–2016) (in Crore ₹) and Percentage in Total Income (in %)	Percentage Increase/ Decrease (in %)	Income for Previous Year (2014–2015) (in Crore ₹) and Percentage in Total Income (in %)
Academic receipts	7.08 (2.03%)	−2.02	7.22 (2.24%)
Grants in aid/subsidies	319.17 (91.94%)	+7.79	296.09 (91.93%)
Income from investments	10.43 (3.005%)	+30.78	7.97 (2.47%)
Interest earned	1.51 (0.43%)	−41.95	2.61 (0.81%)
Other income	8.87 (2.55%)	+9.39	8.1 (2.51%)
Prior period income	0.51 (0.014%)	+60.28	0.31 (0.01%)
TOTAL	347.12 (100%)	+7.78	322.05 (100%)

Source: JNU, Annual Accounts (2015–2016).

The total income for the current year (2015–2016) is ₹3.4712 billion (see Table 14.3). A 7.78 per cent increase from the previous year (2014–2015), which had a total income of ₹3.2205 billion.

The grants-in-aid/subsidies for the current year (2015–2016) were approximately ₹3.19 billion (91.94% of the total income), compared to the approximately ₹2.96 billion (91.93% of the total income) for the previous year (2014–2015). The grants-in-aid/subsidies for the current year (2015–2016) witnessed a 7.79 per cent increase from the previous year (2014–2015). This is the reason for maintaining the high academic standards of the university, as this money is being used directly for teachers and students to enhance learning outcomes leading to good quality in education. The university receives almost 90 per cent of its total receipts as grants and subsidies.

The income from investments for the current year (2015–2016) was approximately ₹100 million (3.005% of the total income), compared to the approximately ₹70 million (2.47% of the total income) for the previous year (2014–2015). The income from investments for the current year (2015–2016) witnessed a 30.78 per cent increase from the previous year (2014–2015). Such investments lead to more resources for the university, which can be used to ameliorate the quality of the institution.

For ensuring quality, we see that JNU spends about 72 per cent of its expenditure on human resource, in the form of salaries and wages, provident fund, medical reimbursements, and so on (see Table 14.4). This helps JNU attract and retain quality manpower. We also see that academic expenses comprise about 7 per cent, to support the

Table 14.4 *Establishment, Academic, Administrative and General Expenses of JNU for 2015–2016*

Expenditure	Expenditure for Current Year (2015–2016) (in Crore ₹)	Percentage in Total Expenditure (in %)
Establishment expenses	352.0	71.6
Academic expenses	34.7	7.0
Administrative and general expenses	67.6	13.7
Miscellaneous including transport, repair and incidentals	37.64	7.65
Total expenditure	492.0	100.0

Source: JNU accounts.

Table 14.5 *Academic Expenses*

Particulars	Financial Year (2015–2016) (in Crore ₹)	Percentage of Total Academic Expenses (in %)
Research*	25.94	74.8
Examination expenses	4.4	12.7
Student welfare expenses	3.8	10.9
Miscellaneous academic expenses	0.54	1.6
Gross total	34.7	100.0

Source: JNU, Annual Accounts (2015–2016).

Note: Salary expenditure is not included in the academic expenses.

*Research includes research activities, fieldwork and participation in conferences, laboratory expenses, seminars and workshops, scholarship/stipend to doctoral students, and journals and publications.

faculty in undertaking academic activities. Administrative and general expenses comprise 13 per cent of the total expenditure, to augment the functioning of the academic activities of the university. This is how JNU maintains quality, by adequate investment. We now look at the academic expenses in detail in Table 14.5. The table represents the academic expenses for JNU for the financial year 2015–2016. We see that almost 75 per cent of the academic expenses are invested on research. This investment includes laboratories, which are central to scientific inquiry and experimentation in natural sciences, as well as field work in social sciences, which is the backbone for empirical investigations. Participation in conferences, seminars and workshops are necessary in order to share insights from one's research and strengthen one's understanding by vetting ideas, and research forms an important part of the JNU ecosystem with adequate financing, leading to enhanced quality. The expenditure on journals and publications is also substantial, which feeds into research and also an output of research. The heavy investment on research justifies JNU in being an intense research university with high standards of quality.

Academic activity reaches full circle only once the evaluation results reach the hands of the scholar. A total of 12.68 per cent of the total academic expenses is used to undertake this important final activity of the academic cycle. This improves the quality of education and research through appropriate investment.

Given the high opportunity cost, especially in higher education, the support from the university in terms of decent fellowship and good student-welfare facilities becomes critical for students to excel. We see a major investment in the total student welfare expenses at about 11 per cent.

The diversity of heads under which academic expenses takes place, that is, from students to teachers, and laboratory to field work among others, reflects that it is meticulously taken up. The academic expenses of JNU can be a good model for other institutions to re-prioritize the expenditure in order to enhance academic quality.

CONCLUSION

The analysis reveals that JNU has been given gracious grants by the government through the UGC, and it has been able to utilize, generate and mobilize the funds judiciously. This could be a pace setting model for financing of other universities. Nearly 30 per cent of the budget is retained for non-salary expenses, and a good share of the academic expenses is devoted to research-related activities. The contours of higher education have undergone a sea of change. The public funding of higher education is shrinking rapidly. As reflected in the chapter, most of the aspects related to quality have a subtle or upfront link with financing. The state cannot abdicate itself from its responsibility of funding higher education as this sector generates umpteen positive externalities. In India, the higher education sector is dominated by the private, who carries out its financing cryptically and not for public consumption. More worrisome are the concerns of quality in the impervious structures of the private.

Since quality and financing are positively correlated, decreasing public funds to higher education institutions in India by the government is a huge challenge. On one side, we aspire to go global and world class, and on the other, we experience receding public grants. In a developing nation like ours, with a huge demographic dividend, we need to prioritize higher education because it is here that the youth transforms into human capital with externalities which no other sector generates. A nation which prioritizes education and research, develops rapidly with invincible quality. This has already been demonstrated by most advanced nations, and India should also emulate them by financing heavily on quality of higher education.

REFERENCES

GOI (Government of India). (1964). *Report of the education commission: 1964–66*. New Delhi: GOI.

———. (1985). *Challenge of education: A policy perspective*. New Delhi: Ministry of Human Resource Development, GOI.

———. (1986). *Report of the University Grants Commission Pay Review Committee* (Chairman: R. C. Mehrotra). New Delhi: Ministry of Human Resource Development, GOI.

———. (1997). *Report of the University Grants Commission Pay Review Committee* (Chairman: R. P. Rastogi). New Delhi: Ministry of Human Resource Development, GOI.

———. (1998). *National policy on education, 1986: Programme of action*. New Delhi: GOI.

———. (2008a). *Eleventh five year plan (2007–2012): Social sectors*. Planning Commission, GOI, Volume II. New Delhi: OUP. Retrieved 8 May 2017, from http://planningcommission.gov.in/plans/planrel/fiveyr/11th/11_v2/11th_vol2.pdf/

———. (2008b). *Report of the University Grants Commission Pay Review Committee* (Chairman: G. K. Chadha). New Delhi: Ministry of Human Resource Development, GOI.

———. (2013a). *Ministry of Human Resource Development/educational statistics at a glance*. Retrieved 16 May 2018, from http://mhrd.gov.in/sites/upload_files/mhrd/files/statistics/EAG_2013.pdf

———. (2013b). *Twelfth five year plan (2012–2017): Social sectors*. Planning Commission, GOI, Vol. III. New Delhi: SAGE. Retrieved 20 March 2018, from http://planningcommission.gov.in/plans/planrel/fiveyr/12th/pdf/12fyp_vol3.pdf /

———. (2013c). *Rashtriya Uchchatar Shiksha Abhiyan 2013*. Retrieved 20 March 2018, from http://rusa.nic.in/about-us/overview/

GOI (Government of India). (2014). *Ministry of Human Resource Development/ analysis of budgeted expenditure 2010–2013.* Retrieved 12 May 2017, from http://mhrd.gov.in/sites/upload_files/mhrd/files/statistics/ABE_2010-13.pdf/
———. (2017). *Ministry of Human Resource Development/national institutional ranking framework 2017.* Retrieved 16 June 2017, from https://www.nirfindia.org/ UniversityRanking.html/

NAAC (National Assessment and Accreditation Council). *Criteria for assessment.* Retrieved 20 September 2017, from http://www.naac.gov.in/criteria_assessment.asp

Paulsen, Michael B. (Ed.). (2016). *Higher education: Handbook of theory and research.* Vol. 31. Switzerland: Springer International Publishing.

Varghese, N. V. (2015). Challenges of massification of higher education in India. *CPRHE Research Papers Series* (Research Paper No. 1). New Delhi: CPRHE-NIEPA.

Varghese, N. V., Malik, G., & Gautam, D. R. (2017). Teacher recruitment in higher education in India: An analysis of NET results. *CPRHE Research Papers Series* (Research Paper No. 8). New Delhi: CPRHE-NIEPA.

Chapter 15

Qualification Frameworks for Improving Quality and Relevance of Education*

N. V. Varghese

INTRODUCTION

Globalization implies a cross-border flow of capital, people and jobs. The acceptability of skills produced in a country is a necessary condition for migration of the skilled workers to another country. A trust in qualifications plays an important role in the labour market of the migrant workers within a country or between countries. The education and modes of training, curriculum and quality assurance (QA) mechanisms in place are factors influencing acceptability of graduates across borders. This puts pressure on national skill formation to meet global standards. A QA of certifications is an important element in developing mutual trust among qualifications awarded by national agencies. The qualification frameworks (QFs) help overcome the barriers in acceptability of qualifications from one region in another region.

---

* This chapter is based on the two documents which the author prepared (Varghese, 2015a, 2015b).

The QFs ensure standards in skill training, facilitate comparability of skills, improve employability of graduates, and promote mobility of workers within the country and across borders. Most countries in the world are operating under the national QFs (Cedefop, 2015). The level of knowledge, skills and competencies acquired are important elements which make a graduate from one institution acceptable in the labour market. It is expected that the QFs will provide specificity to what is to be the learning outcome at each level of education and better links qualification with employment.

The employability of higher education graduates continues to be one of the major concerns in India. The recent efforts to establish a Ministry of Skill Development & Entrepreneurship (MSDE), initiating the Skill India programme and Pradhan Mantri Kaushal Vikas Yojana (PMKVY) programme are efforts to link education and training with the job market. Any QF is designed to provide: (a) quality assured, nationally recognized and consistent training standards and (b) recognition and credit for all acquisition of knowledge and skills. It is a way of structuring existing and new qualifications (OECD, 2006). India too is in the process of developing and implementing a national qualification framework (NQF). The country initially developed an NQF in vocational education (NVEQF) which was later replaced by the National Skill Qualification Framework (NSQF).

This chapter is organized as follows: The next section discusses the origins and global trends in the move towards developing national and regional QFs. The following section discusses some of the essential characteristics of QFs followed by a major section on Indian efforts to develop QFs focusing on the NVEQF, NSQF and National Higher Education Qualification Framework (NHEQF). The chapter further discusses efforts to ensure quality and relevance of education and training systems through QFs. The final section draws some conclusions.

THE ORIGINS OF QFs

Job descriptions also play an important role in recruitment of prospective employees. Job descriptions indicate only what the employer expects his or her prospective employee to do. The other part of the job description is the profile of the person the employer would like to have to perform the job. This is reflected in terms of the educational and training qualifications possessed by the candidate. In many job advertisements, the skills and knowledge expected from the candidate is specified in terms of qualifications to do the job or the expected standards. This has been the logic behind relying on educational qualifications for screening candidates and recruiting prospective employees.

The job performance of employees in many companies indicated that it varied even when the qualification levels were the same. That gave rise to a mismatch between degrees and the skills the educational institutions certify and the competencies possessed by the candidate. The mismatch between skills expected and skills reflected by the qualifications was a source of lack of confidence in the certification of skills. Employers started losing confidence in the qualifications and degrees awarded by institutions, and there developed a 'crisis of legitimacy' of the existing qualification systems. The QFs are a means to regain confidence of the employers on the education and training systems.

The origins of NQF can be traced to the evolution of competency-based qualification reforms introduced in the UK in the 1980s (Jessup, 1991; Young, 2005) followed by similar efforts in Australia, New Zealand and South Africa (Ensor, 2003). The NQFs in these countries were in response to the demand by the employers for greater participation in skill formation as well as to shape the content of education and training programmes. The second-generation implementation of NQFs started in the late 1990s in Ireland, and it spread to many of the developing countries of Africa, Asia and Latin America (Tuk, 2007). Regional qualification frameworks (RQFs) also developed in the African, European, Latin American and Asian regions. Many of the efforts to develop national and regional QFs were supported by international agencies such as OECD, ILO, the World Bank and the European Union (ILO, 2006). In fact, QFs became a major initiative in reforming national education and training systems since the 1990s.

The Bologna Process involving the largest number of countries and their varying educational systems is the classic example of successful efforts in developing an RQF, namely, the European Qualification Framework (EQF; EC, 2008). The EQF facilitates translation or comparison of qualification levels so that there is no difficulty in identification of skills, inter-country comparisons, and mobility of learners and workers between countries based on qualification descriptors (CINQF, 2011; EC, 2008).

The qualification descriptors are general statements of the typical achievement of learners who have been awarded a qualification on successful completion of a cycle. Dublin descriptors are the most commonly used qualification descriptors. These descriptors help develop and impart competency-based training and outcome-based learning by the educational institutions. Even when the country-level QF is called an NQF, the framework may be developed only in selected sectors. The QFs are more easily developed and are commonly found in technical vocational education and training (VET) domains. These initiatives referred to as sub-frameworks forms part of a broader NQF (Allias, 2010).

SOME COMMON FEATURES OF QFS

QF is a useful tool to compare different national systems, and to promote comparability and compatibility between different systems. It classifies qualifications by levels, and differentiates each level based on learning outcomes that are based on skills, knowledge and abilities, which the holders of the qualifications at a given level will have acquired. The basis for these classifications, very often, is Dublin descriptors. In a typical situation, the level and length (duration of study) are taken into account while awarding a degree. However, in the QFs, it is the skills and learning outcomes are more important than the duration of the study programme.

A qualification in the NQF context is a statement of learning outcomes and associated requirements for awards. Under the QF framework, the skills possessed by the individual (learning outcome) are more important than the mode of acquiring (informal learning, training or institutions) the skills. In the context of QFs, education becomes competency based, focussing on learning outcomes and predetermined standards (Gonczi & Arguelles, 2000). The qualifications are a formal outcome of an assessment and validation process, which is obtained when a competent body determines that an individual has achieved learning outcomes of given standards.

The NQF provides a structure of well-defined and nationally accredited qualifications which are awarded at the end of a study programme. It attempts to bring together education and training under a single unified system. A qualifications framework is designed to provide (a) quality assured nationally recognized and consistent training standards, and (b) recognition and credit for all acquisition of knowledge and skills. It is a way of structuring existing and new qualifications (OECD, 2006). One of the distinctive characteristic of the NQFs is that the qualifications they contain are independent of the institutions that offered the programmes. In simple terms, this means that educational and training qualifications become 'national property' rather than being owned by the education and training institutions themselves.

As discussed in the beginning, there is no uniform pattern of implementing the QFs. Some countries may start developing NQF in any one of the sectors and may progressively move to other sectors, while others may start with developing a comprehensive NQF. Needless to add, a comprehensive NQF approach helps in developing a strategic and complete vision of the education and qualifications, and their alignment with skills and competencies. For example, India started with developing QF in the domain of vocational education and later extended to other domains.

NATIONAL QUALIFICATION FRAMEWORKS IN INDIA

Nearly 62 per cent of India's population is in the working age group of 15–60, and more than 54 per cent of the total population is below 25 years of age (MSD&E, 2015). At present, not more than 10 per cent of the youth has received any vocational training. Nearly 12.8 million people enter the workforce every year, and the existing skill development capacity can accommodate only 3.1 million (IAMR, 2012; Mehrotra, 2015). Further, nearly 93 per cent of the workforce is in unorganized sectors, and nearly 83 per cent of the new entrants in the workforce have no opportunity for skill training.

The country experiences paucity of skilled workforce on the one hand and lack of relevant skills among the educated on the other. Between 2013 and 2022, the employment is expected to increase from 461.1 million to 581.9 million workers, implying an additional employment of 120.8 skilled human resources. It is estimated that only 4.7 per cent of the workforce in India has undergone skill training by 2015 (MSD&E, 2015). These numbers reflect the nature and extent of challenges faced by the country in providing opportunities for gainfully employed.

While the large share of the youth population and the resulting demographic dividend is impressive, the difficulty is to translate this positive trend into an asset. The new initiatives such as Make in India and Skill India Missions aim to train nearly 10 million youth by 2020 by numerous training providers and certifying agencies. Given the multiplicity of agencies offering training, there is a need to clearly define skill levels and standardize the training arrangements so that the certification of skill levels imply minimum variations.

India is committed to an inclusive policy on educational development. The strategies to ensure inclusiveness include measures to reduce and eventually eliminate regional, gender, and social disparities, and disparities between differently abled children. Since the access conditions have improved and a major share of the age-group children are already in the schools, the focus of policy interventions has been shifting to improving quality and relevance. The focus on relevance refers to the nature skills acquired by students while they pursue their studies in schools and institutions of higher education. The revised scheme of vocationalization of education seeks to emphasize on the students acquiring vocational skills to improve their employability. These vocational courses are developed based on the studies and surveys carried out by the national skill development mission.

Indian higher education institutions vary in terms of the content and level at which courses are offered. These result in a lack of comparability of outcomes associated with different qualifications across institutions. The title of qualifications, their contents, level and duration of the study programmes vary making it difficult for establishing equivalence of certificates issued from different institutions. It constrains mobility of students and their employability.

The QF will be able to address the issue of the diversity of Indian education and training systems. The expectation is that an NQF will help the country to move towards developing nationally standardized, and internationally comparable and acceptable qualifications. It is expected that the QF will help developing a set of qualifications corresponding to the skill levels for each level that are accepted across the country and that can be developed through multiple pathways.

Since there was no central agency to be entrusted with the task of developing QF in India, individual ministries started working on development of a QF. The Ministry of Labour and Employment developed the national vocational qualification framework (NVQF) and the Ministry of Human Resource Development conceptualized the NVEQF. An inter-ministerial committee was formed by the Cabinet secretariat to use these two frameworks while developing a national skill qualification framework (NSQF) by the National Skill Development Agency (NSDA). The University Grants Commission (UGC) is in the process of developing an NHEQF.

National Vocational Education Qualification Framework

VET is offered by different ministries and agencies, although the Directorate General of Employment and Training (DGE&T) of the Ministry of Labour and Employment (MOL&E) has the overall responsibility for offering VET. It is estimated that India has around 95,000 industrial training institutes (ITIs) in public and private sectors which can provide short- and long-term training to around 1.3 million candidates (British Council, 2014). During the 11th five-year plan, the government developed a national skill development policy and established a national skill development corporation (NSDC) in 2009. The Ministry of Human Resources Development (MHRD) and MOL&E developed an NVEQF, which states

> NVEQF is a descriptive framework that organizes qualifications according to a series of levels of knowledge along with skills. These levels are defined in terms of learning outcomes, that is, the competencies which the learners must possess regardless of whether they were acquired through formal, non-formal or informal education and training. (MHRD, 2012, p. 1)

The NVEQF is organized as a series of levels of competency/skills arranged in an ascending order from Recognition of Prior Learning (RPL) Levels 1 to 10. Each level on NVEQF is described by a statement of learning called level descriptor. The NVEQF level descriptor provides indication of learning outcomes specified in National Occupational Standards (NOS). The NVEQF takes into account RPL, engagement with industry through their involvement in the design, development and delivery of courses. The NVEQF also will develop a competency-based curriculum package consisting of syllabus, student manual, trainers guide, training manual, multimedia packages and e-material.

A credit framework to certify skill competencies and general education learning requirements will be developed by the certifying agencies. Facilities for credit accumulation and transfer of credits will be part of this arrangement. The NVEQF will integrate formal, vocational, education and job market. The AICTE will be the nodal agency for implementation from Level 3 to Level 7. It provides students multi-level entry/exit system for them to seek employment after plus 2 levels.

The NVQEF will be based on nationally recognized occupational standards, skill mapping, and multi-entry and exit points. It will have industry-linked learning trades with 50 of the courses on hands-on practice, project work with cross movement of faculty between industry, and vocational courses. It will permit credit accumulation, credit portability from multiple agencies leading to certification, accreditation and QA. It is expected that '[t]he National Vocational Education Qualifications Framework (NVEQF) would be assimilated into the National Skills Qualification Framework, once that framework is notified for the country' (MHRD, 2012, p. 1).

National Skill Qualification Framework

The National Skills Qualifications Framework (NSQF is a competency-based framework that organizes all qualifications according to a series of levels of knowledge, skills and aptitude (MOF, 2013). These levels, graded from 1 to 10, are defined in terms of learning outcomes which the learner must possess, regardless of whether they are obtained through formal, non-formal or informal learning. NSQF in India was notified on 27 December 2013. All other frameworks, including the NVEQF released by the Ministry of HRD, stand superseded by the NSQF.

Under NSQF, the learner can acquire the certification for competency needed at any level through formal, non-formal or informal learning. In that sense, the NSQF is a QA framework. In fact, what NQSF assures is standardized, consistent and nationally acceptable outcomes of education and training across the country through a national QA framework.

The NSQF is anchored at the NSDA, and is being implemented through the National Skills Qualifications Committee (NSQC) which comprises of all key stakeholders. It is expected that the recruitment rules of the public sector enterprises and government agencies may be amended to define eligibility criteria for all positions in terms of NSQF levels. By 2018, it will be mandatory for all training/educational programmes to be NSQF-compliant, and all training and educational institutions shall define eligibility criteria for admission to various courses in terms of NSQF levels.

The NSQF is a nationally integrated education and competency-based skills framework with provision for multiple pathways including mobility between technical and general education. It also provides for entry to labour market and to exit the labour market to acquire more skills, and to re-enter the labour market again after acquiring higher-level qualifications. The key features of the NSQF include multiple entry and exit, horizontal and vertical mobility, outcome-based learning, credit accumulation and transfer, life-long learning, competency-based curriculum aligned to NOS, RPL, and third-party assessment and certification.

National Higher Education Qualification Framework

The UGC is planning to develop a comprehensive NHEQF for the entire higher education sector (1). While the need for introducing NHEQF to facilitate transparency and comparability of qualifications at all levels among different higher education institutions is very well recognized, developing a NHEQF for a country like India is a huge task, given the size of the sector, diversity of institutions and programmes of study.

HEQF can be defined as a comprehensive framework that develops and classifies qualifications based on a set of criteria, approved nationally and comparable with international quality standards, specifies academic levels and learning outcomes, and is aligned to a credit system based on the time taken and the academic workload of students to complete the study programme. The objective is to create an integrated national framework for learning outcomes by recognizing and accrediting qualifications offered by different institutions engaged in higher education and skill training in India.

The NHEQF will take into account the work done earlier in the context of NVEQF and NSQF, and build on those frameworks. The level descriptors in other QFs have already indicated the role of higher education qualifications. Therefore, it is important to rely on the work already done by other QFs in India and establish comparability and consistency with those efforts.

It is expected that NHEQF will be comprehensive and overarching, and will cover all programmes of study offered in institutions at the post-secondary education level (PSE), that is, it should incorporate all study programmes offered beyond 10+2 levels of education or confined to education provided by universities and institutions offering degrees and diplomas. Some of the post-secondary courses are not part of the higher education system (equivalent to ISCED4 level).

Another important issue is the number of regulatory bodies/agencies in higher education in India. Higher education in India is regulated by several agencies such as UGC, AICTE, MCI, ICAR, BCI, DEC, etc. The qualification structure and the duration of time invested by students to obtain the first and second degrees (undergraduate and graduate studies) vary among the study programmes regulated by these agencies. There is a need for consultations and regular meetings between these regulatory bodies to arrive at a more comparable understanding on learning outcomes and level descriptors.

The NHEQF should place competencies in a comprehensive framework. This is more difficult in India also because of the fact that a major share of expansion is accounted for by the private institutions. An important and necessary exercise India needs to undertake is to develop a matrix mapping of qualifications certified and the corresponding skills and competencies. This is a difficult and time-consuming exercise given the multiplicity of providers and diversity of study programmes offered by them. However, such an exercise can be a reliable starting point to move towards a comprehensive NHEQF taking into account all education and training programmes offered by all providers.

NHEQF needs to include all study programmes offered at the post-secondary level including all types of qualifications and skill formation—technical vocational education and training, academic programmes and professional programmes. All programmes must provide clear, measurable and observable learning outcomes. Learning outcomes includes knowledge, skills and competence.

Learning outcomes, quality standards and assessment procedures are accountability measures, and they need to be clearly defined. The level descriptors will help in this process. These accountability measures are also important to help institutions to put targets for improvements in the contents and quality of study programmes. The level descriptors should indicate an individual's knowledge, professional skills and responsibility level. Assessment and validation of learning outcomes needs to be carried out systematically by a recognized body/bodies. Outcome of a formal assessment and validation process will be certification of qualifications. The accreditation bodies for general and technical higher education will be relied on for QA.

SKILL FORMATION TO IMPROVE RELEVANCE AND QUALITY IN EDUCATION

The NSQF is the basis for organizing skill training in India. It specifies the learning outcomes and the quality standards to be achieved in education and training programmes. The policy framework for skill development envisages that skill components will be integrated with formal education by introducing vocational education classes from Grade 9 of the secondary education onwards. In higher education, skilling will be integrated with polytechnics, offering NSQF-aligned vocational courses and bachelor of vocational study degrees. The existing ITI and polytechnics will be modernized and linked to formal educational qualifications, and also aligned to the emerging competency-based demand for skills in the employment market. All formal and vocational education including skill training will have to align themselves with NSQF by December 2018.

The strategies envisaged for expanding institutional arrangements for skilling include full utilization of existing capacities in the institutions, utilizing facilities of schools and colleges during holidays, and expanding skilling facilities both in the public and private sector. New ITIs, advanced training institutions (ATIs) and multi-skill institutes (MSIs) will be set up with public–private partnership (PPP) mode with strong linkages with industry.

Curricula, Assessment and Certification

Sector skills councils (SSCs), which are industry-led bodies helpful in identifying industry relevant skills, are established. The SSCs will be responsible for development of NOS and qualification packs (QPs) for various job roles in a sector. The outcome standards for each job role will need to be clearly defined and notified as per NSQF. Development of standards by SSCs will be under the aegis of the NSQC under NSQF. All NOSs and QPs developed by the SSCs will be examined and reviewed by the NSQC and, thereafter, conferred the status of 'national standards'. All skill training in the country will necessarily align itself to these national standards.

A QA framework for NSQF is being developed. The QA framework for certification and assessment will set minimum standards and provide guidance for effective, valid, reliable, fair and transparent assessment within the context of the NSQF. RPL is a part of the assessment and certification process. At present, the National Council for Vocational Training (NCVT) provides a national framework for setting curricula for various vocational courses, and it also prescribes standards for equipment, scale of space, duration of courses, methods of training, conducting all-India trade tests and awarding national trade certificates. The CBSE and other school boards will certify skill-based vocational courses with certification at NSQF level for students completing 10 + 2 level of school education. All the learners continuing diploma courses after 10 + 2 for two semesters will be awarded NSQF Level 5, those completing two years will be awarded advanced diploma and those who complete three years of further study after 10 + 2 will be awarded a B.Voc. degree (UGC, 2012). The skill component of the courses will have 60 per cent weights and will be assessed by the SSCs, while the general education component of the course will be assessed by the concerned educational institutions. The UGC has recommended a 10-point letter grade and equivalent grade point 9 for assessment of students.

The NSQF assures quality in higher education in terms of awarding credits and allowing transfer of credits by evaluating each level and every form of education. Each of the 10 levels of skills formation represents a distinct set of knowledge, complexity and autonomy. These levels define the professional knowledge, professional skills, core skill and responsibility to be attained by any person to be certified. Each qualification at the NSQF level may be defined in terms of curriculum contents, notional contact hours, duration of studies, workload, trainer quality and the type of institution attended. This may imply standardization of course contents, syllabus, study duration and credits, and developing a qualification register.

Management of Implementation of NSQF

India created a Ministry of Skill Development and Entrepreneurship (MSD&E) in 2014 to co-ordinate skill development efforts in the country. The other central ministries/departments, state governments and industry/employers are expected to fulfil the roles and responsibilities pertaining to their domain as laid down in the National Policy for Skill Development and Entrepreneurship.

The MSD&E will be mapping the existing skills and their certification, providing academic equivalence of skill sets. The NSDA, which was created as an autonomous body, has been made part of the

MSD&E. The NSDC was set up as a non-profit company for coordinating and stimulating private sector initiatives in skill development. To ensure that the skill development is in line with the needs of the industry, SSCs have been set up. SSCs are industry-led bodies, and will identify skill requirements and help in facilitating affiliation, accreditation, and certification process.

The National Skill Development Mission will be launched to implement and co-ordinate all skilling efforts in the country towards the objectives laid down in the policy. The mission will be housed in MSDE, and the key institutional mechanisms for achieving the objectives of the mission will be divided into a three-tier structure at the centre to steer, drive and execute the mission's objectives. The mission will consist of a governing council at apex level, a steering committee and a mission directorate (along with an executive committee) as the executive arm of the mission.

At state level, states will be encouraged to create State Skill Development Missions (SSDMs) along the lines of the National Skill Development Mission with a steering committee and mission directorate at the state level. States will, in turn, be supported by district committees at the functional tier. The mission directorate will be supported by three other institutions: NSDA, NSDC, and Directorate General of Training (DGT) all of which will have horizontal/vertical linkages with the mission directorate to facilitate the smooth functioning of the national institutional mechanism. NSDA was set up as a society in June 2013.

National Skills Research Division (NSRD), under NSDA, will be established to serve as the apex division for providing technical and research support to the Mission. This division will act as a think tank for MSDE and be the core skill development hub, which will connect implementation of the mission with academic research and data. Its four key functions will include research, policy advisory/inputs, career support and knowledge exchange networks. NSDC, a PPP was set up in 2008 as a Section 25 company under the Companies Act 1956 with shareholding of the Government of India (GOI) 49 per cent and private sector 51 per cent. It will be the nodal organization for all private sector initiatives in the short-term skilling space.

Financing Skill Development Under NSQF

National Skill Development Fund (NSDF) has been set up by the GOI with the objective of encouraging skill development in the country. A public trust set up by the GOI is the custodian of the fund. The Fund acts as a receptacle for all donations, contribution in cash or kind from all contributors (including the government, multilateral organizations, corporations, etc.) for furtherance of the objectives of the fund. To channelize the interest of a plethora of organizations to participate in the mission of Skill India, a strategic vehicle to create a multiplier effect on skilling has been devised. A Resource Optimization for Skilling at Scale Platform has been proposed by the government to act as a demand-responsive and flexible vehicle to tackle the issues of skills shortages through skill development, job creation and placement at scale. It will serve as the aggregator vehicle for pooling the funds of multilateral agencies, companies, foundations, NGOs and individuals for skilling interventions by leveraging the existing infrastructure and resources. The platform will also be subjected to timely audits to ensure that the contributions are used for the intended purpose.

To attract funds from industry, companies will be encouraged to spend at least 25 per cent of their corporate social responsibility (CSR) funds on skill development initiatives directly or through the NSDF. Further, industry should earmark at least 2 per cent of its payroll bill (including for contract labour) for skill development initiatives in their respective sectors. These funds can be channelized for skill development activities either through respective SSCs or through NSDF. All government schemes across sectors will be encouraged to apportion a certain percentage (10%) of the scheme budget towards skilling of human resources in local regions in the required sector. These funds could be used for implementation directly or be routed through NSDF. The government may consider other options including cess etc. to raise funds for meeting the requirements of this sector. End-user funding through a basic fee paying model will also be a key medium for funding training activities. However, the government believes that the inability to pay training costs should not stop any desirous citizen in the country from acquiring any certified skill training. The government will promote grant of scholarships, rewards and skill vouchers (SV) for funding of training costs. It will also be ensured that for all government schemes, direct benefit transfer (DBT) will be used as a mechanism for payment disbursement.

A Credit Guarantee Fund for Skill Development and a National Credit Guarantee Trustee Company (NCGTC) has been set up to support the initiative of loans for the purpose of skilling and will be used to leverage credit financing in the skill landscape. It will be further expanded to ensure greater outreach and access to all citizens. Similarly, a Credit Guarantee Fund for Entrepreneurship Development worth ₹30 billion per year has already been initiated under Prime Minister MUDRA Yojna through NCGTC.

CONCLUDING OBSERVATIONS

The QFs have become a major international trend in reforming national education and training systems since the 1990s. Although most countries are moving towards developing QFs, the nature of QFs vary among countries. Some have developed comprehensive QFs covering all levels and forms of skill formation. Some others have developed sectoral QFs, mostly in areas related to technical and vocational education. Very rarely do we come across QFs only for higher education sector separately.

A common practice seems to be that countries start with vocational qualifications framework to build towards NQFs. There are efforts to develop RQFs. The RQFs are being developed in the Caribbean region, in the European higher education area by the EU, Southern African Development Community (SADC) and in Asia. The funding support from international agencies is at times driving the development of NQFs and RQFs.

India is in the process of developing sectoral QFs. The country has already developed a NVQF and developed another QF replacing the earlier one. The new QFs is called the NSQF. This came into existence in 2013. The NSQF is being implemented by the newly created ministry of skill development and entrepreneurship. Further, India is also in the process of developing an NHEQF.

The NSQF is the most advanced in terms of developing a framework and preparing a plan for implementation. It envisages relying on the existing institutions, creation of additional facilities and establishing PPPs in funding, managing and ensuring that the skills and competencies developed are relevant for the industry. Since these QFs are in the initial stages of conceptualization and implementation, it is not yet time to make an assessment of the success or failure of their implementation.

While QFs are welcomed by the employers, the professoriate has concerns about dovetailing teaching and learning in institutions of higher education purely from a skill-development perspective. It may be argued that the universities have a larger role than skill inculcation. Research and teaching are the major functions of universities, and they are engaged in knowledge generation rather than confining themselves to knowledge transmission and skill training. It is feared that an over-emphasis on skill formation may distort the research priorities of institutions of higher education; it may make colleges and universities training institutions and it may, in the long run, bring down the country's competitiveness in the global context.

REFERENCES

Allias, S. (2010). *The implementation and impact of national qualifications frameworks: Report of a study of 16 countries.* Geneva: Allais Skills and Employability Department, ILO.

British Council. (2014). *Skills assessment in India: A discussion paper on policy, practice and capacity.* New Delhi: British Council.

Cedefop. (2015). *The shift to learning outcomes: Policies and practices in Europe.* Luxembourg: European Centre for the Development of Vocational Training. Retrieved 15 March 2018, from http://www.cedefop.europa.eu/EN/publications/5030.aspx

CINQF (Council of Implementation of National Qualification Framework). (2011). *Report on the referencing of the national qualifications framework to the European qualifications framework.* Brussels: European Union.

Ensor, P. (2003). The national qualifications framework and higher education in South Africa: Some epistemological issues. *Journal of Education and Work, 16*(3), 325–346.

EC (European Commission). (2008). *The European qualifications framework for lifelong learning (EQF).* Luxembourg: Office for Official Publications of the European Communities.

Gonczi, A., & Arguelles, A. (2000). Introduction. In A. Arguelles & A. Gonczi (Eds), *Competency based education and training: A world perspective* (pp. 9–13). Mexico City: Grupo Noriega.

IAMR (Institute of Applied Manpower Research). (2012). *A proposed national qualification framework for vocational education for India*. New Delhi: IAMR.

ILO (International Labour Organization). (2006). *Guidelines for development of regional model competency standards (RMCS)*. Geneva: ILO.

Jessup, G. (1991). *Outcomes. NVQs and the emerging model of education and training*. London: The Falmer Press.

Mehrotra, S. (2015). Employment of tertiary-level graduates in India. In N. V. Varghese & G. Malik (Eds), *India higher education report 2015* (pp. 251–274). London and New York, NY: Routledge.

MHRD (Ministry of Human Resources Development). (2012). *National vocational education qualification framework (NVEQP)*. New Delhi: MHRD.

MOF (Ministry of Finance). (2013). *National skill qualification framework (NSQF)*. (Notification dated 27 December 2013). New Delhi: Department of Economic Affairs.

MSD&E (Ministry of Skill Development and Entrepreneurship). (2015). *National policy for skill development and entrepreneurship 2015*. New Delhi: MSD&E.

OECD (Organisation for Economic Cooperation and Development). (2006). *Moving mountains: The role of national qualifications systems in promoting lifelong learning*. Paris: OECD.

Tuk, R. (2007). *Introductory guide to national qualifications frameworks: Conceptual and practical issues for policy makers*. Geneva: Skills and Employability Department, International Labour Office.

UGC (University Grants Commission). (2012). *Guidelines for curricular aspects, assessment criteria and credit system in skill based vocational courses under NSQF*. New Delhi: UGC.

Varghese, N. V. (2015a). *A note on national higher education qualification framework (NHEQF) in India*. Note submitted to the UGC. New Delhi: CPRHE-NIEPA, mimeo.

———. (2015b). *Indian efforts towards developing a national qualification framework (NQF)*. Paper presented at the Expert Meeting on Developing Regional Guidelines for National Qualifications Frameworks in Asia and the Pacific organized by UNESCO, Bangkok, 27–29 July 2015.

Young, M. (2005). *National qualification frameworks: Their feasibility for effective implementation in developing countries*. Geneva: ILO.

About the Editors and Contributors

EDITORS

N. V. Varghese is the Vice-chancellor, National University of Educational Planning and Administration, and also the founding director of the Centre for Policy Research in Higher Education at NUEPA. Formerly, he was the Director, International Institute of Educational Planning, Paris.

Anupam Pachauri is Assistant Professor at the Centre for Policy Research in Higher Education at the National University of Educational Planning and Administration. At CPRHE, she leads a national research project 'Quality of Higher Education in India—A Study of External and Internal Quality Assurance at the Institutional Level'.

Sayantan Mandal is Assistant Professor at the Centre for Policy Research in Higher Education at the National University of Educational Planning and Administration. At CPRHE, he leads a national research project on teaching–learning in higher education in India.

CONTRIBUTORS

N. Jayaram is Professor at the Master of Public Policy Programme at the National Law School of India University, Bengaluru. He is former Director of the Institute for Social and Economic Change, Bengaluru (2006–2008).

B. S. Madhukar is the Founder Director, Quality Assurance Cell, University of Mumbai, and presently Adviser at National Assessment and Accreditation Council (NAAC), Bengaluru.

Santosh Panda is Professor of Distance Education at Staff Training and Research Institute, Indira Gandhi National Open University, New Delhi.

K. Pushpanadham is Professor of Educational Management at the Department of Educational Administration, Faculty of Education and Psychology, Maharaja Sayajirao University of Baroda, Vadodara, Gujarat.

Furqan Qamar is Secretary General, Association of Indian Universities (AIU); former Vice-chancellor, Central University of Himachal Pradesh and University of Rajasthan; and former Advisor (Education), Planning Commission.

M. Rajivlochan is Professor at the Department of History and Director, Internal Quality Assurance Cell, Panjab University, Chandigarh, Punjab.

Meeta Rajivlochan is in the Indian Administrative Service, MH-90, and has served as Administrator for eight years in some of India's best institutions of higher education and research.

Vimal Rarh is Associate Professor at SGTB Khalsa College, University of Delhi, where she is the Project Head of 'Guru Angad Dev Teaching Learning Centre' of MHRD, created under the Pandit Madan Mohan Malaviya National Mission on Teachers and Training (PMMMNMTT) scheme of the Government of India. She is also the Principal Investigator for e-PG Pathshala project of UGC and MHRD in chemistry, and the Deputy Director of Centre for e-Learning at SGTB Khalsa College.

Chiranjib Sen is Professor at the School of Continuing Education and University Resource Centre, Azim Premji University, Bengaluru. He was a Professor at and the Founding Chairperson of the Centre for Public Policy (CPP) at IIM Bangalore. He was the member of the task force on faculty shortage and design performance appraisal systems, MHRD, Government of India, in 2011.

G. D. Sharma is currently the CEO at the Society for Education and Economic Development, and is a former Professor, National Institute of Educational Planning and Administration.

Aarti Srivastava is Associate Professor, Department of Higher and Professional Education, National University of Educational Planning and Administration.

Mariamma Varghese is former Vice-chancellor of the SNDT Women's University and a Senior Consultant to NAAC.

Index